Table Of Contents

KV-193-273

Preface

Economic events have taken on a new importance in our lives—an importance so compelling as to make the study of economics necessary for coping with these troubled times. The ways that economic events affect our incomes, the prices we pay, the taxes we bear, the standard of living we aspire to, and even the length of the lines we now stand in for gas, make these economic events both more obvious to us and yet—paradoxically—more of a mystery. Yes, it is true that we are more aware of the effect of economic actions on our lives, but, by and large, we remain as much in the dark as ever to the causes and cures of these problems.

Economists normally attribute this lack of economic knowledge to simple ignorance. If the people in the gas lines or the voting booth just understood Economics 101, the economists suggest, they would understand the problems and trade-offs and be able to suggest valid solutions, or at least understand why easy solutions cannot be found. This is a convenient stand for economists to take, but a disturbing one. Economics classes these days are among the largest and most popular on American campuses. A relatively large part of the voting population has been exposed to Economics 101, but continues to act as if the principles discussed there never existed.

What is the cause of this problem? One possibility is that people learn nothing in economics classes. This suggestion is easily dismissed. A second answer may be that they learn something in economics, but don't be-

lieve it. There may be a grain of truth to this. Economic models often come across as being ivory tower constructions that have little in common with the real world, which economists often discuss but apparently (to students) seldom visit. A final hypothesis is that students learn something in economics classes, but don't know what it is. They become proficient in dealing with economic models, but don't understand how to use them in analyzing the real world. The awesome power of economic analysis becomes, to them, just a pile of sticks to be crossed and plotted. Machines made with these sticks seem of little value and of uncertain strength to the student.

This text is written with the assumption that the real problem with economics courses (and textbooks) is that students spend too much time learning to manipulate a variety of complicated models and, because of this, never really understand the principles behind those models. They cannot, therefore, be expected to apply those principles in five, ten, or even twenty years. Because they have forgotten the charts, graphs, and models, they have forgotten the economics behind them.

This text looks at economics from a different perspective. Economics is built on a foundation made of a few simple but powerful ingredients. Our goal here is to teach those essential building blocks, and then see how they can be used to analyze a variety of economic decisions and activities.

WHAT THIS BOOK IS ABOUT

This book is about microeconomics. Microeconomics is the economic analysis of individual decisions. Everywhere individuals must cope with the essential facts of scarcity and choice. The analysis of these choices rightfully occupies our time since the causes and consequences of these decisions affect every part of our lives.

Microeconomics is the study of exchange. Exchange is the system by which we expand our horizons and improve economic welfare. Exchange is the most important game we play because it is not a zero-sum affair. For every winner there is also another winner. Losers are not necessary in this league.

Microeconomics is also about markets. Markets are the structures that make exchange possible and convenient. Markets are the price-setters, the income-producers, and the key decision-makers of a modern economic system.

Microeconomics is the study of prices. Prices are the rates of exchange. Depending on the exchange rate, exchange can benefit one side more than another, encourage new exchanges, or discourage old ones. We are all affected by the power of price as an incentive and as an allocator.

To help you understand this and learn how it affects you, this text is written with an emphasis on a number of important ideas:

Understandable presentation.   This text is written for the reader. The ideas, concepts, and theories presented are discussed in a simple, direct way that makes them easy to read, easy to study, and easy to understand.

Emphasis on basic principles.   This text isolates a few fundamental ideas in economics and then uses them again and again to analyze economic problems. The unifying threads here are exchange, trade-offs, and opportunity cost. By looking at microeconomics through these glasses, the economic issues become more clearly visible and less obscured by complex models.

Understandable discussions of producer and consumer choice.   Economics texts frequently go overboard in discussing how businesses and consumers make choices. This text concentrates on simple models of these choices, while also presenting the more complicated traditional analysis (hopefully, in an easily understandable way).

Emphasis on resource markets.   A special feature of this text is a full section discussing resource markets. These markets (and the decisions that underly them) are becoming increasingly important to the economic world. Labor, capital, natural resources, and energy are in many ways the keys to economic activity in general. The principles necessary for understanding these markets are not difficult, and the gains from analyzing them are large.

Discussion of government policies.   Government affects every part of the economic world. This text takes the time to look at the rationale for government actions, the effects of those actions, and the winners and losers that result when government steps in.

SPECIAL FEATURES OF THIS TEXT

This text has several special features designed to make it more useful to both student and instructor. Each chapter contains a *Real World Economics* section, which presents applications in the form of fictional news stories. News articles (many of which are based on real world events) are followed by an economic analysis of those events using tools and concepts presented in the chapter. These sections ask the student to apply the tools and ideas of the chapter, and can form the basis for good class discussions besides helping the student recognize economic theory disguised as real world behavior.

Each chapter begins with a *Preview,* which presents a number of questions that are answered in the following pages. This gives the reader an idea of what topics to be on the lookout for as the chapter is read.

Each chapter ends with a number of important features. A chapter *Summary* lets the reader check to see if all the principle points of the text have been absorbed. *Discussion Questions* are then presented to give the student the chance to think in greater depth about the topics covered. These questions provide, as well, a good basis for classroom discussions of the material. A number of objective questions are presented in *Test Yourself* sections. Answers to these sample questions are at the end of the text. *Suggestions for Further Reading* can also be found at the back of the book. Students who pursue the suggested readings will learn even more about economics and the way that economists think. Instructors can vary the breadth and depth of their courses by using these readings.

These features of the text make it a self-contained guide to microeconomics that can be used in a wide variety of classroom situations.

ACKNOWLEDGMENTS

Any work of this nature benefits from the contributions of a host of individuals whose names do not, alas, appear on the title page. I wish to thank the administration of the University of Puget Sound for providing an atmosphere of freedom and creativity in which to think, write, and teach. Thanks must go, as well, to my colleagues, Ernie Combs, Bruce Mann, and Doug Goodman. Each commented on the concept of the text and provided useful reactions to individual chapters. Through their comments and disagreement, they improved the quality of this text significantly. Several reviewers also provided constructive criticism and deserve thanks. My editors at Academic Press worked hard on this book and must share credit for it. Finally, thanks to my wife Sue, who contributed in every way to make this book possible.

This volume is dedicated to the students who use it. I hope that it helps them see the invisible hand.

Introduction

WHAT IS ECONOMICS?

What is economics, anyway? The answer depends on whom you ask. You could answer that economics is what economists do, but this response does not enlighten us much, since economists do all kinds of things in virtually every type of occupation. Some folks say that economics is a way of thinking—a way of analyzing problems and looking for answers. This is not far wrong. You will discover in reading this book that economics is made up of a few basic principles that are enormously powerful when applied to real world situations.

A good working definition is that economics is a social science that examines the problems of scarcity and choice; the study of the production and distribution of goods and services in a world of scarce resources. Some resources (natural resources, goods and services, time, talent, and so on) may not be scarce in a physical sense, but they are always scarce in that the amount available is never enough to satisfy all our varied needs and desires. Since we can't have everything at once, choice is necessary. Society must determine what goods to produce and how to distribute them.

Economics is important. Anyone reading the daily newspaper or listening to radio or television newcasts is bound to conclude that many of today's most pressing social problems—energy, poverty, unemployment, inflation—are fundamentally economic problems. We must understand something of economics to see how society copes with these problems.

People are becoming more and more aware of the economic aspects of their lives. Enrollments in economics courses have zoomed in recent years. Technical topics once discussed only by professors are now dealt with by politicans and joked about on the *Tonight* show. This book is designed to help you understand how the economic world works, how it affects you, and how society deals with economic problems.

WHY STUDY ECONOMICS?

Why should you study economics? There are lots of reasons. Businessmen and women find that economics helps them explain the forces that affect business conditions. The study of economics helps the business person understand how prices change, the impacts of changing markets, and the effect of government policies on production, sales, and profits.

Consumers need to understand economics for different reasons. Consumers must make decisions that affect buying, working, income, and taxes. They need to know how the system works so that they can better deal with it. Economics also helps consumers understand why things happen to them (Why has the price of gasoline risen? Why isn't more produced? Why did the concert sell out before I got my ticket?). An informed consumer can better cope with the economic world.

Students of history, political science, sociology, psychology, and literature will benefit by understanding how economics works because it can help them better understand their own fields. Economic pressures are not the only forces at work in our complex and interrelated social system, but economic forces are powerful. Someone who is interested in human behavior and the human condition needs to understand how these economic forces work and what impacts they have on society.

Students of public policy benefit from an exposure to economics because it makes them more aware of the economic consequences of their decisions. Government policy is all tied up with economics these days. Politicians set prices and determine production and distribution schedules with the laws that they pass. Are these decisions good? To evaluate public policies we must know something of how they affect producers, consumers, and others. This involves a knowledge of basic economic factors.

You may decide to study economics for its employment possibilities. Economists are widely employed in a variety of occupations. They work in business, finance, research, government, teaching, and other fields. Scratch any area where important choices must be made, and chances are the tools of economics can be applied.

Finally, economics is good general training because it is really the study of individual and societal decision making. Economics takes difficult problems and tries to analyze them and come to conclusions concerning what takes place and, more importantly, why things happen.

Economics is, then, very basically, a way of thinking and analyzing problems.

MICRO VERSUS MACRO

This book deals with a part of economics called microeconomics. Microeconomics analyzes the production and distribution choices that are made by individual decision makers. Microeconomics looks at the way that producers determine which goods to produce, how much to produce, which resources to use, and how government policies affect these choices. Microeconomics also looks at how individuals and households decide which goods to purchase, how much to buy, how much time to spend working, and how many dollars to borrow, lend, or save. Finally, microeconomics looks at how consumers and producers come together in markets where goods and services are exchanged and prices are set.

Microeconomics is different from macroeconomics. Whereas microeconomics looks at how individual decisions are made, macroeconomics examines the consequences of all these decisions taken together. Macro looks at the issues of inflation, unemployment, and the government policies that are used to deal with these and other national problems.

Macro and microeconomics are not two competing tribes of economists, they are merely different ways of looking at the same world. Macro looks at the health and stability of the forest; micro examines the characteristics of the individual trees. Each tells us something about how the forest works. This text, as its title suggests, will talk about the trees—the topics of microeconomics.

Introductory Microeconomics

Part 1
The Economics of Exchange

1
Scarcity and Choice

This chapter introduces some of the basic problems with which economics deals. Questions that will be answered in this chapter include the following:

What are the basic economic problems that face society?

How do we deal with these problems?

What is the role of economic growth?

Economics: the social science that studies the production and distribution of goods and services in a world of scarce resources

Economics is useful stuff, but economists sometimes seem like a pretty dismal group. Normal in most other respects, economists have the uncomfortable habit of finding dark clouds surrounding every otherwise silver lining. The economists' motto ''There is no free lunch'' is not a particularly friendly one. This seeming pessimism has something to do with the way that economists view the world.

Given Aladdin's lamp (and the three free wishes that the genie provides) most people would dream only of the luxuries now available. To the economist, however, this seeming abundance is really a problem of scarcity. A world of wants and just three wishes! What dreams to fulfill? What wishes to forego? How to choose? To the economist, even Aladdin's lamp is a problem of **scarcity** and **choice**.

Scarcity: the situation that prevails when desires exceed resources

Choice: the problem of deciding among several alternatives, not all of which can be obtained at the same time

THE PROBLEM OF SCARCITY

We all face the problem of scarcity. Because there are not enough resources to satisfy all our wants, we must live with the uncomfortable reality of the **trade-off**. When we choose to produce one good, spend time doing one activity, or purchase one item, the finite nature of resources means that we are implicitly choosing to give up all the other things that could have been done with that time, talent, and resources. In life we are always trading one item for another. College students choose to spend four or more years studying, and so choose *not* to spend that time working at a full-time job, for example.

Trade-off: the situation that prevails when one or more options must be given up when a choice is made

Having one thing means giving up all the other goods and services that could have been produced or purchased instead. Economists call the value of the best foregone option the **opportunity cost** of a decision. The concepts of opportunity cost and trade-off are familiar to all of us. Everyone at one time or another in their childhood was faced with the problem of a small pocketful of coins and a large counterful of candy. If you buy one you must give up the other. We face that problem still, and the decisions are made no easier by the maturity (and fuller pockets) that we have gained since childhood.

Opportunity cost: the value of the best foregone alternative when a decision is made

Economists use a **model** called the **production possibilities curve** (PPC) to illustrate the problem of scarcity, the reality of the trade-off, and the concept of opportunity cost. Let's begin by building a production possibilities curve for a hypothetical student.

Models: simplified descriptions of real world processes designed to increase the understanding of real world behavior

Joe College has only a few hours left to study before the Big Economics Exam. His scarce resource is time. Being a less-than-typical student, Joe hasn't read the textbook yet and so must try to devour (and retain) as many pages of economics as possible.

Production possibilities curve (PPC): a graphic device illustrating the maximum possible combinations of goods that can be produced with given technology and available resources

As if this weren't enough of a problem, Joe must also turn in an English term paper just before the exam. Typically (for Joe), he hasn't done this assignment either, and so he must try to get as much written as possible in the short time remaining. Let's look at the options available to Joe College in trying to pass both Economics and English.

Joe's ability to read economics and write his English term paper are illustrated in Figure 1. Shown here are Joe's **production functions** for economics reading and term paper writing. Production functions show the relationship between the resources used (Joe's time) and the production that results (economics pages read and English pages written). Joe's production functions display several characteristics that we find for producers in the real world. First, note that production increases as more and more resources are used. In the first hour, for example, Joe can read 20 pages in his economics text and, if he continues to read for a total of 5 hours, his total economics production rises to 52 pages. Likewise, the more time Joe spends writing his English paper, the more pages he generates.

But Joe faces a problem. The more he reads, the slower his reading gets. In the first hour he can read 20 pages, but in the second hour fatigue starts to set in and his reading speed declines—he reads only 15 additional pages in the second hour. In the third hour the amount of additional work that he does—what economists call his **marginal product**—declines even more. By the fifth hour, Joe is completely zonked with economics and can only manage to read 2 pages per hour. The phenomenon of declining marginal product is called the **law of diminishing returns**.

Joe experiences diminishing returns in writing his English paper, too. In the first hour he can write 10 pages, but in the second hour writer's block begins to set in and he scribbles only an additional 8 pages. By the fifth hour

Production functions: show the relationship between the resources used and the production that results

Marginal product: the amount of additional production that results when an additional unit of a resource is used in production, all else held constant

Law of diminishing returns: the economic law that holds that, in general, additional resources used in production are less productive than the resources already in use; declining marginal product. Like other laws, diminishing returns does not hold in every case

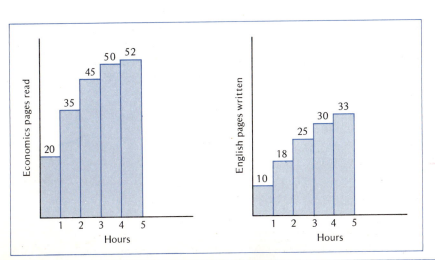

FIGURE 1-1: JOE COLLEGE'S PRODUCTION FUNCTIONS
These graphs illustrate Joe College's ability to read economics books and write English papers. Joe's efforts are subject to the law of diminishing returns. The more time he spends on any one project, the smaller is the addition to total production that his time provides.

(see Figure 1) he is writing only 3 pages per hour. His total page number is still increasing, but he is not as productive as he was in the first several hours.

So far, we have discovered what Joe College *could* do if he had 5 hours available for reading economics and 5 hours available to write his English paper. Unfortunately, in the time that it has taken to explain this, Joe has wasted an hour watching a rerun of *Star Trek*. He now has only 4 hours left before he must turn in his English paper and take the economics exam. How should he use the scarce resource of time in the 4 hours left? What are his options?

Figure 2 illustrates Joe College's problem. This is a production possibilities curve that indicates the maximum amount of reading and writing that he can do in the 4 hours, assuming that he starts work now and doesn't settle in to watch reruns of M*A*S*H.

If Joe spends all 4 hours reading economics, he can study a total of 50 pages, but he will not be able to do any work on his English paper. The production possibilities curve (PPC) illustrates this by noting that Joe has, as one of his options, the combination of 50 economics pages read and 0 English pages written. He could, instead, spend 3 hours reading economics (he will be able to read 45 pages, according to the production function of Figure 1) and, in the remaining hour he can write 10 pages of his English paper. Thus 45 pages read and 10 pages written is another point on the PPC.

If Joe spends 2 hours reading economics and 2 hours writing his paper, then he can have 35 pages read and be able to write 18 pages. By allocating his time differently, he could also read 20 pages and write 25, or read nothing and write a 30-page English paper (check these combinations on the PPC and Joe's production functions).

FIGURE 1-2: PRODUCTION POSSIBILITIES CURVE (PPC)
This production possibilities curve illustrates the maximum amount of reading and writing that Joe can do in 4 hours.

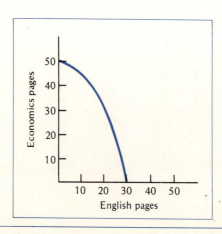

By drawing a curve connecting the points that we have found in Figure 2 we have constructed the production possibilities curve showing the options Joe College faces. The points on the PPC represent the maximum possible combinations of English writing and economics reading that Joe can achieve with his 4 hour limited time resource. These are the **efficient** combinations of reading and writing because Joe cannot produce more of *both* products at the same time. When Joe is on the PPC, he is working as hard as he can and not wasting resources through inefficiency. Combinations of reading and writing that fall inside the PPC represent **inefficient** production. For example, if Joe wanted to, he could waste time watching television and end up producing only 20 pages of reading and 10 pages of writing. We say that this combination is inefficient because, by using resources more fully, Joe could read more and write more, too. Alas, many of us spend too much of our time in the inefficient area of our personal PPCs.

The area to the right of the PPC is the **impossible zone**. These are combinations of reading and writing that cannot be achieved with the resources available. For example, Joe may want to read 50 pages of economics *and* write a 25-page English paper. But this is a point in the impossible zone because in order to achieve this, Joe will have to spend 4 hours reading and 3 hours writing—he will need to spend 7 hours working efficiently. Since he has only 4 hours before his deadline, this combination of reading and writing is impossible for him to achieve.

So, what will Joe do with his time? He would like to achieve point F in Figure 3, where he reads 50 pages of economics and writes a 25-page paper as well. Sadly, we have just shown that this is impossible unless his ability to read and write suddenly changes (his production function changes) or more

Efficient: an efficient use of resources is said to occur when it is impossible to use resources differently to produce more of every good or service

Inefficient: a method of production that does not produce the maximum possible totals of goods and services from available resources

Impossible zone: the area that lies outside the production possibilities curve; combinations of goods and services that cannot be produced with existing production methods and available resources

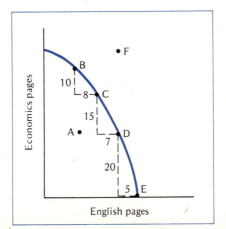

FIGURE 1-3: CHANGING TRADE-OFFS
From an inefficient point like A, it is possible to produce more of one good without producing less of another. Once on the PPC, however, a trade-off is necessary. Because of the law of diminishing returns, the trade-off changes as we move from B to C to D to E. Some points like F are impossible with the resources available.

time becomes available. He will probably end up at point A, where he wastes so much time trying to figure out what to do that he winds up with the inefficient combination of 20 pages read and 10 pages written.

CHANGING TRADE-OFFS

Joe is hopeless, but for the sake of illustration let's examine the options available to him if he works hard for 4 hours. Joe is aware that he faces a trade-off—the more economics he reads the fewer English pages he can write. This trade-off is clear, but it is also a changing trade-off. Suppose for a moment that Joe has decided to spend 3 hours on economics and 1 hour on English. He can therefore produce 10 pages of English and 45 pages of economics (point B on the PPC in Figure 3). What happens if he chooses to spend more time on English and less time on economics (a movement from point B to point C)? If Joe spends an hour less on economics and an hour more on his English paper he will gain 8 additional pages of English essay, but he must give up the 10 pages of economics that he could have read instead. The opportunity cost of the 8 pages of English paper is the 10 pages of economics Joe could have read in the same amount of time.

Let's suppose that Joe perceives this trade-off and, because he is worried about his English grade, decides to spend the extra time on his paper and so moves to point C. What is the trade-off if he spends *even more* time on English? As Figure 3 shows, if he devotes an additional hour to English (moves from point C to point D on the PPC), the amount of economics reading that he gives up increases (from 10 to 15 pages) but the amount of English paper that he gains declines (from 8 to 7 pages)! The law of diminishing returns makes the trade-off different. Each hour that he takes away from reading the economics text produces fewer and fewer pages of English paper. Thus Joe must give up more economic reading to get less English paper when he moves from C to D.

The trade-off is even more severe if Joe decides to devote all his time to writing the English paper. As he moves from point D to point E, Joe gives up the 20 pages of economics reading that he could have done, but gains only 5 pages of English paper. Each additional page of English paper has an opportunity cost of 4 pages of economics since that is the amount of reading that Joe must give up when he chooses to write more.

Joe now faces a problem of choice. The PPC illustrates the scarcity of time with the resulting trade-offs between the English paper and study for the economics test. Joe must balance the trade-off between his interest in each subject and the grades that each is likely to bring. For now, we'll let Joe ponder his choice—we shall explore a model of how he might choose the best point on his PPC later in this text.

SCARCITY AND CHOICE FOR THE INDIVIDUAL

The problem that Joe College faces with scarce time and the necessity of choice (given changing trade-offs) are not unique to him. We all face the problem of scarcity and choice when we spend our income. Our finite pocketbook must be stretched to cover our infinite desires for goods and services. The trade-offs that we face are shown in Figure 4. Suppose an individual (Joe College again) has $100.00 per week to spend on beer and pizza when the price of beer is $2.00 per six-pack and the price of pizza is $5.00 per pie. If he spends all his income on pizza, Joe can buy 20 pies (but he will get pretty thirsty). If all his income is spent on beer, he can have 50 six-packs, but he will get hungry (or pass out!) in short order. The PPC in Figure 4 really represents Joe's **purchase possibilities curve**, since it shows all the combinations of beer and pizza that Joe can afford (with no money left over) when the prices of beer and pizza are as stated. The purchase possibilities curve is also commonly called the **budget line** because it shows the different combinations of goods that can be purchased within a given budget (total spending) limit.

Joe's problem here is to decide on the amounts of beer and pizza to consume given the options available on the PPC. His choice is made easier, however, because the trade-off is not variable. So long as prices remain constant, two pizzas (which cost a total of $10.00) can always be traded for five cartons of beer (which also cost $10.00). The trade-off is uniform because money does not display diminishing returns—the last dollar buys just as much beer as the first. The purchase possibilities shown in the figure change whenever either income (the budget limit) or prices change.

Purchase Possibilities Curve: a graphic device showing the maximum possible combinations of two goods that can be purchased with given income and prices

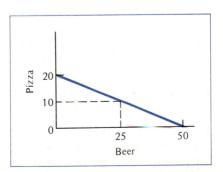

FIGURE 1-4: A PURCHASE POSSIBILITIES CURVE (BUDGET LINE)
This special kind of PPC shows the different purchases that are possible with a given amount of resources (income) and given prices. This PPC shows the combinations of beer and pizza that can be purchased with $100 when beer costs $2 and pizza costs $5.

SCARCITY AND CHOICE FOR THE BUSINESS FIRM

Producers face the same problems as individuals in dealing with scarcity and choice. Businesses are bound by the limits of the PPC and must choose from a number of possibilities and evaluate hard trade-offs.

Old McDonald had a farm (e-i-e-i-o) and on this farm he had some soybeans (e-i-e-i-o). Actually, McDonald can raise either soybeans or corn on the land available. McDonald's problem is complicated. Whenever he chooses to produce more soybeans he must give up larger and larger amounts of corn because he, like Joe College, faces the increasing opportunity cost phenomenon that is brought on by diminishing returns. In addition McDonald has to worry about the prices he can get for each crop. Trading more corn for fewer soybeans may make sense if the price of corn rises and the price of soybeans falls. But if the prices should move in the opposite direction, then McDonald's income will take a nose dive and he will have to live on IOUs, not e-i-os.

A similar problem is faced by most other businesses. Over the long run, General Motors may be able to expand its plants to produce as many cars and trucks as its customers need (this is much the same idea as the farmer buying more land). In the short run, however, the trade-off persists for the firm. When making production plans for the coming year, GM must decide whether to produce more trucks or to produce more cars. If they guess wrong, the company managers may be stuck with lots full of unsold cars, or trucks, or both. This may mean that in the future GM will have to shut down factories and lay off people until the surplus cars and trucks are purchased. This moves General Motors to the interior of the PPC where resources are inefficiently used or unemployed. GM is most profitable when it is on the PPC and so will try to plan production and undertake marketing to stay there.

SCARCITY AND CHOICE FOR SOCIETY

Society has more resources at its command than any individual or single firm, yet it faces the same trade-offs and problems of scarcity and choice. National economies cannot have everything they want at the same time: guns *and* butter; equality *and* efficiency.

One societal choice is illustrated in Figure 5. This societal PPC illustrates the trade-off between environmental quality and production. Sometimes it is possible to produce more goods and services without harming the environment. This is shown by a movement from the interior of this PPC to the curve itself. Once all such technological improvements have been made, however, we are left with a choice of which to give up: environmental quality or production, income, and employment.

A major American city faced this problem only a few years ago. The city

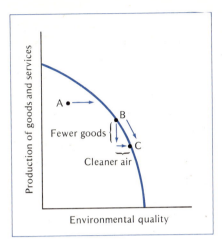

FIGURE 1-5: PPC FOR SOCIETY
This PPC shows the trade-off that society faces between environmental quality and the production of goods and services. Sometimes it is possible to improve the environment without giving up consumer goods (a movement from A to B). More often, however, society must decide between goods and services and environmental quality. (Should society move from B to C?)

imposed environmental protection standards on a steel mill located in the area. The intention of the city leaders was to increase environmental quality by cleaning up the water and air. If that city had been at point A in Figure 5, then it might have been able to increase environmental quality without decreasing production by using some unemployed resources or making better use of the resources already employed. The steel mill, however, informed the city that this was not the case. In reality, the city was at point B—balanced on the PPC between production and environmental quality. To increase environmental quality, they told the city, would make the plant unprofitable and it would have to be closed, reducing production and income and increasing unemployment severely in the area.

How should the decision whether to move from B (with high production but low environmental quality) to C (with lower production but a cleaner environment) be made? In this particular case, the matter went before the voters. They had to decide which was more important: incomes and employment or cleaner water and air. Because they could not have both at the same time, they had to choose higher incomes and dirtier air. Was their decision correct?

The concepts illustrated in the societal production possibilities curves can also shed some light on why some actions may be politically popular and why others find no popular support. Two presidents in the last 60 years have attempted to rapidly expand government spending: Franklin D. Roosevelt (FDR) and Lyndon B. Johnson (LBJ). FDR became very popular, while LBJ suffered political setbacks. What might have caused this very different reaction from voters? We can see at least a few of the reasons by examining the societal PPC illustrated in Figure 6.

FIGURE 1-6: POLITICAL AND
ECONOMIC TRADE-OFFS
*In 1932 the economy was in a deep
depression, and so it was possible to
increase production of government
goods without giving up private
goods—no trade-off was necessary. In
1967, however, the economy was
producing on the PPC. When
production of government goods
increased, production of private goods
had to fall. This created winners and
losers—the underlying fact of a
trade-off.*

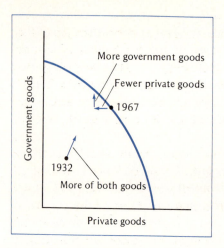

When FDR increased government spending, the U.S. economy was
mired deep in the Great Depression. Many resources (people, factories,
natural resources) were unemployed and restless. This put the economy at
the point labeled 1932 in the PPC illustrated here. As Roosevelt moved to
increase the amount of government goods produced (in an attempt to put
people back to work) he did not have to reduce the amounts of private
goods also produced. In fact, because of the interdependent nature of the
economy, the increase in the amount of government goods produced
actually caused the amounts of private goods to increase as well! No one
lost, while some were able to gain. This action of creating winners without
also creating losers made Roosevelt very popular and it was one of the
reasons he was reelected to the presidency three times. LBJ was not so
lucky.

In 1967 the U.S. economy was operating at full employment. In terms of
our picture, full employment corresponds to a position on the PPC. No
increase in production in one sector of the economy was possible without a
corresponding decrease in another. Hence, when LBJ undertook his
increase in production of government goods (the "Great Society" programs
for the poor and the Vietnam War), a trade-off was necessary. In order to
increase the production of government goods, a reduction in the amount of
private goods was necessary. As it turns out, this caused inflation (since
there were fewer private goods but many people trying to buy them) and
created losers in those who had to forego consumption of private goods.
LBJ's programs created winners—like Roosevelt's—but the programs were
different in that they also created losers. These losers made their discontent
known.

Economic growth is an important topic because as economies grow, their production possibilities expand and they escape the bounds of resource limitations. Economies can expand their PPCs by either acquiring more resources or by finding new ways of making things that allow more items to be produced with current resources. We all constantly try to expand our personal PPCs because we want to increase the amounts of goods, services, and leisure that are available to us.

This process of economic growth also applies to society. The economy can grow in many ways. Economic growth can take place, first of all, because we have more resources at our disposal. Discoveries of natural resources, increases in the labor force, and expansion of the number of factories and machines available all tend to increase the total amounts that can be produced. Improvements in the ways that goods are produced, as well, can expand the PPC. As labor becomes more skilled and machines are refined and new production processes invented, the PPC grows. Much of our economic growth, as shown in Figure 7, can be attributed to the impact of improving technologies and increased productivity.

Economic growth is highly desirable, but it is not costless. To expand our PPC over time means making other, hard trade-offs. In particular, economic growth may only take place if we are willing to invest in machines, technology, and research that make growth possible. In order to grow then, we must divert resources from the production of consumer goods (hamburgers, boats, new cars) to the production of business goods (machines, factories, new inventions). This trade-off, like any other, is an uncomfortable one. Students, who give up income now in hopes of a better life later, have first-hand experience with the trade-off involved.

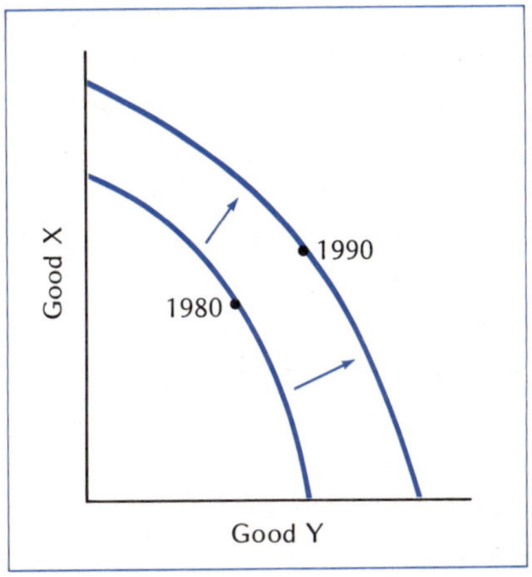

ECONOMIC GROWTH

FIGURE 1-7: ECONOMIC GROWTH
Economic growth (outward movements in the PPC) allows us to have more of everything. Economic growth takes time, however, and in the short run trade-offs still prevail.

REAL WORLD ECONOMICS: JIM DANIELS HAS A HANGOVER?

WHISKEY MAKER CAN'T SATISFY DEMAND FOR TENNESSEE SIPPIN' WHISKEY

TENNESSEE—Jim Daniels has a drinking problem and if it doesn't improve the consumers of this brand of whiskey may soon be forced to take the pledge.

The drinking problem that the folks at the Jim Daniels Distillery have is not that they drink too much (the distillery is located in a dry county). Their problem is the amount that their customers down. Jim Daniels literally cannot bottle the stuff fast enough to meet the demand for this premium-priced Tennessee sippin' whiskey.

Too many customers is not considered a problem for most businesses. The problem is a severe one in the whiskey business, however, because of the time necessary to produce a bottle of whiskey. Most whiskeys must sit quietly in oak barrels for a minimum of four years before they are ready to bottle and market. The amount of whiskey available this year, therefore, depends on the business decisions that distillery managers made four and more years ago.

Jim Daniels, because it is a premium whiskey, spends even more time in the barrel and so the quality of today's production was determined seven and eight years ago. Jim Daniels' producers had anticipated rising demand for their relatively expensive product, but were not prepared for the increases that have recently materialized. Since higher production will take several years to hit the market, friends of Jim Daniels are going to have to pay higher prices or switch brands until the shortage can be met.

The makers of Jim Daniels figure that they could sell more now but they would have to face a trade-off. Jim Daniels comes in two qualities, the top of the line Black Label, and the less expensive Green. The difference between the two bottles amounts to several dollars and one year in oak (the Black Label is aged a year longer and is therefore, supposedly, smoother sippin'). Jim Daniels could produce more of the Green Label in order to satisfy today's customers, but doing so would leave less Black Label for next year's market.

The folks at the Jim Daniels distillery (and their customers) face an uncomfortable dilemma. The more they drink now, the less they will have for later—at least until the current crop of Tennessee whiskey matures and is ready to drink. Here in Tennessee, people hope that whiskey-drinkers across the country will still prefer Jim Daniels when that time comes.

ECONOMIC ANALYSIS

The problems faced by the hypothetical Jim Daniels Distillery are in no way unique. This story illustrates the concepts of scarcity, choice, and trade-offs. Whiskey drinkers notice the scarcity first: The shelves are empty or the amount they can buy is limited. They must pay higher prices, or shift to the consumption of other beverages (in reality both things happen—the higher price rations the scarce good by seeing that only those who are willing to pay the most get it; others buy something else).

The Jim Daniels producers find the scarcity uncomfortable, too. The high price that their whiskey brings makes them wish they could produce more. But, like many other producers, their ability to expand production is severely limited. Farmers, auto manufacturers, and a variety of other producers also find it difficult to increase production drastically in the short run. Over longer periods, they can expand their factories or stores (Jim Daniels will have more to sell in several years if it puts more whiskey in barrels now). In the short run,

however, large increases in production may be difficult.

Jim Daniels faces another problem, however. They can either sell part of their whiskey now (as Green Label) and so satisfy today's customers or they can leave it in the barrel for another year and sell it as the more expensive Black Label to tomorrow's drinkers. They can't do both, however.

What is the solution? The makers of Jim Daniels must weigh the trade-offs and balance today's profits against the profits of the future. Business success depends largely on making the right choice when faced with the problem of scarcity.

SUMMARY

1. The basic problems that society faces are scarcity and choice. These problems are illustrated by the production possibilities curve. Once efficient production is achieved, it is impossible to have more of one item without giving up another. This trade-off makes the problem of choice difficult, and the problem is not made easier by the existence of diminishing returns. Because of the law of diminishing returns, the trade-off between goods is not constant. In general, the more of one good that we have, the greater the amount of all other goods that must be given up to get more.

2. We deal with the problems of scarcity and choice by analyzing the trade-offs and evaluating opportunity cost. By weighing the opportunity costs of individual decisions, economic actors eventually can decide which resources to have and which to give up.

3. Economic growth is important because it expands our options. Economic growth expands the bounds of the production possibilities curve and makes possible the attainment of combinations of goods and services that were previously impossible with given resources and production processes.

DISCUSSION QUESTIONS

1. The law of diminishing returns holds that as more and more resources are used in producing a good, they become less and less productive or effective in production. Can you think of examples where the concept applies? Can you think of areas where the law of diminishing returns does not hold? Give examples of each. What is the difference between these two types of production processes?

2. We say that *negative* marginal returns prevail when more resources used results in *less* total production. Give an example of a situation where negative marginal returns prevail. How do you suppose negative returns are related to the law of diminishing returns?

3. Recall the example of Joe College facing the problem of reading his economics text and writing an English paper. The production possibilities curve illustrated the options available to him and the trade-offs he faced. How would Joe actually decide which combination of reading and writing to do? What factors would he take into consideration? How do *you* decide, when in a similar situation?

4. The purchase possibilities curve in Figure 4 shows the combinations of beer and pizza that Joe can buy with $100.00 if beer costs $2.00 and pizza is priced at $5.00. How does this curve change if the amount to be spent rises to $120.00? When the price of pizza falls to $4.00? What will happen to this PPC if, at the same time, the amount to be spent increases from $100.00 to $200.00 and the prices of beer and pizza rise to $4.00 and $10.00, respectively? What does this tell you about what happens to *your* PPC when your income rises, but prices rise (inflation takes place) at the same rate?

5. "Economic growth is good because it allows us to help the poor without harming other income groups. When the economy is growing, all parties can benefit at the same time; none need lose." Does this statement make sense? Use a PPC to illustrate your answer.

TEST YOURSELF

Determine whether each of the following statements is *true* or *false*. Be able to defend your choice.

1. Opportunity costs are not constant in a world of diminishing returns.

2. If diminishing returns did not exist, the production possibilities curve would be a straight line.

3. The fact of high unemployment rates suggests that the

United States is operating on the boundary of its production possibilities curve.

4. There are no trade-offs in economic growth; nothing must be given up in order to get more.

5. The law of diminishing returns holds that additional resources reduce the total amount of production.

6. The production possibilities curve shows the total amounts of various goods attainable, given certain quantities of the scarce resources.

7. Opportunity cost can be defined as the amount that it would cost you if you did something else.

8. Because of the law of diminishing returns, as more and more of one good is produced, less and less of any other goods need to be given up.

9. The PPC does not move unless the amounts of resources available change.

10. We are not always on the production possibilities curve. When resources are used inefficiently or are unemployed, we fall below the PPC and produce less than we otherwise could.

2
Specialization
and
Exchange

Economics is the study of the problem of scarcity and choice. This chapter looks at how choices can be expanded through the process of exchange. Questions that this chapter will answer include the following:

What determines how exchange takes place?

Who gains from exchange? Who loses?

How does exchange lead to specialization?

How does money make exchange easier and more efficient?

What factors can limit the amounts and kinds of exchanges that take place?

Each of us is bound by the limits of personal and societal production possibilities curves. It is impossible to escape the reality of finite resources and infinite desires. Still, we must cope with these problems and make choices that leave us as well off as possible. This chapter deals with a means of expanding our choices and escaping from the limits of the PPC: **mutually advantageous exchange. Specialization** and **exchange** can expand the limits of choice and help consumers, firms, and society achieve production and distribution combinations that would be impossible otherwise.

In this chapter we examine the economic factors that lead to exchange, the role of exchange in specialization, and the gains that exchange makes possible.

Mutually advantageous exchange: exchange that benefits all trading partners

Specialization: use of resources that results in the more efficient production of one good

Exchange: the voluntary trading of goods or services

A BARTER ECONOMY

Barter economy: an economy where exchange takes place without money; goods are exchanged for each other directly

A good way to understand how exchange makes us better off is to look at an economy where exchange takes place without money; one good is traded directly for another. Such a pure exchange system is called a **barter economy.** Barter economies have existed everywhere in ancient societies and still prevail in many primitive (and some not so primitive) areas.

To get a good understanding of how exchange makes people better off, let's go back in time and examine the plight of the first ancient people to discover exchange. The inventors of exchange are two cave people: Bruce and Ernie (their names have been changed to protect the real inventors).

Being typical cave people, Bruce and Ernie spend most of their time scratching abstract art on cave walls and running around yelling "Look out for the dinosaurs!" But they have to eat, too, and so some time is spent finding food. The principal sources of food for Bruce and Ernie are fish and fruit gathered from the wild.

Like modern men, Bruce and Ernie face the problems of scarcity and choice. With limited time available, these cave people can gather only limited amounts of fruit and fish. They have to figure out how much time to spend on each activity and carefully weigh the trade-offs. Their production possibilities curves are illustrated in Figure 1.

Bruce is not very good at either fishing or gathering fruit. If he spends 1 hour fishing, he catches, on an average, only 1 fish. One hour spent gathering fruit, on the other hand, yields only 1 bowl of fruit. Assuming that Bruce has 10 hours per day available to get food, this gives him the PPC illustrated in Figure 1. Bruce can have 10 fish per day, 10 bowls of fruit, or any of the combinations (such as 5 fish and 5 fruit) shown by the PPC.

Ernie faces the same basic problems—scarcity and choice—but his choices are less restrictive because he is a better breadwinner. One hour of Ernie's time produces 2 fish or 4 bowls of fruit. If he has 10 hours available,

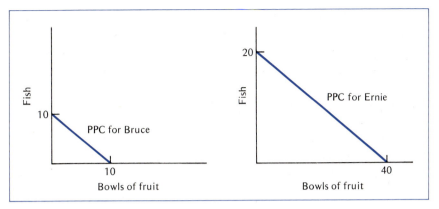

FIGURE 2-1: PPCs FOR BRUCE AND ERNIE
These production possibilities curves show the amounts of fruit and fish that the cave people, Bruce and Ernie, can produce for themselves without trade. These PPCs are straight lines due to the assumption of constant returns in this example.

then he can have either 20 fish per day or 40 bowls of fruit or any of the combinations shown on his PPC in Figure 1.

Notice that the PPCs drawn here are straight lines (compared with the curved PPCs in the last chapter). This is because we are assuming that the law of diminishing returns does not hold for Bruce and Ernie. Each hour, whether spent gathering fruit or spearing fish, is just as productive as the last hour. This assumption—that Bruce and Ernie's efforts bring **constant returns**—will make our calculations easier and will not detract from the usefulness of the example.

Constant returns: the condition prevailing when each resource adds as much to production as the one before it; equal productivity of resources

The production possibilities curves in Figure 1 show the limits of production and consumption that Bruce and Ernie each face if they eat only what they are able to gather. Would trade (fish for fruit) make them any better off? Would they want to trade? What would they trade for?

Let's examine the trade-offs that the two cave people face. It takes Bruce an average of 1 hour to catch 1 fish. This time could have been spent, instead, picking 1 bowl of fruit. The opportunity cost of the fish, then, is the 1 bowl of fruit.

What does it cost Ernie to catch a fish? Because Ernie is a better fisherman, it takes him only an average of ½ hour to catch a fish. He can gather 4 bowls of fruit in 1 hour, and so the time it takes him to catch 1 fish could have been spent filling 2 bowls with fruit. Therefore, his opportunity cost is the 2 bowls of fruit.

Despite the fact that Ernie has an **absolute advantage** in spearing fish (he can catch twice as many as Bruce in a given amount of time), he must give

THE THEORY OF COMPARATIVE ADVANTAGE

Absolute advantage: the ability to produce more total output with a given amount of resources

Comparative advantage: the ability to produce a good or service at a lower opportunity cost

up more fruit per fish than Bruce in doing so. Bruce has a **comparative advantage** in catching fish. The opportunity cost of a fish is 1 bowl of fruit for Bruce versus 2 bowls for Ernie.

Ernie, on the other hand, has a comparative advantage in gathering fruit. When Ernie gathers a bowl of fruit, it takes him just ¼ hour, which could have been used to catch an average of ½ fish (if he can catch 2 fish in one hour, he can catch ½ fish in 15 minutes). Bruce faces a higher opportunity cost. When Bruce fills a bowl with fruit, it takes him an entire hour. Thus gathering a bowl of fruit costs Bruce 1 fish. The cost of a bowl of fruit is less for Ernie (opportunity cost of ½ fish) than for Bruce (opportunity cost of 1 fish).

The theory of comparative advantage holds that when trading partners specialize in the production of the good in which they have a comparative advantage, mutually advantageous exchange can take place. Both sides of the exchange are made better off and society is better off as well. Bruce has a comparative advantage in catching fish and Ernie has a comparative advantage in gathering fruit. Let's see if the theory of comparative advantage holds in this case.

MUTUALLY ADVANTAGEOUS EXCHANGE

We can see gains from trade using the production possibilities curves shown in Figure 2. (The details of this exchange are also worked out in Table 1.) Here we assume that, before trade, both Bruce and Ernie spend 3 hours fishing and the remaining 7 hours gathering fruit. This means that Bruce is able to produce 3 fish and 7 bowls of fruit and Ernie has 6 fish and 28 bowls of fruit.

Now, suppose that both Bruce and Ernie specialize in the production of the good in which they have the comparative advantage. This means that Bruce spends all his time fishing and is able to catch a total of 10 fish. Ernie spends all his time gathering fruit and so is able to gather a total of 40 bowls of this commodity.

Specialization has now taken place, but how does this benefit the trading partners? It will only help them if they trade. Suppose, again, that Bruce and Ernie agree to trade fish for fruit at an **exchange rate** of 1 fish for 1½ bowls of fruit. This is an exchange rate that will be acceptable to both Bruce and Ernie since, at this exchange rate, Ernie can buy fish for less than it would cost him to catch them himself and Bruce can sell the fish at a profit by receiving more fruit than his opportunity cost.

Since Bruce has specialized in producing fish, he must trade to get fruit. Suppose that he decides to keep 4 fish for his own use. How many bowls of fruit can he trade for? If the exchange rate is 1 fish for each 1½ bowls of fruit,

Exchange rate: the ratio of goods in exchange; the rate at which two goods trade

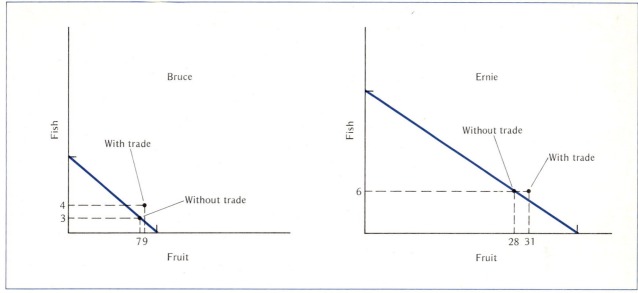

FIGURE 2-2: GAINS FROM TRADE
*By specializing in the production of the good in which they have a comparative
advantage (and trading that good for other items) both trading partners can gain
by achieving combinations of fruit and fish that they would have been unable to
consume in the absence of trade.*

then the 6 extra fish can be traded for a total of 9 bowls of fruit. By
specializing in producing fish, Bruce can trade for a total of 9 bowls of fruit
and still have 4 fish left. Notice that, without exchange, Bruce could have

TABLE 2-1

GAINS FROM TRADE

	Bruce		Ernie	
Item	Fish	Fruit	Fish	Fruit
Without trade (each spends three hours fishing, seven hours gathering fruit)	3	7	6	28
With trade (each specializes in good with comparative advantage)				
Production	10	0	0	40
Offered for trade	−6			−9
Received in exchange		+9	+6	
Net amounts available with trade	4	9	6	31
Gains from trade	+1	+2	0	+3

produced only 3 fish and 7 bowls of fruit. As a result of trade, Bruce ends up with both more fish and more fruit! He has escaped the bounds of his production possibilities curve in Figure 2. Exchange has allowed Bruce to gain from specialization. If Bruce has gained, however, Ernie must have lost, right? No!

Ernie is now specializing in the production of fruit. This means that he gathers a total of 40 bowls of fruit every day. He trades 9 of these to Bruce (at the exchange rate of 1½ bowls of fruit for each fish) and receives in return a total of 6 fish. Is he worse off on account of this exchange? Figure 2 and Table 1 indicate that he is not. Ernie still gets a total of 6 fish, just as before he started trading, but now he has even more fruit than before. Since he produces 40 bowls of fruit and trades only 9 of them, he is left with a total of 31 bowls of fruit and 6 fish. Ernie, too, escapes the bounds of his production possibilities curve through the process of specialization and exchange. The distribution of the gains from trade is shown as the bottom line in Table 1.

THE GAINS FROM TRADE

Several parties gain from exchange when it takes place as we have shown here. Obviously, both sides to the exchange gain, for why else would they trade? No one forces them to trade. The fact of voluntary exchange is evidence of its mutually advantageous nature. (Not all exchanges are voluntary, of course—coercion is sometimes a fact of life.)

The parties to exchange gain because they can achieve higher levels of consumption. Our cave people found they could consume both more fish and more fruit with trade than they could without it.

This consumption gain from trade is made possible by a production gain. Specialization along the lines of comparative advantage results in a more efficient use of resources. Finite resources are stretched to do more work. We can see this in the example just discussed. Without trade, a total of 9 fish and 35 bowls of fruit can be produced. Through specialization, more total fish (10) and more total fruit (40 bowls) are produced.

This is really an amazing result! The amount of resources available to Bruce and Ernie has not changed. The production functions for fish and fruit are still the same. Nothing about how production is carried out changed when trade began. Yet, through the more efficient use of resources that trade promotes, increases in total production and total consumption are possible!

Gain from trade is possible whenever the opportunity costs of production are different for two individuals, firms, or nations. This idea is illustrated for two countries in Figure 3. Suppose we have two hypothetical countries, the United States and Saudi Arabia. Each of these countries has the potential to produce as much oil or wheat as it wants—if it is willing to bear the trade-off. The trade-off is shown by the PPCs in Figure 3.

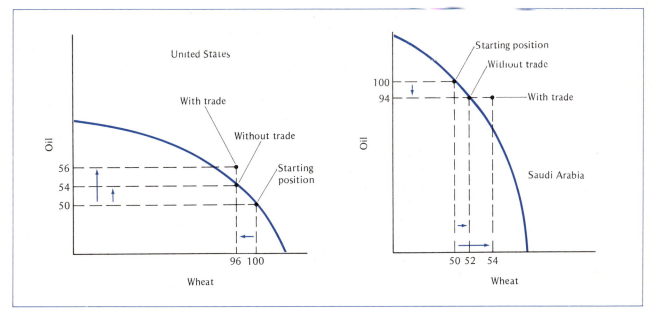

FIGURE 2-3: **COMPARATIVE ADVANTAGE AMONG NATIONS**
This example shows how both the United States and Saudi Arabia gain by exchange. Comparative advantage explains the trade that takes place among individuals, firms, and nations.

Without trade, the United States can produce 100 units of wheat and 50 units of oil. The United States can produce more oil (increase oil production from 50 to 54 units), but only at a cost of less wheat production (96 units, down from 100). Since resources are limited, an increase in oil production must necessarily take resources from other areas.

Saudi Arabia also faces a production possibilities curve. Without trade they can have 100 units of oil, but the remaining resources will produce only 50 units of wheat. They can have more wheat, as shown in Figure 3, but only if they are willing to give up more and more oil.

Saudi Arabia and the United States face essentially the same problem as the cave people Bruce and Ernie, except that their dilemma may be even worse. In the real world, the law of diminishing returns prevails (hence the curved PPCs in Figure 3). Because of diminishing returns, more and more oil must be given up to increase wheat production in Saudi Arabia and, similarly, the United States must be willing to sacrifice more and more wheat as it tries to increase oil production.

This situation is more realistic than the one Bruce and Ernie faced, but the analysis is still the same. Trade that takes place according to the theory of

comparative advantage will benefit both trading partners. The United States has a comparative advantage in the production of wheat and Saudi Arabia has a comparative advantage in the production of oil (work this out from the numbers given in Figure 3—calculate the opportunity costs of wheat and oil for each nation).

Suppose that trade takes place at the exchange rate of 1½ units of oil for each unit of wheat. Then the United States can produce 100 units of wheat and trade 4 of them to Saudi Arabia in exchange for 6 units of oil. The United States is better off, as Figure 3 suggests, because it is able to attain a level of consumption that could not be achieved without trade.

Saudi Arabia also gains. It can trade 6 units of oil for four units of wheat. Since it would have cost the resource equivalent of 6 units of oil to produce just 2 units of wheat on its own, Saudi Arabia is better off by the exchange. This benefit is shown, as well, in Figure 3 as Saudi Arabia, too, is able to attain a consumption level of wheat and oil that would have been impossible without trade.

SPECIALIZATION IN THE REAL WORLD

Complete specialization: when an economic unit produces only one good or service; specialization in one aspect of production to the exclusion of all others

Incomplete specialization: specialization that is not complete; production becomes specialized, but some other goods are also produced

Trade that takes place in the real world, like the United States–Saudi Arabia example above, is based on the theory of comparative advantage. People, firms, and nations tend to specialize in the production of goods in which they have a comparative advantage and trade accordingly. In the real world, however, **complete specialization** is seldom the case. With complete specialization, a person produces only the item in which he or she has the comparative advantage and trades this good for all others. In general, we observe **incomplete specialization** in the real world.

Incomplete specialization takes place when economic units (people, firms, nations) devote most of their resources to the production of goods in which they have a comparative advantage, but not all of them. The chef may spend most of his or her time preparing food, and the carpenter building cabinets, but each may still use some resources to perform tasks in the other's area of specialization.

Incomplete specialization is a result of the law of diminishing returns. As Saudi Arabia produces more and more oil for trade, for example, the opportunity cost of the oil rises. At first, little wheat must be given up to produce more oil. But, as diminishing returns to oil production set in, Saudi Arabia finds that more and more wheat is sacrificed for each additional unit of oil produced. Finally, the opportunity cost of the additional oil is so high that it is unprofitable to increase production. At this point, further specialization in oil production for Saudi Arabia would not make sense. It would still produce some wheat and devote most of its resources to producing oil.

The same idea prevails in the United States. The United States could produce all wheat, but the cost would be too high. As more and more resources are devoted to wheat production, the opportunity cost of that wheat (in terms of the oil given up) would climb. Finally, the opportunity cost would be simply too great and further specialization would stop here, as well. Rising opportunity costs, then, limit the degree of specialization. That specialization which does take place, however, increases total consumption and production and results in a more efficient use of world resources.

COMPARATIVE ADVANTAGE IN THE REAL WORLD

All of this makes very nice theory, but does it, in fact, work out in the real world? The answer is yes! A great many things that we observe in the real world are explained by the idea of comparative advantage and specialization.

Most college students are concerned about career choice. This choice is exactly the matter of choosing an area of specialization: doctor, lawyer, teacher, accountant, economist. Most students hope to take advantage of some natural comparative advantage or to acquire one through training.

Many forms of business organization result from the ideas of comparative advantage and specialization. Managers often hire specialists to make out payrolls, perform data processing services, or maintain buildings. Smaller firms, by specializing in these kinds of activities, can do them at a lower cost than larger, seemingly more efficient firms.

This process of specialization is apparent to anyone who owns a car. Ford may have its name on the hood, but other people have their names on the lights, batteries, tires, filters, and many other items. By specializing, each of these suppliers can produce at a lower cost. Ford, too, specializes—in producing the major components of the car, assembling all the parts, and marketing the product.

Nations also get into the act. Because of differences in climate, geography, natural resources, and culture, comparative advantages can extend to whole nations. Thus nations with few natural resources (like Japan) may have an absolute disadvantage in making manufactured goods but can still achieve a very profitable comparative advantage in their production.

THE ROLE OF MONEY

Coincidence of wants: the condition prevailing when the items that one person wishes to receive are the same as those the other person wishes to exchange; the condition necessary for exchange

Money: anything generally accepted in exchange for goods and services and in payment of debt

Exchange is beneficial even in a simple economy, but exchange can also be very complicated and costly in such a barter system. These problems can limit the gains possible from specialization and comparative advantage.

One problem that barter faces is the necessity of a **coincidence of wants** among trading partners. Bruce may want to trade fish for fruit, for example, but Ernie may want to have goat's milk instead. Despite his comparative advantage in fishing, Bruce may have to learn to catch and milk goats before he can get the fruit that he wants through trade. When there is no coincidence of wants, the idea of comparative advantage may be an interesting theory but is of little use in a practical sense.

Another problem that traders face in a barter economy is that of information. In order to know if he or she is paying a fair price, a buyer must know the alternatives. In a barter system, this means that you know all the exchange rates of all available goods. This can get very complicated.

In a 2-good society, exchange rates are easy to remember. The smart trader must know the price of fruit in terms of fish and the price of fish in terms of fruit. This is easy to figure out. But add a third good—milk. Now the intelligent trader has to know the price of fish in terms of fruit and milk, the price of fruit in terms of fish and milk, and the price of milk in terms of fruit and fish. For 3 goods you must know a total of 6 separate exchange rates.

The problem gets even worse when we add more goods. With 4 goods, a total of 12 exchange rates must be mastered. For 5 goods, the total is 20 exchange rates. And for a relatively simple economy with just 1000 goods a wise trader would need to know and keep track of almost a million different exchange rates! It's no wonder that barter societies never get very large. Anyone who spends the time necessary to master all the exchange rates would have no time left to actually produce anything to trade.

Exchange is a beneficial phenomenon, but the mechanics of exchange can get very cumbersome. The solution to this problem is **money**. Money is anything that people accept in exchange for goods and services and in payment of debt. It can be rocks, beads, shells, gold coins, paper currency, or bank accounts.

Money facilitates exchange in several ways. First it does away with the problem of coincidence of wants. Since everyone wants money, a producer need only be concerned about getting money, not the goods that someone else might want to trade. Second, money simplifies exchange by reducing the amount of information that an intelligent trader needs. Instead of knowing hundreds of thousands of exchange rates, the trader only needs to know the price of each good in terms of money—the amount of money it takes to buy each item. If there are a thousand goods, then, the consumer need know just a thousand prices.

Because money simplifies exchange, it increases the gains from trade and it makes specialization possible. In fact, the extent of specialization that takes place on account of money is truly remarkable. In some factories, workers specialize in tightening a certain bolt or connecting a certain wire. How could they possibly specialize to that extent in a barter economy? Likewise, some doctors specialize in performing specific operations and lawyers specialize in certain aspects of the law. Such beneficial specialization would be impossible in a world without money.

LIMITS TO EXCHANGE

Beneficial exchange is possible whenever opportunity costs differ for two traders, but when the costs of exchange exceed the possible gain, trade cannot take place. What kinds of costs are we talking about here? Information costs, for one. The existence of money lowers the amount of information that a trader needs to have about exchange rates, but other types of information are still necessary. Anyone who has shopped for a new car can attest that there is a great deal to know before a wise purchase can be made. What are the features and defects of each model? What kind of deal can one get? What will the dealer in the next town offer to pay for one's trade-in? Should one wait until later in the year to get a better deal or buy now and save? Getting this kind of information is time-consuming and costly, but necessary to efficient trade. The lack of information can hamper exchange.

Information costs may be even higher and more significant in other areas. Most people earn income through the basic transaction of exchanging their time, effort, and talents for money. This exchange is called employment. Many people are unable to complete this exchange because they cannot find the employer who requires their skills. The job opening may be in another city and may not be advertised or otherwise publicized. The costs of this very common type of unemployment are high.

High transaction costs can also limit trade. Because buying and selling a house is a very complicated matter, for example, most people employ real estate agents to handle all the details. The agent is an example of specialization. By doing nothing but dealing with real estate sales, the agent can deal with the sales more cheaply and more efficiently than the traders could themselves. But the high cost of putting through the transaction, whether an agent is paid or not, reduces the gain that both buyer and seller realize, and increases the price of the goods exchanged. Exchange is therefore discouraged.

High transportation costs can also discourage or destroy exchange. Some parts of the country may have a natural comparative advantage in the production of sand, gravel, and cement, for example. Yet, we seldom hear of sand being imported from Arizona. The high costs of transporting the raw material exceed any gain that specialization or exchange create.

Finally, taxes and government regulations can reduce or destroy comparative advantage. Any tax, because it diverts part of the gains of exchange from the traders to the government, tends to discourage exchange. A high enough tax can destroy trade. Government regulations that make exchange more costly reduce trade, too. Thus laws that require pharmacies to keep detailed records of their customers' purchases, for example, increase the price of those drugs and so reduce the gains that these exchanges make possible. Some government rules, such as criminal laws concerning the sale of narcotics, are designed to halt exchange by increasing the transaction costs involved.

DISTRIBUTION OF THE GAIN

Any voluntary exchange benefits all traders concerned. Many different mutually advantageous exchange rates are possible, however, and the distribution of the gain is different with each one. Two traders who both gain, therefore, may still disagree about exchange rates as each attempts to derive a larger share of the benefits available.

The distribution of the gains from trade, for example, is exactly the question that keeps labor and management apart in wage contract negotiations. Both employers and employees realize that their exchange (labor for wages) makes both sides better off. But at what rate should work be exchanged for wages? The higher the wage rate, the greater the share of the gain that labor receives. If wage rates are low, the employer reaps more of the benefits of the exchange. If the wage rate falls low enough, however, workers cease to gain from the exchange and will look for work elsewhere. If the wage rate rises high enough, employers will find no gain and may seek other lines of work themselves.

The practice of haggling over a price is nothing more than two traders trying to decide on an exchange rate and dividing the gains from exchange. This process is perhaps easiest to see when a new car is purchased. There is a certain amount of gain here, which can either end up as profit for the car dealer or savings for the purchaser. The negotiations between buyer and seller key on the distribution of this gain.

This chapter has concentrated on the theory of comparative advantage as an explanation for trade among individuals, firms, and nations. While comparative advantage explains much of the trade that takes place, it is important to note some other reasons for trade that go beyond this theory.

One explanation for much of the trade that takes place in the world today is the existence of differing tastes and preferences among the traders involved. In the case of the cave people Bruce and Ernie, trade was beneficial even when their relative preferences for fish and fruit were ignored. When we take into account the fact that people like some goods more than others, we find that comparative advantage is not necessary for some exchanges.

A simple example of this kind of trade occurs all the time and can be called the "lunchbox paradox." School children come to school endowed with whatever their parents have decided to make for lunch. In a sense, there is no opportunity cost (as far as the children are concerned), yet despite the lack of the traditional comparative advantage conditions, lunch time trade in apples, oranges, and peanut butter sandwiches is brisk. The reason for this trade is clearly that kids who like apples more than oranges are able to find others who like oranges more than apples. Trade is based on differences in taste and is still mutually advantageous.

Other trades occur due to force. Criminal activities aside ("your money or your life" is an interesting problem in opportunity cost), governmental rules force many exchanges that might not otherwise take place. The military draft, for example, has at various times forced young men to trade their time and talents (and sometimes their lives) for minimal wages. Recent experience with an all-volunteer military system in the United States indicates how unpopular this exchange is in the absence of force. Other kinds of trades are forced as well. The government can force a person to sell property against his or her will (to make room for a highway, for example), or to sell property to pay debts or taxes. And, as already noted, governmental price regulations often dictate exchange rates at which trades must take place.

Traditional or cultural values represent a final reason for exchange. A simple example of this is the custom of tipping people for performing services (such as haircutters, waiters, or cab drivers). In some cultures this exchange is expected and the lack of a tip is cause for scorn. In other cultural settings, tipping is viewed as an insult. The extent of gain from this exchange, it seems, depends on who you are, where you are, and the tradition that has grown around it. Many other exchanges are similarly mandated or prohibited by traditional and cultural factors.

In the developed nations of the world, most important exchanges take

OTHER REASONS FOR EXCHANGE

place through the use of markets and market prices. The next chapter will help us understand how these markets work.

REAL WORLD ECONOMICS: BULLISH ON WALL STREET

WIN OR LOSE, BROKERS TAKE THEIR CUT

NEW YORK—Ask a typical stock trader on Wall Street who her best friend is and she will likely tell you that it is her stockbroker— especially if stocks have just risen in value. Ask her who her worst enemy is and the answer may be the same if the stock market has just taken a tumble.

Stockbrokers are used to this love–hate relationship, but that doesn't make the ups and downs in the market any easier to take. The truth is that brokers, unlike their clients, make money no matter which way the stock market turns. Brokerage fees are paid whenever stocks are traded. Thus a typical stock transaction will involve two brokerage fees—one paid to an agent for purchasing the stock shares, and another to the selling broker. In this way, the broker makes his living buying (when his clients think the market is moving up) and selling (when his clients fear falling stocks).

Brokers may make money even when stocks fall, but they prefer buying to selling because clients who make money come back and buy more. Losers may be gone for good and with them, their broker-age fees.

Stock fees are determined on the basis of the number of shares exchanged, the price of the shares, and a number of other factors. Because these fees can be high, they cut into the profits of a stock trader. Many stock players find that they must gain 5 percent on a deal just to pay off the broker. Losers (those who see stock prices fall) lose even more when they sell stocks because they must also lose to the house—their broker gets a cut of losses as well as any profits. Like the house in Las Vegas, it seems, stockbrokers have a system to beat the odds.

Why do stock traders put up with this situation? The brokerage hous-es have made themselves indispen-sable. They provide research, data, and stock quotes in a matter of minutes. They also make financial services more convenient for stock traders.

Their biggest service, however, is simply making the stock transac-tions possible. With stock owners scattered all over the world, a stockholder in Tulsa would be hard pressed to locate and come to terms with a buyer in, say, Boise. Yet, through the miracle of the computer and the specialized stock brokerage organization, just such a transaction can take place quickly and efficiently.

Stock brokers, then, play the role of middlemen. They bring together buyer and seller and therefore earn their fees by doing this at low cost. As much as buyers and sellers may resent brokerage fees, they still have to realize that any gain on Wall Street would probably be impossible without the help of their friendly neighborhood broker.

ECONOMIC ANALYSIS

The stock market is an example of a market where mutually advantageous exchange can take place, but might not without the existence of middlemen. Middlemen bring together buyers and sellers, supply information to both, and earn a fee for doing so. Real estate agents, wholesalers, and other middlemen abound in the economy.

Why is a middleman necessary in the stock market? There are a number of problems here that require their services. The first problem is one of information. The intelligent securities trader needs to have a wealth of information in order to make a decision to buy or sell stocks and bonds. Since it would be costly and time-consuming to obtain all this information for oneself, stock trading without brokers would be limited to wealthy players with little else to do.

Instead, brokerage houses specialize in information—about stocks, the economy, and the market. By specializing, they do a better job (at a lower cost) of putting together this costly information than most traders would be able to do themselves. Stock traders make use of

this comparative advantage when they pay their fee. Stock owners typically specialize in occupations of their own (doctor, lawyer, salesperson) and trade cash for the product of the brokerage houses. This is an example of the theory of comparative advantage at work.

But this still doesn't explain why stock brokers are as important as they are. The missing piece involves the costs of transaction on the stock market. Finding a buyer for a particular amount and kind of stock is a costly business—especially with buyers and sellers scattered all over the world. Without middlemen to aid in the search, it is likely that the transactions costs would be so high that few exchanges would result. The brokers specialize in connecting buyers and sellers and so reduce transaction costs to the point where the active stock market we see today (where tens of millions of shares can change hands on any given day) is possible.

So why do stock traders put up with relatively high brokerage fees? Two reasons seem clear: First, traders realize that their costs would be much higher without the brokers. So high, in fact, that mutually advantageous trade might be impossible. The second reason is that every trade involves some kind of gain to both sides and the broker makes this exchange inexpensive and profitable.

---

1. Exchange takes place whenever there is a difference in oppor-

tunity costs among traders. Even when one trading partner has

SUMMARY

an absolute advantage in the production of all goods, there can still be a comparative advantage that makes trade beneficial. This difference makes specialization and exchange an efficient way to allocate resources and achieve production and consumption combinations that are not possible without exchange.

2. All partners to an exchange gain. It is one of the miracles of economics that exchange creates winners without creating any losers. The distribution of the gain among trading partners depends on the exchange rate that prevails and the opportunity costs of the traders.

3. Exchange leads to specialization. When exchange takes place, individuals, firms, and nations can achieve greater consumption combinations by specializing in the goods in which they have comparative advantage and then trading for other goods that they need. This specialization leads to greater total production. In the real world, however, incomplete specialization is more common than complete specialization. The law of diminishing returns limits the extent to which producers can benefit from specialization.

4. Money encourages exchange and increases the potential for specialization. Money lowers the amount of information needed for exchange and lessens the need for a coincidence of wants. Without money (in a barter economy) the degree to which specialization and exchange can take place is very limited.

5. Even mutually advantageous exchange can be limited or discouraged by factors such as information costs, transaction costs, or government taxes and regulations. These costs reduce the gain and can bring exchange to a halt.

DISCUSSION QUESTIONS

1. How is the law of diminishing returns related to the shape of the productions possibilities curve? Show how the property of constant returns gives the straight-line PPC shown in Figure 1.

2. The record books show that Babe Ruth was one of the best pitchers in baseball during the early part of his career. Despite this, he was seldom allowed to pitch. Use the theory of comparative advantage to explain this seeming paradox.

3. Dean Chance was also an excellent baseball pitcher, yet he was seldom allowed to go to bat. What makes Chance different from Babe Ruth? What does this say about absolute advantage, comparative advantage, and specialization?

4. Doug and Gail are students. In

a given period of time, Gail can solve 3 marketing problems or work 5 accounting problems. In the same time, Doug can work 2 marketing problems or solve 4 accounting problems. If Gail and Doug form a partnership when they graduate, who should be the salesperson and who should be the accountant (based on their abilities to solve marketing and accounting problems)?

5. Give an example of an exchange rate in Problem 4 where Doug gains, but Gail does not; Gail gains, but Doug does not; both gain; both lose.

TEST YOURSELF

Indicate whether each of the following statements is *true* or *false*. Be able to defend your choice.

1. If a firm has an absolute advantage in production of cars, then it follows that they have a comparative disadvantage in the production of trucks.

2. It is possible for an individual to have the comparative advantage in all types of production.

3. Comparative advantage always results in specialization.

4. When there are transaction costs, it is possible for people to be middlemen because they have a comparative advantage in the mechanics of exchange.

5. These middlemen, because they charge for their services, tend to prevent exchange.

6. Exchange makes one trader better off only if it makes the other trader worse off.

7. The existence of money means that more information about other prices is necessary in order for exchange to take place.

8. Diminishing returns reduce the gains that can be made through specialization.

9. Suppose that in a given amount of time Joe can make 2 cakes or cut the grass in 1 yard. In the same amount of time, Joan can make 4 cakes or trim the grass in 2 yards. Both have the same preferences for cakes and cutting grass. Mutually advantageous trade between these two is impossible.

10. In the previous problem, trade will not increase total production by Joe and Joan.

3
Demand and Supply: The Micro Side

This chapter presents one of the most basic economic tools: the supply and demand model of how markets operate and how prices are set and changed. When finished with this chapter you should be able to answer the following questions:

What is meant by demand?

What factors determine the amounts of goods and services that people demand?

What is meant by the term supply?

What factors determine the quantities supplied?

What is the equilibrium price?

What factors can make prices change?

Market: a general term describing the economic institutions where exchanges of goods and services are made

Exchange is the basic activity that takes place in the economy. Exchange, as we have seen, produces numerous benefits. In this chapter we examine the economics of exchange from the perspective of **markets**. By studying markets and the way they work, we can better understand how exchange affects the economy and how economic events affect us.

THE ROLE OF THE MARKET

Economists spend a lot of time talking about the advantages of letting markets make production and distribution decisions. Exactly what is a market and what tasks does it perform?

The first thing to understand about markets is that they are easy to see but difficult to touch. Take the market for canned tuna, for example. Where is this market? What does the market do?

WHERE IS THE MARKET? The answer is that it is nowhere and everywhere. It is nowhere in the sense that there is no single place where all the sellers and buyers of canned tuna meet to make exchanges. This is impossible since the various buyers and sellers are scattered around the world. Buyers can purchase tuna at millions of outlets. Sellers, too, exist in widely separated areas. The market is the sum of all these groups' actions. When you go to the supermarket to buy tuna (or order a tuna sandwich at a lunch counter) you are entering the tuna market because your actions affect the amount of tuna left for other buyers and the price that all buyers will pay and the sellers will receive.

WHAT DOES THE MARKET DO? The market sends a series of signals throughout the economy. The tuna market, for example, tells us whether tuna is valuable (a high price) or worth little. It tells us whether more or less tuna should be produced and whether additional workers should train for jobs in the tuna industry. The market determines the distribution of income between tuna producers, tuna consumers, and all others. In short, the market decides what should be produced, who should receive these goods, and who should receive income from the sales.

HOW THE MARKET WORKS

When exchange takes place through markets, many buyers and sellers come together. The basic forces in a market are conflict and competition. Conflict arises because the two sides of the market process have different ends in mind. Sellers (the supply side of the market) are interested in gaining profits, which provide them with higher income and allow them to expand their businesses or attract new investors. They want to get the highest possible price for their goods or services to achieve the greatest gain from exchange.

Buyers (the demand side of the market) are interested in just the opposite result. They wish to pay the lowest possible price for the goods that they buy. A low price gives buyers a larger share of the available gains.

As sellers push for the highest possible price and buyers lobby for bargains, the resulting conflict is resolved only because of the second characteristic of the market: competition. Both buyers and sellers face competition. A seller who asks too high a price is soon without customers if others are willing to sell for less. Each seller's livelihood is threatened by every other seller. Producers must grasp for any advantage. Often they try to lure customers by offering goods of a higher quality than those produced by competitors. More often the competition focuses on price.

Buyers, too, face rivals. Items that are scarce go to the highest bidder. Individuals who are unable or unwilling to back their desires with dollars find themselves allocated out of the market. Prices rise when goods are scarce, and goods in abundance are cheaper because the competition bids the price down.

The combination of competition and conflict makes the market work. Sellers try to get the highest possible price for their wares, while noting that, if the price is too high, competitors will get all the business. Buyers haggle to find bargains, but must be aware that the goods go to the highest bidder. These forces set most of the prices that we pay. In some markets, competition breaks down as, for example, when monopolies or governmental price controls exist. We shall examine these market failures in later chapters.

THE CONCEPT OF DEMAND

Demand: a description of the buyer side of the market; demand looks at how the amounts and kinds of goods and services people wish to buy are determined

Demand is the easiest side of the market for most of us to see because this is the part of exchange where we seem to be most actively involved. Demand is a total description of how people feel about the things that they buy—and how these feelings determine how much of any particular good they desire to purchase. Demand, then, is not a purely economic phenomenon. Psychology, sociology, and information theory all are involved in our concept of demand. So are many other, seemingly unrelated factors.

Since demand is such a broad concept, it is useful to simplify it from the start. Demand depends on a virtually endless number of things, but a list of five key determinants of demand covers most of the important ideas.

1. PRICE. How much of an item we wish to purchase depends very much

Price: the amount of money required in exchange for a unit of a good or service

Inverse relationship: an inverse relationship is said to exist between A and B if an increase in A results in a decrease in B (A and B move in opposite directions)

Substitution effect: when the price of an individual good changes, consumers tend to purchase more of relatively cheaper goods and less of relatively more expensive substitutes

Income effect: when the price of an individual good increases or decreases, this affects the consumer's ability to purchase that good and all other goods. This change in purchasing power has an impact on the quantity of goods demanded and is called the income effect

Income: the amount of money received in a given period of time

Direct relationship: a direct relationship exists between A and B if they increase or decrease together, i.e., an increase in A implies an increase in B

Substitutes: goods that perform the same function are termed substitutes; coffee and tea, hamburgers and hot dogs, and pens and pencils are examples of pairs of substitutes

on the **price** of that item. The price determines how much we can afford to purchase within our budget, and allows comparison with other goods at other prices, which may be desired as well. In general, the amount that we wish to purchase is inversely related to price. When prices are low, we purchase more. High prices mean less buying.

The reason for this **inverse relationship** between price and the amount desired is not hard to imagine. Two factors influence the purchaser's decisions. As the price of any one good rises, consumers buy less of that good and shift purchases to other items. This is called the **substitution effect**. Rising prices also cause people to buy fewer goods in general because their purchasing power falls—they can't afford to buy as many goods or services. This is the **income effect**.

When the price of an item falls, on the other hand, the substitution and income effects increase the amount desired. People substitute cheaper goods for more expensive ones and buy more because they can afford more at the cheaper price.

2. INCOME.
Income is as basic to our buying decision as price. In general, the more income we have, the more of any particular item we would like to purchase (a **direct relationship** between income and quantity desired).

There are, of course, a few items that have a negative income effect. That is, as income rises, our desired purchases fall and vice versa. These goods have a low social status or an aura of cheapness. Beans, for example, are purchased less frequently as income rises. Most goods and services are normal, however, in that our desire for them responds positively to increases in our purchasing power.

3. PRICES OF OTHER GOODS.
The way we feel about buying one item is heavily influenced by the prices of all other goods and services available to us. Some things we classify as **substitutes**. Substitutes are goods that satisfy the same need or desire. Water, coffee, tea, and beer, for example, are substitutes since all satisfy our thirst. Fords and Chevys are substitute forms of transportation. Houses and apartments, while different in many ways, are substitute forms of shelter.

The amount of a good that we wish to purchase tends to vary directly with the price of its substitutes. Thus, for example, the amount of Coke desired declines if the price of Pepsi falls, and rises if Pepsi becomes more expensive. When the price of a substitute falls, we switch purchases to the cheaper item. This switching of purchases is strong among goods that are very similar in their ability to satisfy our desires, and weak among goods that are imperfect substitutes for one another.

Other things are **complements**—they are used together to satisfy some want or need. The list of complements is endless: bread and butter, toast and jam, bacon and eggs (just for breakfast), as well as pencils and erasers, and economics books and headache remedies.

The basic idea of complementarity is that since the goods are used together, our desire for the two goods rises and falls together, too. When the price of bacon falls, for example, the amount of eggs purchased will rise since the two are often consumed together. If eggs become more expensive, however, less bacon may be sold. There is, then, an inverse relationship between the amount of a particular good that we want and the price of its complementary good or goods.

Merchants take advantage of the relationship among complements. Stores often put some particular item on sale at a lower price (wall paint) in the hope of selling more of the complementary items (brushes, rollers, drop cloths) at their regular prices.

4. TASTES AND PREFERENCES.
Changes in the nature of our desires (what we want, when we want it, what is fashionable) have a direct effect on the kinds and amounts of goods that we wish to buy. As tastes and preferences change, our purchases change as well.

Sometimes our desires change very gradually. Blue jeans, for example, were once mostly worn by cowboys and workmen who needed the strength and durability of that kind of pant. Slowly, blue jeans gained acceptance among social and economic groups that had previously shunned them. Finally, they became almost a uniform for young people, and eventually even appeared in the White House.

But changes in tastes and preferences can be rapid, too. A few years ago a rumor suddenly got started that a major hamburger chain was making its burgers moist and juicy by adding a secret ingredient to the meat: worms. The rumor was wrong, of course, but the effect on the amount demanded was significant: the hamburger stores were deserted until customers became convinced that wormburgers were not being sold. The demand for hamburgers took a nosedive and then returned to normal, all in a few weeks. The reason was the burger-eating public's changing perceptions of the product that they were consuming.

Most changes in tastes and preferences are less abrupt than this, but they may occur for roughly the same reason. As people acquire new information about products, or styles and living fashions change, the amounts and kinds of goods purchased can be expected to change as well.

5. EVERYTHING ELSE.
Everything else? Sure. A whole world of things can affect our demand for goods and services. Weather, for example. The

Complement: goods that are used together are called complements; toast and jam, coffee and sugar, and hamburgers and french fries are all examples of complements

demands for umbrellas, snow tires, suntan oil, and irrigation water are affected by changes in the weather. Expectations concerning future prices is an "everything else," too. If people hear that the price of heating oil is going to increase next month they are likely to try to fill their fuel tanks now before the increase comes due. And if customers expect lower prices in the future (as they might just before the traditional January white sales) they rationally delay purchases.

THE DEMAND CURVE

Demand curve: a curve that shows the quantity of a good or service that buyers wish to purchase at every possible price

These five factors describe the general concept of demand. Unfortunately, demand is too complicated a concept to use directly to analyze problems that may occur in the market. For this reason, the concept of demand is simplified by a graphical tool: the **demand curve**.

The demand curve maps the way that the quantity demanded over a certain period of time varies as the price of the good in question varies. For simplicity, we shall assume that income, the prices of all other goods, tastes and preferences, and everything else is fixed or held constant. Then, in this relative vacuum, we can examine the effects of price changes on the quantity demanded.

FIGURE 3-1: A DEMAND CURVE FOR APPLES

As the price of apples falls from 30¢ to 10¢, the quantity of apples that people want to purchase increases as the income and substitution effects take place. The demand curve shows the quantity demanded at every price.

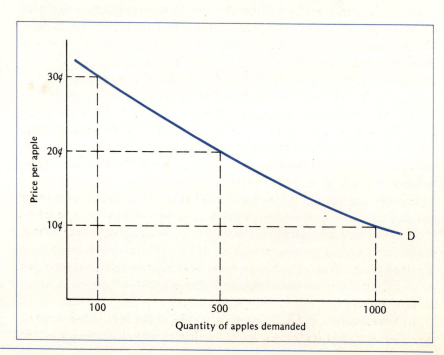

A hypothetical demand curve for apples is shown in Figure 1. This graph shows the amount of apples that people wish to purchase at different prices. Such a demand curve could actually be constructed by polling consumers in an area to determine what their likely behavior would be at different apple prices. But, whether it is actually compiled or not, the demand curve still exists in the sense that the behavior suggested by the demand curve exists.

The demand curve in Figure 1 shows that, at a relatively low price of 10¢ per apple, there will be a relatively large quantity of apples demanded—1000 apples. As the price of apples rises to 20¢, fewer apples are sold (only 500). The reasons for this are clear. At 20¢ per apple, some people cannot afford to purchase as many apples as before. They may substitute other foods for the now more expensive apples. Or they simply may not be willing to spend that much in exchange for apples and so voluntarily withdraw from the market. Essentially, people will only pay 20¢ for an apple if they feel that they get at least 20¢ worth of satisfaction from it. The falling quantity demanded here indicates that only 500 apples give people at least 20¢ worth of satisfaction, while 1000 apples are considered worth 10¢ each. At 30¢ each, only 100 apples are desired. The substitution and income effects further reduce the quantity demanded as price rises.

In discussing the demand curve, it is important to distinguish between *demand* (the entire curve) and the *quantity demanded* (the amount that buyers wish to purchase at any given price). Demand (the demand curve) changes only when one of the underlying determinants of demand changes. The quantity demanded, however, changes whenever the price changes (a movement along the curve). When economists talk about a change in demand, therefore, they mean a change in one of the underlying assumptions of the demand side of the market. The demand curve shifts, as we shall see below. Different amounts are demanded at any given price. When economists discuss a change in the quantity demanded, however, they suggest no such major change in buying behavior. A change in the quantity demanded occurs whenever price changes—none of the other underlying factors need change for this to result.

To build a demand curve, we are forced to hold constant a whole list of factors—like income and the prices of other goods—which are, in real life, likely to be changing all the time. What effect will a change in one of these parameters have on the demand curve?

We divide the determinants of demand now into two categories: changes that increase the quantity desired and changes that reduce the quantity demand at any price and so reduce demand.

An **increase in demand** is shown by a shift to the right in the demand curve because this movement indicates that at any given price a larger

Increase in demand: a change in income, tastes, or some other determinant of demand that causes the quantity demanded of some good to rise at every price (shown by a shift to the right in the demand curve)

amount is demanded. In Figure 2, for example, 500 apples were orginally desired at a price of 20¢ each. After the increase in demand (shifting the demand curve from D_0 to D_1) a larger amount, 700 apples, is demanded.

What can cause such an increase in demand? Anything that makes the good in question more desirable or necessary. For example:

☐ An increase in the income of apple eaters.

☐ An increase in the price of pears (an apple substitute).

☐ A decrease in the price of cheddar cheese (which is often consumed together with apples and is, therefore, a complement).

☐ A medical discovery that an apple a day keeps the doctor away.

☐ A successful advertising campaign by an apple marketing organization that causes people to be more aware of apples.

Decrease in demand: a change in income, tastes and preferences, or some other determinant of demand, which causes the quantity demanded to be lower at every price (shown by a shift to the left in the demand curve)

A **decrease in demand** occurs when something happens to make a good less desirable. This is illustrated in Figure 3 by a shift to the left in the demand curve. Here, demand has fallen from D_0 to D_2. At a price of 20¢ per apple, only 300 (as compared to 500) apples are required, with similarly lower quantities demanded at other prices.

FIGURE 3-2: INCREASE IN DEMAND
An increase in demand occurs whenever something happens to make a good more desirable. It means that people are willing to purchase more of the item at any given price.

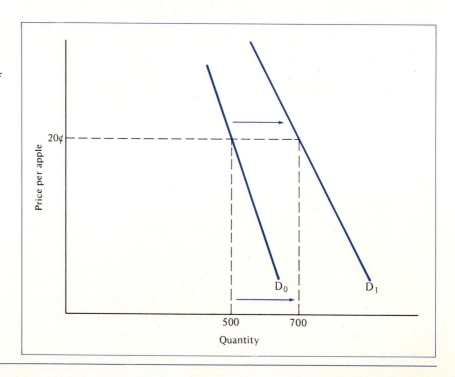

A fall in demand can occur due to a wide variety of factors, among them:

☐ A decrease in the incomes of apple eaters.

☐ A fall in the price of other kinds of fruit.

☐ A rise in the prices of flour, butter, sugar, and cinnamon (ingredients used in making apple pie and, so, possible complements of apples).

☐ A rumor starts that apples cause constipation, producing reduced demand for apples.

☐ A fad that involves eating prunes instead of apples in order to avoid doctors.

Demand (and, therefore, the demand curve) is a description of what buyers would like to do. It shows us the amounts that they would like to purchase at different prices. This does not show how much they actually receive, because only one price will prevail in the end. But that one price will be influenced heavily by the nature of demand and supply.

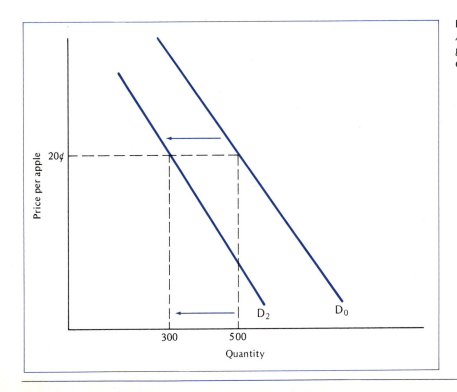

FIGURE 3-3: DECREASE IN DEMAND
A decrease in demand occurs when a good becomes less desirable. A smaller quantity is demanded at every price.

THE CONCEPT OF SUPPLY

Supply: a description of the seller side of the market; supply looks at the factors that determine the amounts and kinds of goods and services offered for sale

Supply is a complete description of how producers determine the amount and kinds of goods and services that they wish to produce and exchange. While we normally think of ourselves as demanders, everyone is actually involved in both demanding goods and in supplying something, such as time, talent, know-how, and experience. Even people who are unemployed or who don't work for whatever reason are involved in supplying some of these services at home (we call these nonmarket activities, however, since they don't earn a paycheck). Like demand, the concept of supply can be a very complicated one, but a little intuition will go a long way toward helping us understand the factors that determine how much of something is offered for sale.

While the supply decision depends on a multitude of factors, it is useful to look at five of the most important ones.

1. PRICE.
We generally assume that there is a direct relationship between price and the amount produced—a higher price induces greater production and a lower price reduces the amount made available. Why is this so? Let's suppose that the price of pizza suddenly rises by $1 in your area. How will the pizza producers respond to this? First, note that pizza making is now more profitable. Assuming that nothing has happened to increase the costs of making pizza pies, each pizza now earns $1 more profit. This induces pizza barons to expand production. Local junk food shops may start selling pizza as well as burgers and fries in an attempt to gain a cut of the profits, too. And smart businessmen and women may open new pizza places to gain some of the profits. The quantity of pizza supplied will thus rise as the price of pizza rises.

The law of diminishing returns plays a role here, too. As the pizza makers expand production, they have to hire more workers and increase the use of pizza machines. In general, they will not be able to produce the additional pizzas as efficiently (which means as cheaply) as they did before. The rising price is necessary in order to pay for the increased production because diminishing returns drive up costs as production rises.

Lower prices have just the opposite effect. Lower prices cut profits and cause producers to look for something else to sell, selling less of the lower-priced item in the process.

2. PRICES OF INPUTS.
Inputs: factors of production; goods and services that are used in the production of other goods and services (labor, raw materials, and so on)

Inputs are goods and services that are used to make other goods and services. Flour, water, shortening, yeast, heat, and labor are inputs, for example, in the production of bread. Inputs make outputs.

The costs of these inputs affect the amount of any good offered for sale.

As input costs rise, it becomes less profitable to produce a good, and so smart sellers produce a little less and look for a more profitable line. When input costs fall, on the other hand, profits rise and so production goes up.

Examples of the effect of input prices on the quantity supplied are not hard to find. A rise in the minimum wage has a substantial impact on the sellers of fast foods (who traditionally employ lots of young workers at about the minimum wage). As wage rates rise, the fast food business becomes less profitable. Many sellers respond to this by hiring fewer workers and reducing the hours that their business is open. In this way, they reduce costs during low profit hours and keep profits as high as possible. But they also sell fewer burgers, fries, and chicken. The higher input prices make the sellers lower the quantity of fast food they wish to supply.

3. AVAILABILITY OF INPUTS. A large number of inputs are necessary for even relatively minor production operations. A professor, for example, wouldn't seem to need very many tools in order to produce education services. Yet, most profs would be hard pressed to operate without such basic inputs as blackboard, chalk, heat, lights, chairs, texts, and . . . oh, yes . . . students!

The availability of the proper kinds of inputs at the right time with the correct skills or properties has a large impact on the amounts and kinds of goods offered for sale.

4. TECHNOLOGY. The way that inputs are combined to produce outputs is at the very heart of the concept of supply. Changes in **technology** affect the goods produced and sold as well as the demands for the various kinds of inputs involved.

Technology: the process by which inputs are combined to produce goods and services; changes in technology involve changes in the processes that are used to make goods and services

Changes in technology are very important. Improved technology allows us to produce more things with the same resources or to produce better things. Much of the growth in American industry can be attributed to improved technologies.

The power of improving technology is not to be denied and it shows up in the unlikeliest of places. Even the familiar hamburger has benefited from the march of science. Burger shops, which were once slow and inefficient, operated by one or two people, have now made way for the modern McDonald's and similar chains, which use specialization of labor and modern machinery to increase the amounts and kinds of fast foods they can sell.

5. EVERYTHING ELSE. All sorts of other things can affect the production process and sales. You should have no trouble coming up with dozens of examples, but here are two to start things off. The weather is a very basic

everything else that can affect the supply decision. Weather has a large impact on the amounts of agricultural goods made available each year. Too much rain, not enough rain, too much heat, not enough heat: all these situations can reduce agricultural yields and so reduce the supply of fruits and vegetables.

A second example of everything else is government regulation. The government has broad powers to regulate the production and distribution of goods and services to protect the public interest. Goods can rise and fall in price, appear or disappear from store shelves, or change in design in response to changing government regulations. This everything else is beginning to have a large impact on the goods that we purchase. Environmental regulations, for example, have significantly affected the supplies of automobiles, coal, clean air and water, and nuclear power, to list just a few.

THE SUPPLY CURVE

Supply curve: a curve that shows the quantity of a good or service that producers wish to sell at every possible price

The **supply curve** is a simplification of the concept of supply, which allows us to more clearly see the consequences of a change in one of the determinants of supply on the market process. The supply curve holds the costs and availability of inputs constant, assumes no change in technology or anything else, and examines the relationship between the quantity supplied and the price at which the goods are sold.

There are many possible shapes that a supply curve can assume. Figure 4 shows the normal representation of a supply curve for apples. This curve is upward-sloping, showing that, as the market price of apples rises, more and more apples are offered for sale in a given period of time. Conversely, if the price of apples falls, more apple growers find this business unprofitable, and so fewer apples are made available.

This upward-sloping supply curve probably characterizes the supply situation in most industries. In general, higher prices are needed, at least in the short run, to induce increased production, and lower prices cause fewer goods to be supplied. We shall examine the origins of supply curves in detail in later chapters.

CHANGES IN SUPPLY

The quantity of any good or service that firms provide depends mostly upon the price of that good, the costs of production, and the amount and availability of inputs necessary to the production process. Anything that acts to change the costs of production or the availability of inputs causes the supply relationship to change.

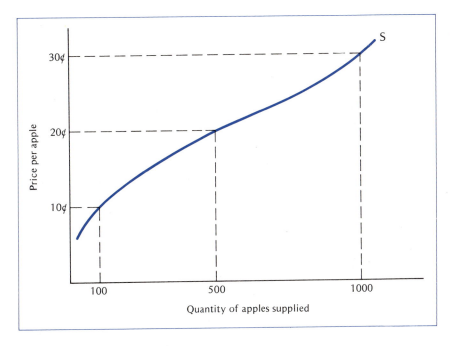

FIGURE 3-4: A SUPPLY CURVE FOR APPLES
The supply curve shows how the amount of goods offered for sale varies with price. Higher prices mean higher profits, all else being equal. They also encourage firms to produce. The quantity supplied is high when prices are high and declines as the selling price falls.

Changes that make production cheaper or that increase the amounts of goods that can be produced with the same resources cause supply to increase. An **increase in supply** is pictured in Figure 5 as a shift to the right in the supply curve. An increase in supply can be caused by numerous factors, among them:

Increase in supply: a change in the costs of production, technology, or some other determinant of supply that causes the quantity supplied to increase at every price (shown by a shift to the right in the supply curve)

☐ Reduced labor costs (which make production more profitable and cause more to be produced).

☐ Reduced raw material costs (which have the same effect on profits and production).

☐ Increased availability of inputs (which makes it easier to produce if there have been some shortages in the past).

☐ A labor-saving invention that reduces costs.

☐ The lifting of a government regulation that had added to costs.

An increase in supply is a change in one of the determinants of supply that induces producers to increase the quantity supplied at any price. Note here we distinguish between the concept of supply—which is a description of the entire supply process—and the *quantity supplied* at any given price. Quantity supplied rises whenever price rises. Supply (the supply curve) rises

FIGURE 3-5: INCREASE IN SUPPLY
Supply rises when goods become more profitable or easier or cheaper to make.

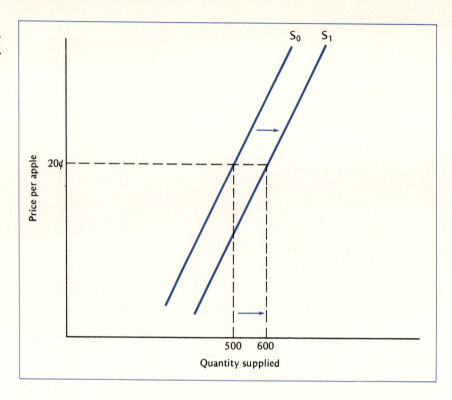

only when something has happened—like a reduction in the costs of production—to alter the entire supply relationship.

A **decrease in supply** occurs whenever something happens to either increase the costs of production or hamper the ability to produce (as in the case of a shortage of necessary inputs). A decrease in supply occurs when the quantity supplied is decreased at any price. A decrease in supply is pictured in Figure 6 as a shift to the left in the supply curve.

Many factors can cause supply to fall, among them:

□ An increase in the price of vital raw materials (which reduces profit and so discourages production).

□ A strike, which reduces the availability of labor.

□ An increase in the taxes that businesses must pay.

□ The imposition of costly environmental regulations.

Supply changes whenever one of the underlying determinants of supply is altered. Note that the supply curve shows the amounts of goods that

Decrease in supply: a change in costs of production, technology, or some other determinant of supply, which causes the quantity supplied to be less at every price (shown by a shift to the left in the supply curve)

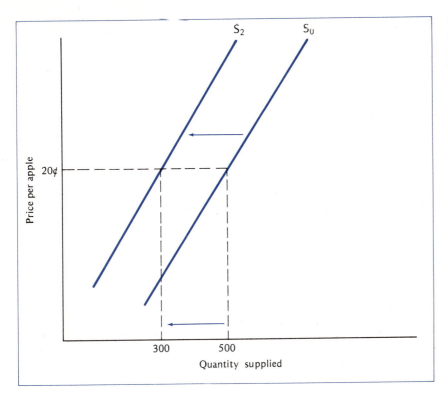

FIGURE 3-6: DECREASE IN SUPPLY
Supply falls when a good becomes more costly to produce or less profitable to make and sell.

producers would like to sell at some particular price. There is no guarantee that the public will cooperate and purchase that amount. In the end, that decision is made by the market.

The *market* is where all the action is. In the market, the conflict and competition that characterize exchange come to the fore. To better understand how markets work, pretend for a moment that you have been transported to a medieval street market. There is a large crowd milling around the marketplace waiting for the buying and selling to begin.

On one side of the street are the producers. They make up the supply curve for this market. Each knows how much of the day's goods—apples—that they can profitably sell at any given price. The supply curve that they form is shown in Figure 7.

On the other side of the street are the buyers. There are many of them, too, with widely different preferences, and each has decided how many apples he or she will buy at any given price. They make up the demand curve of Figure 7.

THE MARKET AT WORK

FIGURE 3-7: THE MARKET FOR APPLES
The supply and demand curves show how many apples people would like to buy and sell at different prices. The market determines the final amounts and the selling price.

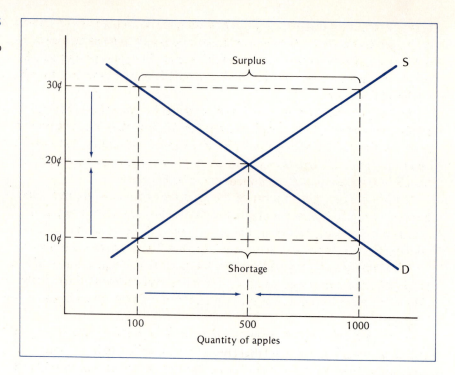

In the middle of the street, standing on a soapbox, is the auctioneer. His job is to call out prices. He will continue to call out prices until all the buyers and sellers are satisfied with the results of the exchanges that take place at that price. When an equilibrium is achieved (in the sense that all desired exchanges can be successfully completed), the auctioneer can go home.

The market opens at 10:00 A.M. sharp. The auctioneer calls out his first price, 30¢ per apple, and buyers and sellers form huddles and examine the results of the call (see Figure 7). Thirty cents is a comparatively high price for this market, and so the growers are willing to sell 1000 apples. But, since the price is so high, the consumers are only interested in buying 100 apples. There is a **surplus** or **excess supply** equal to 900 apples. Some of the sellers quickly calculate that, at this price, there will be no buyer for their apples and they will be left holding the bag. Since they want to do business, the holders of the surplus apples offer to put them on sale and demand that the auctioneer call out a lower price. The auctioneer quickly calls out a very low price: 10¢ per apple.

At 10¢ per apple, apples are cheap, and the buyers announce that they are willing to purchase 1000 of them. But the sellers are not so pleased. At

Surplus: a situation where the quantity supplied exceeds the quantity demanded

Excess supply: a situation where the quantity supplied at a particular price exceeds the quantity demanded at that price

such a low price it does not pay most of them to produce apples and many of the producers find it is more profitable to produce something else or to hold their apples and hope for a better price later. Those few producers who have particularly profitable harvesting methods are willing to sell 100 apples at this price.

A quick tally indicates that, at this price, there is going to be a **shortage** or **excess demand** of apples. People want to buy 1000 apples, but there will be only 100 available, creating a potential shortage of 900 apples. Some of the apple buyers, realizing that at 10¢ an apple they will go home empty-handed, demand that the auctioneer call a higher price.

Shortage: a situation where quantity demanded exceeds quantity supplied

Excess demand: a situation where the quantity demanded at a particular price exceeds the quantity supplied at that price

The auctioneer spends most of the next two hours calling our prices between 10¢ and 30¢ per apple, but each time there is either a surplus or a shortage. Eventually, however, the auctioneer calls out a price of 20¢ per apple. At this price something unique happens. The producers discover, in their huddle, that they are willing to sell a total of 500 apples (some of the producers, unwilling to sell for such a low price, start to leave). On the other side of the road, the buyers discover that, together, they are willing to buy 500 apples.

At the price of 20¢ per apple, the quantity that producers are willing to sell exactly equals the amount that consumers are willing to buy. There is no shortage, and no surplus either. The auctioneer has found a price that will clear the market.

This is actually how markets work in the real world, although the buyers and sellers do not necessarily all gather in one place, and no actual auctioneer exists. The goal of the market is to find a market-clearing price, which economists call the **equilibrium price**.

The market responds to shortages and surpluses. When too much of a good is offered for sale, a surplus is created and the goods are put on sale, causing the price to fall. When not enough to produced, buyers bribe the sellers to produce more by offering them a higher price.

Equilibrium price: the one price where the quantity supplied equals the quantity demanded; neither a surplus nor a shortage exists at the equilibrium price; all exchanges desired at this price can be completed

Eventually, the equilibrium price is found such that no surplus or shortage exists, and that price holds. All desired exchanges at the equilibrium price can be completed. In compact and highly organized markets, like the New York Stock Exchange, this price is arrived at quickly and easily. In other, less organized markets, like the market for used cars, the price is found eventually.

The magical property of the equilibrium price is that it is the only price at which quantity demanded is equal to the quantity supplied. While buyers prefer a lower price and sellers would be pleased if they could charge more, at the equilibrium all exchanges can be accommodated.

Once the market equilibrium is found, shortages can occur only if something happens to increase the amount that buyers wish to purchase, or to reduce the amount offered for sale. In either case, a shortage is a sign that the price is too low. When the shortage becomes apparent, market forces bid up the price to its equilibrium level.

Surpluses signify the opposite situation. A surplus exists when the quantity demanded at a particular price is less than the quantity supplied. This happens when people reduce the amount they wish to purchase, or when sellers increase the amount they offer for sale. Surpluses indicate that the price is too high. In response to the excess supply, sellers bid down the price of their goods in search of a market-clearing situation. The equilibrium price is arrived at eventually.

CHANGING MARKETS

The equilibrium price prevails in a market until something happens to alter demand and supply and create a new equilibrium. By learning to recognize factors that can change either demand, supply, or both, you can predict what will happen to market prices and quantities exchanged.

FIGURE 3-8: AN INCREASE IN DEMAND
An increase in demand creates a shortage. Price and quantity rise as the market moves to a new equilibrium.

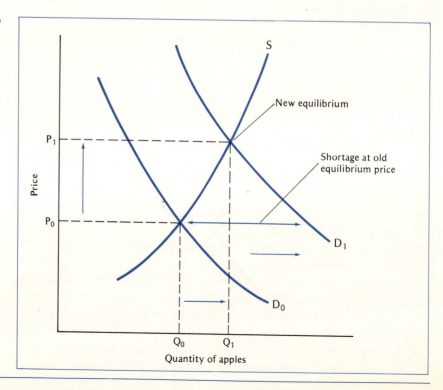

Suppose, for example, that the price of oranges rises. An increase in the price of oranges reduces the quantity of oranges that consumers want to buy and, assuming that people treat apples as a substitute for oranges, at least part of the falling purchases of oranges will be made up with rising apple buying. The demand curve for apples shifts out and to the right as shown in Figure 8. More apples are demanded here, but nothing has happened to increase the amount of apples that buyers bring to market (the apple supply curve). The increase in demand creates an initial shortage of apples.

In response to the apples shortage, sellers begin to ration the scarce fruit by raising the price. As the price of apples rises, the quantity of apples supplied rises (a movement along the supply curve). A new equilibrium is achieved, as Figure 8 shows, but at a higher price with a large quantity of apples exchanged.

This is not the only way that the apple market can be thrown out of equilibrium, of course. Another possibility is shown in Figure 9. Here, an unusually good harvest of apples has disrupted the market. The large apple crop shifts the supply of apples out and to the right. This increase in the apple supply creates a surplus of apples. At the old equilibrium price, the amount of apples that consumers want to buy is far less than the new, larger

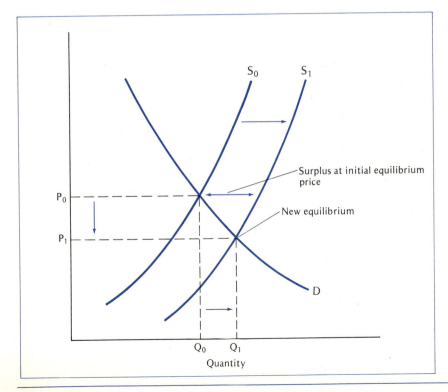

FIGURE 3-9: AN INCREASE IN SUPPLY
Rising supply creates a surplus at the initial equilibrium price. Price falls as a result of the surplus. A new equilibrium is found at a lower price and higher quantity than before.

quantity of apples that are brought to market. Apple prices drop due to the surplus. As price falls, consumers purchase more apples and bring the market into equilibrium.

SUMMARY OF MARKET ACTIONS

The analysis of the market is largely one of examining the components of demand and supply to see how they combine to produce a shortage, surplus, or equilibrium. Since our pictures model the real world, they can be used to tell us a great deal about how economic events occur in the economy. Since the model is so simple we can summarize the basic market movements in only a few paragraphs.

An *increase in demand* occurs whenever the quantity of a good that people wish to buy increases at any price. The increase in demand causes a shortage of that good, bidding up its price. The higher price induces higher production. We can summarize this chain reaction as follows:

$$\uparrow D \rightarrow \uparrow P \rightarrow \uparrow Q$$

An *increase in supply* occurs whenever a good becomes more profitable to produce, and therefore more of it is offered for sale. The increase in the amount supplied causes a surplus of the good. To get rid of the surplus, sellers put the item on sale and its price falls. The result is

$$\uparrow S \rightarrow \uparrow Q \rightarrow \downarrow P$$

A *decrease in demand* occurs whenever a good becomes less desirable as, for example, when some substitute item falls in price. The falling demand creates a surplus of the good. As dealers' shelves and stockrooms fill up, sellers get wise to the surplus and offer a lower price to clear out the goods. The lower price discourages further production of the item involved. The result of a fall in demand is

$$\downarrow D \rightarrow \downarrow P \rightarrow \downarrow Q$$

A *decrease in supply* will have the opposite effect. As costs rise, businesses cut back unprofitable production, creating a shortage. This shortage bids up price. The result is

$$\downarrow S \rightarrow \downarrow Q \rightarrow \uparrow P$$

An *increase in demand* accompanied by a *decrease in supply* causes prices to rise substantially. The increase in demand causes prices to be bid up. The fall in supply means that firms are attempting to pass increased costs of production on to consumers. Together, they cause a large increase in

ECONOMIC ANALYSIS

Normally, higher and higher quantities demanded produce higher prices, yet in this case, we find that higher sales come at a lower price. How can this be? The answer is shown in Figure 1. It is not the demand curve that has been at work here, but supply.

As changing technology lowers the costs of producing pocket calculators and other electronic devices, competition among producers forces down price. The improved technologies shift supply out and to the right, bidding down prices as quantity exchanged increases.

At the high initial prices only a few people can gain by buying pocket calculators. This explains the high price and the small number sold. As supply increases and price falls, however, more and more people find that they can gain by trading for pocket calculators. Today the quantity demanded is huge because of the low price.

How low will the price of these pocket gizmos go? The answer depends on what happens to demand and supply. If supply continues to increase as it has in the past, we can expect the price to fall even lower. However, if supply should level off and demand should increase, then the price of pocket calculators could stop falling and even rise. Predicting changes in price here involves guessing what will happen to the supply and demand for this product in the future.

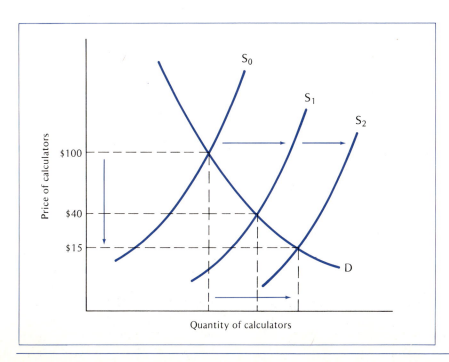

FIGURE 4-1: THE CALCULATOR MARKET
Technological advances cause the supply of calculators to increase repeatedly. This results in lower prices with larger quantities purchased.

REAL WORLD ECONOMICS: COFFEE AND TEA

CAFFEINE INFLATION? TEA PRICES RISE AS FROST ATTACKS BRAZIL COFFEE CROP

Heavy frosts last month destroyed a large part of the coffee harvest in Brazil. This is bad news for people who drink coffee in the United States. It may be even worse news for those who drink tea.

Tea drinkers can expect to pay 10 to 20 percent higher prices for their cup of tea in a few months, according to industry officials. And some types of tea may be in short supply, even at the higher prices.

Why should frosts in Brazil have such an impact on the price of tea? Did those frosts also hurt the tea harvest? No. Tea grown in the Far East and elsewhere was unaffected by Brazil's low temperatures. The tea harvest today is about what it has been for several years. Therein lies the problem.

In the past, problems with the coffee harvest have resulted in higher coffee prices. When coffee gets very costly, however, even addicted Americans drink less coffee and more of the relatively less expensive tea. These sudden swings in the tea market cause the prices of all kinds of tea to rise, too, and some of the more popular types inevitably run out.

"We're hoping that the cold weather lasts a good long time," Dar G. Ling, a tea industry official, commented concerning the Brazilian situation. Tea-drinking consumers, however, should pray for an early thaw.

ECONOMIC ANALYSIS

The situation described here is fairly common in markets where demands are interrelated. Coffee and tea are treated as substitutes by many people. When the price of one changes, impacts are felt in the market for the other. This is shown in Figures 2 and 3.

The damage to the coffee crop causes the supply of coffee to decrease (the coffee supply curve shifts back and to the left as in Figure 2). A shortage of coffee prevails and bids up the price of coffee.

While many coffee drinkers are willing to pay the higher price for their brew, some drop out of the market as price rises. A higher price causes a smaller quantity demanded—a movement along the coffee demand curve. Many of those who no longer buy coffee switch to tea as a substitute. This increases the demand for tea (Figure 3), which creates a shortage of tea and also increases the price.

Just the opposite result prevails when goods are complements, such as coffee and cream. As coffee prices rise, and people drink less coffee, they also use less cream. Hence, the demand for cream (Figure 4) falls and, with it, the price of cream.

Markets can be related in other ways, too. Often the product of one market is used as an input in the production of another good. Coffee, for example, is used in the manufacture of coffee liqueurs. When coffee beans become more

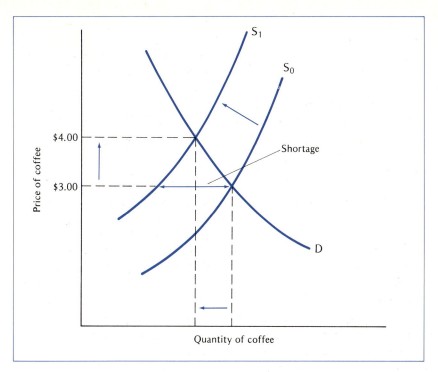

FIGURE 4-2: RISING COFFEE PRICES
Frosts in Brazil reduce the supply of coffee. This forces up the price of coffee, and has impacts in many other markets as well.

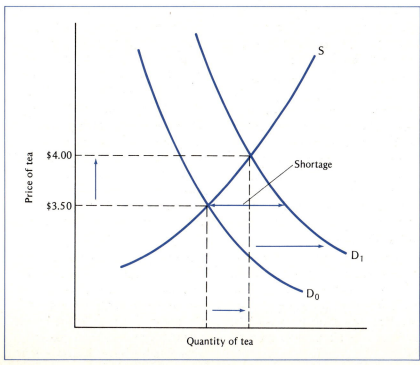

FIGURE 4-3: RISING TEA PRICES
Tea is a substitute for coffee. Many people who refuse to pay higher prices for coffee switch to tea instead. This increases the demand for tea, bidding up its price, too.

FIGURE 4-4: COFFEE AND CREAM
*Rising coffee prices affect the market
for cream, too. People who no longer
drink coffee will purchase less cream.
The demand for cream falls and so
does its price.*

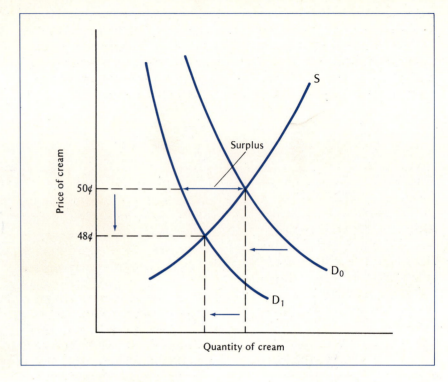

**FIGURE 4-5: MARKET FOR COFFEE
LIQUEUR**
*Since coffee is more expensive, this
will increase the costs of everything
made with coffee. These prices will rise
as well.*

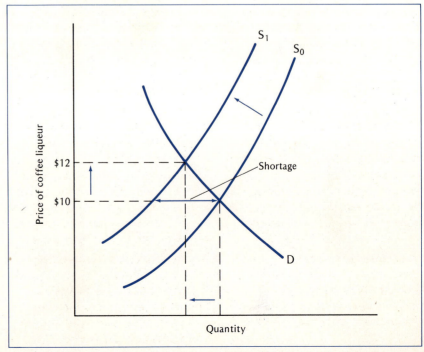

expensive, costs of production rise for coffee liqueurs—this is shown in Figure 5 as a reduction in the supply of the liqueurs. Here, again, the higher coffee prices cause a higher price of another good.

Since markets are connected in so many ways, it is not surprising that a change in the price of any major good in the economy sends shock waves spreading into other markets throughout the world.

AIRLINE PROFITS RISE AS DISCOUNT PRICES SWEEP INDUSTRY

Airlines are charging less these days and enjoying it more. Despite heavy discounting of air fares, which began in 1978, airlines find that they are posting higher and higher revenues and making record profits.

"When we cut prices, we knew we were taking a risk," airline official Kitty Hawk commented. "We knew we would have more customers at a lower price, but we weren't sure if we could get enough new passengers to make up for the lower per-seat revenues."

This worry seems to have been a false one. The problem that airlines now have is finding enough seats to serve the customers attracted by lower fares. They have accomplished this largely by ordering new, more economical jets for the future and by squeezing more seats on the planes now in service.

"Our passengers don't complain about a loss of a few inches in shoulder room when they know that they are saving as much as half over a regular fare," Ms. Hawk said.

ECONOMIC ANALYSIS

The question that the airlines faced in cutting prices was one of figuring out the **elasticity of demand** for their product. Economists know that the demand for some products is very responsive to price—a small change in price produces a large change in quantity demanded. We say that these goods have an **elastic demand**—a demand that is very responsive to price changes. The airline industry is one case of a market where an elastic demand prevails. Small reductions in fares result in large increases in sales— the quantity rises so much that more revenues are generated, even with lower prices!

Goods with elastic demands are often goods with many substitutes. When price rises a little, consumers shift to available substitutes. With higher air fares, lots of travelers would use trains, buses, private cars, or simply stay home and not fly as often. With lowered air fares, however, travelers shift to planes.

Not all products have demands that behave this way. The demand for some products is **inelastic** or unresponsive to price. Even large swings in price have little impact on the quantity demanded. Goods

REAL WORLD ECONOMICS: CUT-RATE AIR FARES

Elasticity of demand: a measure of the responsiveness of quantity demanded to changes in price

Elastic demand: a good has an elastic demand if quantity demanded is responsive to changes in price. The elasticity coefficient is greater than one

Inelastic demand: a good has an inelastic demand if quantity demanded changes relatively little when price changes; elasticity coefficient is less than one

that are considered necessities or that have few close substitutes are inelastic. Cigarettes, gasoline, electricity, and water are examples of goods with relatively inelastic demands.

Economists have developed a statistic called the **elasticity coefficient** to measure the responsiveness of market demand. The elasticity coefficient E is defined to be

$$E = \left| \frac{\% \text{ change in quantity demanded}}{\% \text{ change in price}} \right|$$

The bars on either side of this fraction indicate that an **absolute value** is being taken. That is, the sign (plus or minus) of the fraction is ignored and only the actual values themselves are computed.

We can use the following formula to measure the elasticity of demand between two points by calculating the percentage change in prices and quantities.

$$E = \left| \frac{(q_0 - q_1) \div (q_0 + q_1)}{(p_0 - p_1) \div (p_0 + p_1)} \right|$$

The quantities at the two points on the demand curve are q_0 and q_1, and p_0 and p_1 are their corresponding prices.

An elasticity coefficient that exceeds one ($E > 1$) indicates a responsive or elastic demand since quantity changes proportionally more than price. An elastic demand curve is illustrated in Figure 6 for airline seats between two specific destinations.

At a price of $100 per seat, 100 seats are demanded per week for this particular flight. If the price is lowered to $75, the quantity demanded rises to 150 seats per week. At the lower price, many more people are willing to pay to fly on this route. The elasticity coefficient tells us that the demand for this product at these prices is elastic:

$$E = \left| \frac{\% \text{ change in quantity demanded}}{\% \text{ change in price}} \right|$$

$$= \left| \frac{(100 - 150) \div (100 + 150)}{(\$100 - \$75) \div (\$100 + \$75)} \right|$$

$$= \left| \frac{(-50) \div (250)}{(\$25) \div (\$175)} \right|$$

$$= \left| \frac{-20\%}{14\%} \right| = 1.4 > 1$$

Since this elasticity coefficient exceeds one, the demand is elastic by definition.

Why should someone care if the demand is elastic or not? There is a close relationship between elasticity of demand and the way that the total revenue from selling a good changes with price. Total **revenue** is the total amount spent on a particular item (price multiplied times quantity). When a good has an elastic demand, as in Figure 6, there is an inverse relationship between price and revenue. That is, when price falls, total revenue rises and as price goes up total revenue goes down. We can see this in Figure 6. At the initial price of $100, revenue was $10,000 (100 seats sold at $100 each). When the price goes down to $75, total revenue actually goes *up* to $11,250 (150 seats at $75 each) because the change in quantity demanded

---

Elasticity coefficient: the elasticity coefficient is defined to be

$$E = \left| \frac{\% \text{ change in quantity demanded}}{\% \text{ change in price}} \right|$$

Absolute value: the value of a number regardless of its sign. The absolute value of both +4 and −4 is 4, for example

Revenue: the amount of money spent on an item; price times the quantity bought and sold

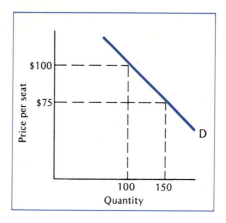

FIGURE 4-6: ELASTIC DEMAND FOR AIRLINE SEATS
For this demand curve, a 25 percent reduction in price causes a 50 percent increase in the quantity demanded. This is called an elastic demand. As price falls, notice that total revenue rises.

is so much larger than the change in price.

The airlines were uncertain about lowering prices because they feared that the demand for their product might be inelastic (as pictured in Figure 7). This demand curve is drawn much steeper than the one in Figure 6 to suggest that the demand curve lacks responsiveness to changes in price.

We can verify that this demand curve is inelastic at these prices by computing the elasticity coefficient. When the price drops from $100 to $75, demand increases, but only from 100 seats to 105 seats. The elasticity coefficient is

$$E = \left| \frac{\% \text{ change in quantity demanded}}{\% \text{ change in price}} \right|$$

$$= \left| \frac{(100 - 105) \div (100 + 105)}{(\$100 - \$75) \div (\$100 + \$75)} \right|$$

$$= \left| \frac{(-5) \div (205)}{(\$25) \div (\$175)} \right|$$

$$= \left| \frac{-2\%}{14\%} \right| = 0.1 < 1$$

Since the elasticity coefficient is less than one, the demand for this product is inelastic.

When a good has an inelastic demand, there is a direct relationship between price and total revenue. When price rises, total revenue rises as well. Price cuts, however, result in lower total revenues. We can see this in Figure 7. At the higher price ($100), total revenues are high—$10,000. At the lower price of $75, however, total revenue is less—$7875.

In discussing the elasticity of demand for a particular item, like airline tickets, remember that our conclusions regarding elasticity apply only to a specific range of prices. That is, a good may have an inelastic demand at a certain price, but an elastic demand at prices very much higher or lower than this. The elasticity coefficient can change at different parts of the demand curves.

The problem of the airlines is now clear. If they increase supply and lower price (as shown in Figure 8), the impact on profits will depend

**FIGURE 4-7: INELASTIC DEMAND FOR
AIRLINE SEATS**
*This is an example of an inelastic
demand curve. As price falls by 25
percent the quantity demanded rises by
only 5 percent. Total revenue falls as
price falls.*

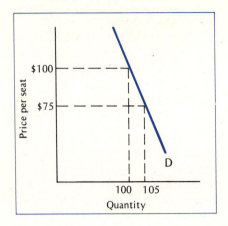

**FIGURE 4-8: HOW THE AIRLINES DID IT
IN 1978**

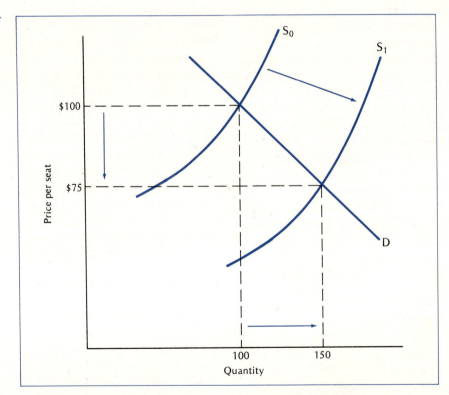

on the elasticity of demand for their product at the current price range. If demand is elastic at these prices, then total revenues are higher at the discount price and airline profits can rise.

As the news story shows, the demand for airline seats is elastic, and so increased supply and lower fares result in higher revenues for the airlines, and more and more air travel for the public.

CIGARETTE TAX BURNS SMOKERS, NOT TOBACCO FIRMS

STATE CAPITAL—When state cigarette taxes rose from 6¢ per pack to 10 and then 13¢ here this year, many cigarette distributors were concerned that they might be taxed out of business. Their worries, however, seem to have been needless.

"We were pretty worried when cigarette taxes took such a big jump," Elmer Lungrot, a tobacco distributor, notes. "We weren't sure that we could pass on such a big increase in costs to our customers. Many of us thought that we'd have to either absorb most of the tax ourselves or lose customers."

Instead, cigarette sellers have suffered a minor loss, but most of the tax, although officially paid by wholesalers when they purchase special cigarette tax stamps, is actually being paid by consumers.

"We were able to pass most of the tax on to the smoking public with only a little loss in revenue," Mr. Lungrot added. "I guess the smoker got burned by this tax increase, because we haven't been affected all that much."

ECONOMIC ANALYSIS

Who bears the burden of a tax on a good like cigarettes? In general, part of the tax is paid by consumers in the form of higher prices (as the tax is passed on to them) and part is paid by sellers, who sell fewer goods and receive a lower price for them after the tax is paid. This is illustrated in Figure 9. As-

sume that, without any tax, the equilibrium price of cigarettes is 50¢ per pack. Now, let's impose the 13¢ per pack cigarette tax all at once. The tax (which is paid by the seller) shifts the supply curve for cigarettes up by a vertical distance equal to the 13¢ tax.

This shift shows that the quantity of cigarettes initially offered for sale at 50¢ per pack will now be sold at 63¢. In other words, sellers raise their prices by the full amount of the tax. Does this mean that consumers pay all the tax? Not necessarily.

If sellers raise their price to 63¢, they find some consumers are unwilling to pay the higher price. A smaller quantity is demanded, creating a surplus of cigarettes at 63¢ (see Figure 9). This surplus forces the price of cigarettes to fall to 61¢—still above the pretax price of 50¢, but below the price that the cigarette sellers would like to charge.

Who has paid this tax? Both producer and consumer bear part of the burden here, with most of the tax being paid by the smoker. Because of the tax, cigarette smokers are now paying 61¢ per pack for smokes, up from 50¢ before the tax was imposed. This 11¢ increase in price represents the **consumer burden** of the tax. Here, the consumer is paying most of the 13¢ state tax.

The producer bears part of the burden, too. Before the tax, the sellers were receiving 50¢ per pack for their goods. After the tax they receive 61¢, but must pay 13¢ to the

REAL WORLD ECONOMICS: CIGARETTE TAXES

Consumer burden: the part of a tax that consumers pay in the form of higher prices for the taxed goods

FIGURE 4-9: TAX ON A GOOD WITH AN INELASTIC DEMAND

Because the demand for cigarettes is relatively inelastic, there is little drop in quantity demanded when the tax is enacted. Most of the cost of the tax is passed on to buyers in the form of higher prices. Only a little of the tax is borne by producers.

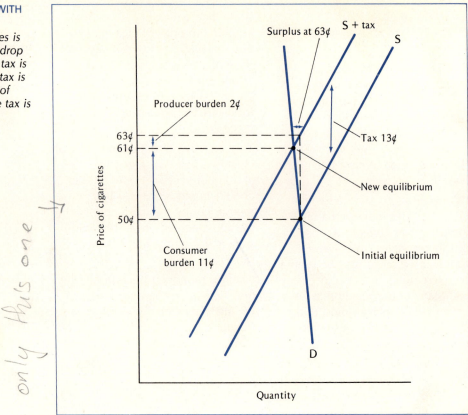

state tax authorities. The seller, therefore, receives 2¢ less after the tax than before. The **producer burden** of the tax is equal to 2¢.

Figure 9 shows what happened in the news story. Most of the tax was passed on to smokers, with only a little of it actually coming out of the producers' pockets. Is this the case with every tax? No. The distribution of the tax burden depends on the elasticity of demand for the product involved. This can be seen by comparing producer and con-

sumer burdens in Figure 9 with those shown in Figure 10.

Because the demand for cigarettes is inelastic, the sellers can raise their price a great deal and experience only a small decrease in quantity demanded. This is not the case if cigarettes have an elastic demand as pictured in Figure 10. Because demand is very responsive to price here, if the cigarette producers raise the price very much, they encounter a huge decline in quantity demanded. In order to

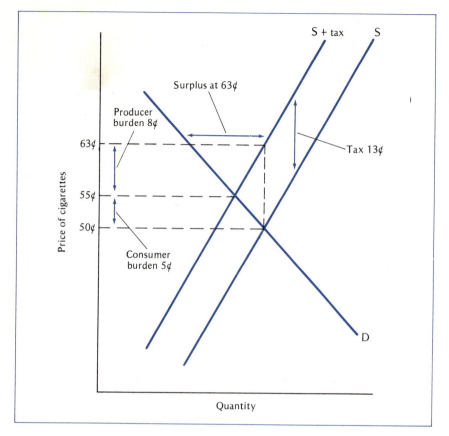

FIGURE 4-10: TAX ON GOOD WITH ELASTIC DEMAND
In this case, if producers pass too much of the tax on to the consumers, demand will fall. To avoid a surplus, the producers bear the largest part of the burden in the form of lower after-tax revenues.

avoid a surplus of cigarettes, then, prices rise only a little (from 50 to 55¢) and so the producers receive a much lower price. The consumer still bears part of the burden but the larger portion falls on the producer, who receives 8¢ per pack less.

The distribution of the tax burden, then, depends on the elasticity of demand for a product (at least in the short run—over the long run changing demand and supply can alter this analysis). Only in very unusual cases is the entire burden of a tax borne by either producer or consumer. One such exceptional instance is illustrated in Figure 11. Here the market for a good with a **perfectly inelastic demand** (elasticity coefficient is zero) is illustrated. No matter what happens to price, the same quantity is demanded. This is the type of demand that may exist for goods that are absolute necessities—like heroin to a drug addict or insulin to a diabetic. Since there is no change in quantity demanded when price rises, the complete burden of the 13¢ tax falls on the consumer in this case.

Perfectly inelastic demand: the situation which prevails when the same quantity is demanded at every price

FIGURE 4-11:   TAX ON A GOOD WITH PERFECTLY INELASTIC DEMAND
If cigarettes have a perfectly inelastic demand, all of the tax is passed on to consumers in the form of higher prices.

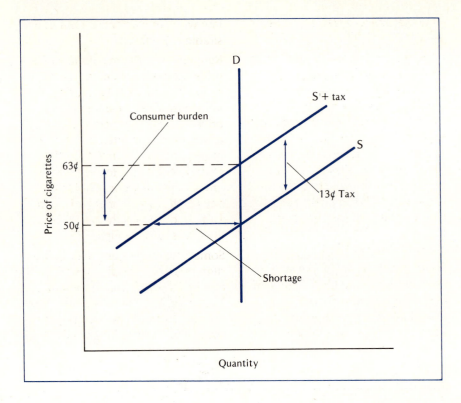

REAL WORLD ECONOMICS: RENT CONTROLS

RENTS ARE CHEAP HERE, BUT APARTMENTS COST A FORTUNE

NEW YORK CITY—Rents on apartments are cheap in this city. Or not so cheap. It depends on whom you ask.

New York has had government controls on rents for many years. Laws specify when rents can be raised and by how much. These rent controls have resulted in apartment rents that are less than in many comparable cities (many of which are now considering rent control laws). So the controls have been effective. Or have they?

The problem, many New Yorkers

claim, isn't the rents, but the cost. "Just try to find an apartment!" one subway rider explains. "There just aren't any available. If you can find one you can be sure that it's either so run down that you wouldn't want to live in it or else you have to offer to pay the landlord under the table to get it."

The housing shortage here is real. Apartments in many parts of town are in constant short supply. Others are run down. Paradoxically, instead of more apartments appearing to handle the shortage, some buildings are being torn down or abandoned. As a result, there are actually fewer apartments in town now than there were several years ago.

"You just can't afford to be a land-lord in this city anymore," one frustrated building owner ex-plained. "I can't afford to fix up these buildings at the rents the law says I have to take. So I'll let them run down and get what I can. I'd like to fix these places up—this property could be a good invest-ment. But with these rent controls, I'm stuck in a no-win situation."

ECONOMIC ANALYSIS

Sometimes government rules are used to short-circuit the actions of the market. When this happens, the results are often unfortunate. Rent controls are an example of a

law with good intentions but unde-sirable side effects.

Rent controls are an example of a **price ceiling**. A price ceiling is simply a maximum legal price. Rent controls set maximum legal prices for rents on houses and apartments. The intention of these price controls is admirable—the government wants to keep prices low so that the poor can afford to pay for the price-controlled good. This is not always the result, how-ever, as shown in Figure 12.

Some time in the past, the equilib-rium rent for a certain type of apartment was found to be $400. To keep prices from rising, the gov-ernment froze prices—refused to allow rents to rise. This would

Price ceiling: **a maximum legal price**

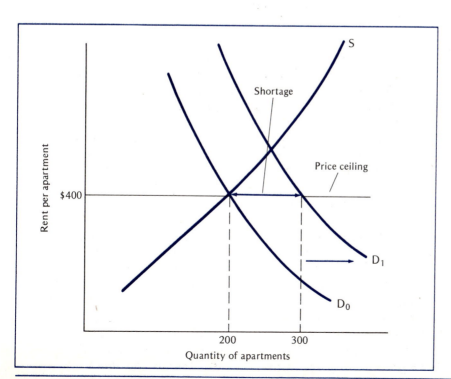

FIGURE 4-12: IMPACT OF A PRICE CEILING
Price ceilings tend to cause shortages because they do not allow prices to rise. This prevents a greater amount from being supplied when demand rises.

have had no impact on the market if both demand and supply had stayed constant. This is seldom the case, however.

As the demand for apartments rises, no increase in supply is forthcoming. Apartment house owners cannot afford to supply more apartments unless rents are allowed to rise. Since they are frozen at $400, the only result is a shortage of apartments. Those who already have apartments benefit because they get relatively low rents, although the condition of their apartments may suffer. Those without apartments, however, are left out in the cold. If they are to find a place to live, they must either know someone who can get them a deal or be willing to bribe a landlord to rent to them. Sometimes even this isn't enough, and they must settle for an apartment that is falling apart because the owner can't afford upkeep at current rental levels.

Rent controls, then, are a mixed bag. They help those who can manage to avoid the unpleasant side effects of the controls but hurt others by creating a shortage of rental units, reducing the quality of the apartments available, and forcing illegal payments to apartment managers.

REAL WORLD ECONOMICS: PRICE FLOORS

Subsidy: a government payment to an individual or group, generally designed to encourage certain economic actions

BILL TO GUARANTEE EGG PRICES NEARS PASSAGE IN CONGRESS

WASHINGTON, D.C.—A bill that would stabilize the incomes of America's egg producers came one step nearer to passage today when it gained support in a key subcommittee vote.

"We are pretty sure now that the egg price supports will pass in some form," Representative Orson Henhouse, who is sponsoring the legislation, commented. "The question now boils down to which way we go about guaranteeing egg producers a fair price."

The committee has two proposals before it. Under the provisions of one plan the federal government would support posted egg prices through a variety of public purchase plans. A second proposal, widely supported by consumer groups, calls for federal subsidy of egg sales as a better way of guaranteeing price. Egg industry lobbyists have come out against the latter subsidy proposal on the grounds that it provides inadequate protection for egg producers. They may, however, be willing to compromise for the subsidies if they cannot muster enough votes for their first choice.

The committee staff is studying these proposals to see if a compromise plan can be reached to speed this bill through the entire House.

ECONOMIC ANALYSIS

We shall do the committee's work and analyze the difference between these two plans, but first let's take a look at **price floors** in general. Prices in certain industries (particularly in agricultural production) can vary widely from year to year. These unstable prices create problems for those involved in production since planning is difficult and unexpectedly low prices several years in a row can force some producers out of business.

In response to these and other problems, the government in the United States and elsewhere has repeatedly stepped in to try to stabilize farm incomes through a variety of means, most commonly by guaranteeing farm prices—setting a price floor for a particular good. When a price floor is put in place, the power of the market is reduced. While the buyers are free to pay more than the minimum price, they cannot buy goods for less than the legal minimum. This creates problems, as Figure 13 shows. Here we see a hypothetical egg market where the equilibrium price is 95¢ per dozen. If the price is allowed to go to 95¢ the market clears. Now, suppose Congress enacts a price floor of $1.20. If $1.20 is the minimum legal price for eggs, the market cannot clear and a surplus of eggs shows up. Producers, responding to the high egg price, work their hens overtime and produce a large quantity of eggs. Consumers, however, won't buy many eggs at this high minimum price. The result is eggs rotting in storage houses.

Simply setting a price floor, then,

Price floor: a minimum legal price

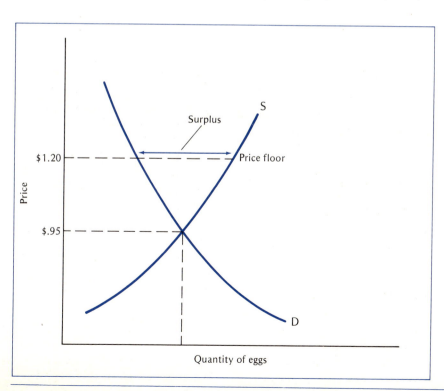

FIGURE 4-13: PRICE FLOOR FOR EGGS
If the equilibrium price for eggs is 95¢, a price floor of $1.20 creates a surplus of eggs on the market.

doesn't necessarily solve the problem of the egg producer. Some sellers benefit from the higher price (those who are able to sell their eggs), but others lose since their eggs can't be sold at so high a price. Consumers lose as well, since they are forced to pay more for eggs.

There are two ways to solve this problem. The first is shown in Figure 14. Here, the government steps in to buy the surplus eggs. The demand for eggs is artifically increased by a new government demand for the eggs. In effect, the government promises to buy any unsold eggs at the floor price. In this way, all the eggs produced are sold (and so all egg producers ben-

efit) with the surplus eggs going to the government instead of going to waste. The U.S. government has often undertaken policies like this. The extra goods are either stored (impossible with eggs) or given away to schools, the poor, or needy foreign countries. In this plan, the egg producers get what they want (higher incomes), but consumers lose since they must pay more for eggs and, in addition, must bear the higher taxes necessary for the government to buy the egg surplus.

An alternative plan is shown in Figure 15, where the consumer burden is reduced. Here, the price that farmers receive is the same—$1.20—but the *way* they get their

FIGURE 4-14: GOVERNMENT PRICE SUPPORTS
Under one plan, the surplus eggs are bought by the government, increasing demand from D to D*. Price rises to $1.20. Egg producers win, egg consumers lose.

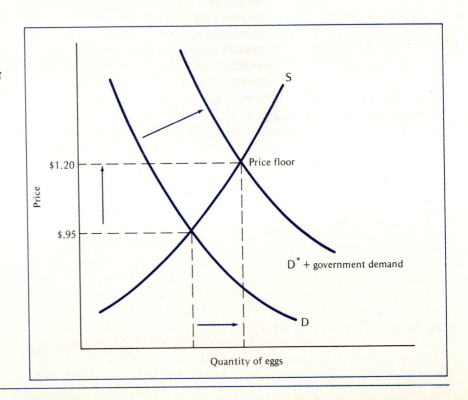

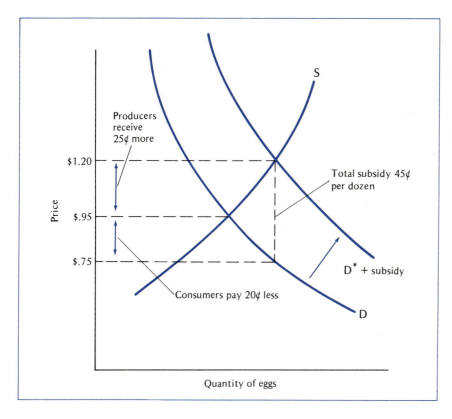

FIGURE 4-15: SUBSIDIZING EGG PRODUCTION
If a subsidy is granted to egg producers, consumers pay less than the equilibrium price, but producers receive more. The D curve shows the amount that consumers pay for eggs. The producers receive 45¢ more than this—the government subsidy is 45¢ in this example.

money has changed. In this second plan, the government agrees to pay the farmer a subsidy of, say, 45¢ for each dozen eggs sold. When a subsidy is used, the egg producers sell their goods for a low price and still make money since the price they actually receive (including the subsidy) is much higher.

All of this can be seen in Figure 15. Here, there are two demand curves that are relevant. The first is the market demand curve D, which shows the price that consumers are willing to pay for each quantity of eggs. A second curve D* shows the price that the producers actually receive for the eggs

(the amount that the consumers pay plus the 45¢ subsidy). As the figure shows, with a 45¢ subsidy, egg producers can sell all the eggs they want and still receive $1.20 per dozen. The market price for the eggs will be just 75¢, however, since that is the maximum amount that consumers are willing to pay for this quantity of eggs.

As far as the egg producers are concerned, the government purchase program shown in Figure 14 and the price subsidy plan of Figure 15 have the same end result. They receive $1.20 per dozen eggs in each case and they are able to sell all that they want at this price.

For consumers, the plans are very different (this accounts for the news story's note that consumer groups support the subsidy proposal). In either case, taxes have to be raised because both plans call for increased government outlays. In the case of the first proposal, however, the government steps in to buy eggs to keep their price high (hurting egg consumers). Under the subsidy proposal, government payments to egg producers keep the price of eggs artifically low. Egg buyers gain when this happens.

Why should the egg producers favor the first plan over the second? In the two figures we find little difference in the output and the amount the producers receive. In the first plan, however, they are protected against falling consumer demand for eggs. If consumers purchase fewer eggs the government must step in and purchase more of them.

With the subsidy plan, egg ranchers receive a fixed subsidy, but if demand falls, so will the price that they receive. The forces of the market can still cause problems. Since they are trying to avoid the verdict of the market, the subsidy program, which is better for consumers, may be viewed as worse by the producers.

APPENDIX: MORE ABOUT ELASTICITY

The concept of elasticity is one of the more useful ideas in microeconomics. This brief appendix gives more details to help you better understand elasticity.

One of the mistakes that students commonly make in thinking about the elasticity of demand is to assume that steep demand curves are inelastic while flat demand curves are more elastic. The slope of a curve may be useful at times in telling something about elasticity, but this is not always the case, as Figure 16 shows.

Here we have two demand curves, one fairly flat and the other steeply pitched. Which is more elastic? Despite appearances, their elasticity is exactly the same! Each is, in fact, the elastic demand for airline tickets previously pictured in Figure 6. Why does one look elastic while the other appears more inelastic? The only difference is in the scale on the horizontal axis used to measure quantity demanded.

Since differences in scale can make demand curves look different, what can we conclude about the elasticity of demand for a product just by looking at its demand curve? Nothing. To really know if a demand is elastic or inelastic, we must go through the calculations outlined in the text.

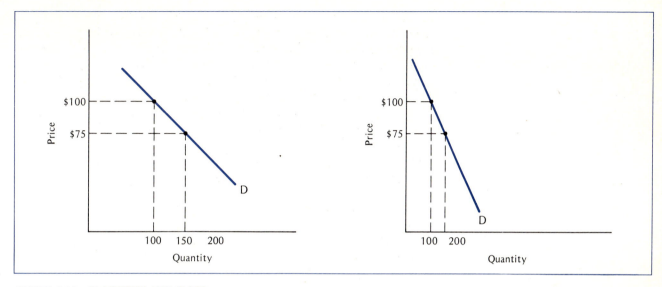

FIGURE 4-16: ELASTICITY AND SLOPE
The slope of a demand curve is not necessarily an indication of the elasticity of demand for the product involved. Both of these demand curves are elastic (they are the demand for airline seats discussed in this chapter). Because the scales that measure quantity are different, however, one has a greater slope and so "appears" less elastic. The elasticity coefficient is the same for both.

ELASTICITY AND PRICE. Another surprise is that the elasticity of demand for a good is not always the same—even on the same demand curve. Elasticity often changes with price. This is illustrated in Figure 17.

When a good is cheap, its demand may be very inelastic. Because salt is so very inexpensive, for example, people treat it as a necessity—they have no reason to seek higher-priced substitutes. Even a relatively large increase in price has little effect on the quantity demanded. When price is very high, however, consumer behavior changes. If the price of salt increases from 20¢ per pound to, say, $5.00 per pound, you can bet the elasticity of demand will be different. At $5.00 per pound, people will be very aware of salt substitutes. Even a relatively small increase in salt's price then would lead to a relatively larger change in the quantity of salt demanded.

Figure 17 shows a straight-line demand curve that is both elastic and inelastic, depending on the price of the good. Use the formula in the text to calculate the elasticity of demand in both ranges to see that the figure is correct.

FIGURE 4-17: ELASTICITY OF DEMAND AND PRICE
Elasticity is different at different prices as this figure indicates. At high prices, the demand for goods is often inelastic. As price falls, however, elasticity increases. In this figure, demand is completely inelastic when price is $100 and completely elastic when price is $0. Calculate elasticity in each range of this straight-line demand curve to prove that elasticity does change as price changes.

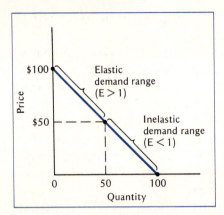

FIGURE 4-18: ELASTICITY OF SUPPLY
Supply curves can display different price elasticities. A relatively inelastic supply indicates that price changes induce relatively small changes in quantity supplied. An elastic supply curve indicates that small changes in price bring about relatively large changes in quantity supplied. A perfectly inelastic supply indicates that quantity supplied is the same at all prices. A perfectly elastic supply means that any quantity can be supplied at the price shown.

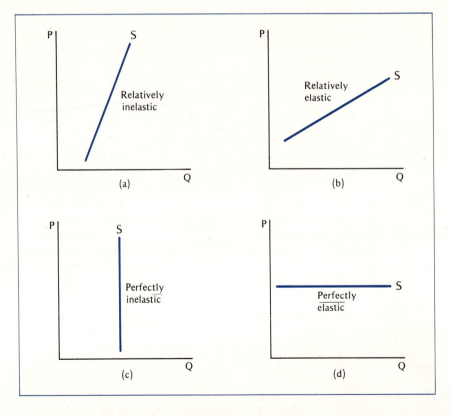

ELASTICITY OF SUPPLY. The concept of elasticity can also be applied to supply curves. The elasticity of supply is a measure of the responsiveness of quantity supplied to changes in price. An inelastic supply is one where quantity supplied changes relatively little when price is increased or decreased. An elastic supply is one that is relatively more responsive to changes in price.

Figure 18 shows several supply curves (with the same price and quantity scales) of differing elasticity. Just as with elasticity of demand, the supply elasticity is not determined by slope alone. And elasticity can change along a given supply curve depending on the price quoted.

Looking at the supply curves of Figure 18, we see that market conditions are influenced by the elasticity of supply. Suppose, for example, that demand increases in each of the supply cases noted in the figure. Show, as an exercise, that the market price increases more in the inelastic supply cases. Can you explain why this is the case?

A final note about elasticity is appropriate. When economists talk about the elasticity of demand or supply, they are limiting their conclusions to the short run, the elasticity at a given price, and only small changes in price.

SUMMARY

1. Markets are connected in many ways. The demands for goods that are substitutes or complements are very much related. An increase in the price of one good, for example, tends to cause an increase in the price of its substitute. This, however, may cause the price of a complement to fall as well. Rising and falling prices can also affect other markets because they may affect the costs of production of other goods.

2. A change in the price of a good can have different impacts depending on the nature of the demand for that good. Economists look at the elasticity of demand for goods. An item with an elastic demand is one where a small percentage change in price causes a relatively large percentage change in quantity demanded. Goods with inelastic demands also exist. If demand is inelastic, then a large proportional change in price has a relatively small change in quantity demanded. Elasticity of demand is important to firms because of the relationship between elasticity and total revenue. For goods with elastic demands, price and total revenue are inversely related. For goods with inelastic demands, price and total revenue are directly related.

3. A tax affects markets differently depending on the elasticity of demand for the taxed product. If the good has an inelastic demand, then most of the tax is passed on to consumers in the form of higher prices. Only a relatively small proportion of the tax is borne by producers in

the form of lower after-tax revenue. If the taxed good has an elastic demand, on the other hand, relatively less of a tax is borne by the consumer in higher prices and relatively more is borne by producers.

4. Supply and demand analysis does not always work because of governmental price floors and ceilings, which set prices independently of market forces. While these programs have their advocates, in an economic sense they are often undesirable because of the problems they cause. Price ceilings (like rent controls) cause shortages of goods and services. Price floors (like farm price supports) create surpluses. Each creates winners, but losers are created by these laws as well.

DISCUSSION QUESTIONS

1. Suppose that there were to be a new discovery of oil in the United States. What impacts would this have on the following markets: oil, natural gas, automobiles, airlines, hamburgers?

2. You are a merchant and you are trying to improve business by putting some items on sale for a short period of time. Under what circumstances would this be a good idea? When might you lose money doing this?

3. Governments often impose price floors—minimum legal prices. The minimum wage is an example of such a price floor. Suppose that the minimum wage is set below the equilibrium wage in the labor market. What economic effects will this action have on employers, employees, and unemployment?

4. The following is a list of items that are typically taxed by state governments. Who bears the burden of the tax in each case? Gasoline, alcohol, automobiles, hotel rooms, theatre admissions.

5. Suppose the government wants to take actions that will reduce the retail price of beef products. Congress has decided to accomplish this goal through the use of subsidies. Does it make any difference if the subsidy is paid to the beef producers (they receive a government payment when they sell beef) or to the consumers (who get a subsidy when they buy beef)? Explain your reasoning.

TEST YOURSELF

Indicate whether each of the following statements is *true* or *false*. Be able to defend your choice.

1. When we observe rising quantity supplied in a market, it must follow that price has risen.

2. If the price of Coke rises, it

must be because of some increase in the cost of producing Coke.

3. If the cost of Coke rises, then the price of Pepsi will surely fall.

4. If a good has an elastic demand, then falling price does not necessarily mean rising profits.

5. If a good has inelastic demand, then rising price generally means rising revenues for producers.

6. If the government wants to raise the largest amount of taxes, it should tax goods with inelastic demands.

7. If the government wants to place most of the burden on producers, it should tax goods with inelastic demands.

8. Price ceilings tend to produce surpluses.

9. Both price floors and ceilings are examples of situations where the market is not allowed to set prices itself.

10. Price floors and ceilings always cause shortages and surpluses.

Part 2
Consumer and Producer Choice

5
Consumer Choice

This chapter looks behind the demand curve to see how consumers decide which kinds and amounts of goods and services they will purchase. This chapter will also help you understand the basis for economic decisions in general and will answer the following questions in particular:

What costs and benefits do consumers consider when making a demand decision?

What is utility and how do economists use it to anlayze consumer choice?

Why is the demand curve for an individual item downward sloping and what factors cause a person's demand to change?

What other decisions does the consumer make? How do costs and benefits affect consumer choice in these areas?

The 1978 raisin harvest was rotten. Rain at the wrong time ruined much of the crop and raisin prices doubled. Consumers responded to these higher prices in a number of ways. They bought fewer raisins—an obvious choice. They increased purchases of items that can be substituted for raisins in cooking and daily use. The Christmas 1978 fruitcakes were heavy on walnuts and light on raisins—in spite of the fact that the price of walnuts increased at the same time!

The tools of supply and demand are useful in explaining events in the raisin, walnut, and fruitcake markets. But they don't tell us the whole story. In order to really understand how markets work, we must look behind the curves to see the individual behavior that the curves represent. How do individuals choose how many raisins to buy? What governs this consumer choice? When prices change what determines the kind of change in consumer behavior which results? In short, how do people make the choices that we see as market demand? What economic factors influence these choices?

Consumer choice is an interesting problem because it exactly demonstrates the economic facts of scarcity and choice. The consumer has scarce resources and must choose how to use them in a world with millions of options. How is this choice made? This chapter looks at the decision-making process that results in your demand for raisins, walnuts, and a world of other things.

HOW MUCH TO BUY?

Suppose that you arrive at a fast food store with $2.00 to spend on lunch and are faced with a two-item menu. Tacos cost 50¢ and root beer can also be purchased at 50¢ per serving. How do you decide how many tacos and how many root beers to buy? The question may seem trivial. You simply decide and say, "Give me three tacos and a root beer." But how do you arrive at this decision? What factors enter into the choice that results in your demand for tacos and root beer? Why do you choose to have a third taco instead of a second root beer (since you can't have both)?

Economists suggest that all economic decisions involve a weighing of the benefits that a decision makes possible versus its costs. Put very simply, you buy a third taco (instead of a second root beer) because the benefits that a third taco makes possible exceed the cost.

CONSUMER BENEFITS: UTILITY

People make decisions that affect their time and income to improve their overall well-being. Suppose that we could put a meter on you that would measure this well-being. It would show an increase when your well-being increased (because you ate a taco, for example) and would decline when well-being went down (because, say, of a poor grade on an economics exam). If we then put any arbitrary scale on this utility meter we could measure ups and downs in well-being and compare the effects of different actions on the consumer.

The concept of **utility** is built on the idea of measuring changes in well-being. When the consumption of a good or service improves well-being, we shall talk about this as causing an increase in utility. The greater the increase in well-being, the greater is the utility rating assigned to that activity. The particular scale used to measure utility is unimportant. Any way of measuring will do, so long as better choices receive higher utility ratings and choices that are equally good are assigned equal utility numbers.

Utility: a measure of well-being, used to compare choices

The idea here is *not* that we all go around with utility meters attached to our heads and carefully watch them to see that we are making the right decision. But we, as individuals, know what actions make us better off and which ones make us worse off. That is, the meter exists, but it exists only deep within each of us. By seeing how individuals would behave if the utility meter were visible, we gain insights into actual consumer choice behavior.

Suppose we put a utility meter on you and watch what happens to your well-being as you consume, say, seven tacos. What might we observe? Chances are that the readings on the utility index would look something like the readings displayed in Figure 1.

Assuming that you like tacos to begin with (that they give you positive utility and so increase your well-being), we would expect to see your total utility rise as the number of tacos you eat increases. Using the scale shown here, the first taco causes total utility to increase by 15 points. When two tacos are eaten at the same sitting, total utility goes up to 25. The third taco increases total utility to 30, and so on. The utility scale used here is arbitrary—any scale will do so long as the numbers provide an accurate ranking of your preferences (things you prefer get higher utility scores).

Figure 1 shows that total utility increases as the number of tacos eaten at one sitting rises. But it also shows something even more interesting. Notice that the first taco caused the utility needle to rise by 15 points, but that the second taco was not nearly so well received. Consuming the second taco caused utility to rise from 15 to 25. The second taco has **marginal utility** of just 10. The lower utility index shows that, while you enjoy the second taco, it doesn't add to your well-being as much as the first. And the third taco, as Figure 2 shows, provides even lower marginal utility. Because at this point you begin to get tired of tacos (or your desire for tacos is nearly satisfied), the third taco adds relatively little to well-being and therefore carries a relatively low marginal utility. Eventually, eating tacos adds nothing to utility. As

Marginal utility: the amount of additional utility derived from an additional unit of a good or service

FIGURE 5-1: UTILITY FROM TACOS
Utility is a measure of well-being.
Utility rises as the number of tacos
consumed rises.

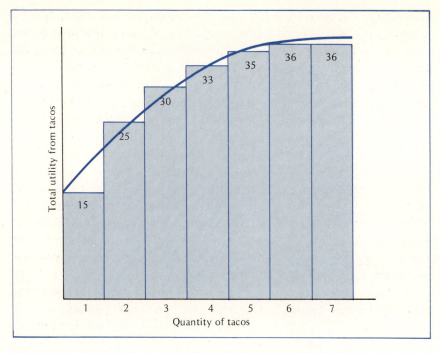

**FIGURE 5-2: DECLINING MARGINAL
UTILITY**
Each of the first 6 tacos increases
utility, but by successively smaller
amounts. This phenomenon is known
as declining marginal utility.

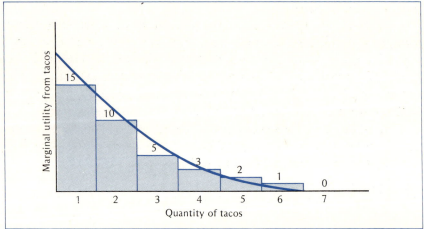

Figure 2 indicates, the seventh taco adds nothing to well-being and an eighth taco (at one sitting) might actually make you worse off—provide negative marginal utility.

Chances are that consumption of most items affects well-being in this way. In general, we prefer more goods to less because higher consumption increases total utility (makes us better off, within limits). But the greater the amount of any item we consume, the less each additional unit adds to our well-being in a given period of time. Sometimes marginal utility falls off quickly (the marginal utility of the second haircut in one afternoon is very small) and sometimes it declines only slowly (the marginal utility of the twentieth peanut may still be relatively high given the addictive nature of that food). Marginal utility may even increase for a while (sometimes the second beer tastes better than the first). But, in general, consumers react to tacos, root beer, and most other items in the ways described here.

MAXIMIZING UTILITY

Given this information, it is now possible to simply determine the amount of tacos and root beers you might choose to purchase. The marginal utility that different quantities of root beer consumed at one sitting provide is shown in Figure 3. Here, again, root beers add to total utility but the fact of diminishing marginal utility is apparent, too. The fourth root beer provides significantly less utility than the first, second, and third.

Supposing that tacos and root beer each cost 50¢ and that you have $2.00 to spend. How many tacos and root beers should you purchase? To get an idea, let's divide the $2.00 into four 50¢ allotments and find the best way to spend each, given the goal of maximizing total utility from tacos and root beer consumption.

How should you spend the first 50¢. Look at the marginal utility ratings for tacos and root beer in Figures 2 and 3. If you spend the 50¢ on tacos, you can buy 1; the first taco has a marginal utility (MU) of 15 points. The same amount spent on the first root beer provides MU equal to just 10. The choice? Obviously, the first thing you buy is a taco because you "like it the best"—it has the highest marginal utility available.

How do you spend your next 50¢? The choice is slightly changed. You can either purchase 1 root beer (MU = 10) or a second taco, which also provides MU = 10. Since these two add equal amounts to utility, you are

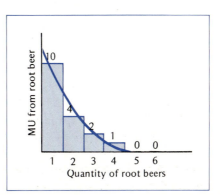

FIGURE 5-3: MARGINAL UTILITY FROM ROOT BEER
The marginal utility from root beer also declines. We can compare the MU shown here with that shown for tacos in Figure 2 to determine which good the consumer prefers.

indifferent between them. You could flip a coin to decide—the decision wouldn't affect your total level of satisfaction. Suppose, for the sake of argument, the coin comes up heads and you purchase another taco. You still have $1.00 left to spend, so what else do you buy?

With the next 50¢ you can either purchase the first root beer (MU still equal to 10) or you can buy a third taco. Because you are now getting full of tacos (the MU of the third one equals just 5), the money is better spent on root beer. With the last 50¢, the choice is the third taco (MU = 5) or a second root beer (MU = 4). The best choice is to go with tacos again. As a result of this action, you end up having 3 tacos and 1 root beer for lunch, and the total utility that this provides (15 + 10 + 10 + 5 = 40) is the maximum that you can achieve, given the preferences shown here, the amount of money available, and the prices of root beers and tacos. (Check this statement out: try to find an affordable combination of root beers and tacos that provides greater total utility.)

Conceptually, we can measure the benefits from any action in terms of the utility (or marginal utility) that that action provides. And we can, as shown above, see what combinations a consumer might choose by building up total utility, spending income bit by bit to maximize total utility. But what factors really produced this choice? To fully understand what is going on here, we must understand not only the benefits, but also the costs of consumer choice.

OPPORTUNITY COST

What does it cost to buy, say, the third taco? The easy answer is to simply quote its price. The third taco costs the same as any other taco: 50¢. This answer is correct, but it doesn't go far enough. With a fixed budget (we assume just $2.00 is available to spend on lunch), the allocation of 50¢ to buy the third taco means that other goods (root beer) worth 50¢ must be foregone. Figure 4 shows the budget line that the consumer faces at the lunch counter. With $2.00 to spend on tacos and root beers that cost 50¢ each, the choice must fall within these purchase possibilities. If all income is spent on tacos, 4 can be purchased. If 4 root beers are desired, 0 tacos can be purchased. The other combinations possible are shown in the figure. Any increase in the number of tacos consumed dictates a reduction in root beer.

The cost of an item is therefore not just its money cost, but also its opportunity cost. The opportunity cost of an action is the foregone benefits of the best alternative choice. The money price of a good tells us which other items must be given up in order to consume this good. But the real cost of a taco is not 50¢, it is the utility of the root beer (or other desirable items),

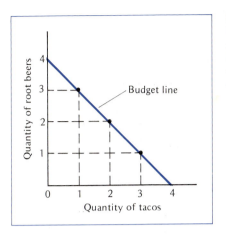

FIGURE 5-4: THE BUDGET CONSTRAINT
With $2.00 to spend and both tacos and root beer selling for 50¢, the budget line tells us the different combinations of the two goods that can be purchased.

which is foregone when the taco is purchased. The cost of the taco is its opportunity cost.

Can we calculate this opportunity cost? Opportunity cost is not difficult to figure if we know the choices that the consumer faces (shown in Figure 4) and the utility of the items given up (see Figure 3).

The budget line in Figure 4 shows all the different possible choices that the consumer in this example can make. Assuming that money itself yields no utility (so that there is no advantage in holding it) and that no other choices exist, all $2.00 will be spent on either tacos or root beers. The choices, then, are those on the budget line.

Our business here is to calculate the opportunity cost of consuming different amounts of tacos. To do this, we need to first see what goods are foregone when a taco is consumed and then look at the utility that the goods given up provide. This foregone utility is the opportunity cost.

Suppose that the consumer decides to eat one taco. What must be given up? As Figure 4 indicates, the consumer has enough money to purchase either 0 tacos and 4 root beers or 1 taco and 3 root beers. In eating the first taco then, the consumer is giving up the utility that the fourth root beer would have provided. The fourth root beer, as Figure 3 shows, has a marginal utility of just 1. We plot this opportunity cost in Figure 5.

What is the opportunity cost of the second taco? The choice to eat one more taco requires drinking one less root beer. Since the third root beer (which must be foregone) yields MU = 2, this is the opportunity cost of the second taco. As an exercise, you should continue this opportunity cost calculation to see that the curve in Figure 5 is correct.

The opportunity cost of consuming tacos increases as the number purchased rises. As more tacos are purchased, fewer root beers are left. Each additional root beer given up has a higher marginal utility than the one

FIGURE 5-5: MARGINAL OPPORTUNITY
COST (MOC)

*Each additional taco consumed
requires that more and more root beers
be foregone. Consuming the first taco,
for example, means giving up the
fourth root beer, which has MU = 1.
This is the opportunity cost.
Consuming the fourth taco, however,
requires giving up the very first root
beer, which has a high marginal utility.
Thus the marginal opportunity cost of
the fourth taco is greater than that of*

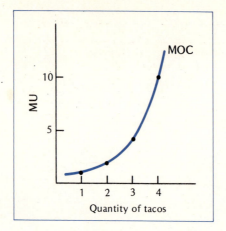

before. The opportunity cost of the fourth taco is therefore higher than that
of the first.

CONSUMER EQUILIBRIUM

Marginal benefit: an item's marginal utility

Marginal opportunity cost: the opportunity
cost of consuming an additional unit of a good
or service

How many tacos should you buy? You make your decision based on a
comparison of the **marginal benefits** (MB) you get from each taco (as
measured by their marginal utility) versus the **marginal opportunity cost**
(MOC) of each taco (the utility of the foregone root beers). Logically, you
should *buy* tacos so long as their benefits exceed their cost (and as long as
your money holds out). If the opportunity cost of a taco exceeds its benefits,
you get more utility by buying root beers (or other goods) instead of tacos.

Using the information presented earlier, we can graph the costs and
benefits for tacos. The marginal benefits are the marginal utility (from Figure
2) that tacos provide. The marginal costs are the opportunity costs of each
taco in terms of the utility of the foregone root beers, as plotted in Figure 5.
These marginal costs and marginal benefits are calculated in Table 1 and
plotted in Figure 6.

Purchasing the first taco is clearly a good idea because, as Figure 6
shows, the benefits that the first taco provides exceed its opportunity cost.
Eating the first taco increases utility by 15 points. In consuming it, however,
you are forced to give up the fourth root beer. The opportunity cost of the
first taco is therefore the utility of the fourth root beer that cannot now be
purchased. Since 1 taco increases utility by 15 points, while giving up the
root beer lowers utility by just 1 point, this decision makes sense.

If eating 1 taco is a good idea, how about 2? Again, as Figure 6 shows, it
is to the consumer's benefit to make this purchase since the benefits are

TABLE 5-1

COSTS AND BENEFITS

Item	Marginal Benefit	Item Foregone	Marginal Cost Opportunity Cost (Utility of Fore-gone Item)	Do Benefits Exceed Cost?
First taco	15	Fourth root beer	1	Yes
Second taco	10	Third root beer	2	Yes
Third taco	5	Second root beer	4	Yes
Fourth taco	3	First root beer	10	No

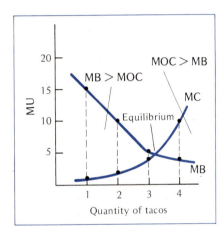

FIGURE 5-6: EQUILIBRIUM FOR THE CONSUMER
The consumer weighs the marginal benefits (MB) or marginal utility of buying tacos against the marginal opportunity cost (MOC), or opportunity cost of that action. Consumers continue to buy so long as marginal benefits exceed marginal costs. Here, the best choice for the consumer is to buy 3 tacos (1 root beer is purchased with the remaining funds).

greater than the cost. With $2.00 to spend, buying the second taco (MU = 10) means giving up the third root beer (MU = 2). The benefits of this purchase exceed the opportunity cost, making this a wise choice, too.

If 2 tacos are good, what about 3? The third taco increases utility by 5 but means giving up the second root beer, which privides MU = 4. Three tacos and 1 root beer are therefore a good choice.

What about buying a fourth taco and skipping root beer altogether? As Figure 6 shows, this would be a bad decision. The fourth taco's MU is just 3, while its opportunity cost (the MU of the first root beer) is a much higher 10. Trading the last taco for the first root beer, therefore, is a decision that costs more than it benefits the buyer.

Since the consumer is best off consuming all goods that have marginal benefits (marginal utility) exceeding their marginal cost (in terms of opportunity cost), the utility-maximizing decision is the one shown in Figure 6: Purchase tacos (or any other good or service) until the marginal benefit equals the marginal opportunity cost (assuming partial units like ⅓ taco are possible) or so long as MB is greater than MOC (if partial units cannot be purchased).

We call this the **consumer equilibrium.** Buying any more tacos would be a bad decision (MOC exceeds MB), but purchasing fewer would mean giving up benefits that are greater than the cost.

Consumer equilibrium: the situation that prevails when the consumer allocates resources to maximize utility

When the consumer equilibrium is reached, all items purchased provide benefits at least as great as their opportunity cost. At this equilibrium, the consumer maximizes total utility, given prevailing income and prices. This equilibrium is stable in the sense that there is no incentive to the consumer to alter buying behavior and do anything else. Any movement away from the equilibrium would only make the consumer worse off—so long as prices, income, and preferences do not change.

CHANGING CONSUMER CHOICE

Once the consumer has reached this equilibrium, the demand decision only changes if something happens to alter either the benefits that different goods provide or the opportunity costs involved. Two possible changes are illustrated in Figures 7 and 8.

Anything that lowers the opportunity cost of an item increases the consumers' purchases of it. This is illustrated in Figure 7. Suppose that this consumer was initially in equilibrium, purchasing a quantity Q_0 of bread. At this quantity the benefits of the last loaf of bread just match the opportunity cost of purchasing it.

Opportunity costs can fall, as Figure 7 shows, for several reasons. Suppose that the price of bread falls. Now, buying a loaf of bread means giving up less money, and therefore fewer other goods. A lower price directly lowers opportunity cost.

The opportunity cost of bread falls indirectly if the prices of other items rise. Suppose, for example, that the price of beer increases substantially. Now consuming a loaf of bread involves giving up less beer. A dollar spent on bread buys just as much as before, but a dollar spent on beer doesn't go as far. The opportunity cost of buying bread is reduced.

Events that increase opportunity cost, as shown in Figure 8, reduce consumption. Suppose, for example, that there is an increase in the price of beer. Since beer costs more, more of other goods must be foregone in order to purchase beer. This increases the opportunity cost of beer and reduces the utility—maximizing quantity of beer demanded as shown in the figure. A reduction in income would also increase opportunity cost and reduce consumption of beer.

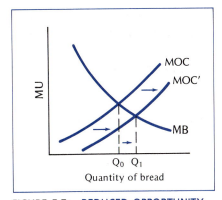

FIGURE 5-7: REDUCED OPPORTUNITY COST INCREASES CONSUMPTION
Here the consumer initially maximizes utility by consuming amount Q_0. If opportunity cost falls, quantities greater than Q_0 will have benefits that exceed the new, lower costs. The utility-maximizing consumer increases consumption to amount Q_1.

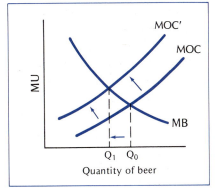

FIGURE 5-8: INCREASED OPPORTUNITY COST REDUCES CONSUMPTION
Here an increase in opportunity cost causes consumption to fall. Goods that were previously rational to purchase now are not because the higher opportunity costs exceed their benefits. Quantity falls from Q_0 to Q_1.

Since individuals alter their behavior based on changes in opportunity costs, we can analyze the economic decisions that go into making a demand curve by looking at how changing prices alter demand. By examining the way that consumers determine how much to buy at different prices, we can draw an individual's demand curve and understand more about the factors that can cause it to shift or change. The basic facts are shown in Figures 9 and 10.

At a price of 50¢ per taco, the consumer we have been discussing is willing to buy 3 tacos (given a budget of $2.00 and root beers that cost 50¢). If the price of a taco rises to $1.00, however, the quantity demanded falls. At $1.00 each, buying 1 taco means giving up 2 root beers, not 1. This increases the opportunity cost of buying tacos, as Figure 9 shows. With higher opportunity costs, it is no longer a good idea to buy 3 tacos since the benefits that the second and third tacos supply are now less than their opportunity costs. The quantity of tacos demanded at $1.00 falls to just 1.

If the price rises even further, taco demand will fall even more. At a price of $2.00 per taco, for example, the purchase of even 1 taco requires giving up the utility that 4 root beers provide. At this high opportunity cost 0 tacos are purchased since MOC exceeds MB for every taco (even the first one). When opportunity cost gets high enough, consumption stops completely.

CHANGING PRICES: DEMAND CURVES

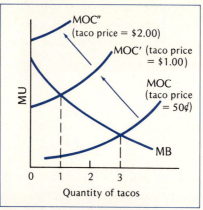

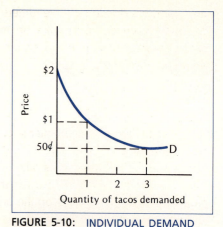

FIGURE 5-9: CHANGING PRICES
As the price of tacos rises, the opportunity cost of a taco increases. This reduces the quantity of tacos demanded until, at a price of $2.00, the opportunity cost is so high that cost exceeds benefits for all tacos and the quantity demanded is zero.

FIGURE 5-10: INDIVIDUAL DEMAND CURVE
By plotting the quantities demanded in Figure 9 against the prices shown there, we derive the individual's demand curve for tacos.

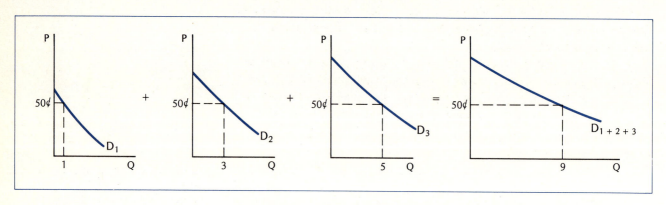

FIGURE 5-11: MARKET DEMAND IS THE SUM OF INDIVIDUAL DEMANDS
By adding together the quantities that individuals wish to purchase at different prices, we can construct a market demand curve.

If we plot the prices and quantities discussed above, we get an individual's taco demand curve as shown in Figure 10. As taco prices increase, the opportunity cost of tacos increases as well. Rational consumers therefore demand smaller and smaller quantities of tacos at higher prices. The normal downward-sloping demand curve results.

Market demand is the sum of all the individual demands for a particular good. Since individuals have differing incomes and preferences, their individual demand curves take on many different shapes, as Figure 11 shows. The market demand is obtained by adding the various quantities demanded at different prices.

SUBSTITUTES, COMPLEMENTS, AND INCOME EFFECTS

Events that alter the consumer's cost–benefit calculation also change consumer choice and affect individual and market demand curves. Let's try to understand how these shifts take place.

In an earlier chapter we learned that the quantity of a particular item demanded depends, in part, on the prices of substitutes and complements. How does this relationship work?

An increase in the price of a substitute, as Figure 12 shows, reduces the opportunity cost of purchasing a good. Shown here is the consumer choice to buy Coke. Part of the opportunity cost of buying Coke is, of course, the amount of Pepsi that is given up when the decision is made to buy the substitute Coke. If the price of Pepsi rises, the opportunity cost of a Coke is reduced. Since Pepsi costs more, each dollar spent on Pepsi doesn't go as far. A dollar spent on Coke, therefore, has a smaller trade-off in terms of the Pepsi foregone. With lower opportunity cost it is desirable to purchase more Cokes than before at the going price. We see this as an increasing shift in the Coke demand curve.

Just the opposite changes occur if the price of a complement changes (see Figure 13). Complements are goods or services that must be consumed together or at the same time. One pair of oddball complements is gasoline and hamburgers. Since many people drive to hamburger stores, it is

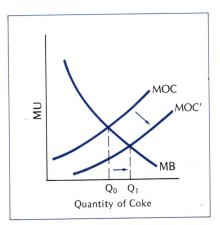

FIGURE 5-12: INCREASE IN PRICE OF SUBSTITUTE
If the price of Pepsi rises, then the opportunity cost of buying a Coke declines (since fewer Pepsis are given up for each Coke purchased). This reduction in opportunity cost (from MOC to MOC') causes the quantity of Coke purchased to rise from Q_0 to Q_1.

FIGURE 5-13: INCREASE IN PRICE OF COMPLEMENT
An increase in the price of gasoline increases the opportunity cost of a hamburger since consumers must purchase gasoline in order to buy hamburgers. At the higher opportunity cost, consumers reduce purchases of hamburgers (even though the price of the hamburgers is unchanged).

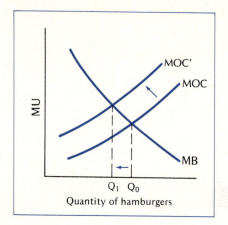

generally necessary to use hamburgers and gasoline together (although we consume them separately).

If the price of gasoline goes up, the price of the hamburger has not changed, but the opportunity cost has increased. In order to buy a hamburger, we must give up money for both the hamburger and the gasoline necessary to go to the store to make the purchase. This is a double opportunity cost. An increase in the price of gasoline, therefore, increases the number of other goods we must forego in order to purchase a hamburger, and the quantity of hamburgers demanded falls as shown in the figure.

Changes in income affect the problem of consumer choice by altering opportunity costs. Opportunity costs change because the opportunities themselves change. When income is low, for example, the fact of limited income makes opportunity costs high in many cases. If a poor person buys a new car, for example, that purchase requires giving up goods that are dear—food, clothes, shelter. The opportunity cost of a Mercedes Benz is therefore very high and we observe few very poor people tooling around town in fancy cars.

As income rises, the opportunity costs change. If our hypothetical poor family wins a lottery and becomes instantly rich, their behavior will change because opportunity costs have changed. When income is high, buying a fancy new car does not mean that vital food must be foregone. Rather the richer family gives up items of lower marginal utility (a third winter coat, Persian rugs, or meals at expensive restaurants) when making this purchase. Rising income reduces opportunity cost by expanding the set of possible purchases. In general, higher income reduces opportunity costs and increases demand as pictured in Figure 7, and falling income increases opportunity costs, as Figure 8 shows.

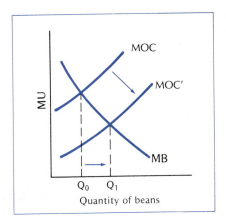

FIGURE 5-14: NEGATIVE INCOME
EFFECT
*As income falls, the opportunity cost of
beans falls too, since other, preferable
items can no longer be purchased and
are therefore no longer "given up"
when beans are bought. The quantity
of beans demanded rises.*

This sort of income effect does not hold in all cases, however. Sometimes the demand for an item increases as income falls, as Figure 14 shows. Here we look at the decision to purchase a less desirable good such as beans. Because beans are considered to be inferior to other items (like meat) they provide relatively low utility to many people and are consumed in relatively small quantities. But when income falls a strange thing happens.

As income drops, certain other more desirable items leave the budget picture entirely. Families living on unemployment benefits, for example, do not realistically have the option of buying expensive steaks and roasts as they might with higher income. Since their lower income means that they can no longer afford these items, these goods no longer enter into the opportunity cost calculation. The poor person does not give up steak when buying beans; rice and potatoes with lower marginal utility are foregone instead.

Falling income, then, lowers the opportunity cost of things like beans while increasing opportunity costs elsewhere. With lower income, fewer steaks are given up because the consumer can't afford them anyway. With opportunity cost falling, the quantity of beans consumed increases, as Figure 14 shows. Can you think of other items where this negative income effect occurs as well?

In general, three things affect consumer choice: income, prices (of goods and their substitutes and complements), and preferences. Changing preferences are reflected in changing utility values assigned to goods. Goods that

CHANGING PREFERENCES

FIGURE 5-15: THE EFFECT OF
ADVERTISING
*By using sports figures to advertise low
calorie beer, brewers were able to
make people more aware of the beer
and increase the benefits (marginal
utility) that the beer provides.
Consumers responded to the higher
perceived benefits by increasing the
quantity of beer demanded.*

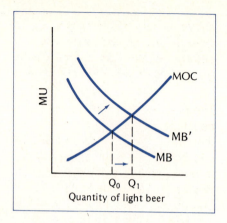

we like more or that become more popular or useful have increased
marginal utilities. Goods that experience falling popularity have lower
utility.

Consumer preferences can change for many reasons. One factor that can
alter consumer choice is advertising. The effect of a successful advertising
campaign on consumer choice is shown in Figure 15.

Low-calorie beer (light beer) was marketed for years before it became a
popular item. Because it was viewed as weak (it has less alcohol) and a poor
substitute for real beer, it provided low benefits (low marginal utility) to its
users and, as the figure shows, was not in high demand. In the mid-1970s,
however, one brewer began a new advertising campaign that featured
sports stars and emphasized the fact that lo-cal beer is less filling—and so
you can presumably drink even more of it than regular beers. This new
information changed people's perceptions of light beer. Because people
assigned a higher utility to the new beer, and derived higher benefits from it,
they rationally increased their purchases of it. The advertising, by increasing
the perceived benefits from this product, altered the benefit–cost calculation and increased its sales. Most advertising is designed to work this way.

We have seen that consumers make decisions by comparing benefits
with opportunity costs. This is how people decide how to allocate scarce
income. But consumers have more than just income to spend: they also
must allocate their time. In a world with more and more to do, the decision
of how to spend time is becoming increasingly important. Not surprisingly,
the way that consumers decide how much time to spend on work, leisure,
and other activities involves the same kind of cost–benefit comparisons we
have already noted.

TWO-HOUR WAIT COMMON

WASHINGTON, D.C.—Gas lines are growing longer and tempers shorter in the nation's capital as the current gasoline shortage hits D.C. drivers at the start of the summer driving season.

Even with gasoline prices at their legal maximum, current demand exceeds supply at the gas pump. Those gasoline stations that opened over the holiday weekend (an estimated 95 percent were closed) immediately drew long lines. Some drivers reported waiting over three hours to buy gasoline. A two-hour wait was not uncommon.

"I don't care about the price," commented Roscoe Gashog, who waited for over an hour to put fuel in his 1972 Pontiac station wagon, "I'm willing to pay as much as I have to for gas. But I don't think it's fair to make people wait in long lines like this. It's a conspiracy."

Many of the drivers polled in lines here reported that they would spend less time on the road this summer, which should reduce the gasoline shortage. It isn't the price of gasoline that is keeping them off the road, however. The reason most noted is the desire to avoid spending long hours in gas lines like those found here this week.

ECONOMIC ANALYSIS

Government price controls have strange and unusual consequences. As we saw in the last chapter, price ceilings (like those which prevail on gasoline) create shortages when the equilibrium price rises above the ceiling price. When a shortage occurs and price is not allowed to rise, how are the scarce goods distributed? Who consumes less?

The problem that government planners face is shown in Figure 16. If there is not enough gasoline available, how can consumers be made to purchase less of it? The quantity of gasoline demanded falls if the opportunity cost of the gasoline can be increased. There are two ways of doing this: through price or through congestion.

The simplest way to reduce gasoline sales is to let the price of gasoline rise to the equilibrium level. The higher gas price increases the opportunity cost of fuel: Since more money must be paid for gas, each gallon purchased comes at a cost of more and more other goods foregone. Eventually, the opportunity cost is so high that the quantity demanded falls to the supply available.

For a variety of reasons, however, this solution is not favored by politicians. Higher gasoline prices are paid by consumers (who have lots of votes) and go to oil companies (who have just a few votes). The rational congressman, making a cost–benefit decision, may vote to keep gasoline price ceilings low, even if a shortage does arise.

But if price is not used to ration gasoline, some other method must be used to increase opportunity cost and make drivers use less gasoline. The method used here, as the news story suggests, is congestion.

REAL WORLD ECONOMICS: GAS LINES GROW LONGER IN NATION'S CAPITAL

FIGURE 5-16: REDUCING GASOLINE CONSUMPTION

In order to reduce gas demand, the opportunity cost of gasoline must increase. This can be done either by letting the price of gas rise or by letting long gas lines form. The time spent in these lines is another cost of buying gas and reduces the quantity demanded, too.

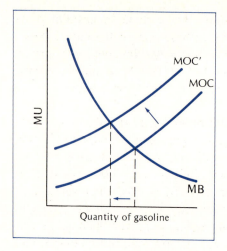

With just a few stations open, gas buyers must line up and wait long periods of time in order to buy fuel. These lines increase the opportunity cost of gasoline by increasing the amount of time that must be spent. The time spent waiting in line has an opportunity cost. Each hour in the gas line is one less hour that can be used to work, rest, run errands, or perform chores. This higher opportunity cost causes people to conserve gasoline not so much to save *money* but to save *time* (and frustration). The opportunity cost—in terms of time and money—is simply too high not to conserve.

Who gets the gasoline when goods are rationed in this way? Those with the time, not necessarily those with the money. This forces some uncomfortable trade-offs, such as doctors leaving hospitals understaffed on Monday so that they can sit in line to get fuel to get them to work the rest of the week.

The moral here is that, either way, the shortage is solved by rising opportunity cost. This occurs either directly—with price increases—or indirectly by forcing other trade-offs.

APPENDIX: INDIFFERENCE CURVE ANALYSIS

Indifference curve: a graph that shows all the different combinations of two goods that produce the same total utility

Consumer choice is essentially the problem of picking the best bundle of goods and services from all available combinations given a certain income and the prices that currently prevail. This kind of choice lends itself particularly well to analysis using a graphical device called an **indifference curve.** This appendix presents a reprise of the discussion of consumer choice using the indifference curve tools.

Indifference curve analysis may look complicated, but the ideas involved are really very simple. The method is simply this: The first step is to determine which choices are available. This is done by examining the choices available on the budget line (purchase possibilities curve). Next, indifferences curves are drawn, which make clear the consumer's preferences. Finally, this picture is examined to find the choice that is preferred from among those choices available within the consumer's budget.

BUDGET LINES. The first step in this process is to examine the feasible choices, given the prices of goods and income available. Suppose that the particular consumer choice in question involves hot dogs and hamburgers: How many of each should be purchased? Assume that $5.00 is available to spend on these items and that hot dogs cost 50¢, while hamburgers sell for $1.00. The possible combinations that the consumer can choose among in this case are shown by Figure 17. If all income is spent on hot dogs, 10 can be purchased. If all $5.00 goes to buy hamburgers, the consumer can purchase 5. Other combinations of hot dogs and hamburgers (such as 3 hamburgers and 4 hot dogs) can also be had, as the figure shows. Each point on the budget line represents a combination of hot dogs and hamburgers that has a total cost equal to the $5.00 available.

The budget line (and therefore the set of possible consumption possibilities) shifts if either price or income changes. Such shifts are shown in Figures 18 and 19. Suppose, for example, that the price of hamburgers falls to 50¢. The maximum amount of hot dogs that $5.00 purchases does not change, but the maximum possible purchase of hamburgers rises from 5 to 10. This causes the shift in the budget line shown in Figure 18. New choices are now available—more hamburgers (and, with the money left over because hamburgers are cheaper, more hot dogs) can be purchased than before.

Rising income causes a different shift in the budget line. Suppose the

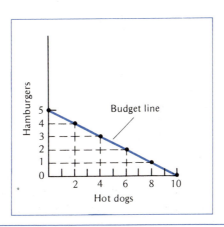

FIGURE 5-17: BUDGET LINE
The budget line shows the combinations of hamburgers and hot dogs that can be purchased with $5 given prices of $1 and 50¢ for hamburgers and hot dogs, respectively.

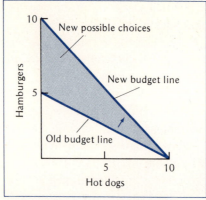

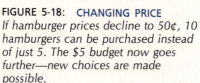

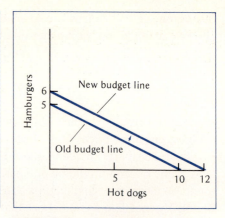

FIGURE 5-18: **CHANGING PRICE**
If hamburger prices decline to 50¢, 10 hamburgers can be purchased instead of just 5. The $5 budget now goes further—new choices are made possible.

FIGURE 5-19: **CHANGING INCOME**
An increase in income from $5 to $6 makes possible larger quantities of both hot dogs and hamburgers. The new choices are shown by the new budget line.

amount available to spend on these two items rises from $5.00 to $6.00. This affects both the maximum amount of hamburgers and hot dogs that can be purchased. The parallel shift in the budget line shown in Figure 19 results. New choices become available as income rises and, conversely, declining income reduces total choice.

The budget line simply tells us which choices are possible with given income and prices. The consumer can afford any of the combinations on the budget line. Which one is chosen depends on preferences.

INDIFFERENCE CURVES. The analysis of this chapter relies on marginal and total utility curves, like those in Figure 20, to supply information about consumer preferences. We can gain more information from these pictures, however, by using total utility relationships to construct indifference curves. To build an indifference curve, begin with a graphical framework like that of the budget line. In Figure 21, the quantity of hamburgers consumed is given on the vertical axis and the number of hot dogs on the horizontal scale. An indifference curve is built by asking the question: Which combinations of hamburgers and hot dogs would the consumer be indifferent toward? That is, which combinations yield the *same* total utility so that it makes no difference which is chosen?

To answer this question we must begin with specifics, so suppose that we plot all the combinations of hamburgers and hot dogs that result in a total

FIGURE 5-20: UTILITY FROM HAMBURGERS AND HOT DOGS

These figures show the utility that a typical consumer might derive from hamburgers and hot dogs. Note that utility increases as consumption of each good rises, but that diminishing marginal utility prevails.

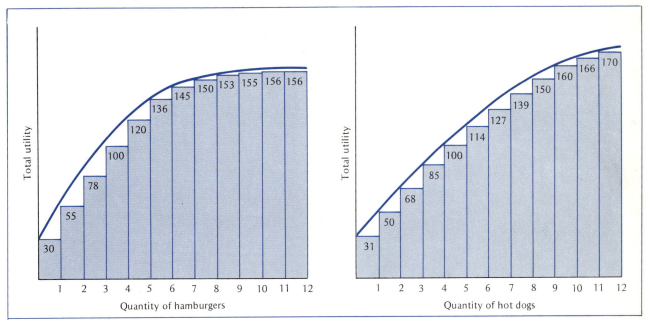

utility of 250 points. A glance at Figure 20, which shows the total utility curves for hamburgers and hot dogs, suggests that many combinations are indifferent in this sense. The consumer whose preferences are shown here is indifferent between having a combination of 8 hamburgers and 5 hot dogs or having 4 hamburgers and 9 hot dogs. Either of these combinations yields a total utility of 250 points.

When all the combinations of hamburgers and hot dogs that yield a total utility of 250 are plotted, as in Figure 21, the result is an indifference curve of utility 250. This curve shows all the various combinations of the two goods that yield that single level of total satisfaction.

DIFFERENCES IN UTILITY. Having constructed an indifference curve for a total utility level of 250, it is now relatively simple to build one for any other level of satisfaction. A total utility of 200, for example, can be achieved by consuming any of the following combinations: 8 hamburgers and 2 hot dogs; 4 hamburgers and 5 hot dogs; 1 hamburger and 12 hot dogs.

As seen in Figure 22, the indifference curve for a total utility of 200 lies

FIGURE 5-21: AN INDIFFERENCE CURVE
FOR HAMBURGERS AND HOT DOGS
**FIGURE 5-21: AN INDIFFERENCE CURVE
FOR HAMBURGERS AND HOT DOGS**
*This indifference curve shows the
different combinations of hamburgers
and hot dogs that would produce
identical total utility of 250. The shape
of the indifference curve reflects the
fact of diminishing marginal utility in
consumption of both goods.*

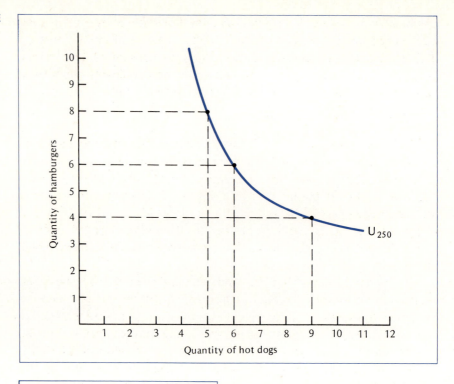

**FIGURE 5-22: A FAMILY OF
INDIFFERENCE CURVES**
*There is one indifference curve for
every possible total utility. Every
combination on a given indifference
curve yields a like total utility.
Combinations on "higher" indifference
curves are preferred because they give
higher total utility.*

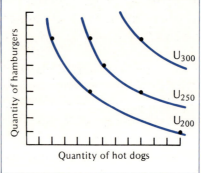

closer to the origin than the 250 indifference curve. This reflects the fact that
more is preferred to less. Because the combinations on the 250 indifference
curve involve either more hot dogs or more hamburgers (or more of both
items) than the combinations on the 200 curve, the choices on the 250
curve are preferred to those on the 200 curve. Likewise, those choices on a
utility 300 indifference curve are preferred to those on either the 200 or 250
indifference maps.

Using indifference curves, it is possible to divide the world into those combinations of items yielding the same level of utility (those on the same indifference curve) and those yielding different levels of utility (those on different indifference curves). Determining the consumer's best choice becomes a matter of inspecting to find the highest attainable indifference curve (corresponding to the highest attainable level of utility) that can be reached.

CONSUMER EQUILIBRIUM. The problem of the consumer is easier to see if we add the rest of the consumer problem: prices and income constraint. Suppose that, given prices and income, the budget line for a consumer looks like the one shown in Figure 23. Here we have assumed that hamburgers cost $1.50 each and hot dogs cost $1.00 and there is a total of $15.00 to be spent. The consumer can purchase either 10 hamburgers or 15 hot dogs or any combination of hot dogs and hamburgers on the budget line shown.

Which combination of hot dogs and hamburgers yields the highest total satisfaction? To find out, let's look at the possible choices and try to pick the best one. One possibility is point A in Figure 23, which is a combination of a lot of hot dogs and just a few hamburgers. Since this combination is on the U_{200} indifference curve, we know that it provides a total utility of 200. Is this the best choice? The answer is clearly no. By consuming fewer hot dogs and more hamburgers it is possible to move from point A to the preferred point B (still on the budget line) and increase utility from 200 to 230. This trade-off moves the consumer to a higher indifference curve, and so makes the consumer better off.

If the consumer prefers to have fewer hot dogs and more hamburgers, then is a point like C, which is a combination of lots of hamburgers with only a few hot dogs, the utility-maximizing combination? The answer again is no. By consuming fewer hamburgers and more hot dogs, the consumer can move from C to D and find a higher indifference curve.

What about a point like E? This combination of lots of hamburgers and lots of hot dogs gives a very high level of utility—it's on the U_{300} indifference curve—but this combination does not fall within the consumer's income as given by the budget line. As a result, combination E is impossible for the consumer to obtain.

The consumer's best choice is the combination of hot dogs and hamburgers given by point F in Figure 23. We can tell that this is the optimal choice by looking at the alternatives. Suppose that we consume fewer hamburgers and more hot dogs. What is the result? Utility falls from 250 to a smaller total as we move toward a combination like B. This is not a good consumer choice. What happens if we consume fewer hot dogs and more hamburgers? Again, this brings about a lower total utility as we move along

FIGURE 5-23: CONSUMER CHOICE
The best choice for this consumer, given income, relative prices, and preferences is the combination of hot dogs and hamburgers given by point F. At point F, the consumer attains a 250 level of total utility. This is the highest indifference curve possible given these prices and income. Other combinations, such as A, B, C, or D, yield lower total utility. The combination represented by point E is better (on a higher indifference curve) but cannot be purchased with given income.

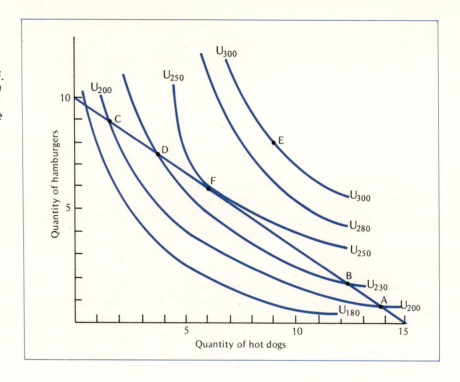

Tangent: a pair of lines or curves that have only one point in common, but do not intersect or cross, are said to be tangent to one another

the budget line toward point D. Point F is the utility-maximizing point, because any trade-off only makes the consumer worse off.

We can tell, by inspection, that F is the best choice for this consumer, given preferences, relative prices, and income, because it is on the highest attainable indifference curve. At this point, the highest indifference curve is just **tangent** to the PPC.

CHANGING INCOMES. Now that we have graphically derived a method of determining the utility-maximizing choice for the consumer, what good is it? Well, for one thing, this tool will allow us to examine in more detail the ways that consumer choice is affected by changing economic conditions.

What impact, for example, does a change in income have on the consumer choice? As shown in Figure 24, an increase in income expands the budget line, shifting it out parallel to the old budget line. While there is no change in the prices of the two goods, the absolute amounts that can be purchased have increased.

Point A in Figure 24 represents the utility-maximizing combination before the increase in income. Is it also the best choice after the income increase? No, now there are many combinations that lie on higher

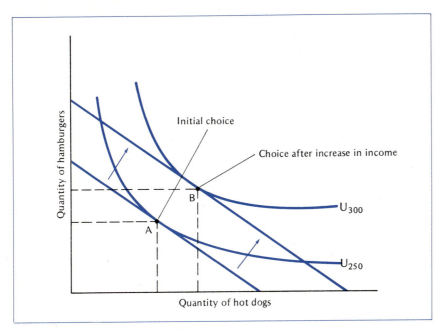

FIGURE 5-24: INCREASE IN INCOME
Higher income shifts the budget line out. Now both more hamburgers and more hot dogs are possible. As a result, we normally expect consumption of both goods to increase.

indifference curves than point A. The new, higher level of total utility is achieved at point B, where the indifference curve is tangent to the new budget line.

An increase in income affects choices, but not relative prices. The consumer will change behavior in order to achieve the highest indifference curve within the new, higher budget line. Note that consumption of both goods increases as income rises. At the same relative prices, more of both goods is demanded. This tells us two things. First, this reminds us that an increase in income shifts demand curves by generating an increased demand at any given price. The larger quantities also are an indication that neither of these items is what economists call an **inferior good**. An inferior good is one that has a negative income effect—when income rises the amount consumed actually falls. For example, in Figure 25 inferior goods tend to be low-status items like beans or hamburger, which are cheap substitutes for more expensive goods. As income rises, people switch from inferior to normal goods, causing the negative income effect as shown here.

Inferior good: a good with a negative income effect; a good that experiences falling demand when income rises

CHANGING PRICES. Consumer choice also changes whenever prices change. This accounts for the existence of the demand curve: Changing prices alter opportunity costs and bring about different quantities demanded. This is illustrated in Figure 26, which looks at the consumer choice to buy concert tickets.

Suppose that the price of concert tickets is a relatively high P_1. At this

FIGURE 5-25:   AN INFERIOR GOOD
An inferior good is one with a negative income effect—less is consumed when income rises. If hot dogs were an inferior good, this is what would happen as income rises.

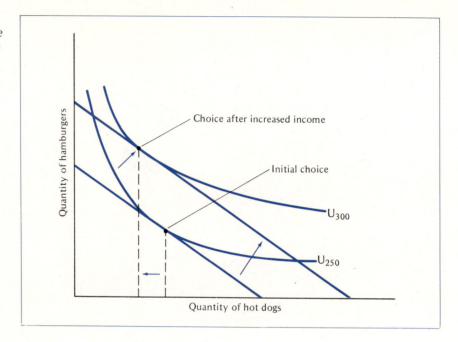

price, as the budget line shows, only a few concert tickets can be purchased. Consequently utility is maximized when Q_1 concert tickets are purchased.

When the price of concert tickets falls to P_2, the budget line shifts out. Now, because of their lower price, more concert tickets can be purchased and more of everything else is affordable, too. We expect an income effect (more of everything purchased because money goes further at low prices) and a substitution effect (cheaper concert tickets purchased because of their lower opportunity cost). The result is that a higher quantity Q_2 is purchased at the lower price P_2.

When price falls again, to P_3, these same forces work again to affect consumer choice. Again, we expect to see an income effect and a substitution effect at work. As Figure 26 shows, this results in an increase in the purchase of concert tickets to Q_3. As the price of concert tickets falls, the number purchased rises.

This is exactly the behavior that we have come to expect, and when we plot the prices against the quantities, as has been done in Figure 27, the result is the downward-sloping demand curve. An individual's demand curve (and the market demand curve that arises from many individuals acting together) is nothing more than the consequence of utility-maximizing behavior in the face of changing prices.

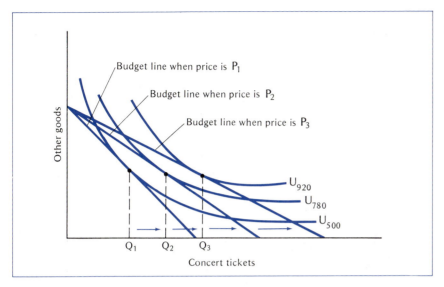

FIGURE 5-26: FALLING PRICES, RISING DEMAND
As the price of concert tickets falls, the consumer can afford to purchase more of them. This shifts the consumer's purchase possibilities curve out and the consumer's total utility rises as the quantity of concert tickets rises.

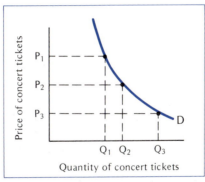

FIGURE 5-27: THE DEMAND CURVE FOR CONCERT TICKETS
As Figure 26 showed, lower prices bring about increased quantities of concert tickets demanded. When this is plotted, as above, the demand curve for concert tickets is formed.

TAXES AND CONSUMER CHOICE. The imposition of taxes by the government affects consumer choice just as a change in income or prices would. In general, two types of taxes can be imposed, with different effects on choice. Income taxes take a proportion of spendable income away from the consumer. Sales and excise taxes are collected only when the consumer purchases taxed items. The impact of these two types of taxes is shown in Figures 28 and 29.

Suppose that all consumer purchases are divided into two types of items: food items and nonfood goods. The consumer is initially in equilibrium at a utility level of 60. If an income tax is imposed, as Figure 28 shows, the ability to purchase both types of goods is affected. Because the government takes part of income as taxes, both less food and less nonfood items are affordable. The income tax shifts the budget line in exactly the same way that a reduction in income would.

FIGURE 5-28: EFFECT OF INCOME TAX
The income tax reduces spendable income. The budget line shifts in to reflect the fact that fewer goods and services can now be purchased. Consumer choice changes as shown.

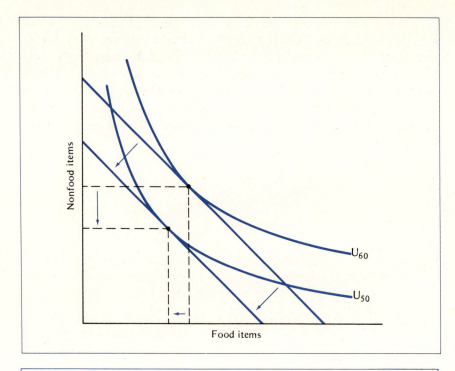

FIGURE 5-29: A SALES TAX
A sales tax that applies only to nonfood items has no effect on the price of food, but increases the cost of nonfood items. The budget line shifts as shown with consumer choice shifting away from taxed goods toward those where tax payments aren't necessary.

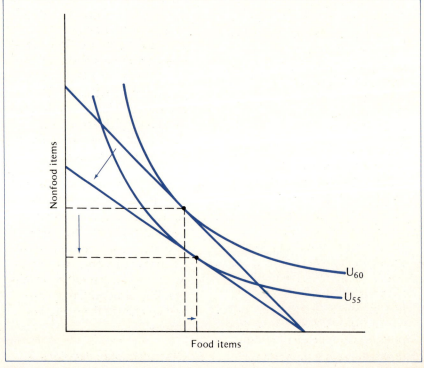

A sales tax on nonfood items alters the decision process in a different way, as Figure 29 shows. A dollar spent on bread goes just as far as ever with this tax but fewer nonfood goods can be bought because the purchase of a radio or other such item requires the payment of the sales tax in addition to the purchase price. The sales tax increases the effective price of nonfood items, as the figure indicates. All else being equal, the sales tax discourages the demand for nonfood items and encourages purchases of the nontaxable food items.

SUMMARY

1. The consumer choice decision is made by comparing the costs and benefits that any individual action provides. In purchasing an item, for example, the good acquired provides benefits in terms of use, satisfaction, and utility. Because resources are finite, however, the decision to purchase one item requires that other goods be foregone. This opportunity cost must be compared with the benefits from any action. If benefits outweigh the opportunity costs, the choice is a good one.

2. Economists describe the benefits that a particular good provides as being the utility derived from that good. Utility measures are used simply to measure relative preferences. If good A is preferred to good B, for example, A will have a higher utility measure number. Goods that are equally desired (the consumer is indifferent between them) will get equal utility numbers. The scale of the utility index is unimportant. Most goods experience diminishing marginal utility as more is consumed.

3. An individual's demand curve for an item is generally downward sloping to reflect the fact that, at higher prices, opportunity costs are higher and so utility is maximized at a lower quantity consumed. When price is lower, the benefits from the purchase of a good outweigh the lower opportunity cost, resulting in higher total purchases. Market demand curves are the sum of individual demands for goods and services.

4. The demand curve for a particular good changes whenever something happens to alter the benefits and costs that enter into the consumption decision. Changes in income, preferences, or prices alter either marginal utility or opportunity cost and so change the consumer choice.

5. Other consumer decisions are

made using the same benefit–cost comparison. Consumers decide how much time to spend working, on leisure, and on other activities (such as waiting in gas lines). Benefits from these activities are weighed against the opportunity costs in each case to arrive at a decision. Government policies alter opportunity costs and so affect the results of the consumer choice.

DISCUSSION QUESTIONS

1. Suppose that hamburgers cost $1.00 and french fries are 50¢. If you have $3.00 to spend and the marginal utilities of these two items are as shown below, how many french fries and hamburgers should you buy? Explain your reasoning.

Quantity	Marginal Utility	
	Hamburgers	French fries
1	50	20
2	40	10
3	20	5
4	5	0
5	0	0

2. Poor people and rich people consume different items. In particular, poor people often buy low-quality items while the rich buy better-made products. Does this difference in behavior reflect a difference in preferences? Can you explain this behavior in any other way?

3. Suppose that you observe the price of a good (movie tickets) rising with no decrease in the quantity demanded. Can you explain this behavior using the tools of this chapter? What conditions must be present for this to happen?

4. This chapter began with a story about changing conditions in the markets for raisins and walnuts. Can you explain the types of consumer behavior described here using the tools of this chapter? What happens to opportunity cost in each case? Why?

5. Can you think of a circumstance such that an individual consumer might have an upward-sloping demand curve for an item (larger quantity demanded at a higher price)? Use the tools of this chapter to describe how this wacky behavior might come about.

TEST YOURSELF

Indicate whether each of the following statements is true or false. Be able to defend your choice.

1. Consumers make choices based on costs and benefits.

The benefits are the utility gained, and the costs are the number of dollars given up to make the purchase.

2. If the consumption of pizza

displays diminishing marginal utility, the fifth slice of pizza provides less utility than the tenth one.

3. If two goods provide the same utility, then the consumer is indifferent between them.

4. The opportunity cost of an item is the utility that the best alternative choice would have provided.

5. When the price of bread rises, the opportunity cost of bread rises and consumers must choose from among a smaller set of attainable goods.

6. When the price of bread rises, the opportunity cost of bread increases, but the opportunity cost of its complement, butter, falls.

7. When the price of bread rises, the opportunity cost of bread substitutes falls.

8. A rise in the wage rate increases the opportunity cost of leisure.

9. The opportunity cost of a decision includes both the goods given up because of an expenditure and the other activities that are foregone because of the time that any activity requires.

10. Price is the only way to allocate a scarce resource.

6
Production and Cost

This chapter begins our look at producer choice by examining the production process and the relationship between production and costs for the firm. This chapter answers questions about the economics of business including the following:

Why do firms exist? What is the motive of the firm?

What costs does the firm consider when making a production decision? What determines these costs?

What is the relationship between production and costs?

What measures of cost are useful to the firm and why?

How are the costs of production different in the long run from those in the short run? Is this difference important?

The three most important economic activities are production, consumption, and exchange. Nearly every move we make is related to one of these three very much interrelated activities. We have learned, in the last few chapters, about the gains from exchange and the ways that markets facilitate this mutually advantageous process. In the preceding chapter, some of the principles governing consumer choice were explored. The goal of the next four chapters is to learn more about production processes and the factors that influence producer decisions. We begin this study by looking at some basic principles of production that are common to most producers and which will help us later analyze the producer choice problem.

WHO ARE THE PRODUCERS?

Firm: a group of people organized to produce and sell goods and services

Sole-proprietorship: a firm with a single owner

Partnership: a firm with two or more owners

Corporation: a form of business organization where a firm has many owners each of whom has only limited liability for the debts of the firm

Stockholder: part-owner of a corporation

Just who are these producers whose choices we are setting out to analyze? Actually, everyone is engaged in production in some form or another. Most folks produce some goods and services for their own consumption and others that are sold (mutually advantageous exchange at work). When people band together in order to produce more complex goods or to produce items more efficiently, we call the resulting organization a **firm**.

Firms come in many different shapes and sizes. The most basic sort of business organization is called a **sole-proprietorship**. This is a business owned by a single individual who takes all the risks and potentially receives all the gains from that business operation. A **partnership** is a more complicated form of business organization where two or more individuals share risk and gain (if any). Finally, a **corporation** is the most complicated type of business organization. When business is organized into a corporate structure, the business may be owned by several (indeed, hundreds of thousands!) individuals. Each owner or **stockholder** shares in any profits of the firm, but bears relatively less risk in case of failure. Whereas each owner of a partnership is individually responsible for all debts of the firm, individual owners of corporations are not. For this reason, these businesses are sometimes called limited-liability corporations since each owner's liability is limited to the initial investment in the business.

Gilbert and Sullivan's amusing operetta *Utopia Limited*, deals with the paradox of the limited-liability corporation—proving that economics can be fun and musical, too!

Most firms in the United States are partnerships or sole-proprietorships. Most market production, however, takes place through corporations, leading to the conclusion that corporations tend to be larger producers than the other forms of business organization.

What are firms aiming at? What is the goal of the firm? Production is, of course, at the root of it all. And exchange, through which gain is made. In simple terms, the firm seeks to win a portion of the gains from production and exchange. We commonly measure the firm's portion of this gain as **profit**. Profit is equal to the difference between the costs of production and the amount of money that the firm receives in exchange for the goods and services produced. Firms, economists suppose, aim to maximize profits through business decisions. If profits are maximized, then the owners of the firm receive the maximum total amount of income (profits), which can then be used to purchase consumer goods or to finance other production activities.

Profits may not be the only star that guides producer decisions, however. Firms may respond as well to other motives that are more complex. Why, for example, should major corporations give money to charity, or sponsor cultural events, or participate in other activities that are unlikely to show a profit? Giving to the poor, as Ebenezer Scrooge might have noted, doesn't help balance the firm's books, but it does contribute to a healthier environment. Some businesses may sacrifice profits in order to achieve other, less immediate goals.

Businesses may try to maximize sales or their share of a given market. Or, they may simply try to stay in business and earn some minimum income for the operation's owners. In this text, we shall assume that the owners and managers of firms are guided by the profit motive and seek to maximize this gain from exchange (while remembering that other goals are possible and likely).

MOTIVES OF THE FIRM

Profit: the difference between revenues and costs to a firm

Production is the act of combining **inputs** to produce **outputs**. The variety of inputs involved in even a relatively simple act of production is intriguing. According to the can, for example, Campbell's cream of chicken soup contains, as inputs, chicken stock, chicken, wheat flour, corn starch, cream, vegetable oil, dried dairy blend (whey, calcium caseinate), salt, unbleached palm oil, chicken fat, water, monosodium glutamate, margarine, yeast extract, and natural flavoring. Even this lengthy list, however, severely understates the kinds of inputs found in this common product. Together with these ingredients, many hours of labor, machine time, heat, refrigeration, as well as a can and label are needed to make production possible.

The recipe by which inputs are combined to make outputs can be complicated, indeed. And that recipe clearly varies from product to

PRODUCTION AND COSTS

Input: resources used by firms in production

Output: the result of the production process

product. Yet certain broad principles are common to most types of production.

Some production ingredients we can call **fixed inputs**. These are production tools whose use does not change, in the **short run**, when the quantity produced changes. Many of the fixed inputs are machinery or capital items. In making the soup, for example, Campbell's Soup Company utilizes a soup factory of fixed size, a fixed number of mixing containers and cooking pots, and the like. In the **long run**, Campbell's might add new cooking facilities or replace some equipment in response to market conditions. In the short run, however, these inputs are fixed in size, type, and quality.

Other items used in production are called **variable inputs**. These items, like the chicken in the soup, are variable in two ways. First, the amount used depends on the quantity of goods produced. If Campbell's decides to make less chicken soup this month, for example, it will use less of the variable input, chicken. Thus the quantity of variable inputs used by the firm depends on the level of production. Individual inputs are also variable in the sense that one can often be substituted for another in the production process. If vegetable oil becomes very expensive, for example, Campbell's might be able to substitute unbleached palm oil in order to reduce production costs. Firms generally try to combine these variable inputs with the fixed ones to minimize the costs of production. By keeping costs down, they hope to keep profits up. (The nature of production and the goal of cost minimization is explored in more detail in the appendix to this chapter.)

Because there are two types of production inputs, there are also two types of production costs that firms must bear. Some costs paid by the firm are called **fixed costs**. Fixed costs are the costs of the fixed inputs of production. The cost of the machinery, the rent on the factory, minimum utility, and service costs, which must be paid in the short run, regardless of the quantity produced, are viewed by the firm as fixed costs. Fixed costs, because they do not change with production, are shown by a horizontal line in Figure 1.

Variable costs are those payments for variable inputs that depend on the quantity of goods or services produced. As more output is produced, more variable inputs are needed and so variable costs rise as shown in Figure 1. The total cost of production for the firm is the sum of these variable and fixed costs.

In looking at the costs of production, remember that any firm bears two forms of cost when production takes place. The kinds of costs that we are most familiar with might be called **explicit costs** or money costs. These are costs that must be paid out-of-pocket. For example, when Campbell's makes more chicken soup, it must buy more chicken; thus incurring a

---

Fixed inputs: resources whose use does not change with the level of production in the short run

Short run: a period of time such that some inputs and costs are fixed

Long run: a period of time long enough so that firms may alter plant, size, technology, and so on

Variable inputs: resources whose use depends on the level of production

Fixed costs: costs that do not vary with the level of production in the short run

Variable costs: costs that depend on the level of production in the short run

Explicit costs: costs that the firm must pay to other firms or businesses

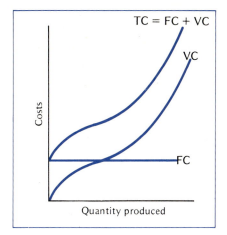

FIGURE 6-1: FIXED, VARIABLE, AND TOTAL COSTS
The total costs (TC) of the firm depend on two types of costs. Fixed costs (FC) are the same regardless of the amount produced. Variable costs (VC) increase or decrease as the quantity produced increases or decreases. Total cost is the sum of the fixed plus variable costs of production.

variable explicit cost as it writes a check to a chicken seller. But Campbell's also bears a different, implicit cost. This is the **opportunity cost** of production. When money is invested in a new cooking kettle, or more chicken wings, for example, the firm and its owners give up the return that those resources would have paid in the next best use. When the owner of the firm spends his or her time managing production, the wages that could have been earned in the next most profitable employ are given up as well. Economists hold that these opportunity costs must be considered in any production decision. The economist therefore adds both explicit and implicit (opportunity) costs when compiling the kinds of cost information shown in Figure 1.

Opportunity cost: the cost of an economic action as determined by the value of the opportunities foregone

In counting opportunity costs as a cost of production, the economist (unlike the accountant who ignores opportunity cost in compiling the firm's books) is correctly stating costs in two ways. First, from the view of the firm, any decision that affects resource use *does* come at a cost, the cost of the return that is given up. Efficient management dictates that this opportunity cost must be recognized in making decisions. In addition, the inclusion of opportunity cost correctly states the cost of production from society's point of view. When resources are employed in a given way, both explicit and opportunity costs must be considered. The economist's calculation takes this into account.

This discussion of business costs has focused on costs in the short run when some factors of production are fixed. In the long run (a period of time long enough for firms to adjust plant size, production technology, and the like to changing economic conditions) all costs are variable. That is, in the long run, Campbell's can alter the amount of chicken in the soup, the number of factories that it uses, and the soup production process.

DIFFERENT VIEWS OF PRODUCTION COSTS

Firms (and economists) find it useful to look at production costs in several different ways. Let's look at the costs of a typical small firm to see how these different views add to the panorama. Figure 2 shows total, variable, and fixed costs for a tiny firm that produces decorated birthday cakes. As the figure indicates, the firm pays $5.00 per day fixed costs (equipment rental) plus variable costs, which go from just $1.00 if only 1 cake is produced to a total of $11.00 if 7 cakes are made. Thus total cost rises from $6.00 for 1 cake to $16.00 if a total of 7 cakes are made per day.

While these total cost figures provide information necessary to business decision-making, they do not tell the whole story. Another measure of production cost is useful to the owner, manager, or economist: **marginal cost**. Marginal cost is defined as the change in total cost that occurs when production is changed by 1 unit; in other words, it is the cost of the last (or next) item produced.

The relationship between marginal cost and the level of production typically displays the behavior indicated in Figure 3, which is derived from the birthday cake cost data. Note that since $5.00 fixed costs must be paid anyway, the first cake produced adds $1.00 to the total cost and so has a marginal cost of $1.00. When a second cake is produced, the total cost rises

Marginal cost: the change in total cost resulting from a one-unit change in production

FIGURE 6-2: COSTS OF PRODUCING BIRTHDAY CAKES
In this example, fixed costs of $5.00 per day must be paid regardless of the number of cakes produced. Variable costs increase as production rises.

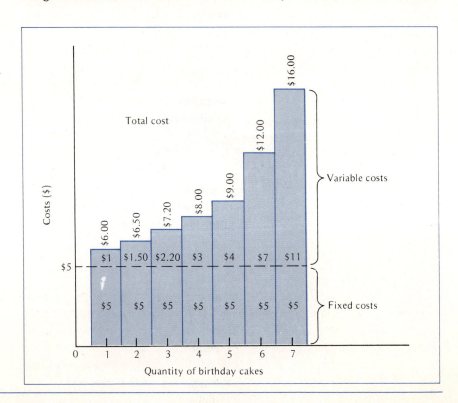

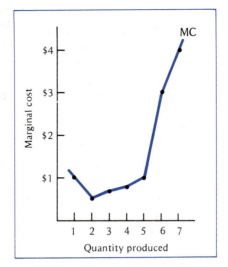

FIGURE 6-3: MARGINAL COSTS OF PRODUCTION
The marginal cost (MC) of producing birthday cakes is shown here based on the costs given in Figure 2. Marginal cost is the change in total cost when production is changed by 1 unit.

to $6.50—an increase of 50¢. The marginal cost of the second cake is therefore 50¢.

Often, when production takes place, marginal costs decrease as the quantity produced rises. This is because the higher level of production makes possible specialization and increased efficiency in production, which results in lower costs. However, marginal costs do not fall forever. At some point the law of diminishing returns take force. As more and more variable inputs are combined with a set amount of the fixed inputs, inefficiencies in production take place. Production expands beyond the level that is most efficient given the level of fixed inputs (the law of diminishing returns is sometimes referred to as the **law of variable proportions** since the diminishing returns result from the differing proportion of variable to fixed inputs).

Law of variable proportions: the marginal product of any one input changes as the quantity used varies relative to other inputs

When the point of diminishing returns is reached, marginal costs begin to rise. As shown in Figure 3 and Table 1, the marginal cost of the third cake is greater than that of the second one and the marginal cost of the fourth one is higher yet. The U-shaped marginal cost curve is commonly encountered in all types of businesses. As production increases, given a fixed stock of

TABLE 6-1

Quantity	Fixed Cost	Variable Cost	Total Cost	Marginal Cost
0	$5.00	—	$5.00	—
1	5.00	$1.00	6.00	$1.00
2	5.00	1.50	6.50	0.50
3	5.00	2.20	7.20	0.70
4	5.00	3.00	8.00	0.80

Average cost: total cost divided by the quantity of production; the mean cost of production

machinery, equipment, and so on, marginal costs eventually rise. You are invited to calculate the remaining marginal costs from Figure 2 to check the accuracy of the numbers indicated in Figure 3.

Another useful way to view business costs is to calculate the **average cost** of production. Average cost is obtained by dividing the total cost of production (or, in the case of average variable cost, the total variable cost) by the number of units produced. Average cost curves for the birthday cake example are derived from Table 2 and are illustrated in Figure 4. You should calculate these average figures, using the information in Figure 2, to see that the curves are correct.

The firm needs to know something of its average costs in order to tell if it is earning a profit at a particular price. So long as the price that it receives for its product is greater than the average total cost (ATC) of that output, then **economic profits** are earned. If, however, price is less than ATC, the firm earns a negative economic profit (loses money). If price just equals ATC, then the firm breaks even.

Economic profits: profits in excess of the opportunity costs of the firm

Accounting profits: profits calculated ignoring opportunity cost as a cost to the firm

Notice that *economic profits* were referred to in the last paragraph. Economic profit differs from the **accounting profit** we normally concern ourselves with. When the economist calculates profit, opportunity cost, as previously noted, is included as one of the items in total cost. Thus if a firm

TABLE 6-2

Quantity	Fixed Cost	Variable Cost	Total Cost	Marginal Cost	Average Total Cost	Average Variable Cost
0	$5.00	—	$5.00	—	—	—
1	5.00	$1.00	6.00	$1.00	$6.00	$1.00
2	5.00	1.50	6.50	0.50	3.25	0.75
3	5.00	2.20	7.20	0.70	2.40	0.73
4	5.00	3.00	8.00	0.80	2.00	0.75

FIGURE 6-4:   AVERAGE COST CURVES
Average cost curves take on this typical U shape. Average total cost (ATC) exceeds average variable cost (AVC) because it includes fixed costs of production, which are not included in the variable cost.

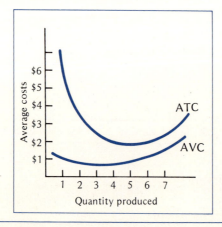

earns zero economic profits, it is simply earning no profits in excess of the return available from the next best business opportunity (since this return was included as a cost item). Accounting calculations, however, ignore opportunity cost as a business expense. Thus a firm that shows a zero economic profit is earning accounting profits equal to profit available elsewhere in the economy. A firm that earns zero accounting profits, however, is normally earning a negative economic profit.

Average variable cost (shown in Figure 4) is also important because firms normally must receive a price for their output that is at least high enough to pay for variable costs. If price falls below average variable costs, the firm may be forced to shut down.

We shall use these cost curves in the next few chapters when examining the producer choice problem. Figure 5 shows the relationship between marginal costs and average costs. Note that average cost falls when marginal cost is less than average cost, and rises when marginal cost is greater than average cost. This relationship is easy to understand if we think about it in a slightly different way. Suppose that, instead of average cost, we are looking at your average exam score in this class. Suppose, for the sake of example, that your exams currently average 80 percent. Now suppose that your next (marginal) score is less than your average (say, 70 percent). What will happen to your class average? If your marginal score is less than your average, it will pull the average down with it. Note that the same is true with costs in Figure 5. Now, what will happen if your marginal exam scores suddenly improve—rising far above your average—to 95 percent. These high marginal scores will pull your average up. This, again, is illustrated in

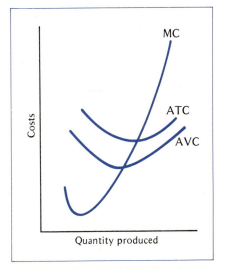

FIGURE 6-5: MARGINAL AND AVERAGE COSTS
Average costs fall so long as marginal cost is below average cost and rises when marginal cost exceeds average cost. For this reason, the marginal cost curve intersects each average cost curve at its minimum.

the case of cost curves in the figure. High marginal costs pull up average costs. Low marginal costs push the averages down.

Using marginal and average cost curves, we can analyze most of the types of events that can affect production for a firm. For example, an increase in the cost of labor (a variable input) will increase marginal costs, average variable costs, and average total cost. An increase in the fixed costs of production, however, will increase ATC but will have no effect on either marginal or average variable cost (work this out to see that it is true).

COSTS IN THE LONG RUN

Our analysis of production costs has thus far been concerned with the way that costs vary with production in the short run. In the long run, however, firms can adjust to changing business conditions by altering their production process, the size of the firm, and variable and fixed (only in the short run) inputs. In the long run, firms alter the use of all inputs at their command to find the cheapest (and, therefore, the most profitable) method of doing business.

The difference between the costs for the firm in the short run and the long run is illustrated in Figure 6. Suppose that a firm is currently producing an amount Q_0 and wishes to expand production to a greater quantity Q_1. In the short run, with many variables fixed, the law of diminishing returns suggests that the extra production will come at a very high marginal cost. Thus average costs rise to AC_{SR} as production increases to amount Q_1.

In the long run, however, the firm can alter its production process and plant size to adjust for the new, larger amount produced. This long-run adjustment process results in economies of production that lower total and average costs. Thus, in the long run, the firm's average cost falls back to AC_{LR} in Figure 6.

FIGURE 6-6: SHORT AND LONG-RUN AVERAGE COSTS

In the short run, quantity Q_1 can be produced only at a very high average cost because the marginal cost of production is very high. In the long run, however, plant size and production methods can be altered to reduce average costs.

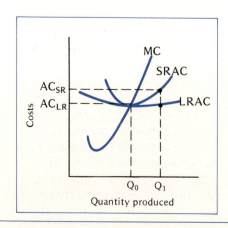

In the short run, firms use different combinations of variable inputs to produce a given amount of goods and services at the lowest total cost (since reducing total costs also increases profits). In the long run, the same cost-reducing motivation is possible, with the difference that more inputs are variable as the firm adjusts to changing economic conditions.

We can learn a lot about the way firms behave by examining their cost curves. In the next three chapters, the activities of monopolies, competitive firms, and firms that engage in imperfect competition will be examined by looking at their cost curves.

ELECTRONIC TOYS TOP CHRISTMAS GIFT LIST

Electronic toys and games are at the top of the nation's gift list this year according to department store mogul Bergdorf Batman. "The current interest in outer space games and toys is part of the trend toward electronic recreation," Batman said, "but the falling price of all electronic consumer goods is an important trend, too."

Despite higher production levels than in years past, the prices of electronic games have fallen dramatically in the past several years. Industry experts look for even lower prices in the future as this gift market grows.

ECONOMIC ANALYSIS

In the short run, production costs (and therefore market prices) normally rise as the level of production expands. In the long run, however, this is not always the case. In the long run, in fact, increased production can cause costs and prices to actually fall. Is this always the case? No. It all depends on how the efficiency of production changes as production expands—a relationship that economists refer to as **returns to scale**.

Figure 7 shows how different firms can experience different returns to scale. Figure 7a illustrates the situation that the news story describes in the electronic games industry. As individual firms expand here, they are limited, in the short run, to a rising average cost curve.

But, in the long run, the firm finds that it can take advantage of a more efficient factory size, increased specialization, and better technology when producing a larger number of goods. Thus the higher output, in the long run, can be produced at lower costs. The long-run average cost curve for this firm is downward sloping, indicating that even greater expansion of the firm results in even lower average costs.

This is a desirable situation from the consumer's point of view since lower costs generally spell lower prices. Economists say that firms like this experience **increasing returns to scale** since, when the scale of production is increased, resources are even more productive, giving lower long-run costs.

REAL WORLD ECONOMICS: TOYS AND GAMES

Returns to scale: the relationship between inputs and outputs over the long run

Increasing returns to scale: a firm that experiences falling long-run average costs

FIGURE 6-7:   RETURNS TO SCALE IN THE LONG RUN
*Firms that experience long-run increasing returns to scale have decreasing
long-run average cost (LRAC) as shown in (a). For other firms, constant returns to
scale, as shown in (b), are the case. Finally, some firms experience rising average
costs in the long run and are said to display decreasing returns to scale as shown
in (c).*

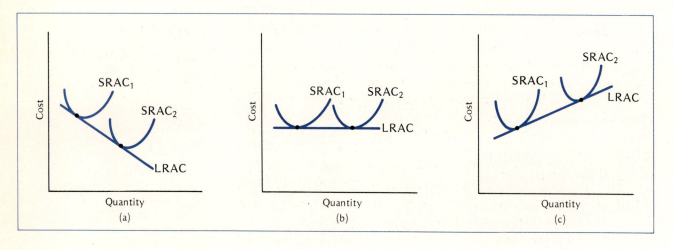

Constant returns to scale: constant long-run
average costs

Decreasing returns to scale: rising long-run
average costs

This is not the case for all industries or firms, however. Figure 7b
shows the case of a firm experienc-
ing **constant returns to scale**. In
the short run, average costs still
rise as production increases. In the
long run, however, average costs
can be brought back down to their
original level as factories are expanded or changed and technology
is adjusted for the larger capacity.
Average costs are constant, over
the long run, if a firm experiences
constant returns to scale.
A final possibility is shown in Figure 7c. This firm displays **decreasing returns to scale**. As production
expands, even in the long run,
costs still rise because the additional resources used by the firm are
not as productive at the larger
scale of production.

The electronics industry seems to
have experienced increasing returns to scale, hence the lower
costs and prices that we have observed in recent years. For most
other firms, however, economists
suspect that constant returns to
scale might be more common. But
beware! Don't expect prices to fall
back to their 1975 levels just because constant returns to scale
might exist in an industry. This
analysis of long-run costs looks just
at the technology of production.
We have assumed that, in the long
run, the prices of raw materials,
equipment, and labor are constant.
In the real work world, of course,
the prices of these things can be
expected to change constantly,
with rising prices seeming to be the
case more often than not. So, de-

spite the possible existence of constant returns to scale (and therefore constant long-run average cost curves), stable prices are not necessarily in the cards—even if the dealer is an electronic device!

APPENDIX: PRODUCTION THEORY

This appendix presents a simple economic model that describes how production takes place and how production decisions involving inputs and outputs are made. To better understand the production process, we must look a little deeper into the properties of the production process.

The production function describes the way production takes place. It is essentially a recipe detailing the ways that inputs are combined to produce outputs. This recipe varies, of course, depending on the type of good or service produced. The ingredients and processes necessary to produce a haircut, for example, are far different from those that result in radial tires, digital watches, chemical fertilizers, or baked beans. To further complicate matters, there are often many different recipes used to produce essentially similar goods. The production function for candy, for example, may vary depending on the availability and prices of raw materials and whether the production takes place in a large or small factory.

Production is a complicated process and one that takes many different forms. However, economists have observed certain common production properties. By examining these properties and building on them, we can construct a general model of production activity that is useful in explaining the economic behavior of producers.

TOTAL AND MARGINAL PRODUCT. To gain insights into the concepts at work in production, let's model a very simple production process. Suppose that a firm rents fields that contain strawberry plants. The act of production that we wish to describe is the harvesting of these berries. This production requires just two kinds of inputs: land (and the berry plants growing on it) and labor (the people who gather the berries and deliver them to sellers). This is, of course, an oversimplified picture of how this production takes place. Many other inputs come into play when the berries themselves are produced (seeds, fertilizers and insecticides, and machines) or harvested (containers and fuel for transportation). Let us suppose that all of these other factors are givens of the problem and see how the production function relating inputs of land and labor to outputs of strawberries might look.

What is the relationship between inputs of land and labor and outputs of berries? Suppose that we hold the amount of land to be harvested constant and change just the number of workers hired to gather berries. The resulting relationship between workers and berries harvested will look similar to that pictured in Figure 8.

Given a certain amount of land available, the amount of berries gathered depends directly on the number of workers hired to pick berries. **Total product** rises as the amount of labor employed increases. This is as we might expect. Four berry pickers can be expected to produce more than 2 pickers.

But something perhaps unexpected is seen in Figure 8. While 2 pickers are better than 1, they are not twice as good. The first berry picker adds a great deal to total product. The first picker's **marginal product** is relatively high. This is not difficult to understand—with a field of berries waiting, the first worker here need not search very far for berries to pick.

The second picker also has a high marginal product, but not as high as the first (see Figure 8 again). Picking behind the first worker, the second berry picker must search a little harder for ripe berries. This process is more time consuming and therefore results in a smaller addition to the total production of berries.

The third picker adds even less to total product since this worker, in a sense, must compete with the others for berries. Note that this diminishing marginal product does not mean that the third worker is less able or less efficient in gathering strawberries. Total production does not rise very much when the third picker is hired because the problem of a larger number of workers laboring in a fixed-size field results in **diminishing marginal product**. As the figure shows, the problem continues as more and more workers are hired until, at some point, total production doesn't rise (and may even fall) when additional workers are employed.

The hypothesis of diminishing marginal product applies to labor in this example and probably prevails with respect to most inputs in most kinds of productive processes. As more and more of any single input is added to

Total product: the total amount of output produced with given inputs

Marginal product: the addition to total product resulting from the addition of one input to the production function

Diminishing marginal product: a situation where the addition to total product of a unit of input declines as the number of inputs used increases

FIGURE 6-8: TOTAL AND MARGINAL PRODUCT

Total product increases as the amount of labor used by the firm rises (all else held constant). But each additional worker adds less to production than the one before. The phenomenon of diminishing marginal product is therefore observed.

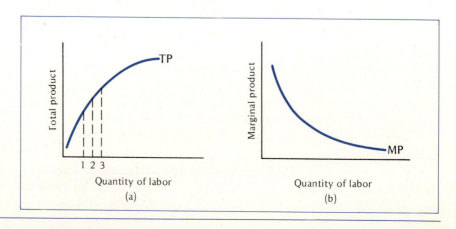

production, all else held constant, marginal product can be expected to fall. This is the law of variable proportions at work. As more of one input is added to production, the changing proportions between the variable and fixed inputs cause diminishing returns to exist.

ISOQUANT CURVES. Even with just two inputs—labor and land in this example—there are still many ways that these factors can be combined to produce output. Which combination should the firm choose? Lots of land with only a few workers? Some of each?

We can begin to analyze this problem by building an **isoquant** for a particular firm. The term isoquant comes from the Greek root *iso* meaning the same and *quant* or quantity. Isoquants are figures that show all the different ways to make the same quantity of total output.

Isoquant: a graphic device showing all the different combinations of two inputs that can be used to produce the same level of total output

What does an isoquant look like? An isoquant for the strawberry field example is illustrated in Figure 9. Suppose that the strawberry firm has determined that the profit maximizing output of strawberries is 300 *flats* per day. It knows how much to produce, but how should production take place? This is not an easy choice. There are many different ways of gathering the berries that meet the goal of **technical efficiency**, that do not waste resources. These different combinations are listed on the Q_{300} isoquant.

Technical efficiency: a production process that does not result in wasting of resources

One way to produce the required amount of berries is to use a relatively small amount of land (Q_1 acres), but to pick it over very thoroughly, using a large quantity of labor q_3. An alternative method is to use many more acres of berry bushes (Q_3) and fewer workers (q_1), who because they have plenty of room and many ripe berries to choose from, can fill their baskets quickly. Finally, it is possible to gather the 300 flats of berries using Q_2 land and q_2 workers.

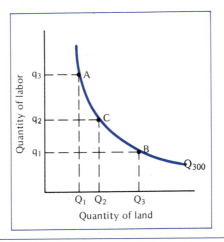

FIGURE 6-9: AN ISOQUANT
This figure shows the different combinations of land and labor that can be combined to produce 300 flats of berries per day.

Note that the isoquant shows only the technically efficient production recipes. It may be possible, for example, to gather the 300 flats of berries by using both large quantities of land (Q_3) and a large number of workers (q_3). But this would be a wasteful use of resources since the same work can be done (according to the isoquant) using less land, less labor, or fewer of both resources. The isoquant shows only those combinations that are efficient in the sense that it is impossible to produce the same quantity using less of both resources.

ISOCOST LINES. All the production possibilities on the isoquant are technically efficient, but the producer is really interested in the unique combination that displays **economic efficiency**—the cheapest (least-cost) way of producing the 300 flats of berries per day.

We can see how much the different combinations cost by drawing **isocost** lines. Isocost lines are figures that show all the different combinations of inputs having the same total cost. Isocost lines for the berry problem are pictured in Figure 10.

Suppose that worker wages are $20 per day and that land rental costs $100 per day. Given these input prices, isocost lines look like those in the figure. The $C_{\$1000}$ isocost, for example, shows that the firm can purchase either 50 workers (at $20 each) or 10 acres of land (at $100 each) or some combination of the two (25 workers and 5 acres of land) and each combination has a total cost of $1000. There is a different isocost for each possible total cost figure. By using isocosts, the economist can tell those

Economic efficiency: a production process that achieves production at least cost

Isocost: a graphical device showing all the combinations of two inputs that can be purchased for the same total cost

FIGURE 6-10:   ISOCOST LINES
Isocost lines show the different combinations of two inputs that can be purchased at the same total cost. All of the isocost lines are parallel because, at constant prices, the trade-off between land and labor does not change. Total cost increases as the amounts of land and labor used increase.

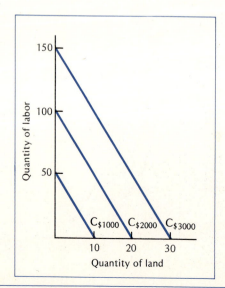

combinations of inputs having the same total cost (lying on the same isocost) and those having different total costs (lying on different isocost lines). The isocost line is built on the assumption of fixed prices. When prices change, as we shall examine shortly, the isocost line shifts to reflect changes in total cost.

PRODUCTION CHOICE. Of all the possible input combinations, which is the economically efficient one? Figure 11 suggests a way of finding out. Here, the Q_{300} isoquant is shown and a number of isocost lines are drawn in as well. You can determine the cost-minimizing use of land and labor by inspection.

Suppose that the berry firm chooses to use many workers on just a little land—point A in the figure. As the isoquant shows, this is an efficient way of picking berries—in the sense that no resources are wasted—but not a particularly cheap one. This production method uses a large quantity of relatively expensive labor. Because it uses much labor—and much of that labor has a relatively low marginal product—this is an inefficient way of producing berries from an economic point of view. The total cost here is $3000 (point A is on the $C_{\$3000}$ isocost line). This gives an average cost of $3000/300 = $10 per flat of berries, which is not going to yield much profit. As the figure shows, the firm can gather the same quantity of berries (stay on the same isoquant) and pay lower total costs by substituting land for labor.

If less labor and more land is cheaper, should the firm change its methods and work at point B? The answer in this case is no. Producing at point B requires using a lot of land and much of the land has low productivity. The

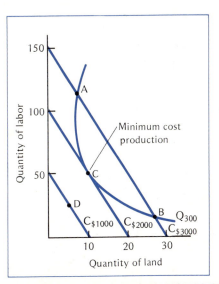

FIGURE 6-11: COST MINIMIZING PRODUCTION
The firm can produce 300 flats of berries per day using any combination of inputs on the isoquant shown here (i.e., combinations A or B). The combination of inputs at point C is economically efficient, however, since it produces the 300 flats at least cost. Points like D involve lower cost, but don't produce the required quantity.

fact of diminishing marginal product again boosts total cost. Point B is also on the $C_{\$3000}$ isocost line, and so total cost here is very high.

The firm would like to keep total costs as low as possible. Therefore, they would really like to produce at point D, which is on the $1000 isocost. Alas, at point D, production is less than the required 300 flats per day.

The profit-maximizing input used is that shown for point C in Figure 11. At this combination the quantity 300 is produced at the lowest possible total cost. Graphically, this occurs where the isoquant is just tangent to an isocost line. At any other point (A or B) on the isoquant, it is possible to achieve the same total product at lower cost by moving toward point C. At C, total cost is minimized and profits are as great as possible.

At point C total cost is $2000 (it is a point on the $C_{\$2000}$ isocost line) so that average total cost per flat is $2000/300 = $6.67. This is the cost that the firm will use in building its cost curves as discussed in this chapter.

Why is point C the cost-minimizing combination of land and labor? Essentially, it is a question of the prices of inputs and the marginal productivity of inputs. At point A, $1.00 spent on labor brings in a low marginal profit, while $1.00 spent on land yields many more berries in marginal product. At combination A, therefore, it makes sense to substitute more productive land for less productive labor. At point B just the opposite forces are at work. One dollar spent on land yields only a few berries (because of diminishing marginal product) while $1.00 spent on labor adds relatively more to production. Labor is substituted for land.

At the economically efficient point C, $1.00 spent on land produces the same marginal product as $1.00 spent on labor. It is not possible to produce more (or cheaper) by changing the production recipe. This is the best production combination for the firm.

Finding the combination that displays economic efficiency, therefore, involves calculating the opportunity costs involved. If you hire one more worker, how much land will you give up? Will the additional worker produce more than the land would have? By calculating the trade-offs and opportunity costs, the firm is able to choose the best production combination.

INPUT SUBSTITUTION. The particular blend of inputs used changes whenever production trade-off is altered. One reason for change is if the productivity of the different inputs changes. Suppose, for example, that a new berry picking technique is devised that increases the marginal product of berry pickers. This alters the shape of the isoquants and, at the going prices for land and labor, increased numbers of the more productive workers are substituted for the relatively less productive land.

Another factor that changes the trade-off and alters opportunity costs is a change in the prices of inputs. Suppose, for example, that the rent of berry land increases. This changes the shape of the isocost lines as shown in Figure 12. Because land is now more expensive, less land can be purchased with a given total cost. The isocost lines become steeper to reflect the change in the relative price of land.

The trade-off between land and labor is changed when prices change. If, at the start, land rents for $100 per day and wages are $20 per day, then renting one more acre of land means giving up wages for 5 workers. If the rent on land rises to $125 per day, then renting another acre has an opportunity cost of over 6 workers—the productivity of more workers must be foregone to gain the output of the additional acre of land.

This changing trade-off alters the production choice, as Figure 12 shows. At the old input prices, the firm minimized cost by producing the 300 flats of berries per day using input combination C. The total cost here was $2000, an average cost of $6.67 per flat. When the price of the land input rises, however, the isocost lines change shape and the old production combina-

FIGURE 6-12:   RISING LAND COSTS
When the cost of land increases from $100 per acre per day to $125 per acre per day, the isocost line shifts to reflect the new trade-off. At the new prices, the firm minimizes costs by producing at E instead of C. More labor and less land is used here, but total costs still rise.

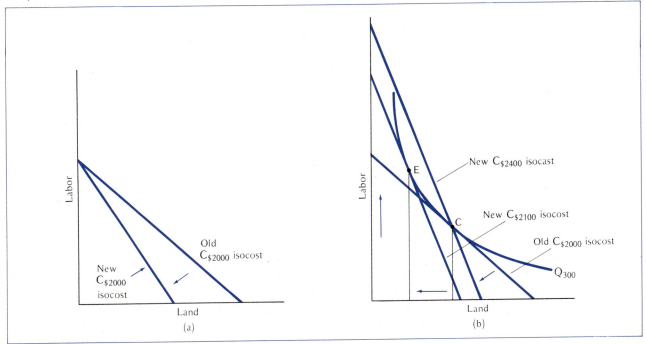

tion is no longer the least-cost one. After the changing prices, production takes place at combination E, which uses more labor (because its price has not changed) and less land (because its price has increased).

Note that the berry firm shown here was able to avoid part of the increase in costs by shifting from higher cost land to relatively lower cost labor. If it had continued to produce at point C, in Figure 12, its total costs would have increased to $2400 (and average costs would rise to $8.00 per flat). By substituting labor for land the firm reduces the increase in total cost. At point E, total cost is now $2100 (point E is on the $C_{\$2100}$ isocost line). Average cost still rises from $6.67 per flat to $2100/300 = $7.00 per flat. But this is still better than the $8.00 that would have occurred if the production recipe had not been changed.

CHANGING PRODUCTION OVER TIME.
In the short run, the use of land, labor, capital, and other inputs changes in response to changes in productivity or prices that alter the opportunity costs and trade-offs among the productive inputs. Over the long run, changes occur because of the nature of the production function. This is illustrated in Figure 13.

As firms expand production, they move to higher and higher isoquants and the production process changes. The same basic recipe used to produce 300 flats of berries per day may not be the best one if 3000 flats per day are required. Even if input prices stay constant, the relative amounts of land, labor, and other inputs used can change. Sometimes, as Figure 13a shows, capital becomes more and more efficient as production increases. The firm then becomes capital intensive in its production techniques. At other times, however, more of other inputs are used because of their higher productivity when production rises.

Many workers were needed to hand-tool cars in the early part of this century, but were replaced with fewer workers and more machine-intensive production as the number of cars produced rose. Part of this change was, of course, the substitution of less skilled (and therefore less expensive) labor for the craftsmen who produced the first cars. But part of the change to the production line was simply a matter of taking advantage of the fact that machines have relatively low productivity when only a few cars are produced (since any particular machine is operating only a fraction of the time), but much higher productivity when operating full-time to produce many automobiles.

The degree to which input substitution takes place depends on a number of factors. Sometimes firms can alter their use of inputs quickly when economic events warrant it. The berry producer described here, for example, might find it easy to rent more or less land and hire more or less

FIGURE 6-13: PRODUCTION OVER TIME
The relative proportions of different inputs used changes over time as the level of production changes. In some cases, more and more labor is used as output increases (movement to higher isoquants) and sometimes capital is substituted for the labor.

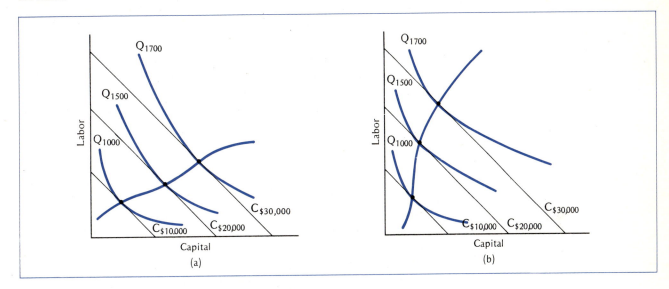

labor as events suggest. But sometimes it is not so easy. If the berry firm owns the land, increasing or decreasing its use may be difficult. If a labor contract has been signed with the berry pickers, changes in the number of workers used may be restricted as well.

Sometimes other barriers prevent input substitution. If, for example, a firm has made large investments in a certain type of technology or production mechanism, it may not have the financial resources to make many changes as the economically efficient production combination changes. Government rules and regulations can also alter the production process and affect costs, productivity, and the ability to substitute in the face of changing economic conditions.

This model of production is simple. It looks, after all, at just two inputs and one output. More complex production processes, which use perhaps thousands of different inputs and produce many different products, are difficult to analyze using these tools. Nonetheless, the basic principles at work here apply to these more complicated processes. The real world of production responds to the trade-offs and opportunity cost motivations described in this chapter.

SUMMARY

1. Firms exist because they can increase efficiency in production. Firms are organized in many different ways according to the size of the firm and the number of owners that firm may have. The principal motive of the firm is to earn profits, although several other motives may also affect business decisions.

2. Firms encounter both fixed and variable costs in production in the short run. In the long run all costs are variable. The firm bears the explicit costs of fixed and variable inputs and, as well, the opportunity costs of production decisions foregone.

3. As production increases, the total cost of production generally increases. The marginal cost of output rises showing that greater levels of production can only be obtained, in the short run, at ever increasing costs. Rising marginal costs mean that average costs display a U-shaped relationship, first falling as production increases, then eventually rising with greater levels of output.

4. In the short run, with some variables fixed, rising production usually means rising marginal and average costs. In the long run, however, all inputs can be viewed as variable and rising average costs are not necessarily the case, depending upon the nature of returns to scale for the individual firm.

DISCUSSION QUESTIONS

1. Table 3 shows cost figures for a hypothetical firm. Fill in the gaps in this table. How do you know what cost numbers to fill in? Are there any blanks that you do not have enough information to calculate?

2. Draw the cost curves for the hypothetical firm illustrated in Table 3. Do the curves display the shape discussed in the text? Why or why not?

3. What effect will an increase in the price of a variable input (such as oil) have on the following: marginal cost, fixed cost, total cost, average total cost, and average variable cost.

4. Show graphically the effect that an increase in the price of a variable input will have on the cost curves in the text. Show how an increase in fixed cost will affect these same curves. How are they different? Why does this difference exist?

5. Why should some firms experience increasing returns to scale while others show constant or decreasing returns? What must be different about their production functions? Do you think that teaching economics (the production of an education service) is likely to display increasing, decreasing, or constant returns to scale? Defend your choice. How could we test to see if you are right or wrong?

TABLE 6-3

Quantity	Fixed Cost	Variable Cost	Total Cost	Marginal Cost	Average Total Cost	Average Variable Cost
0	$100	$ 0	$100	—	—	—
1	100	20	120	20	120	20
2	100	30	130	10	65	15
3	100	—	135	5	—	11⅔
4	100	—	144	—	—	—
5	100	—	160	—	—	—
6	100	80	180	—	30	—
7	—	105	—	25	29²⁄₇	—
8	—	140	—	35	30	17½
9	—	—	—	50	32²⁄₉	21⅑
10	100	270	—	—	—	27

TEST YOURSELF

Indicate whether each of the following statements is *true* or *false*. Be able to defend your choice.

1. Total cost increases whenever variable cost increases in the short run.

2. Average cost is at its greatest when the average cost curve crosses the marginal cost curve.

3. Changes in fixed cost have no effect on marginal cost.

4. Average variable cost rises whenever marginal cost is rising.

5. Firms must consider both explicit and opportunity costs when making production decisions.

6. Firms are sole-proprietorships, partnerships, or corporations, depending upon their long-run returns to scale.

7. Economic profits are less than accounting profits because economists include opportunity cost as a cost of the firm.

8. A firm will earn an economic profit so long as its selling price is greater than the average total cost.

9. A firm that earns zero economic profits also earns zero accounting profits.

10. If increasing returns to scale prevail for a firm, then the short-run average cost curve for that firm is downward sloping.

7
Producer Choice: Monopoly

This chapter begins an analysis of how producers decide how much to produce and what price to charge by looking at the problem of producer choice in its simplest case: the monopoly. Questions this chapter answers include the following:

What is a monopolist? What kinds of economic conditions lead to monopoly?

What quantity does the monopolist choose to produce? What price is charged?

What is the supply curve for a monopolist and what factors change the monopolist's supply decision?

The problem of producer choice is essentially a weighing of costs and benefits from production. The firm weighs the benefits (in the form of revenues) of production against production costs in deciding which and how many goods and services to produce. In this chapter, we examine this benefit–cost calculus from the perspective of a single firm that dominates a market: the **monopoly**.

Monopoly: a market where there is only one seller

This discussion of producer choice begins with the monopoly not because this is the most common form of market organization. True monopolies are relatively rare. Even those that do exist do not always act like monopolists because they are regulated by the government to behave more like competitive firms. Monopolies are discussed first simply because in examining the monopoly we look at the problem of how a single firm deals with the choices and trade-offs that all businesses face in one form or another. Once the monopolist's decision is understood, other forms of business organization can be discussed in terms of how their decisions are similar to or different from the simple monopolist case. In the next two chapters we will examine producer choice in competitive markets and in markets that fall somewhere between monopolies and perfect competition.

This chapter, then, presents some basic information that is useful in understanding all business decisions, and uses that information to show how monopoly firms deal with the particular problems that they face.

WHAT IS A MONOPOLY?

Many people grow up believing that "Monopoly" is a board game manufactured by Parker Brothers, which models the real estate market in Atlantic City, New Jersey. This notion is not far wrong. While the goal of "Monopoly" is to get a monopoly (owning, for example, both Boardwalk and Park Place), the more pertinent fact is that Parker Brothers has a monopoly on "Monopoly." That is, they are the only seller of this popular board game.

This is the key aspect of a monopoly—a market where there is but one seller. With one seller, there is no competition on the supply side of the market. Buyers may still compete for scarce goods, but there is no force of competition among producers. A monopolist (or, at least, an unregulated monopolist) is free to set any price and produce any quantity that is desired, subject to the fact that buyers, although they cannot buy the monopolist's product from others, can always choose not to buy it at all.

This monopoly business sounds like a pretty good deal: How does someone get started in it? The key to monopoly is to restrict competitors from entering the market. How can **barriers to entry** be devised? There are several possible ways. Parker Brothers can keep others from selling "Monopoly" games because they have what is generally termed a **patent monopoly**. In the case of their monopoly, it is really a copyright law at work. **Patents** and **copyrights** are laws that guarantee the producer a monopoly for a specific product for a certain period of time. Because of their copyright, Parker Brothers is the only producer that can market the monopoly game (or even, the courts hold, any game that is much like "Monopoly" but called something else). The copyright gives the producer a monopoly in the sale of a specific item. It does not prevent competition altogether, however. Because it holds the copyright to this book, for example, Academic Press is the only company that can produce it. Yet there are lots of other different economics books on the market to choose from, and so the copyright creates a monopoly in only a very limited sense and competition still prevails.

Patents are a more powerful way to create a monopoly. A patent gives a producer exclusive ownership of an invention or new idea for a period of several years. The producers can sell or license the new process to many producers or use the patent rights to form a monopoly. The Polaroid camera people, for example, for years had a monopoly in instant-picture machines. The problem with a patent monopoly is that the patent eventually runs out and then anyone can use the ideas and processes for free. The key to a patent monopoly then becomes **innovation**. If, by constant innovation and product improvements, the monopolist can keep ahead of the field, a patent monopoly can be preserved indefinitely.

Patent monopolies rely on laws to keep competitors out. Other monopolies rely on economic factors to accomplish this. For some monopolists, the existence of high capital requirements keeps others out of the market. If it takes a huge amount of money to set up a business, this discourages risk-conscious investors. Suppose that you wanted to go into one of the more profitable businesses around—the telephone business. To set up your own telephone exchange would require a high initial investment in poles, wires, computers, and telephones. The start-up costs are probably too high to make such a venture profitable. As a result, Ma Bell faces relatively less competition in the telephone business.

Monopolies can also be formed if all the competitors in a market get together and decide not to compete, but rather to cooperate for their mutual benefit. Such conspiracies are against the law in the United States, but if such a deal were to go undetected, the several firms, acting as one, could exercise monopoly control over the market.

Barriers to entry: factors such as high entry costs or government protection, which prevent competitors from entering a market

Patent monopoly: a monopoly created by the exclusive access to a patented invention or process

Patent: a government grant of exclusive use of a new idea or invention

Copyright: the right to exclusive use of a publication, recording, and so on

Innovation: technological improvements that reduce costs, increase quality, or both

MONOPOLY REVENUES

Average revenue: total revenue divided by the quantity of output

Total revenue: the sum of all revenues from the sale of a product

Marginal revenue: the added revenues that result from the sale of an additional unit

The revenues that a monopolist can expect to receive are determined by consumer demand. The demand curve tells economists how much people are willing to buy at any given price. To the business manager the demand curve relates how much people are willing to *pay* for any amount produced. The demand curve is a source of information concerning business revenues. These revenues can be viewed three different ways. Economists find it useful to look at **average revenue**, **total revenue**, and **marginal revenue**.

Average revenue is the average amount received per unit sold. When all items are sold for the same price (as we assume here), price and average revenue are the same. The demand curve, therefore, is the monopolist's average revenue curve. Figure 1 shows a portion of a demand curve indicating that average revenue declines as production increases. In order to sell larger and larger quantities of a product (here the product is a new invention—a special kind of long-life light bulb) the firm must cut price, thus lowering the average amount received per unit sold.

Using the demand curve, the firm can calculate the total revenues possible from any given level of production. The demand curve shown here notes, for example, that at a price of $10.00 just one light bulb can be sold for a total revenue of $10.00. Two light bulbs are purchased if the price

FIGURE 7-1: DEMAND OR AVERAGE REVENUE (AR) CURVE
The demand curve shows the average revenue that the monopolist can receive for different quantities sold.

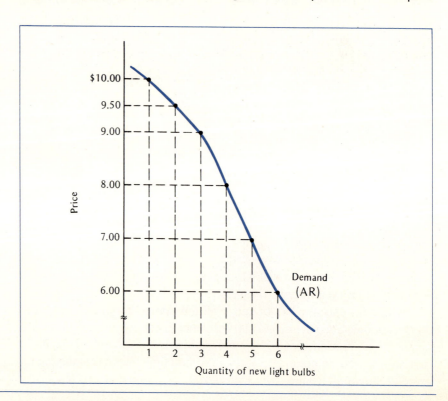

drops to $9.50. Total revenue then rises to $19.00. If three light bulbs are sold at $9.00 each, total revenue is $27.00. Total revenues are plotted in Figure 2.

In this example, total revenue increases as the quantity sold increases. Price has to be cut to get the additional sales, of course, but the larger quantities sold offset the effect of the lower price, increasing total revenues. This seems a reasonable occurrence, but it is not always the case. The relationship between price and total revenue depends on the elasticity of demand for a product. If an item has a relatively elastic demand, as the portion of demand in Figure 1 does, then total revenue rises as the quantity sold rises. On the inelastic portion of a demand curve, however, the price cuts outweigh the increased number of goods sold. More items are sold, but only at a price so low that total revenues actually fall!

Once total revenue has been calculated, we are ready to look at the only information that the monopolist really cares about: marginal revenue (MR). The marginal revenue curve (Figure 2b) shows the additional revenues that come when production changes. When 1 light bulb is sold, total revenues rise from 0 to $10.00. The MR of the first light bulb is therefore $10.00.

FIGURE 7-2: TOTAL AND MARGINAL REVENUE
By making calculations based on the demand curve shown in Figure 1 it is possible to plot the total revenue gained from any quantity sold (a) and the marginal revenue of each sale (b).

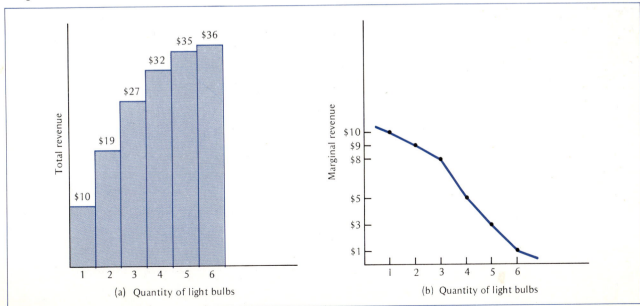

When 2 light bulbs are sold, total revenue rises to $19.00. Selling the second light bulb then adds $9.00 to total revenue. The marginal revenue of the second unit sold is $9.00.

There is an interesting relationship between average and marginal revenue. Compare the marginal revenue curve in Figure 2 with the demand curve in Figure 1. Notice that the second light bulb sells for $9.50 (on the demand curve) but has a marginal revenue of just $9.00. How can an item sell for $9.50 but add just $9.00 to total revenue? The key to this puzzle is that all goods offered for sale at any given time must normally be sold at the same price (the store manager can't generally sell one potato to you for 10¢ and the next one to another customer for 5¢). The firm may be able to sell one light bulb for $10.00 (so the demand curve says), but in order to sell two of them, the price of *both* must be cut to $9.50. While more revenues are earned on the additional items sold, less is taken in on other items that now bear a lower price. This makes marginal revenue generally less than price or average revenue, as shown in Figure 3.

FIGURE 7-3: AVERAGE AND MARGINAL REVENUE CURVES
Marginal revenue falls much more quickly than average revenue. In order to sell an additional unit, the monopolist must lower the price on all items sold. Thus the addition to revenue is much lower than the price of the last unit sold.

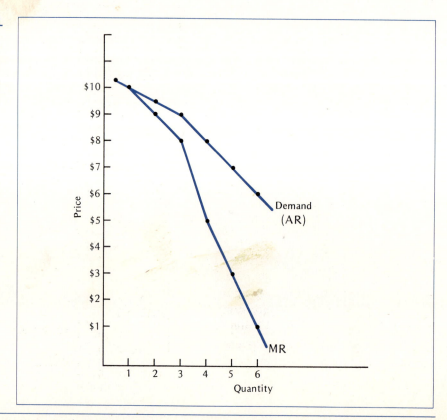

If a firm is interested in securing the highest level of total profits, how much should it produce? A simple but effective test is to examine each item produced and ask the question, "Does the production of this item add more to business revenues than it adds to costs?" If the answer is yes, then that item's marginal revenue (MR) exceeds its marginal cost (MC) and its production is a profitable step. If the answer is no, however, then additional costs (MC) outweigh added revenues (MR) and the item's production results in a financial loss.

To what production conclusion does this decision rule lead us? Figure 4 helps show the answer. This figure shows information about costs and revenues in three ways. Figure 4c shows the marginal costs and revenues experienced at each level of production. Figure 4b plots the total costs and total revenues, which correspond to these same production quantities. Finally, Figure 4a plots the difference between total revenue and total

THE MONOPOLY PRODUCTION DECISION

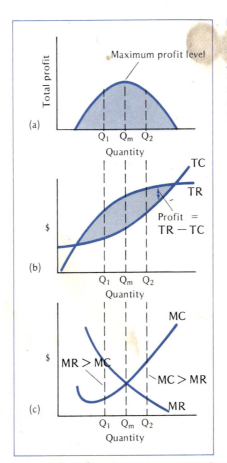

FIGURE 7-4: MONOPOLY PROFITS
Profits for the monopolist are maximized when an amount Q_m is produced. At this production level, marginal cost equals marginal revenue, resulting in a maximum difference between total cost and total revenue—profits.

cost—profit. Using these three diagrams, you can see how increasing or decreasing production affects marginal costs and revenues, total costs and revenues, and profits as well. Since the monopolist decision rule concentrates on marginal values, our discussion focuses on Figure 4c.

If the monopoly produces a small quantity Q_1, it earns a profit. All Q_1 units produced bring in more revenues than costs. But is this the profit-maximizing decision? No. At Q_1, the marginal revenue that one more unit will produce is greater than its marginal cost (MR > MC). Producing another item increases total costs, but total revenues go up more. Therefore, Q_1 is not the best level of production for the monopolist because more profits can be earned by producing more goods (the additional revenues generated will exceed the additional costs).

If more is better, then how about a production level like Q_2? Here, once again, the figure shows that the business generates positive economic profits. Is this the best production level for the monopolistic firm? A glance at the diagram indicates that it is not. At Q_2, the marginal cost of the last unit produced exceeds its marginal revenue (MC > MR). The last unit of output costs more to make than it brings in. It is unprofitable to produce and total profits fall as a result. Total profits will rise if production is reduced so that goods that generate a loss are not produced. The best production choice for the firm, then, is one that produces more than Q_1 but less than Q_2.

The most profitable production level for the monopolist is the quantity labeled Q_m (m for monopolist) in Figure 4. Profits are maximized when the firm produces at the point where marginal cost equals marginal revenue (the MC and MR curves cross).

MONOPOLY PRICING

If the monopoly is going to produce amount Q_m then what price is to be charged? We can read this from Figure 5. Once the production level is chosen, the monopolist charges the highest price that the market will bear. As the demand curve in Figure 5 shows, demanders of the monopolist's product are willing to pay a maximum of P_m, for an output of Q_m. If the monopolist charges more than P_m, there will not be sufficient demand for the producer to sell all that is produced. If the price is set at less than P_m, then there will be a larger quantity demanded than Q_m. At price P_m, the market is cleared (quantity demanded equals quantity supplied) and the monopolist earns the maximum profit available, given the costs and the demand for the product.

The monopoly shown in this figure is earning economic profits because the price that it receives (P_m) is well above the average total cost (ATC) of production at the chosen quantity Q_m. So long as price exceeds ATC, economic profits exist.

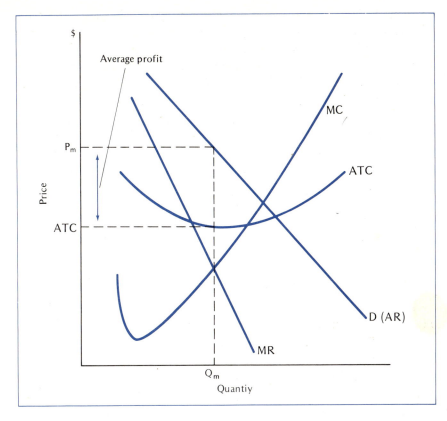

FIGURE 7-5: MONOPOLY PRICING
The monopolist maximizes profits by producing an amount Q_m of output. The monopolist then charges the maximum price that the market will pay for this quantity of production, P_m.

An important point to note here is that in a market with a monopoly supplier, there is no traditional supply curve for the monopoly product. A supply curve shows the different quantities that are offered for sale at different prices. The monopolist, however, is not interested in offering anything for sale at any price other than the profit-maximizing P_m. The supply curve for the monopolist, then, is a single point. If left unregulated or otherwise free to maximize total profits, the monopolist offers just one quantity at one price and sells those goods to the highest bidder. This doesn't mean that the forces of supply and demand break down completely. Changes in costs or demand still have an impact on the market equilibrium. The monopolist is in control here, however.

Will the monopolist always charge the profit-maximizing price P_m? Not always. Sometimes the monopolist will be unable to determine exactly the marginal costs and marginal revenues. If cost and revenue data are unavailable, the monopolist may have to use the trial and error method in finding the profit peak.

Sometimes monopolists intentionally ignore the profit-maximizing price. If the monopolits are worried about government regulation or are concerned about high economic profits attracting the attention of either potential competitors or government regulators, they may try to keep prices (and therefore profits) down in the short run to maintain their monopoly status and enjoy the profits that status provides.

CHANGING COSTS

To see how the monopoly market works, let's examine the impact of factors that would normally change demand or supply when the supplier is a single firm. Suppose that the firm encounters an increase in the cost of production such as higher wages for employees, higher costs for inputs, or a tax on production. We have seen that these kinds of changes in cost can reduce supply (shift the supply curve backward to the left) and bring about lower quantities and higher prices. What impact does it have on the monopolist? Figure 6 will help us answer this question.

The higher costs of production are reflected in higher marginal costs. Because it costs more to produce each additional unit, the marginal cost of

FIGURE 7-6: RISING COSTS FOR THE MONOPOLIST
When costs rise (as with an increase in labor costs or a tax on output) marginal costs rise, causing the profit-maximizing level of output to change. Here, the rising marginal costs cause the monopolist to reduce production and increase the price to the customers.

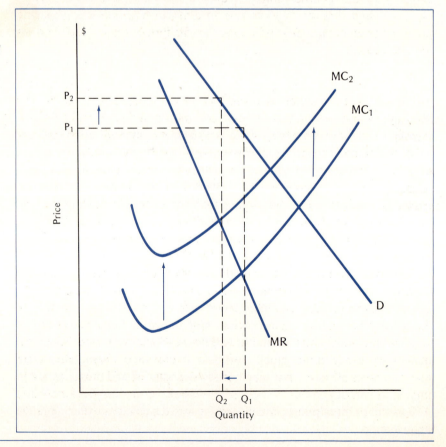

each unit is higher. This changes the monopoly's profit-maximizing level of production. Before the increase in costs, the monopolist achieved highest profits when MC = MR at a quantity of Q_1 units. Now, however, the highest level of total profits occurs at the lower amount Q_2. The monopolist reduces production and, selling the smaller quantity to the highest bidder, charges a higher price to protect the lower profits.

The example just given shows what happens when a change in variable costs occurs. Is there any difference if the change is in fixed costs instead? Yes, indeed there is. An increase in fixed costs increases the total cost of production, but does not directly affect marginal costs, and therefore has no affect on the production and pricing decisions of the monopolist. The same price and quantity will still maximize the now smaller monopoly profit. (Can you show this graphically? Try it!)

This leads us to an interesting conclusion. An increase in variable cost is shared between the monopolist (who receives smaller profits because ATC is increased) and the customer (who pays higher prices). An increase in fixed costs, however, is borne entirely by the monopolist in lower profits—none of it is passed through to customers in terms of higher prices (changing prices or production would only lower profits further since marginal costs are unchanged).

TECHNOLOGICAL ADVANCES

At the start of this chapter we noted that many monopolies are created by innovations—improving technology—and must continue to make technological advances in order to maintain their patent monopoly. How does this affect the monopolist decision? The answer is in Figure 7.

Most technological advances are aimed at either improving quality or reducing cost. A cost-reducing advance is shown here. As innovation reduces marginal cost, the profit-maximizing level of output for the monopolist changes. Before, profits were at their largest at price P_1 and monopoly output Q_1. When marginal cost shifts, however, profits are maximized at a higher level of output Q_2 when sold at a lower price P_2.

Technological advances can benefit the monopoly by erecting a patent or copyright barrier to competition, thus effectively preserving monopoly power in a market. But it can be a mixed blessing, as Figure 8 shows. Here the innovation that reduced marginal cost in Figure 7 reduces profits as well. Before innovation (Figure 8a) marginal costs and price were both high, but so were economic profits. After the innovation (Figure 8b) lower marginal costs allow the monopoly to lower price, expand production, and protect its monopoly. But the costs of innovation in this case have increased ATC to the point where economic profits are actually less than before the innovation.

FIGURE 7-7: INNOVATION AND THE MONOPOLIST
Innovations result in lowered marginal costs. This means that the monopolist maximizes profits by producing a little more and charging a slightly lower price.

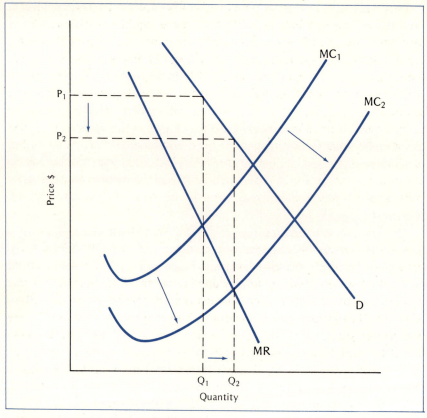

FIGURE 7-8: PROFITS AND INNOVATION
Innovation may reduce marginal costs, but it need not increase profits as this figure shows. Before innovation (a) price far exceeded ATC, indicating the presence of high economic profits. The innovation that lowers MC in (b) also increases average total costs, thus reducing profits.

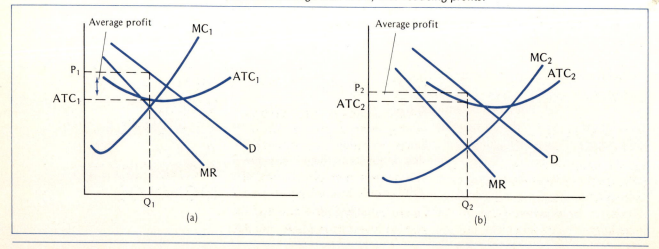

Why would a monopoly voluntarily innovate if this action reduces profits? First, we must be aware that this is not always the case—many times innovation actually increases profits to firms. In the case pictured, however, profits did fall. But the reduced economic profits may still be greater than those that the firm would have received if no innovation had taken place and other firms had entered the market, removing the monopolist's advantage.

Innovation is a risky business. In fact, Joseph Schumpeter, a famous economist, has suggested that innovation and invention are so risky that only monopolies, with their ability to extract high economic profits, may be able to afford the gamble. Monopolies, he suggests, may be highly desirable because of the inventiveness that they are forced (or able) to display!

MONOPOLY IN THE REAL WORLD

In the real world, true monopolies tend to be relatively rare. The kind of monopoly behavior described in this chapter is generally believed by economists to be contrary to the public interest. The high prices that monopolists can charge reduce benefits from exchange that would otherwise exist in markets where monopoly power prevails. As a result, few monopolies are allowed to exist by the government. In those markets where monopolies are necessary—such as in the provision of water and electrical power—they are heavily regulated by the government so that true monopoly pricing and production rules seldom prevail.

If true monopolies don't really exist in the United States to any meaningful extent, why have we taken all this time to analyze their behavior? We have done so because the factors that the monopolist must deal with are basically the same ones that face any firm competing in any market. Having looked at how one firm that dominates a market solves the problem of producer choice, we are now ready to examine the more interesting situation that prevails in competitive markets.

REAL WORLD ECONOMICS: A MONEY-LOSING MONOPOLY

METRO GOING BROKE, ASKS GOVERNMENT AID

BIGTOWN, MASS.—Metropolitan Transit, the county's only major bus line, announced today that it is going broke and will cease operations effective May 1 unless federal, state, or local governments come to the rescue and make up this year's record $2.3 million deficit.

Despite increased fares in recent months, income still has fallen below operating costs for the private corporation, which operates 750 buses and employs a total of 2500 people in the Bigtown area.

Operating losses are a familiar story to investors in Metro, but this is the first time that the company has threatened to cease operations entirely. Bigtown Congressman Al Tuna is reportedly seeking financial help from the U.S. Transportation Department.

ECONOMIC ANALYSIS

Not all monopolies make big bucks. Despite the existence of monopoly power, some firms still lose money. The problem depends on demand and marginal and fixed costs. The problem that Metropolitan Transit faces is illustrated in Figure 9.

Like any monopolist, the bus company operates to maximize profits. This means providing bus services such that marginal revenue equals marginal cost. As the figure shows, this results in a total of 23 million

bus rides per year at a market price of 50¢ each. At this point, Metro is making as much profit as possible. Unfortunately, there are no profits to be made at this or any other price, even for the monopolist. Metro is actually just minimizing its loss.

We can tell how much profit a firm makes by comparing the price (average revenue) it receives with average total cost. If average revenue is greater than average total cost, then a profit is earned. That is, if a bus ride sells for 50¢ and costs an average of just 45¢ to produce, then a 5¢ profit per ride is made. But Figure 9 shows that a profit is not always made.

In this example, the average revenue for the bus monopoly is 50¢, but average total cost is a whop-

FIGURE 7-9: TRANSIT MONOPOLY LOSES MONEY
Even at the "profit-maximizing" production level of 23 million riders, the transit monopoly shown here loses money. Fares are 50¢ per trip, but the average total cost is 60¢. An average of 10¢ is lost per rider. This accounts for the $2.3 million deficit reported.

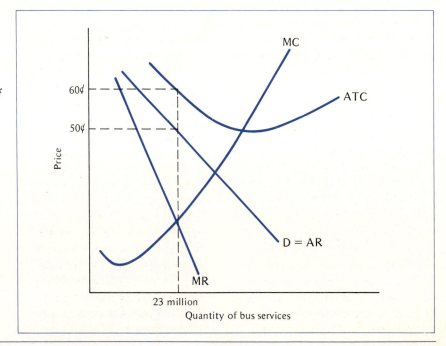

ping 60¢. When losing 10¢ per ride, the bus company can't cut its losses by reducing service and raising the price. Reducing the quantity supplied will mean cutting out bus routes that have a marginal revenue greater than marginal cost—that are profitable. Increasing production above the MC = MR level is also ineffective since the higher output will have marginal cost greater than marginal revenue. Even greater losses result from expanding production in this way.

What is the cause of this problem? This bus company is an example of a monopoly that has very high fixed costs. Many costs, such as debt service and loan payments for the many expensive buses in use, must be made regardless of the number of routes served. Gasoline and labor costs may also be fixed by schedule commitments and union contracts. The variable costs of operating a bus system may be relatively low (making low marginal cost and price possible), but the existence of high fixed costs (which must be paid before any profits are earned) makes most transit systems unprofitable. In fact, most transit systems, like Bigtown's, lose money as a matter of course and are partially or wholly financed by government agencies. Why is the government involved here? This question will be discussed in a later chapter when we look at the public policy aspects of monopolies.

SUMMARY

1. A monopolist is the only seller of a particular product in a given market. As such, the monopoly controls the supply of the product and acts to reap the highest possible profits from the sale of the monopoly good. The key to the creation of the monopoly is the ability to erect barriers to competitors wishing to enter the market. Some barriers, like high initial investment requirements, are natural to a particular industry. Others, like patents, derive from government policy.

2. Businesses make production decisions to maximize the profits they expect to receive from their actions. To do this, they must take into consideration the effect of their decisions on cost and revenues. In general, the firm maximizes profits by producing all items that add more to revenues than to costs.

3. Revenues are determined by consumer demand. The demand curve is also the average revenue curve for a monopolist. Total revenues are calculated by multiplying the demand prices and quantities. Marginal revenue—the change in total revenue that occurs when production changes—is the most important aspect of revenue to the monopolist since it measures the gain from any change in production.

4. The monopolist maximizes profits at the level of output where marginal cost equals marginal revenue. There is no monopoly supply curve as such—monopolists offer for sale only that quantity which maximizes profits and charge the highest price consumers will pay for that product. Any factors that alter marginal cost or marginal revenue change price and output for the monopoly.

DISCUSSION QUESTIONS

1. In looking at supply and demand analysis, we learned that, assuming normally shaped supply and demand curves, an increase in demand normally results in increased price and quantity. The monopolist has no supply curve. How, then, will an increase in demand affect price and quantity in a monopoly market? Explain.

2. Suppose that the government imposes a price ceiling (maximum legal price) in a market characterized by monopoly. Assume that the price ceiling is below the price that the monopolist would otherwise charge. What impact will the price ceiling have on marginal revenue, marginal costs, price, and quantity in the monopoly market? Will production rise or fall? Compare this with the result of a price ceiling in a market with normal supply and demand curves.

3. Using Table 1, construct total revenue, marginal revenue, and average revenue curves for this typical demand curve.

4. A monopolist wishes to increase

TABLE 7-1

Price	Quantity Demanded
$2000	1
1800	2
1500	3
1400	4
1000	5
800	6
500	7

profits, and so he begins an advertising program that features a giveaway—a free ball point pen is given away with each purchase in an attempt to stimulate demand. Explain how this program will affect each of the following: fixed cost, variable cost, marginal cost, demand, marginal revenue, price and quantity produced. Will the monopolist's profits rise or fall? How can you tell?

5. Suppose that the government imposes a license fee on all monopoly producers—they must pay a flat registration fee to the government regardless of their production. How will this kind of a tax on monopolists affect the following: marginal revenues, marginal costs, price, production, and profits?

Indicate whether each of the following statements is *true* or *false*. Be able to defend your choice.

1. Governments encourage the formation of some monopolies through patents and copyrights because monopolies charge very low prices.

2. Monopolies normally produce at the point where marginal revenue equals marginal cost.

3. All monopolies earn high economic profits.

4. An increase in marginal costs causes a monopoly to lower production and increase price.

5. An increase in fixed costs causes a monopoly to lower production and increase price.

6. A monopolist responds to an increase in demand by increasing production and raising price.

7. Through the use of ceiling prices, it is possible to force monopolies to cut price and increase production at the same time.

8. The supply curve of a monopoly is upward sloping, showing that quantity supplied increases as price rises.

9. A monopolist never produces on the inelastic portion of a demand curve.

10. Marginal revenue is generally less than average revenue, a fact that is apparent so long as the demand curve is downward sloping.

TEST YOURSELF

8
Producers in Competitive Markets

The existence of competition alters the problem of producer choice. This chapter examines choice in competitive markets. Questions that are answered here include the following:

How are competitive markets different from monopolies?

What is meant by perfect competition?

Why are competitive firms called price-takers?

How much does a competitive firm produce?

What factors can affect the competitive firm's production decision?

How does the behavior of firms and industries differ in the long run and in the short run?

A monopoly, by virtue of its position as the sole seller in a market, has some control over the problem of producer choice. In most markets, however, this control is not possible. Most markets in the real world are characterized by competition. Many independent producers compete with one another, which makes the analysis of the market at once simpler and more complex.

Perfect competition: a market situation characterized by large numbers of buyers and sellers, identical products, and no barriers to entry or exit

This chapter discusses **perfect competition**—competition among many producers. The next chapter looks at the middle ground between perfect competition and monopoly.

PERFECT COMPETITION

Perfect competition is the description of how an ideal competitive market would work. A perfectly competitive market is one where basic market forces (such as those detailed in the discussion of supply and demand) can work most efficiently. A perfectly competitive market is characterized by the following assumptions:

1. MANY BUYERS.
In a perfectly competitive market there are many buyers, but each is so small relative to the market that any individual buyer cannot affect price. Only many buyers acting at the same time (but independently) have enough effect on the quantity demanded to influence the price that is paid.

2. MANY SELLERS.
There are also many independent sellers. Each seller is but an atom in the scheme of the market (hence the name **atomistic competition** is sometimes applied here). The price that the firm receives for production is determined by the total forces of supply and demand. Unlike the monopolist, no individual firm can have measurable impact on price. Firms in competitive markets are called **price-takers** since they must take the market price as given in making their decisions. Monopolies, on the other hand, are **price-setters**, since they can set whatever price the market will bear.

Atomistic competition: competitive markets where individual buyers and sellers are as small, relative to the market, as atoms are relative to the items they form; another name for perfect competition

Price-takers: competitive firms that must react to changes in market price but have no control over that price themselves

Price-setters: firms, like monopolists, that can set any price for their goods because of their control of the market

3. IDENTICAL PRODUCTS.
A key assumption of perfect competition is that all the goods the many producers offer for sale are identical or at least so similar that differences in quality do not enter into the buying decision. Because there is no quality difference between the products of different sellers, the only factor that enters into the buyer's decision is price. Buyers purchase from whoever has the lowest price. Competition in perfectly competitive markets, then, centers on price rather than advertising or imagery. We shall look at the impact of product differentiation in the next chapter.

4. FREE ENTRY AND EXIT.

In order for perfect competition to hold, firms must be free to enter the market whenever they are drawn in by higher profits, and free to leave the market when losses mount. No natural or artificial barriers exist to prevent firms from joining the competition, and none should prevent firms from leaving to try something different.

5. PERFECT INFORMATION.

All firms in perfectly competitive markets have equal access to information concerning production techniques, market prices, and other factors that enter into the supply decision. In addition, perfect competition assumes that all firms buy inputs at identical prices in markets that are also competitive.

All of these assumptions about perfect competition do not hold in many of the real-world markets with which we are familiar. In some markets there are only a few buyers who can call the tune. Some markets have just a few sellers. Barriers to entry and exit may exist in many places. And products seldom seem identical; it is the difference in goods that attract our attention often as much as the price.

If the assumptions of perfect competition do not always hold in the real world, then why take the time to study it here? Two reasons are apparent. First, there are many markets where the assumptions of perfect competition are met, or nearly so. Agricultural commodities, for example, are the product of thousands of sellers joining with thousands of buyers to exchange nearly identical products. Competition here can be fierce. Natural resource markets can behave similarly. By studying how a firm behaves in a competitive market, we can understand more about how these markets work, how the problem of producer choice is solved by firms in these markets, and how supply decisions are made in markets in general.

There is another reason for studying perfect competition, however. Once we understand how ideal markets work, we can better examine the consequences of actions that violate the assumptions of perfect competition. Why would a firm want to compete on the basis of quality rather than price? What happens when it does so? These are the kinds of questions that we can answer after studying perfect competition. We shall, in fact, examine imperfect competition at length in the next chapter.

Because firms in competitive markets are so small, relative to the much larger market forces, they are forced to view demand in a very different way from the monopolist discussed in the preceding chapter.

The monopoly considers revenue possibilities determined by the market

PRICE TAKERS

demand curve. The monopolist knows that if only a few items are produced they will bring a high price. To sell more, however, means taking increasingly lower prices. The price that is received, then, depends on the amount that is produced. Marginal revenue and average revenue for the monopoly are much different. The monopolist faces a downward-sloping demand curve and makes production and pricing choices within the context of this type of market.

The revenue situation for firms in a perfectly competitive market is much different. The competitive firm may be aware that there is a downward-sloping market demand curve for its product, but cannot take advantage of it. Because the competitive firm is small relative to its market, any change in a single firm's output does not change the supply curve in Figure 1 enough to affect the market price.

The demand curve that an individual firm faces in a competitive market, then, is like the one shown in this figure. The demand curve for the *market* is downward sloping, but each *individual firm* can sell virtually any amount at the market price. Each firm operates on the assumption of a horizontal (constant price) demand curve. This type of demand is called a perfectly elastic demand curve.

Every unit that the competitive firm sells brings the market price. If the firm sells just one item, the price is the market-clearing price. If 1000 units are produced, however, each still sells for the same amount. For the competitive firm then, there is no fall in marginal revenue as the amount sold rises. Average revenue (price) and marginal revenue are constant and equal. They only change if something happens to affect large numbers of buyers or sellers and the market price is changed.

FIGURE 8-1: THE FIRM'S DEMAND CURVE

Each individual firm is a price-taker. Each firm can sell any amount at the market price. Thus, for each firm, additional units can be sold at no decrease in marginal revenue or market price. While the market demand is downward sloping, each firm will behave as if its demand were perfectly elastic as shown here.

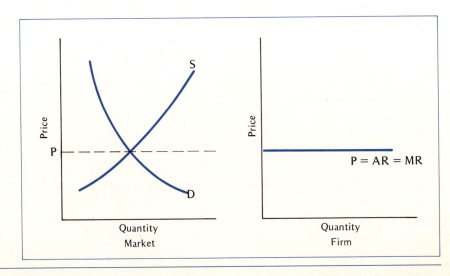

Figure 1 shows the important paradox of perfect competition. While all firms know that demand is downward sloping and that consumers buy more when price falls, each is also aware that the price is set by the huge, impersonal market. Since individual producers have no influence over market price, the producer choice problem centers on the quantity produced. Competitive producers attempt to find the production level that yields the most profits, given prices and costs that they cannot influence.

If the firm in a perfectly competitive market can sell all that is produced at the market price, how much should it produce? All that it can? As little as possible? The competitive firm, like the monopolist, must try to choose the quantity of production that will make profits as great as possible. We can see how this choice is made in Figure 2, which shows the marginal costs and

MAXIMIZING PROFITS

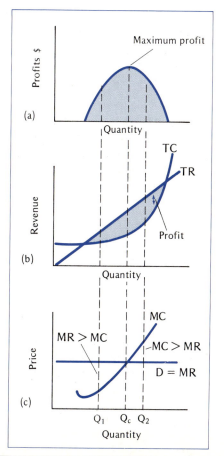

FIGURE 8-2: A PROFIT-MAXIMIZING COMPETITIVE FIRM
A firm in a perfectly competitive market maximizes profits by producing where price equals marginal cost. At this point the difference between total cost and total revenues is greatest.

revenues, total costs and revenue, and profits that the competitive firm achieves at different levels of production. Marginal revenue in this figure is assumed constant and equal to the market price (See Figure 2c). Marginal cost, however, increases as the quantity produced rises. Total revenue (Figure 2b) rises at a constant rate since each unit sold adds an equal amount to the total figure. Total cost rises, too, as shown. Finally, profits (the difference between total revenue and total cost) rise and fall depending on the level of production chosen by the competitive firm.

Suppose that the firm is already producing at level Q_1. At this production level the firm is earning positive economic profit. Is this the best position for the firm to be in? What will happen if the firm increases production by one unit? What happens at the margin? If one more unit is produced, the additional revenues (MR) generated exceed the additional costs (MC) that must be borne. Since this production adds more to revenues than to costs, profits can be increased by increasing production when the firm is at Q_1.

If higher profits come from higher production, then is a level of output like Q_2 the best? Again, the firm needs to look at costs and revenues. The last unit produced at Q_2 has high marginal cost, but provides the same marginal revenue as the first unit sold. Since marginal costs exceed marginal revenues, this last unit costs more to produce than it brings in. This production is unprofitable and total profits rise if the firm cuts its losses and cuts production.

At the low production level of Q_1 then, higher profits are achieved with higher levels of total production. At Q_2, however, too much is produced: higher profits come with less total output. The **equilibrium for the firm**—the profit-maximizing output for an individual firm in a competitive market—comes where the marginal cost of production just equals the marginal revenue received. This is the same production rule (MC = MR) that we saw for the monopolist. There is one difference, however. Since the competitive firm is a price-taker, marginal revenue is constant and equal to the market price. The competitive firm, then, maximizes profits when it produces where marginal cost equals market price. At this point, every unit produced earns a profit and total profits are at a maximum, as Figure 2 shows. To produce one unit more or one unit less will cause total profits to fall.

As with the monopolist, the competitive firm may have trouble discovering exactly what its marginal costs are and so may have to experiment to find the profit-maximizing combination. The production decision, then, is not so cut and dried as we have pictured it here. But Q_c is the profit maximum, and we can be sure that clever managers will quickly discover this production point in the real world.

Does this production strategy always guarantee high profits? The answer to this question is no, as Figure 3 shows. Firms maximize profits by

Equilibrium for the firm: the profit-maximizing (P = MC) level of production for the firm

FIGURE 8-3: FIRM PROFITS IN THE SHORT RUN

Whether or not a firm earns economic profits in the short run depends on price, marginal cost, and the firm's average total cost of production. The firm pictured in (a) earns positive economic profits—price is greater than average total cost—when it follows the price = MC production rule. The firm described by (b) has higher fixed costs. Its economic profits are negative even at the P = MC optimum. The firm shown in (c) earns zero economic profits. Price equals ATC for this firm.

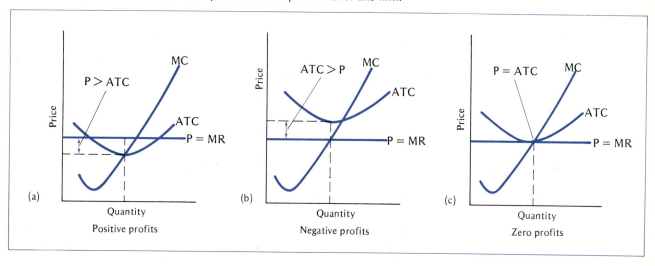

producing where price equals marginal cost, but the amount of profits that this rule yields depends on the relationship between price and average total cost at the chosen production level. If, as in Figure 3a, price exceeds ATC, profits are earned. But it is also possible for firms to earn negative economic profits (see Figure 3b) or to break even—the zero economic situation where price and ATC are equal (Figure 3c).

The profit-maximizing behavior of individual competitive firms gives rise to supply curves both for the firm and for the **industry**. The supply curve for an individual firm is the upward-sloping part of its marginal cost curve. Since the competitive firm sets production levels by equating price with marginal cost, we can determine the quantity a firm will supply by looking at its marginal cost curve.

If marginal cost curves are really firm supply curves, then the market supply can be found by horizontally summing the MC curves for all the firms in an industry as shown in Figure 4. Here we see a hypothetical industry with just three firms. By noting how much each individual firm produces at a given market price, we can calculate the quantity of market supply at that

SUPPLY CURVES

Industry: the collection of all firms that produce a particular product

FIGURE 8-4: SUPPLY CURVE FOR A COMPETITIVE INDUSTRY
Each firm's marginal cost curve is also its supply curve (since it tells the quantity that is supplied at each price). By adding the amount that each firm is willing to sell at any price, we can derive the industry supply curve. At the market price shown, Firm A maximizes profits by producing 100 units, Firm B produces 300, and Firm C's profit maximum occurs when 700 units are produced. For the combined firms then, a total of 1100 units are produced at this price.

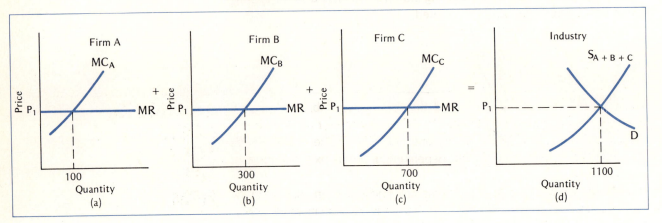

price. When this process is repeated for other prices, the market supply curve shown is derived.

EQUILIBRIUM FOR THE INDUSTRY

For an individual firm to be in equilibrium—a condition such that the firm does not wish to change its behavior—it must be producing at a level that maximizes profits given the going market price. The firm must produce where marginal cost equals marginal revenue (price). In order for all firms in an industry to be in equilibrium (in the short run), another condition must also prevail: The market must be in equilibrium so that there are no market forces acting to change price. Such an industry equilibrium is illustrated in Figure 4.

At the industry equilibrium, each firm in the industry maximizes profits and the market has neither a shortage nor a surplus. If the price is above the market-clearing price, the individual firms produce amounts that, in total, exceed the quantity demanded. As market price falls in response to this surplus, individual firms reduce output, moving the industry toward equilibrium.

If the price is below the market equilibrium, however, the individual firms produce an aggregate quantity that falls below the quantity demanded at that price. As a result, a market shortage prevails, forcing the price up toward equilibrium. As the price rises, individual firms react by increasing output, and eventually both the firms and the market find equilibrium again.

The industry equilibrium can change due to a variety of events that alter either producer or consumer choice. A change in demand, for example, will force a change in market price, causing individual firms to alter production levels until a new equilibrium is reached.

CHANGING COSTS FOR THE FIRM

The equilibrium of the industry and the firm is also subject to change whenever production costs change. Costs can change for all firms in the market, or they can change for just one firm. The market results of the changing costs are much different, depending upon the extent of the cost changes.

Let's first see what happens if a single firm encounters an increase in the cost of a variable input (which translates into an increase in marginal costs). What impact does the increase have on the firm and the market? The answer is indicated in Figure 5.

Before the rise in marginal costs, this individual firm maximized profits by producing at Q_1 where marginal cost equals price. As rising variable costs increase marginal costs, the profit-maximizing quantity falls to Q_2, where profits are now at their highest. (Can you show that there are now greater profits at Q_2 than Q_1?)

When an individual firm in a competitive market encounters rising costs (or falling costs) there is no impact on market price. Unlike the situation in a

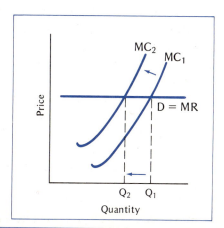

FIGURE 8-5: AN INCREASE IN MARGINAL COSTS
Rising marginal costs make previous production levels unprofitable. In response to rising marginal costs, the profit-maximizing firm reduces production from Q_1 to Q_2.

monopoly market, this is just one of thousands of suppliers deciding to produce a little less. The impact on market supply is too small to be felt. The firm affected produces less, makes less profit, and may possibly leave the industry in the long run if negative economic profits result. When something happens to alter costs throughout an industry, however (like a change in the price of a basic input or a change in business taxes), then both the market and the firm are affected.

Suppose, for example, that labor costs rise for all (or most) firms in a particular market. This has a dual effect, as shown in Figure 6. First, the rising marginal costs cause affected firms to reduce production in order to maximize profits. Because many firms are affected, this decreased production results in a fall in market supply (the supply curve shifts back and to the left). Falling market supply bids up the price of output. As market price rises, firms increase production, since profits get maximized at a higher level of output when prices rise.

We see these reactions in Figure 6 as three movements in firm and industry production. At the initial equilibrium, a typical firm produces Q_1 and total industry output is Q_A. When costs rise, the sample firm cuts back production to Q_2. As many firms behave similarly, market supply falls from Q_A to Q_B, creating a shortage of output at the equilibrium price P_1. Price rises in response to the shortage and, as price increases, the individual firms increase production from Q_2 to Q_3 (and total market supply rises from Q_B to Q_C along the supply curve) until an equilibrium in the market and for the firm is reestablished.

FIGURE 8-6:   THE IMPACT OF RISING COSTS ON THE MARKET
The rising marginal costs for all firms reduce the quantity supplied (shift the supply curve from S_1 to S_2). As market price rises in response to the shortage, the amount produced rises from Q_2 to Q_3.

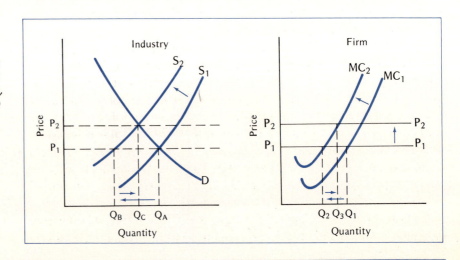

Our discussion of firm behavior in competitive markets has concentrated on the way that producer decisions are made in the short run. In the long run, however two additional changes can take place, to the firm and to the industry. For the firm, the long run provides an opportunity for businesses to alter their use of fixed inputs. In general we expect firms to change their production recipes over the long run to increase profits. Firms alter production techniques, plant size, and other controllable long-run factors in order to minimize average total cost.

SUPPLY
IN
THE
LONG
RUN

While individual firms are minimizing the costs of production, the industry can experience either a growth or decline in the number of firms. In the long run, firms can enter the industry or exit from it. If positive economic profits can be earned, this is a substantial incentive for additional businesses to join the industry. Since the economic calculation of cost includes opportunity cost, positive economic profits represent profits greater than opportunity cost—greater than those which could be earned elsewhere. Investors are likely, in the long run, to take advantage of the potential for these profits. In the long run, as well, firms exit from an industry if higher levels of profit are to be found elsewhere. In the long run the forces of entry and exit alter market supply and push an industry toward a zero profit equilibrium.

Why do zero economic profits prevail in the long run? If positive economic profits exist, firms enter the industry, increase market supply, and so bid down price until the lure of economic profit has disappeared. If negative economic profits are experienced, businesses leave the industry in the long run, causing market price increases until economic profit is again zero and there is no further incentive for firms to either enter or exit. This situation—where individual firms maximize profits by minimizing ATC while the industry adjusts to a condition of zero economic profits—is the long-run equilibrium of the industry.

The effect of these long-run adjustments is illustrated in Figure 7. Here the demand for a product has increased, bidding up the price and establishing a new short-run equilibrium for the industry at price P_1. In the long run, individual firms adjust to this new, higher level of production by altering their relative use of fixed and variable inputs to minimize average total costs. Also, the higher equilibrium price P_1 creates positive economic profits in this industry (can you show why this is true?). Economic profits encourage other firms to enter the market. These dual forces act to increase market supply in the long run to S_1, bidding down price and further increasing equilibrium production levels for the industry.

Does this situation always exist in the long run? The answer is best shown in Figure 8, which shows different types of long-run supply (LRS) curves.

FIGURE 8-7: LONG-RUN SUPPLY

In the short run, an increase in demand raises market price from P_0 to P_1 and production moves up the existing short-run supply curve. In the long run, however, firms seek the optimal production combination and entry takes place in the market. These two factors increase supply in the long run, bidding down price and increasing quantity.

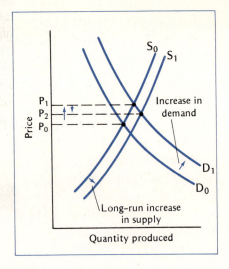

FIGURE 8-8: LONG-RUN SUPPLY CURVES

The long-run supply curve shows how equilibrium price and quantity change over the long run. In the constant cost case (a) the larger quantity is produced at the same cost over the long run. In the two nonconstant cost cases, however, long-run supply curves slope either up (showing rising long-run costs) or down (long-run decreasing costs) as production expands.

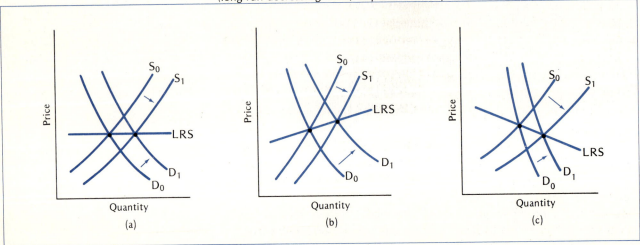

The long-run supply curve shows the relationship between price and quantity supplied for an industry over the long run. While short-run supply curves are still upward sloping, LRS curves take on different shapes depending on the nature of the relationship between costs and output for firms in the industry over the long run.

In some cases costs are constant over the long run. Long-run adjustments bring ATC back to its original level at the new long-run equilibrium. In other cases, however, average costs can either increase (giving an upward-sloping LRS) or decrease (a downward-sloping LRS curve) over the long run. The LRS curves show possible long-run industry equilibrium combinations assuming no external changes in the costs of inputs, government regulations, or other unpredictable factors affecting production. Which point on the LRS curve becomes the equilibrium? As the figures indicate, it depends on demand.

This chapter has looked at the behavior of firms, industries, and markets when the assumptions of perfect competition hold. This is not often the case, however. In the next chapter we examine some interesting exceptions to these rules.

CONSUMER GROUPS CHALLENGE STATE LIQUOR MONOPOLY

STATE CAPITAL—Consumer groups have begun to flood the state legislature here with petitions to allow competition in the lucrative industry of retail liquor stores. The result of the pressure that these groups bring to bear on legislators is unclear at this time, however.

This state, like several others, has a government monopoly on hard liquor. Whiskey by the bottle can only be purchased from the state government monopoly at government stores at government-set prices. These prices are well above those prevailing in neighboring states, which allow competitive private liquor stores.

Consumer groups claim that the state is taking unfair advantage of its position to extract higher prices from liquor consumers. They claim that the state takes enough from the alcohol drinker in the form of high liquor taxes without imposing a further burden of monopoly profits.

A representative from the state revenue subcommittee commented that the antimonopoly groups may have a logical case, but that any change in the state liquor monopoly would necessitate the raising of other taxes to make up for lost revenues. The representative declined to say what other taxes would have to be raised.

ECONOMIC ANALYSIS

This article centers on the difference between a monopoly and competitive markets. Is there a difference, as the consumer group suggests? If so, how large is the difference?

To get a feel for this problem, let's start by making a few reasonable assumptions. First, let's suppose

REAL WORLD ECONOMICS: A MONOPOLY VERSUS A COMPETITIVE MARKET

FIGURE 8-9: MONOPOLY VERSUS
COMPETITIVE FIRMS
*If this market were monopolized, the
firm would produce a low quantity Q_m
and sell it for a high price P_m.
Competitive firms would charge a
lower price and produce a larger
quantity.*

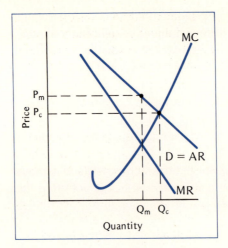

that there is nothing very different about the costs of a state monopoly retailing liquor and the costs that competitive firms would face. Approximately the same cost curves can reasonably be expected to apply to both groups. Let's assume, as well, that the same demand curve is faced (there is nothing that makes people want to buy more or less liquor from a state store versus a private concern). Given these two reasonable assumptions, what is the difference between monopoly and competition?

The state monopoly, if it is operating to maximize economic profits, will produce at a level as shown in Figure 9. The monopoly sells liquor at the level where the additional revenue generated by the sale of one more bottle just equals the incremental cost. At this quantity Q_m and price P_m, the monopoly maximizes profits, and generates high revenues for the state government treasury (which collects the profits).

How does this differ from the situation that would prevail if this market were opened to competition? We have just learned that, in a perfectly competitive market, each individual firm produces at a level where the market price received equals marginal cost. The marginal cost curve for the industry, then, is really the supply curve.

The competitive firms, treated as a whole, would produce where price (from the demand curve) equals marginal cost (the industry's supply curve). As Figure 9 shows, this occurs at price P_c and quantity Q_c.

The consumer groups have a point. If the liquor market were to be made competitive, then we would expect them to charge a lower price P_c and sell a larger amount of liquor Q_c than does this state's current liquor store monopoly. Alcohol users obviously have much to gain by taking away the state's monopoly—they will buy more at a lower price.

The problem of tax revenues still remains, however. Since the current monopoly profits go to the state government (instead of taxing other items) while whatever profits private liquor stores generate are kept by the owners, the state liquor monopoly might still be desirable.

SUMMARY

1. In competitive markets, firms have little control over price. Competitive firms are often called price-takers since they must accept the price that the market gives, rather than setting their own as the monopolist price-setter does.

2. Perfect competition is an economic ideal of a market where competitive forces prevail. In a competitive market, there are many buyers and sellers, each small relative to the market. All sell products of identical quality are sold at the same price. Entry and exit to the market are not restricted.

3. Competitive firms maximize profits by producing where price (equal to marginal revenue for the competitive firm) equals marginal cost. In the long run, firms enter or exit an industry until a level of zero economic profits prevails.

4. Changes in production cost or changes in market demand affect the firm's production decision. Changing marginal costs alter the firm's best output level. Changes in demand alter market price and lead to changes in production and entry or exit from the industry.

5. Prices of goods in the long run depend on conditions in the industry involved. In the long run, supply prices may be constant, rising, or falling. Industries experience differing costs as the number of firms or plant sizes in the industry change.

6. The short-run equilibrium for an industry occurs when individual firms maximize profits and a supply–demand equilibrium prevails in the market, assuring a stable price. In the long run, firms alter fixed inputs to minimize average total costs and new firm entry or exit can take place. Industry profits are zero in perfectly competitive markets in the long run.

DISCUSSION QUESTIONS

1. Suppose that a single firm in a market discovers a technological improvement that leads to lower marginal costs. How does this affect that firm? The market? Market price? Will your answers be different if *all* the firms in the industry use the cost-reducing invention? Why?

2. How will an increase in fixed costs affect a market in the

short run? In the long run? Why?

3. Suppose that the government sets a price floor in an industry. What effect does this floor have on individual producers? On the market? How can a surplus be avoided in this situation? Explain.

4. Would it be profitable for all firms in an industry to form an organization to set prices on quantities (such an organization is sometimes called a cartel)? Can the firms involved gain higher profits from working together instead of working apart?

5. Is competition better than monopoly? Defend your answer. State the advantages and disadvantages (to sellers, to buyers, to others) of each form of market organization.

TEST YOURSELF

Indicate whether each of the following statements is *true* or *false*. Be able to defend your choice.

1. The competitive firm faces a perfectly inelastic demand curve.

2. In a perfectly competitive market, each firm is so small relative to the whole that it can have no impact on market price.

3. The marginal costs and total costs are the same for all firms in a competitive market.

4. Economic profits are positive in the long run in a perfectly competitive market.

5. Accounting profits are positive in the long run in a perfectly competitive market.

6. Economic profits can be either positive, negative, or zero in the short run in a perfectly competitive market.

7. If there are limits to entry, economic profits will be positive in the long run in a market.

8. Rising costs produce higher prices in the short run and decreased quantity supplied.

9. The competitive firm produces where marginal cost equals average revenue.

10. Competitive firms tend to produce larger quantities at higher prices than do monopolists.

9
Imperfect Competition

In many markets producers are neither monopolists nor are they perfectly competitive. This in-between market situation goes by the name imperfect competition. In this chapter we present several views of imperfect competition. When this discussion is completed, you should be able to answer many questions, including the following:

What is product differentiation and why would a firm want to have a differentiated product?

What is price discrimination and why would a producer want to adopt this pricing strategy? Are there limits on price discrimination?

What is a cartel? Are cartels advantageous to their members? To their customers? Are they likely to be long-lived?

What is an oligopoly? How does an oligopoly determine price and quantity produced?

How can government regulations create market imperfections? How do regulations increase profits for producers?

True monopolies are relatively rare in our economy. Those monopolies that do exist do not always behave as monopolists because the government regulates their activities or because they dare not attract the attention of federal antimonopoly prosecutors. The reasons for the government's dislike of monopoly—and the rationale for government action here—will be discussed in greater detail in a later chapter.

While monopoly control is limited, perfectly competitive markets do not fill all the remaining gaps. Even though some markets come close to the ideal of perfect competition where identical goods and prices prevail, still in most markets one or more of the important assumptions of perfect competition fail to hold. These markets, where neither perfect competition nor monopoly control prevails, are examples of **imperfect competition**.

Imperfect competition: market where the assumptions of perfect competition do not hold, but monopolies do not exist either

There is no one kind of imperfect competition, and no one model can accurately describe all the different activities that take place in imperfectly competitive markets. This chapter describes several aspects of producer choice in imperfectly competitive markets and looks at the consequences of each on price, quantity, and the markets involved.

Recall the important assumptions that made perfect competition work. Many sellers are in the market, each small relative to market supply. The same situation prevails among the buyers. All are involved in the exchange of an identical product selling for an identical price. Entry and exit from the market are assured, competition exists on both the demand and supply side of the market, and perfect information prevails. Let's see what happens in the real world when this perfect market breaks down.

PRODUCT DIFFERENTIATION

The first thing that we notice, when comparing the real world with the perfect model, is the lack of identical products. Sure, many items that we buy look and act the same. At the supermarket, for example, one store's apples look much the same as another's. Competition here is likely to be based on price, or imagery, and not on quality. But for other items, it is as much the differences in real or perceived quality as the price that attract our attention.

Product differentiation: the practice of creating a real or perceived difference among similar products in a competitive market

Many producers engage in **product differentiation**. The idea behind product differentiation is simple: If one producer can create a real or perceived difference between his or her product and a competitor's, then customers will buy more of or pay a higher price for the differentiated product.

We see product differentiation at work all the time. Despite tests showing that one beer tastes much the same as another, people still display great loyalty to certain brands of brew. Beer makers, of course, cultivate this loyalty and the image of difference that is necessary for it. The idea is that the customers, when faced with several seemingly identical brews, should reach for their favorite brand, and not just the one with the lowest price.

Product differentiation is apparent in the beer market, but it also exists in many areas of consumer choice. Identical products are more likely to exist among products that businesses purchase rather than those that consumers buy. Businesses are more interested in minimizing cost. Consumers want to maximize utility. A business won't beat its competitors if it buys a different product that is more expensive because of its high advertising costs. The consumer, however, might be willing to pay more if the perceived quality of the good is higher. Cars, TV sets, soups, coffees, clothes (designer labels), and even fruit (Chiquita bananas and Sunkist oranges) are but a few of the items where one producer tries to differentiate its product from that of the competition.

How does a firm go about creating product differentiation? One way, of course, is to actually produce a product that is different (technological improvements, higher standards, tight quality control, longer life, better flavor). The seller with a better moustrap may, indeed, find the world at his or her door.

A second way to create product differentiation is to develop a perceived difference between one product and the next. This can be accomplished by packaging, advertising, or the use of gimmicks. All that may be necessary, in some markets, is an apparent difference in quality in the mind of the consumer. Tests have shown, for example, that brand-name canned goods at the market are of much the same quality as cheaper house brand goods—they are sometimes even packed in the same factory. Yet, consumers habitually buy the national brands, leaving the cheaper substitute behind. There may be no real difference in the products, but it doesn't matter so long as consumers think that there is.

It obviously costs something to produce a differentiated product. A manufacturer of tennis equipment, for example, must spend money to produce a better racket in order to get the customer's attention, spend money to advertise it, or bribe professional players to endorse it. If an item identical to that of the competition is produced, and no effort is made to make it different, it blends into the woodwork and is forced to compete on the basis of low price, and not quality or status.

Often the higher costs of product differentiation act as a barrier to entry. A firm may be quite able to produce a new brand of soap, but is unwilling or unable to make the risky investment in advertising necessary to create "name recognition" and really break into the market. Thus the fact of product differentiation, by discouraging entry, gives existing producers more market power.

When a firm has established a differentiated product, it can engage in what economists call **monopolistic competition**. The firm can behave as a monopolist, to a limited extent, while still facing the problem of competition. The idea is illustrated in Figure 1. Here we see the production decision that the makers of Coca-Cola might face. They compete with the producers of other cola soft drinks. Many people have trouble tasting the difference among these colas. Does this mean that Coke producers sell an identical product at the same price as the others? No, indeed. By advertising their product as "the real thing" and making people aware of Coke, these producers have created a minimonopoly. Many others may sell colas, but these are the only producers of Coke.

Because of product differentiation, the demand for Coke can be separated from the demand for other kinds of colas. If Coke raises its price above that of the competition, it will still sell a considerable quantity, unlike the perfectly competitive firm that loses all its business when the price goes above market price. The reason is that people feel Coke is somehow different from other similar drinks, and they continue to buy Coke even when it is more expensive than, say, Pepsi.

When Coke producers lower their price, as Figure 1 shows, they will sell even more. The producer of a differentiated product, therefore, can calculate the demand for its product and construct the marginal revenue curve that it faces, as indicated in Figure 1. Despite competition from other makers of similar products, Coke can behave like a monopolist with respect to the demand for its differentiated cola drink.

The rationale for product differentiation now becomes clear. By creating

FIGURE 9-1: PRODUCT DIFFERENTIATION
By creating the image of being "different" from its competitors, this firm can exercise monopoly power over the demand for its "different product." This allows it to use monopoly pricing.

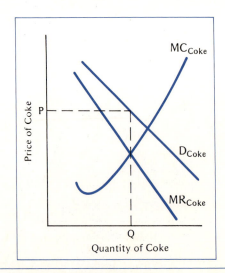

a different product, the monopolistic competitor can behave, within limits, as a monopolist and pursue monopolistic pricing. This means that a price in excess of marginal cost can be charged, yielding economic profits like those monopolies receive. While product differentiation leads to higher costs (for advertising, research, and so on) the economic profits that it makes possible can often (but not always) make the extra expense profitable. Thus the emphasis at the supermarket is on brand-naming and the large amounts of advertising that confront us everywhere.

In recent years, with inflation running at high rates, some kinds of reverse product differentiation have taken place. Some stores have brought out lines of plain-label goods, which are advertised as being inflation-fighters. Because they are not individually advertised, these items are less costly and a better buy. This peculiar type of differentiation has led cost-conscious customers to buy the plain items to save money—sometimes even when these items are priced higher than brand name goods on the same shelf. Product differentiation clearly has many faces.

Because of product differentiation, seemingly identical goods can sell at quite different prices. This is illustrated in Figure 2. Because their products are viewed as different by consumers, the makers of Coke and those of No Name Cola face significantly different demand curves. Coke's price can be raised relatively high and still some will be sold because it is perceived to have better quality or higher status. We might say that the demand for Coke is relatively inelastic. Not so with the demand for No Name Cola. No Name

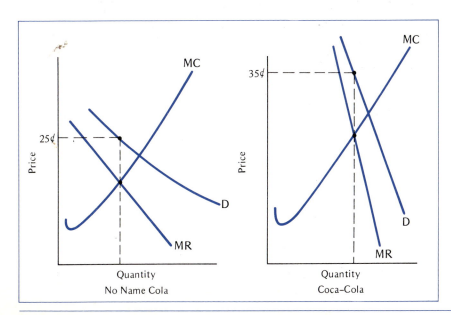

FIGURE 9-2: MONOPOLISTIC COMPETITION
The existence of product differentiation explains why similar products can have different prices in the market place. Here, both the makers of Coke and No Name Cola have similar costs, but sell at different prices because of different demands.

cannot charge a price much different from that of other nonadvertised soft drinks. Any change in price will produce a relatively large change in the quantity demanded. No Name's demand curve is elastic, compared to Coke's.

Because of the difference in demand, Coke and No Name are priced differently. Each producer equates marginal cost with marginal revenue. Because of differences in demand, however, the profit-maximizing price is 25¢ per bottle for No Name Cola and 35¢ for Coke. With its more inelastic demand, Coke can charge a higher price and make larger profits.

This product differentiation scheme is a good one, since it allows firms that are not really monopolists to act, within limits, like monopoly suppliers. Why, then, don't all firms attempt to differentiate their products? Several reasons come to mind. Some products are so similar that attempts to differentiate may be wasted. One supplier's coal, for example, is so much like another's that competition must focus on price (although gasoline producers have somehow succeeded in differentiating remarkably similar brands of gasoline!).

Another reason that some goods remain undifferentiated has to do with the cost of creating the difference. If the cost of differentiation is greater than the monopoly profits that differences make possible, then product differentiation is not such a good deal. This is illustrated in Figure 3. Here, because its product is perceived as different, a producer is able to price at the monopoly level. Even at this price, however, the price received is less than average total cost. By driving up total costs, the advertising that created the difference also created a loss. This firm will quickly go out of business. We might call this the "Billy Beer" effect. President Jimmy Carter's brother, Billy, was hired by a brewer to endorse a brand of beer—named Billy Beer.

FIGURE 9-3: A LOSING PRODUCT DIFFERENTIATOR
Product differentiation allows this firm to behave like a monopolist. Unfortunately, the costs of differentiation are so high that average total cost exceeds average revenue—the firm loses money.

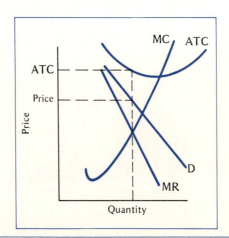

This may have helped the brewer temporarily, but profits still took a nose dive and Billy Beer, although considered very much different, is now a thing of the past.

PRICE DISCRIMINATION

Price discrimination: the practice of charging different prices to different buyers for the same good or service

When perfect competition breaks down, another phenomenon that often occurs is **price discrimination**. Price discrimination occurs when the same (or virtually the same) items are sold to different buyers at different prices. When price discrimination prevails, some folks are charged a high price while others pay a lesser amount. Price discrimination is not a form of competition (like monopoly or monopolistic competition), it is just a type of pricing behavior commonly found in markets where producers are able to exercise substantial power (as in monopoly or monopolistic competitive markets).

Why would a firm want to discriminate in pricing? The answer is suggested by Figure 4. Here, a market is shown with equilibrium price of $10 and equilibrium quantity of 100 units. If everyone pays the same price, then 100 units will be sold at a total revenue of $10 × 100 = $1000. This may be good, but the firms in this market must be aware that some folks are willing to pay a much larger amount to get this item. The demand curve shows that they could sell 40 of them—and take in $800 total revenue—even if the price were raised to $20. The key to price discrimination is to

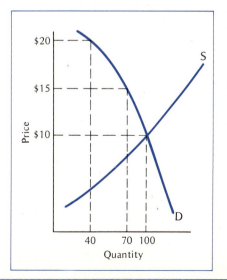

FIGURE 9-4:   PRICE DISCRIMINATION
By charging three different prices for its goods, firms in this industry can increase total revenue from $1000 (if all 100 items are sold at the same $10 price) to $1550. Even greater revenue could be achieved if a larger number of prices could be charged to a larger number of groups.

make each individual or group in the market pay the highest amount possible, charging someone less only if it is necessary to get their business.

The advantage is easy to see. Suppose that the firm in Figure 4 divides its customers into three groups (according to their willingness to pay for the product). Suppose that it charges the 40 richest customers $20 each for the product. This raises total revenues of $800. The diagram shows that 40 is the most it can sell at that price. Now, suppose that, without telling the first group, the firm sells 30 more at $15 (generating $450 total revenue) and, finally, sells the last 30 units at the market-clearing price of $10 (30 × $10 = $300 revenue).

By charging different groups different amounts, this firm is still able to sell 100 units, but it receives a total revenue of $800 + $450 + $300 = $1550 for the sales, instead of the $1000 that it would have realized had all the goods been sold at the market-clearing price of $10. Price discrimination allows a business to increase the total revenues without altering production.

Price discrimination looks like a good deal for the firm, but its use is limited. When you go to the supermarket, for example, the clerk doesn't look you over and then charge a higher or lower price based on what he expects you are willing to pay. In most markets all buyers pay the same price. What makes price discrimination possible? In general, the price-discriminating firm must be able to divide the market into groups with different demand characteristics. If some people will buy at a high price and others buy only if the price is very low, then the seller must divide these groups so that they can be treated differently.

The second key to price discrimination is that the seller must find a way to charge different groups different amounts. This can be done openly, or discreetly through discounts, kickbacks, or other methods. Movie admissions, for example, openly differ for different groups (children, students, adults, senior citizens), but your doctor doesn't openly advertise that a rich patient might be charged more for a visit than a poor one.

Finally, the firm must prevent resale of the item involved. If the lower-price purchaser can resell the good to the high-priced buyer, soon no one will pay the higher price and the dual-price system will disappear.

In what kind of situation, is price discrimination likely? Let's first look at the sale of services. Doctors, for example, are thought to vary their prices for some services (operations, and the like) according to the incomes of their customers. Poor patients of the same physician may pay less per visit than more well-to-do customers. The idea is clear: If doctors' fees were as high for the poor as they are for the rich, the poor might choose to remain sick. The doctor can attract the business of low-income groups without lowering fees gained from high-income patients through price discrimination.

Haircuts and movie tickets are also places where price discrimination is common and accepted. Have you ever wondered why a ticket for a seat in a theater should cost less for a child than an adult (it's still the same seat, after all)? Or why a child should pay less for a haircut when it takes the barber the same amount of time to do the work? The answer is price discrimination. If children were charged as much as adults for these services, it is likely that they would use fewer of them and find cheap substitutes—like home haircuts and television—for haircuts and movies. The dual-pricing system allows these businesses to charge the higher price that adults are willing to pay and, as well, to increase their business by charging others a lower price.

Traditionally, one of the most effective price discriminators has been the airline industry. First-class fares are charged to those who wish status or extra comfort. Coach fares are charged to those who cannot make reservations long in advance or who do not stay in one place very long. Because these first two groups have little option but to use the airlines for travel, they are charged the higher price. Other groups, however, have more options. Vacationers will use the airlines if the price is right, but otherwise will travel by bus, car, or train, or stay home. They are given special discount fares if they make reservations several weeks in advance and stay at their destination more than a few days. It is difficult for the businessperson to meet these restrictions but easy for the vacationer to do so. Thus two prices for the two groups.

The airlines don't stop here, however; they also give further discounts for seats occupied by small children. This encourages family travel and takes advantage of the fact that, at higher fares, kids might not fly at all.

Since it is impossible to resell a haircut or gallstone operation, and it is difficult to resell airline or movie tickets, these markets (and markets like them) are easily used for price discrimination. But what of other areas where resale is easier? Here, a different scheme is used to perform the same function and make price discrimination possible.

One scheme that has been successfully used by several manufacturers is to bring out new items in steps. First a deluxe version is sold at a high price, so that only those who are willing to pay a high price will buy. Next, a less luxurious model is introduced at a lower price. Finally, a cheap model is sold to those who will only buy at a very low price. Polaroid cameras are often sold in this fashion, as are many electronic gizmos. Those who wish to be first to own one pay for that privilege. Those who wait may eventually be able to pay less. Substantially the same product is often sold at several different prices over a period of time as the manufacturer mines every part of the demand curve to achieve the highest total revenue.

The last form of price discrimination that we shall discuss (but by no means the only other way to get away with it) is to sell identical goods at different prices through different retailers. Readers of *Consumer Reports* magazine are familiar with this concept. Often a manufacturer of, say, toasters sells the same item (identical except for brand-name identification and trim) at one price with the manufacturer's brand name, at a second, lower price through, say, Sears stores, and again at a third price under the house brand name of a discount store. This way the manufacturer can sell at the highest price to those who shop department and appliance stores, at a lower price to Sears customers, and at a possibly still lower price to discount store shoppers who would be unlikely to buy at the higher price. If different types of customers patronize the different stores, then shopping habits divide the market into the groups that the effective price discriminator needs.

BENEFITS OF PRICE DISCRIMINATION

On the whole, this discussion has concentrated on the benefits of price discrimination to the producer, but consumers may also benefit indirectly from this pricing practice.

Since price discrimination increases profits, it makes the firm that can get away with it better off. But sometimes price discrimination is necessary in order for the firm to simply stay in business. Recall (in the discussion of monopoly) the plight of the loss-producing monopolist (a transit company was the example used). Even with monopoly power, it was impossible for this firm to earn a profit. If price discrimination occurs, however, revenues increase and the normally unprofitable bus system may be able to stay in business after all. Price discrimination in this case may generate the revenues necessary to keep the firm in business and so give consumers the option to purchase the good or service involved.

Price discrimination may also have a silver lining in that it can cause monopolistic firms to increase production levels. If price discrimination is not available, as in the "Before" picture in Figure 5, monopoly production is relatively small. Compare this monopoly behavior with that displayed in the "After" picture. Here, we allow the monopolist to be a perfect price discriminator. The monopolist auctions each unit produced separately. The first product off the line is auctioned for a very high price, the second item sells for a slightly lower price, and so on until the 120th unit produced sells for $80. When this kind of price discrimination prevails, price and marginal revenue are the same. When the monopolist sells the 120th unit for $80, the firm adds exactly $80 to revenues (the other 119 units still sell for their old prices—the additional production doesn't affect their prices).

The monopolist still maximizes profits where marginal revenue equals marginal cost—but now that occurs at a higher total output of 120 instead of 70 units and at a lower price of $80 instead of $100. This is exactly the price

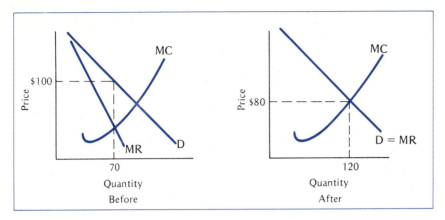

FIGURE 9-5: PRICE DISCRIMINATION AND THE MONOPOLY
Price discrimination can be used to increase monopoly output and lower monopoly price. Once the monopoly is allowed to be a price discriminator, its marginal revenues increase, causing higher production and lower price.

and output that would prevail if the monopoly were replaced with a perfectly competitive market of firms having the same marginal cost curves.

Even when this ultimate price discrimination—each unit sold for a different price—does not take place, the existence of price discrimination generally increases output and lowers price in monopoly or monopoly-like markets. Goods are sold for prices closer to their marginal costs and firms are more efficient in responding to consumer demands.

Price discrimination creates winners and losers. The firms that earn higher profits are winners, obviously. Consumers who are able to pay a lower price than would otherwise be available win, too. But the key to price discrimination is to charge some customers a higher price than would have prevailed on a competitive market. These groups pay the price that makes the other benefits possible.

CARTELS

Thus far our discussion of imperfect competition has concentrated on attempts to reorganize the demand side of the market to secure higher revenues either through product differentiation or price discrimination. In some markets, however, these types of schemes fail. A producer of natural resources or agricultural commodities, for example, must face a more perfectly competitive situation. Product differentiation is difficult, for example, for a wheat farmer since all wheat of a given type is pretty much the same. Price discrimination is hard, too, because of the possibility of resale. Does this mean that perfectly competitive situations will prevail in markets like this? Often the answer is yes, but not always. Producers faced with this situation can increase their combined profits if they form a seller **cartel**.

Cartel: an organization of firms in a market designed to exercise monopoly control by restricting supply

A cartel is an organization of sellers designed to form what is essentially a monopoly situation. The cartel is designed to raise prices by collectively reducing the quantity supplied. The idea behind a cartel is illustrated in Figure 6.

Suppose that there are several firms in the wheat industry in a certain part of the country. If they behave competitively they will sell, say, 120 units of wheat at a price of $5.00 each. This price and quantity are the result of perfect competition. Economic profits, in the long run (when entry and exit take place), are zero. Now, suppose that the firms form a cartel. This cartel might be some sort of trade organization or a cooperative marketing program. If all the producers operate as one—as a monopolist—then they can collectively act to maximize profits by producing, as a group, only until marginal cost equals marginal revenue. They produce fewer goods (saving cost), charge a higher price, and earn economic profits in the meantime. These economic profits—which derive from the monopolistic pricing scheme—can then be divided among the member producers. Each produces less and takes in higher profits by reducing production and joining the cartel.

Many cartels have been organized through the years to take advantage of

FIGURE 9-6:   THE CARTEL STRATEGY
If the firms in this industry behave competitively, they are driven to produce 120 units at a price of $5.00 each. Long-run economic profits are zero. If they form a cartel and restrict production to 100 units, higher prices and economic profits prevail.

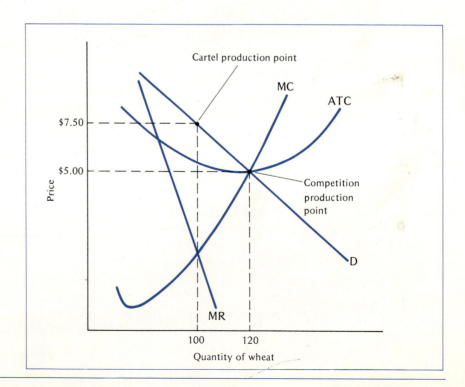

this idea. The Organization of Petroleum Exporting Countries (OPEC) is the most famous of these. OPEC controls the supply of much of the world's oil and reaps huge monopoly profits from its position.

The problem with cartels is that they tend to be unstable. That is, the forces that build cartels also tend to destroy them. Since the force that makes cartels is greed, that is also the death knell for most such organizations.

As a group, cartel members are best off if they restrict collective production. If everybody cuts back, then their collective profits are at their peak and all can gain. Does this mean that it is to each individual producer's advantage to cut back? No! Suppose that one producer cheats and secretly sells one more unit. Will it be profitable to do so? Yes! As Figure 7 shows, added cheater production has a low marginal cost. The cheater increases individual profits by selling secretly, although the profits of the rest of the group fall because the market price is less than if the last unit went unproduced.

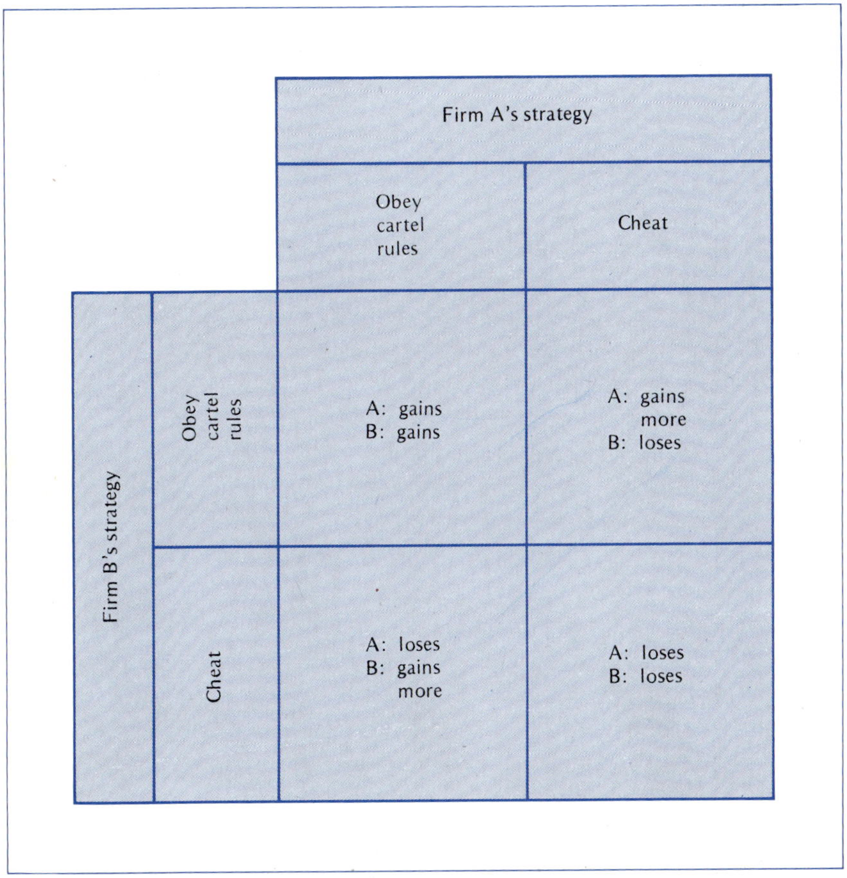

FIGURE 9-7: UNSTABLE CARTELS
All members of a cartel gain when the cartel is organized. But each individual member can gain by cheating (selling more than the cartel quantity) provided all other cartel members obey the rules and restrict production. In the long run, the individual benefits of cheating cause cartels to fall apart.

Cheating is profitable to the individual members of a cartel. The cheating producer gains all the revenue for the extra production, while the loss (in terms of lower market price) is spread among the other members of the cartel. As a group, the members of a cartel have an incentive to control production, but, given the fact that the other members go along with the "rules," each individual member gains by breaking the rules, expanding production, and thereby destroying the cartel. With such large gains from cheating, the theory of cartels holds, it is almost inevitable for large groups of cheaters to sell above their allotment, causing others to protect themselves by also upping production until, finally, fierce competition prevails again.

Cartels may be able to exist for extended periods of time if the gains from membership are very large (as they are for the OPEC producers) or if a way is found to police members in order to discover and punish cheating as soon as it appears. Still, most cartels are probably short-term affairs at best. Greed builds cartels, and it tears them down, too.

OLIGOPOLIES

Oligopoly: competition among just a few firms that together dominate a market

Many markets in the United States and elsewhere are examples of **oligopoly**. Oligopoly markets are basically similar to markets where monopolistic competition prevails with one additional condition: uncertainty. Whereas there may be hundreds or thousands of small firms in a market characterized by monopolistic competition, oligopoly is competition among the few. Because there are only perhaps three or four main producers in an oligopoly market, one firm's actions affect the revenues of all others. This makes any production decision a risky and uncertain one.

Oligopolies are particularly difficult to analyze because producer behavior can vary depending on the type of market involved and the motivations of the managers of the firms. In some markets, it is suspected, the existence of oligopoly leads to a distinct lack of competition. By playing follow the leader or acting as a cartel, oligopoly firms can exercise monopoly control over a market and so earn economic profits. With only a few firms in the market, there may be enough profits available to satisfy all partners in a cartel without inducing the kind of cheating discussed earlier. The steel industry in the United States has sometimes been accused of being this kind of oligopoly. While no illegal cartel agreement exists among steel manufacturers, some have suggested that competition is avoided by having the largest firms set prices and other firms go along.

But the existence of an oligopoly does not necessarily mean that monopoly profits are earned. If the firms in the market choose to compete actively for the available business, they could conceivably drive prices down to the competitive zero economic profit level. This may, in fact, happen in a wide range of markets.

The key to understanding oligopoly is to note the interdependence of firms in such situations. A monopolist can control its own destiny. A competitive firm has no control over market price. But oligopoly producers must be aware that their decisions affect competitors and vice versa. When one firm increases production, for example, this bids down market price, affecting price and quantity decisions for all the other firms in the oligopoly market. Likewise, a reduction in production by one firm affects the prices that all receive.

Oligopolistic firms must therefore calculate the actions and reactions of competitors in making price or output decisions. If United Airlines lowers air fares, for example, over some specific route, will American Airlines keep the same price, lower prices, increase advertising, or offer new service? The profitability of United's move depends on what American, Northwest, National, and other carriers do in return. This high degree of uncertainty may account for what we often perceive as a lack of competition in oligopoly markets. If changes in prices or production have such uncertain results, perhaps managers prefer to avoid risk by sticking to proven strategies.

GOVERNMENT REGULATION

Government regulations can also create market imperfections that reduce competition. In general, there are two types of regulations that governments enact: regulations imposed on industries and firms in order to increase social welfare, and regulations that firms seek in order to increase their profits. The first kind of regulation will be discussed in later chapters. The second kind is discussed here.

Why would a firm seek government regulation? The power of the government can be used in several ways to increase profits and decrease competition that firms face. There are several ways that the government can benefit firms.

1. PRICE CONTROLS. The government can reduce competition in a market by controlling the price that firms charge. Fees in the trucking, moving, and transportation industries, for example, have long been set by the government. While in some cases this may lead to lower prices, government price restrictions, by limiting competition, can create monopoly profits. In any case, these regulations are not always in the best interests of the consumer and may well aid producers.

2. RESTRICTIONS TO ENTRY.

The government can also create monopoly profits for firms if it can limit entry into an industry. Entry is often limited by licensing laws. In many states, for example, a person must pass a government licensing exam in order to enter the following occupations: lawyer, doctor, barber, accountant, pharmacist, architect, nurse, chiropractor, mortician. A firm that wishes to start a new bank or compete on a lucrative airline route will also have to seek government approval. In New York City the number of taxicabs has been firmly controlled by the government for years.

These licensing laws are supposed to be designed to protect the public from shoddy service or unprincipled dealers. Their impact, however, reduces entry into markets. With entry thus restricted, the firms already in these markets can earn positive economic profits and take advantage of limited monopoly power. In general, any industry that can gain control of entry through government action will do so.

3. CONTROL OF COMPLEMENTS AND SUBSTITUTES.

Firms can also use government power to control the prices and quantities of complements and substitutes. By affecting these goods, they can often increase their own profits.

A good example of this has to do with butter and its common substitute margarine. This isn't an attempt to single out the dairy industry for abuse of government controls—many industries have sought to do these kinds of things—but the butter example is particularly interesting. Over the years, butter manufacturers have attempted to reduce consumption of margarine and increase sales, prices, and profits from butter. Methods that have been used include the following:

☐ For many years, laws in some dairy-product-producing states made it actually illegal to sell margarine! Smugglers were forced to sneak across state lines and bring back hot margarine.

☐ By law, restaurants that used margarine instead of butter were sometimes required to inform customers in three ways. First, they had to display prominently a sign stating, "we serve margarine" on the premises. Second, they had to put a similar announcement on the menu itself. Finally, and most ridiculous of all, the margarine had to be served to diners in pats the shape of triangles (butter was served in little squares) so that the consumer would be certain to know that the stuff wasn't the real McCoy.

Fortunately, most of the antimargarine regulations are no longer on the books, having fallen to the pressures of margarine consumers, producers, or both. But they still represent an example of how a substitute can be controlled to increase prices and income of firms in competing industries.

Complements can also be used. Carpenters and plumbers, for example, often try to influence building codes. By specifying the types of construction that legal building must have, the codes can increase the use of workers, lumber, and so on. It's not hard to think of other examples where producers in one market try to affect complements to increase their own profits.

We do not want to leave you with the impression that controls, cartels, and price discrimination affect all markets. Indeed, many markets in modern economies are remarkably competitive. Still, there are ways that competition can be altered or reduced, as this chapter has suggested. It is important for the consumer and producer to be aware of how these imperfections affect the market and why they exist.

FORD FOLLOWS GM IN ANNOUNCING LOWER PRICES ON SUBCOMPACT CARS

DETROIT—Ford Motor Company today announced that it is lowering the suggested dealer prices on its lines of subcompact cars by amounts ranging from 2 to 5 percent, depending on the model and options chosen. This move comes just two days after a similar announcement by General Motors.

"Ford wants to stay competitive in the subcompact field," a company spokesman commented. "If GM lowers its prices, then we must follow suit in order to maintain our competitive edge."

Company officials had no comment as to the effect of the lower prices on fourth-quarter profits of the auto manufacturer.

ECONOMIC ANALYSIS

The automotive industry in the United States (and, indeed, in the rest of the world) is an example of oligopoly at work. In the United States just two manufacturers dominate the new car market: Ford and General Motors. Because there are only a few sellers in the new car market and because any action that one of them takes will affect the profits of all, the problem of pricing in oligopoly is a difficult one. When GM lowers prices, should Ford do the same?

There is no clear answer here. Our marginal cost and marginal revenue curves cannot tell us for sure what is the best price, especially since once Ford has set a price, GM is likely to counter with yet another change.

A method of analysis called **game theory** has been developed by

REAL WORLD ECONOMICS: AUTOMOTIVE OLIGOPOLY

Game theory: a method of analysis that analyzes economic decisions by examining strategies and payoffs as if a game were being played

economists to attempt to deal with oligopoly situations like this one. Using game theory, we try to see all the possible actions of the oligopoly producers. Then the gains and losses to each are noted, and an attempt is made to predict what each will do in playing the competitive game. A game between GM and Ford is outlined in Figure 8.

Suppose that each firm has only two options: cut prices or keep prices the same (they may have other strategies—increasing advertising or increasing prices, for example—but we shall look at just these two). With two options each, there are four possible results: both will keep stable prices, both will lower prices, Ford will cut prices and GM will not, or GM will cut prices and Ford will not.

In the boxes of Figure 8, we show the gains and losses that each producer might expect from the combination of strategies shown. If, for example, both firms hold the line on prices, then neither will gain nor lose. If, however, both firms cut prices, then Ford stands to lose $5 million and GM will lose $15 million (our figures are hypothetical). Both lose because both sell cars for less.

If Ford cuts prices and GM does not, according to Figure 8, Ford will gain $20 million in increased sales and GM will lose $20 million. But if GM cuts prices and

FIGURE 9-8: OLIGOPOLY GAME THEORY

This figure illustrates the "game" that Ford and General Motors play. Each has two strategies. For every action there is a reaction. As a group, Ford and GM would be better off not altering their prices. When each tries to better the other, however, they both end up cutting prices and lowering profits.

Ford strategy \ GM strategy	No change in GM price	GM cuts price
No change in Ford price	GM: no gain or loss Ford: no gain or loss	GM: gains $10 million Ford: loses $10 million
Ford cuts price	GM: loses $20 million Ford: gains $20 million	GM: loses $15 million Ford: loses $5 million

Ford does not, then GM gains $10 million and Ford loses that amount.

Given the numbers shown for this game, what is the result in the oligopoly? If neither firm changes prices the status quo is preserved. However, if Ford thinks that GM will hold its prices, then Ford can gain by cutting prices itself. Ford, therefore, has an incentive to lower prices in this case. However, if Ford cuts prices, then GM can reduce its losses from $20 million to only $15 million by *also* reducing the price of its cars. If Ford cuts prices, therefore, GM will follow suit and both will lose.

We get the same result working the other way. If GM thinks that Ford will hold its prices, then they can gain $10 million by cutting the price of their cars. If they do so, however, Ford can reduce its losses from $10 million to just $5 million by cutting prices, too.

The result of these strategies, therefore, is exactly what was reported in the news story. If GM takes the role of the leader in cutting prices, Ford will be the follower and do the same in order to reduce its losses.

It is interesting to note here that, as is often the case with oligopolies, even a few firms provide heavy competition. While in this example both producers would be best off by holding prices (neither would lose and both would earn high profits), still each is forced by the other and the game that they play into lowering prices and suffering lost profits.

Because the game is different for each oligopoly situation, there is no general economic model to describe their actions. This is unfortunate, since many of our largest industries are essentially oligopolies.

SUMMARY

1. Product differentiation occurs when a firm creates a real or perceived difference between its product and those of its competitors. Once this difference is established, the firm can exercise limited monopoly power—it is the sole producer of the different good.

2. Price discrimination occurs when similar or identical goods are sold to different buyers at different prices. Selling for different prices instead of one market-clearing price allows a firm to increase total revenues without necessarily increasing costs. Profits rise. Price discrimination is common in many markets, but also has limits. Discriminating firms must be able to divide the market into groups of buyers with different demand characteristics and then prevent resale of the item between groups.

3. A cartel is an organization of producers designed to limit competition and exercise monopoly power over a market.

Cartels can be profitable, but are not normally stable because of the individual gains to be had from cheating and exceeding the production specified by the cartel.

4. Oligopoly is competition among just a few large producers that dominate a market. There is no general theory of oligopoly, although game theory enters into the analysis. Oligopolies can be very competitive or behave much like cartels, depending on individual market situations.

5. Firms can sometimes increase profits by using government regulations to affect price controls, erect barriers to entry, or to affect substitute and complement markets.

DISCUSSION QUESTIONS

1. Suppose that firms in oligopoly markets earn high economic profits. Why do these markets stay oligopolies? Why don't other firms enter the industry and force competition for these profits? Make a list of industries where oligopolies prevail and determine what barriers to entry exist.

2. Suppose that Pepsi and Coke have both succeeded in producing differentiated products. What will happen to the price and quantity that Coke produces if Pepsi should suddenly lower its price?

3. "Product differentiation is most likely to occur in oligopoly markets." Evaluate this statement.

4. Show how restricting entry in a market can increase the economic profits of firms already in that market. Use supply and demand tools to show the impact on price and quantity produced.

5. OPEC has proved to be a relatively long-lived cartel. Can you think of any economic reasons for this stability? Can you suggest any noneconomic reasons?

TEST YOURSELF

Indicate whether each of the following statements is *true* or *false*. Be able to defend your response.

1. Product differentiation allows a firm to take advantage of declining marginal revenues for its product.

2. A product-differentiating firm sells at a higher price and produces a smaller quantity than a perfectly competitive firm.

3. Some people pay less to a price discriminator than they would in competitive markets.

4. A producer of a service is more likely to be a price discriminator than the producer of a good.

5. Members of a cartel produce less than competitive firms in the same market.

6. All members of a cartel can gain if they all cheat at the same time.

7. Oligopolies tend to be more competitive than other types of firms.

8. The actions of one oligopoly firm have little impact on other firms in the market.

9. Government regulations are normally imposed on firms, rather than being sought by them.

10. Firms may seek government power to restrict entry into a market and so increase the profits of firms already there.

Part 3
Resource Markets

10
Labor Markets

This chapter discusses a very important resource market: the labor market. It answers questions about work and wages including the following:

What is the labor market and how does it work?

What factors affect the supply of labor?

How does a firm decide how many workers to hire?

Why do different jobs pay such different wages? What is the cause of this wage differential?

How do labor unions affect the labor market?

How do government policies affect the labor market?

The labor market is important because it serves a dual function. It is the market that provides income for most people. While sources of nonwage income exist—rental incomes, dividends and interest payments, and the like—wages and salaries paid through the labor market account for about 75 percent of all income that people receive. It is the labor market, then, that most of us depend on for the income to pursue daily purchases.

From the worker's perspective, the labor market generates income. From the business and consumer view, however, a different function is perceived. The labor market is the place where the basic productive resources of talent and labor are exchanged. Activities here help determine the quantity, quality, types, and prices of the goods and services produced. This is particularly the case in markets for services that are, by definition, highly labor intensive. (Haircuts, teaching, and plumbing services all require, essentially, people). The importance of the labor market is seen here most explicitly, although labor market activities affect all the other markets as well.

There is no one labor market. The economy is made up of many markets—those for accountants, teachers, football players, mechanics, die makers, and more. In each individual market, supply and demand forces prevail. Each market is different in that different labor services, skills, and talents are exchanged. By looking at how labor markets in general operate, we shall uncover basic principles that apply to all such markets. Like any market, to understand the actions of the labor market we must first understand the forces of supply and demand that apply there.

THE SUPPLY OF LABOR

The supply of labor really arises from a demand. People are willing to work because they wish to acquire income. Income is desirable because it purchases the goods and services that increase individual total utility. The supply of labor, therefore, is derived from the demand for goods and services. The labor supply in any market is the sum of the quantities of labor that individual consumers/workers wish to supply at a given wage rate.

Why don't people spend all their time at work, since this would generate the maximum amount of income to purchase the maximum amount of goods? Opportunity cost enters into the analysis here. Not working—leisure activities—generates utility as well. If the goods that an hour's work provides do not yield as much utility as an hour asleep under a tree, then this leisure (or the best alternative activity) is chosen over work. There is a trade-off to be faced. Additional hours at work necessitate fewer hours spent in leisure activities and less time available, as well, to enjoy the goods that work makes possible.

Add to this basic trade-off the problem of diminishing marginal utility. Goods bought with the last hour's wages do not give as much satisfaction as those bought with the first hour's pay. And, as more and more leisure is given up to provide consumer goods, each remaining hour of leisure has a higher marginal utility than the one before it. This is one economic rationale for the overtime premiums that are paid in many labor markets. Workers get an extra wage payment (overtime) when they work more than 8 hours per day because the leisure given up is so valuable while the consumer goods made possible have relatively less marginal utility.

The trade-off between goods and leisure (and so the supply of labor) is affected by a number of factors. The first is the wage rate. The higher the wage, the greater the amount of consumer goods purchased with each hour of labor. The wage rate is, therefore, also the opportunity cost of leisure. The wage tells how much income—and therefore how many consumer goods—must be given up for each hour not spent at work. The higher the wage, the higher the opportunity cost of leisure and the lower the relative price of consumer goods.

Another factor that enters into the choice of whether to work or not is the price of the goods to be purchased. Rising prices lower the worker's **real wage** rate by reducing the amount of consumer goods that can be purchased with each hour of labor. Economists believe that workers respond to changes in this real wage as opposed to **money wages**. If workers collect higher money wages, but inflation reduces the amount that can be purchased—a lower real wage—then workers may respond to the lower opportunity cost of leisure and consume more of it (and provide less work).

Real wage: the wage rate expressed in terms of the amount of goods that can be purchased with an hour's work

Money wage: the wage rate expressed in the number of currency units paid per hour of work

Government policies enter into the labor–leisure choice, as well. Taxes reduce the amount of wage that can actually be spent. An increase in taxes, therefore, lowers the quantity of goods that an hour of work provides. This discourages work by lowering its return and encourages leisure by reducing its opportunity cost. The government affects the labor market in many other ways as well, which will be discussed later in this chapter.

The trade-off between labor and leisure gives us the kind of labor supply curve shown in Figure 1. At a relatively low wage rate W_1, an hour's work yields relatively few consumer goods, adding relatively little to total utility. Because of this, a large amount of leisure is chosen (since it costs little, in terms of the consumer goods given up) and, therefore, little labor is offered for sale out of the remaining time.

As the wage rate rises, the amount of labor supplied generally rises, too. At a higher wage rate W_2, for example, each hour's work provides more income to purchase more consumer goods. Less leisure is consumed and

FIGURE 10-1:   THE LABOR SUPPLY CURVE

The supply of labor arises from the demand for consumer goods. As wage rates increase, each hour of labor (foregone leisure) can be exchanged for a greater number of consumer goods. Thus the amount of labor offered in exchange rises as the wage rate rises. If wage rates rise high enough, income effects may eventually dominate worker decisions, giving the backward-bending portion of the labor supply curve.

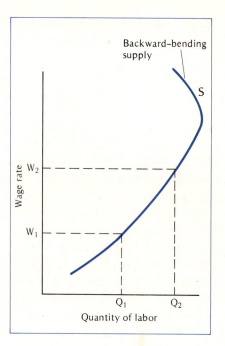

more labor hours supplied. The quantity of labor supplied generally increases as the wage rate rises, giving us the labor supply curve shown here.

Economists suspect, however, that when wage rates are high enough, a backward-bending portion of the labor supply curve is found. Backward bending? What does that mean? If the labor supply curve bends backward it indicates that workers supply *less* labor when wages rise. Why would they do that? The answer, analysts suggest, lies in an income effect. When wage rates rise, workers can afford to buy more consumer goods *and* have more leisure. At the very high wage rates, then, workers can work less and still make more money while also consuming more leisure. This may be the reason why physicians, for example, traditionally play golf on Wednesday instead of reporting for work. At the high wage they receive, they can afford both lots of consumer goods and more leisure, and they maximize utility by balancing the two. Hence the backward-bending portion of the supply curve.

Backward-bending or not, the labor supply curve remains fixed so long as no changes occur in the economic factors that influence the labor/leisure choice. But labor supplies would increase, for example, if taxes were cut, consumer goods prices fell, or if worker preferences shifted from vacations to new cars. Less labor would be supplied, however, if taxes increased, inflation reduced the real wage, or if consumer preferences shifted in favor of nonwork activities.

THE DEMAND FOR LABOR

The demand for labor is generated by firms who wish to purchase the services that labor provides. Their goal, quite clearly, is to hire workers to sell the goods and services that they produce at a profit. Making profits, as we have already learned, means a balancing of revenues against costs.

A profit-maximizing firm, quite logically, hires workers so long as the additional revenues that they bring in exceed the cost of employing labor. That is, workers are profitable to hire if the marginal revenues they make possible exceed their marginal cost. If it costs $5.00 per hour to hire an additional worker, that worker must be able to generate at least $5.00 more in increased revenues to make employment profitable for the business. Workers who cannot add at least $5.00 per hour to revenues are unprofitable to employ at that wage rate. The choice that an employer must make is shown in Figure 2. This figure shows the marginal costs and revenues of labor (c), the total costs and revenues from labor (b), and the total profits from labor employment (a). This decision concentrates on the amount of labor to be hired, all else (number of machines used, amount of other resources employed) held constant.

For an individual firm, the marginal cost of labor is determined by the market. That is, in most labor markets individual firms are price takers in purchasing labor services. This may not be the case for certain large firms, however. These may be able to exercise power as the sole (or one of only a few) buyers of labor. For the typical firm, marginal cost is constant and equal to total compensation, including retirement payments, medical insurance, and other costs of labor.

How are revenues generated? The marginal revenue that a worker produces depends on two things. The first is the **marginal product** of the worker. How many additional goods, given fixed quantities of machinery and raw materials available, does the extra worker produce? One extra unit per hour? Two? The greater the marginal product of the worker, the greater the additional revenue he or she makes possible. As Figure 2 indicates, we normally expect to find diminishing marginal product of labor in the labor market. That is, the first worker, because he or she has many resources to work with, normally adds a great deal to production and has a high marginal product. The second worker, however, has a lower marginal product and, in general, as more and more workers are employed, each adds proportionally less to total production.

Marginal product: the addition to total production of an additional unit of a resource like labor (all other inputs held constant)

FIGURE 10-2: THE LABOR DEMAND DECISION
The firm will employ labor until the marginal cost of the last worker equals his or her marginal revenue. At this point total profits from the employment of labor are at their highest.

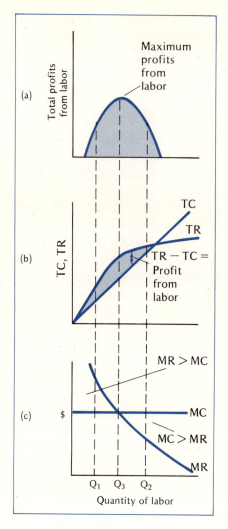

In essence, as more and more workers are combined with a fixed quantity of other resources, problems occur in the production process. Additional workers make use of less productive production methods, get in each other's way, or may spend time in nonproduction as they wait for others to finish a task. The additional workers may be equally as good as the first ones hired, but they add less to total output—and so, have smaller marginal products—because of production inefficiencies. Because of diminishing marginal product of labor, the marginal revenue curve in Figure 2 is downward sloping. Since the tenth worker adds less to production than the first, he or she also brings in fewer additional revenues.

The other major factor that enters into the hiring decision is the price of the output itself. As the final product rises in price, the marginal revenue of labor increases. If a worker can make one additional good, then the value of that labor varies directly with the price of the good produced. Even if marginal product stays constant, the marginal revenue of labor rises with the price of final output.

Given all this, how much labor should a firm hire? The answer, assuming sufficient demand for the goods that labor produces, is shown in Figure 2. Should the firm hire a quantity Q_1 of labor? Since marginal revenue is higher than marginal cost for this number of workers, the workers are generating profits. Each worker produces goods with a higher value than the cost of labor itself. Workers here are paid, say, $5.00 to produce $6.00 worth of goods. Each worker is profitable to employ. But even more workers could be hired who would each also be profitable to put to work—who would also generate marginal revenues in excess of marginal cost.

If Q_1 is too small a number of workers to employ, then is a high quantity like Q_2 the best? To see, we must again compare marginal costs and revenues. At the high employment level of Q_2, the cost of the last worker is greater than the revenue that that worker generates. The marginal cost exceeds marginal revenue. This is situation where you are paying a worker $5.00 to produce $4.00 worth of goods. The worker produces a loss, not a profit. Any worker whose marginal revenue is less than marginal cost (wage plus other compensation costs) should be fired. Quantity Q_2, therefore, is too high a level of labor demand, given the marginal revenues and marginal costs shown in Figure 2.

The profit-maximizing firm hires Q_3 workers. At Q_3 the marginal revenue of the last worker just equals his or her marginal cost. Every worker on the payroll earns a profit (the very last worker breaks even for the firm). Here, total profits from labor are as high as they can be. This is the quantity of labor demanded at the wage rate shown.

CHANGES IN LABOR DEMAND

What makes a firm alter its labor demand? Anything that alters either marginal revenues or marginal costs changes demand in the labor market. Suppose, for example, that inflation causes the market price of the firm's output to rise. What impact will this have? Over the long run rising prices, by reducing the real wage rate, may cause the supply of labor to fall (a smaller quantity of labor offered for sale at each money wage). In the short run, however, employment may increase due to what economists call the **wage-lag effect**. Wages in the labor market temporarily maintain their initial equilibrium level—so that the marginal cost of labor to individual firms does

Wage-lag effect: the increase in employment that takes place because higher output prices increase labor demand for individual firms, causing employment to rise until wage rates also increase

not change. What does change is labor's marginal revenue. The rise in the price of final output increases the marginal revenue of labor, as shown in Figure 3. As the marginal revenue of labor rises, the firm's profit-maximizing level of employment rises, too. A larger quantity of hiring takes place. If this effect is widespread (many firms increase their demand for labor) the market wage rises and reduces the quantity of labor demanded. This same type of shift in the marginal revenue of labor can be caused instead by an improvement in the skills and productivity of workers, which increases the amount that they produce. Investment in more or better machines or production lines can also increase the marginal product of labor and labor's marginal revenue. Marginal revenue rises if workers produce more or if what they produce increases in value.

Other factors can alter the firm's demand for labor, too. Suppose, for instance, that a firm, having already agreed to pay medical insurance premiums, is faced with an increase in these costs. In the long run it may be able to renegotiate the contract with its employees. In the short run, however, it is faced with the problem shown in Figure 4.

Rising medical insurance costs, when borne by the employer, represent an increase in the marginal cost of labor. In this instance, the wage rate itself does not rise, but the cost of labor goes up because of rising nonwage expenses. Rising marginal costs upset the firm's demand for labor. Before the rising medical insurance expense, the firm's profits from the use of labor were at their peak at a quantity Q_1 of labor. After the rising marginal cost, however, the firm reduces labor demand to Q_2. This is, of course, one of the hazards of long-term labor contracts. Here, the rising costs produce unemployment. If, on the other hand, the firm had signed an agreement not

FIGURE 10-3:   THE WAGE-LAG EFFECT
Rising output prices increase the marginal revenue of labor for this firm. This leads the firm to increase employment. If this happens to all firms in a labor market, rising wage rates will reduce employment.

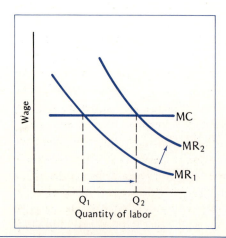

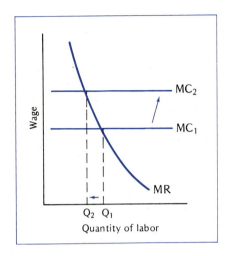

FIGURE 10-4: RISING LABOR COSTS
As the marginal cost of labor rises, this reduces the firm's profit-maximizing quantity of labor. Employment falls as a result.

to lay off employees, it would find that its total profits from labor were reduced and might be forced out of business by more competitive firms.

In this example, rising marginal costs were caused by rising medical insurance expenses. In the real world, a wide variety of factors can account for these rising costs. Increases in wage rates are the most obvious cause of rising marginal labor costs, to be sure, but a number of other factors are of increasing importance these days. Pension contributions, rapidly increasing social security taxes (on both employer and employee), and unemployment insurance taxes all cause marginal labor costs to rise, thus reducing the demand for labor by individual firms.

THE LABOR DEMAND CURVE

Now that we know how the individual firm's labor demand is determined, we can easily construct the market demand for labor as the consequence of profit-maximizing behavior. Suppose that, as in Figure 5, we can draw the marginal revenue of labor curve for all firms combined in a labor market. Assuming sufficient demand for final output, how much labor will these firms demand at a wage rate of W_1? We know that firms maximize the profits from labor by hiring amount Q_1. This combination—Q_1 workers at a wage rate of W_1—can then be plotted on the labor demand curve in Figure 5.

At a higher wage rate, like W_2, firms in this labor market maximize their profits from labor by hiring a smaller number of workers Q_2. We can plot this on the labor demand curve and continue to do so until the entire labor demand curve has been completed. Notice that the demand curve we have derived is nothing more than the marginal revenue of labor curve. At each possible wage rate, firms continue to hire until the marginal revenue

FIGURE 10-5: **LABOR DEMAND CURVE**
The quantity of labor demanded depends on the marginal cost of that labor. As this figure indicates, profit-maximizing behavior by individual firms suggests that the labor demand curve is the same as the marginal revenue of labor curve.

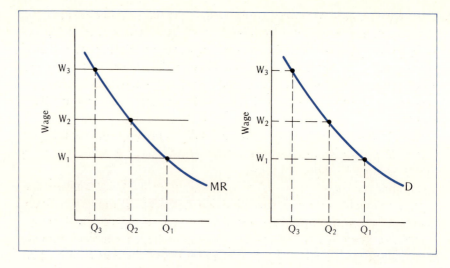

produced by the last worker is just equal to his or her marginal cost. At this point, no additional profits can be gained by hiring more workers and the total profits from the employment of labor are maximized.

It is worth noting that, while we have continued to denote the price of labor by the wage rate, total compensation may be a more appropriate concept since, as modern employers have noted, wages are now only one of many costs associated with employment.

WAGE RATE DIFFERENTIALS

One fact that is apparent as we view labor markets is that there are large differences in wages and salaries among labor markets and among individuals within the same labor market. What accounts for these widely varying payments for labor? In general, we can look to two explanations of wage rate differentials.

Sometimes wage differences come as a result of differences in bargaining power among workers. The wage rate is the payment that takes place when mutually advantageous exchange is made between the worker and the firm. When there are many workers with about the same ability (who can generate about the same marginal revenue) then there is little leverage that an individual worker can exercise over his or her own wages. When a talent is in short supply or the worker is rare or unique, however, this is not the case.

We could call this reason for wage differentials the "Babe Ruth effect." In the late 1920s, the Babe became the first athlete to make more money than the President of the United States (a common phenomenon these days).

There were two explanations for this. First, as the Babe himself pointed out, "I had a better year than the President." This was another way of saying that Ruth's marginal revenue to the Yankees exceeded the President's marginal revenue to the nation, and it was probably true. The other argument is also valid, however. There may have been several people who could have performed the President's job at least as well—but there was only one Babe Ruth.

Scarcity and the power that it gives explains many wage differentials. If a particular type of worker is scarce, he or she can command a larger share of the gains from the labor exchange.

Another, perhaps more typical explanation of wage rate differentials centers on market factors. Why should different prices be found in different markets? The reason is generally one of differing supply and demand factors. This is illustrated in Figure 6 in a comparison of the labor markets for coal miners and retail clerks. In these two labor markets, the demand for labor, based on the marginal revenue a worker produces, is high. Perhaps the coal miner, because of the large store of training and machinery at his disposal, is able to generate a greater addition to total revenue on the margin. This difference in demand then represents part of the wage difference.

Supply factors also enter here, however. Because coal mining is a risky and dangerous occupation available only within a relatively restricted geographical area, the supply of coal miner services is relatively restricted. The supply of retail clerk labor, on the other hand, is taken from a much larger population and is larger, as well, because of the relative lack of health and other occupational hazards. Given these differences in supply and demand, the market wage rates are seen to be much different, too. The

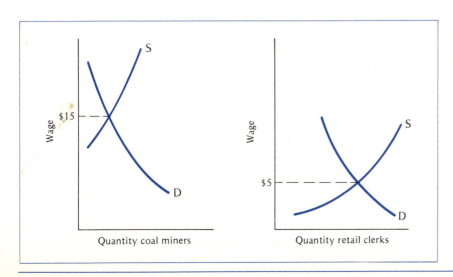

Quantity coal miners

Quantity retail clerks

FIGURE 10-6: WAGE DIFFERENTIALS
Wage differentials can be caused by many factors. As illustrated here, the high marginal revenue of coal miners and the relatively small supply of them accounts for at least part of the difference between coal miner wages and those paid to retail clerks.

equilibrium in the coal market occurs here at an hourly wage of $15.00, while the wage rate for retail clerks in this hypothetical example is $5.00.

How can such large wage differentials exist over time? Surely, people in low-paying jobs would prefer to change labor markets and acquire larger paychecks. Several explanations seem clear. One is that some jobs pay more than others because they are undesirable jobs. Perhaps retail clerks don't rush to become coal miners because they are aware of the risks of that occupation and are not willing to bear them even at the higher wages. Thus differences in the types of work generate the differences in labor supply that make wage differentials possible.

Other explanations are available as well. Geographical separation of labor markets accounts for some wage differences. Wages in the southern part of the United States traditionally have been lower than those in the industrialized north. Part of the reason for this difference is that many people would not move (at large expense) across the country in order to gain the higher wages. Discrimination based on race or sex may be a part of the problem. Wage differences can also result from regional cost-of-living differences, which alter real wages. If it costs much more to buy consumer goods in Washington, D.C., than it does in Portland, Oregon, then this will effect a difference in the supply of labor in these two places, which will eventually result in different wage rates.

Training and educational costs enter into the difference. If one can acquire a higher paying job (move into a different labor market) through training, then a worker's ability to do this may be restricted by the availability of that training or the lack of funds to pay for it. Restrictions to occupational entry such as union rules or government licenses can, by controlling supply, drive up wages, too.

Finally, differences in productivity and changing output prices also affect wage differentials. Part of the reason that wages ran so high during Alaska's oil boom in the 1970s was that, with oil's price soaring, any job that resulted in greater oil production generated much higher marginal revenues. Wage differentials result from a variety of factors. One possible cause of some of today's wage differentials, according to economists, is the existence of labor unions.

LABOR UNIONS

Labor union: an organization of workers designed to increase their market power

Labor unions are organizations of workers in a particular occupation or industry. Labor unions were orginally formed in an attempt to balance market power in labor markets. During the industrial revolution, firms were able to exercise hiring power and take most of the gains from labor exchange by paying less than marginal revenue for worker's services. By forming into groups, workers found that they could achieve a greater share of the gains from exchange here and restore a more competitive market equilibrium.

Unions may have many goals, but it seems reasonable to suppose that their principal aim is to improve the welfare of their members. They can do this in many ways as, for example, by obtaining safer working conditions. Unions can also affect the wages of their members (and indirectly, of nonunion workers) through their impact on labor demand and supply.

If the union is able to negotiate a closed shop agreement with employers, for instance, then only members of the union can work in the industry involved. This action effectively reduces the supply of workers with which employers can deal. With labor supply reduced wage rates naturally rise.

The demand for labor is also affected by union organizations. Unions can use the force of their organized votes to influence legislation to their benefit. Railroad unions, for example, may lobby for safety regulations for trains, which act to guarantee jobs for their members, even if those jobs are sometimes the result of featherbedding—unnecessary to production. Unions may also push for increases in the minimum wage rate. By making unskilled labor more expensive, they may be able to increase demand for its more-skilled substitute: union employees.

Unions, like any organization, are a mixed bag both for their members and also for the economy. Still, they have been an effective force in improving labor conditions in the United States. When unions exist, however, a perfectly competitive model of labor markets cannot hold. The union may act as a labor-supplying monopoly and employers may band together as well to negotiate wages, benefits, and working conditions. The resulting negotiations may best be analyzed using the game theory tools used in the preceding chapter to look at oligopolies.

GOVERNMENT LABOR POLICIES

Government policies affect labor markets in a variety of ways. We have already discussed some of these in this chapter and elsewhere. Government taxes on employees, for example, tend to reduce the supply of labor by lowering the amount of consumer goods that can be purchased with an hour's wages. This discourages work and encourages leisure. Government taxes on employers, such as the social security tax, increase the marginal cost of labor without necessarily increasing its marginal revenue. This causes unemployment, as Figure 7 shows. The social security tax on employers (or unemployment taxes and the like) drives a wedge into the labor decision. The wedge is the difference between the amount that the employer has to pay for labor (MC + tax in the figure) and the amount that

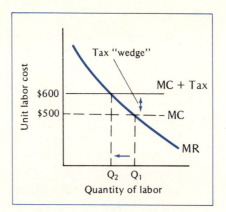

the worker actually receives. The employer may have to pay $6.00, for example, to employ a worker, but only $5.00 of that may be wages and benefits—the rest is taxes and other costs that the worker never sees directly.

This wage reduces the quantity of labor that firms hire. The profit-maximizing firm hires fewer workers with the tax than without it. These taxes create involuntary unemployment even in otherwise efficient labor markets. Without taxes and costs like these, the labor market ensures that, if the equilibrium wage rate is $5.00, all workers who are willing to work and who can earn a marginal revenue of $5.00 or more will find a job. With the $1.00 tax, however, firms will hire only those workers who have a marginal revenue of $6.00 or more. Additional workers whose marginal revenue is in the $5.00–$5.99 range lose their jobs due to the tax wedge in the labor market.

Minimum wage laws also disrupt labor markets. These wage floors, as Figure 8 shows, set wage rates for low-paying jobs at a price well above that which would prevail if the market were free to operate. In setting a price above the market wage, these minimum wage laws create winners and losers. The winners are those who take home more pay and the losers are those who would have had a job at the lower wage but who are unemployed at the higher minimum wage. Since their marginal revenue is less than the minimum wage, no firm can profitably hire them. Unemployment is the result.

Government policies affect the labor market in other ways, too. Unemployment insurance, for example, may actually reduce employment. It affects the market in two ways. First, unemployment payments are funded by taxes levied on employers. These taxes increase the marginal cost of

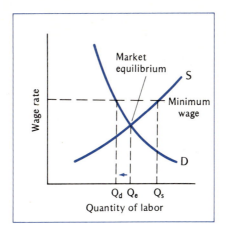

FIGURE 10-8: MINIMUM WAGES
By setting the minimum wage rate above equilibrium, Congress succeeds in raising wages of unskilled workers, but employment falls from Q_e to Q_d. Moreover, additional numbers are drawn into the labor force by the existence of the higher wage. Unemployment results here.

labor and reduce the profit-maximizing quantity of labor purchased by individual firms. The demand for labor is thus reduced. Unemployment payments also reduce the supply of labor. Under a typical unemployment program (and other low-income plans as well) a jobless worker receives a small weekly paycheck from the government. If he or she takes a job, this government subsidy disappears. This increases the opportunity cost of work. When a job is taken, the person involved gives up not only considerable leisure, but a government payment as well. Some workers choose to retain the high leisure and low income instead of making the opposite trade. This acts to reduce the supply of labor.

With government policies here acting to reduce both the demand for and the supply of labor, what is the net impact? We cannot say for sure what the effect on the wage rate is. We can note, however, that the quantity of labor exchanged will surely fall. Is this bad? It clearly depends on whether the lost income and production is worth the gain in economic welfare of those who receive the payments.

It would be a mistake, however, to think that all government programs actually make workers worse off. Sometimes laws can be used to increase the effectiveness of the labor market. Discrimination, for example, may be one cause of the higher unemployment rates that traditionally exist for women and minority groups. Discrimination is, of course, basically unprofitable for the firm since it means not hiring productive and profitable workers because they are women, black, or otherwise don't fit into the narrow mold that the employer desires. Laws that penalize employers for this uneconomic act may restore these affected groups to equality in the market.

A look at recent unemployment figures indicates, however, that if discrimination is the major cause of higher unemployment among women and minorities, then labor markets still have a long way to go before a truly competitive situation prevails.

REAL WORLD ECONOMICS: COST-OF-LIVING CLAUSES

UNIONS SEEK COST OF LIVING PROTECTION IN CONTRACT

WASHINGTON, D.C.—More and more unions are seeking cost-of-living adjustment clauses in their work agreements, a spokesman for the Labor Department noted today in an exclusive interview. "With inflation becoming an increasing burden on the American family, more and more workers are seeking a COL (cost-of-living) clause in their wage contracts in order to insulate themselves from the impact of rising prices. We expect that, if inflation continues at its current rate, almost all the labor force will be covered by some type of COL clause within five years," the labor analyst noted.

The Labor Department is beginning a study of the long-run effects of COL protection of wages and employment. Already the government, by tying minimum wages to a price index, has acted to provide COL protection to many low-income workers.

ECONOMIC ANALYSIS

Since, as this news story notes, COL clauses are becoming more and more common in labor markets, it is important for us to understand how they work and what their likely economic impacts might be. First of all, exactly what is COL protection? Essentially, it is a system designed to increase wages at roughly the same rate that consumer prices rise so that, at least in theory, consumer choice is not altered. If prices double for all goods and income is also doubled, then the individual's real income is not altered and consumer choice is preserved.

While COL clauses manage to provide this protection in theory, they actually fail in the real world for two reasons. First, the government price indices do not include taxes as a price (the price of government services) and so, in recent years, they may have underestimated the inflation rate. In addition, any increase in income granted by the COL clause is reduced by our progressive income tax system. True income protection, therefore, does not really occur. Still, the COL clauses are useful and provide a basic backstop against inflation for workers. One of the things that the news story suggested is that COL clauses may have some impact on labor markets and employment. Let's use some of the tools developed in this chapter to see if we should expect COL clauses to have any impact on the number of workers employed.

A hypothetical labor market is shown in Figure 9. Here, we assume that the labor market is initially in equilibrium at a wage rate

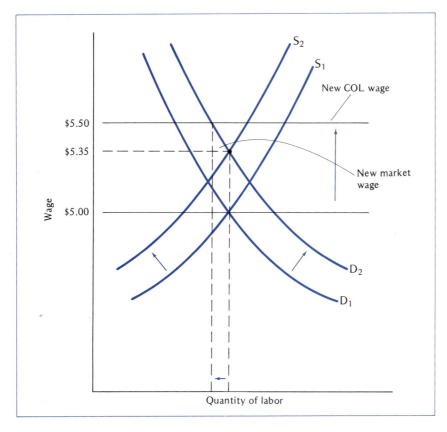

FIGURE 10-9: COST OF LIVING PAY INCREASES
Cost of living clauses in pay contracts automatically increase wages. Inflation also brings about market forces that tend to increase wages. As shown here, however, the COL increase and market forces need not arrive at the same result. Employment falls because the COL wage is greater than the market-clearing wage rate.

of $5.00 per hour. What impact does COL have on this market? Let us first remember that the COL clauses only go into effect when inflation takes place. Inflation is likely to affect both sides of this market. With rising inflation, each dollar of wages buys fewer and fewer goods and services. Thus, at a constant wage rate, the trade-off between leisure and work is altered in favor of leisure, since inflation may not affect the utility gained from leisure, but it reduces the satisfaction to be gained through work. Inflation, therefore, tends to reduce the supply of labor (although there are obviously other factors at work here).

Inflation also has an impact on the demand side. When the prices of goods are rising, the marginal revenue of workers increases, causing the demand for those workers to increase, too. If a worker, in an hour, can build one additional unit of production, for example, then the marginal revenue that the worker produces rises when the price of the good built rises. The demand for labor is increased by inflation.

These two basic forces are caused

by inflation. At once, a worker is more valuable because the price of the things produced is rising, while inflation reduces the return from labor, too. The supply of labor tends to fall while the demand for it rises. What happens to employment? It will vary from market to market. In some markets, as Figure 9 shows, the conflicting forces tend to wash out. In other markets, however, employment can be expected to increase or decrease, perhaps dramatically, because of inflation. Wages, as the figure indicates, should rise anyway during periods of inflation, in response to normal market forces. With a contract-dictated increase (here shown to be 10 percent, assuming that is the inflation rate for the period under consideration) greater uncertainty is generated. There is no guarantee that the labor market

will be in equilibrium at the higher, COL-set wage. Indeed, as the figure suggests, the equilibrium wage could be lower (or much higher) than the COL wage. If the equilibrium wage is below the COL-set wage, then COL protection, like minimum wage laws, may cause unemployment by boosting wage rates above their market equilibrium levels.

There is, of course, more to COL and inflation than this. If labor productivity is changing, or the demand for final products is altered, then even further changes in supply and demand will occur, clouding the labor market picture. We can see the forces at work in labor markets here, but it may be very difficult, in the real world, to isolate the impact of the COL clauses alone.

SUMMARY

1. The labor market is a general description of markets where labor services are bought and sold. Labor markets are important because labor provides goods and services to consumers and income to workers.

2. The supply of labor arises from the consumer's demand for goods and services. In order to obtain these goods, consumers must obtain income through labor. The supply of labor therefore depends on the trade-off between the utility derived from the fruits of labor and the utility derived from leisure. The

labor supply depends on a number of factors such as the wage rate, taxes that reduce take-home pay, the prices of goods to be purchased, and factors that affect the utility of work and leisure.

3. The demand for labor arises from profit-maximizing decisions by firms. Workers produce revenue for firms, but they also cause cost. The profit-maximizing firm will hire additional labor until the marginal revenue of the last worker just equals that worker's marginal cost. Revenue from labor is af-

fected by the productivity of labor and the value of the goods produced. Labor costs include wage rates, nonwage compensation such as pensions and medical insurance, and taxes or other costs associated with the employment of labor.

4. Wage differentials can arise either because of differences in bargaining power between employer and employee or because of basic demand and supply differences among labor markets. Labor unions were formed to increase competition in labor markets by reducing employer hiring power. Some unions may now actually act to reduce competition, however, by acting as labor monopolists, boosting wages and reducing employment.

5. Government policies affect labor markets in many ways. Minimum wage laws set wages for low-income groups, taking this task away from the market and creating unemployment in the labor markets it affects. Taxes can also affect both demand and supply of labor, as do unemployment compensation programs.

DISCUSSION QUESTIONS

1. One of the most interesting wage differentials is that which has traditionally prevailed between men and women in similar jobs. Is there an economic justification for this differential? Explain.

2. Is there an economic reason for firms to base pay raises on seniority? Why should workers with more years on the job receive higher incomes?

3. What impacts do social security payments for retired workers have on the labor force? Does it affect demand? Supply? Both? Explain.

4. "Inflation reduces unemployment." Explain under what conditions this statement is true.

5. Is the market wage rate described in this chapter a fair wage? Define the meaning of a fair wage and evaluate the market as a means of rewarding labor.

TEST YOURSELF

Indicate whether each of the following statements is *true* or *false*. Be able to defend your response.

1. In a competitive labor market, each worker is paid his or her marginal revenue.

2. An increase in consumer preference for leisure would reduce the supply of labor.

3. A decrease in the demand for coffee results in a decrease in the demand for coffee workers.

4. The wage-lag effect describes

the relationship between union negotiations and nonunion wage agreements.

5. Firms will hire workers until their wage rate equals the marginal revenue that they produce.

6. Marginal worker costs can increase even if wage rates are falling in a labor market.

7. Barriers to occupation entry tend to increase wage rates in the restricted occupations.

8. Higher inflation rates normally produce higher wage rates.

9. Unemployment insurance increases employment.

10. All wage rate differentials come as the result of differences in marginal productivity of labor.

11
Capital and Natural Resource Markets

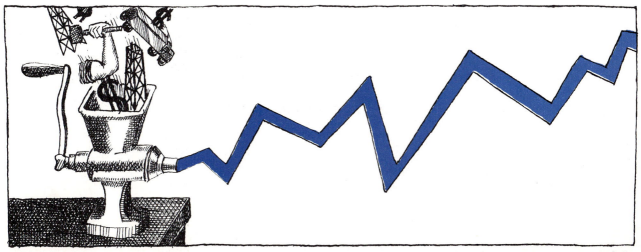

Firms use many inputs besides labor in the production process. This chapter looks at the demand and supply for some of these other productive resources. Capital and natural resource markets are high-lighted. Questions that this chapter answers include the following:

How does a firm decide how much of an input to use in production? What factors affect this decision?

How is the demand for capital different from the demand for other inputs?

What factors affect natural resource supplies to make them different from other input supplies?

Why do some natural resource markets go through boom and bust cycles with market prices rising and falling over a period of years?

Firms use many inputs in the production process. The markets for some of these productive resources are important and interesting because of the economic factors that must necessarily be considered in the decision to demand or supply. This chapter takes a quick look at input markets in general and a few particularly interesting aspects of markets for natural resources and **capital**.

Natural resource markets have become more visible in recent years. Resources that we have come to think of as abundant are suddenly very scarce and this scarcity worries us. This is particularly true in energy markets, which will be treated in more detail in the next chapter, but it applies to all types of resources.

Capital goods are productive resources that are not immediately used up in the production process. While labor disappears as it is used, and other inputs (like lumber, for example) are used up in production, capital goods—machines, trucks, factories, and computers—can be used again and again over long periods of time.

What makes these markets different from markets for other goods or services? To answer these questions—and to learn more about the kinds of economic decisions that all producers and consumers must make—we must look again at the costs and benefits that economic resources provide.

Capital: long-lasting productive resources such as plants, equipment, and factories

THE DEMAND FOR INPUTS

What determines the demand for inputs by a firm? To understand what factors influence the demand for capital, natural resources, and other inputs, we must look again at the problem of producer choice.

Let's look at a specific example to see how the firm might decide how much of an input to use. Suppose that you run a moving company. You rent trucks (a capital good) from a leasing company for a fixed price per day. You can rent any number of trucks that you need (within reason) at that market price. How many should you order?

Basically, the truck rental decision involves weighing costs and benefits. If a truck brings in more marginal revenues than it adds to costs, then the use of a truck is profitable. If trucks rent for $100 per day, then it is profitable to use them so long as their use adds at least $100 per day in additional revenues. If it costs $100 for a truck and the truck brings in only an additional $80 of revenue, however, the truck is not profitable and its use should be avoided.

Suppose that your moving firm has already hired a number of drivers and contracted for gasoline and maintenance. How many trucks should you rent at the $100 per day marginal cost shown in Figure 1? The first truck that is rented allows the firm to go into business. It therefore generates a high

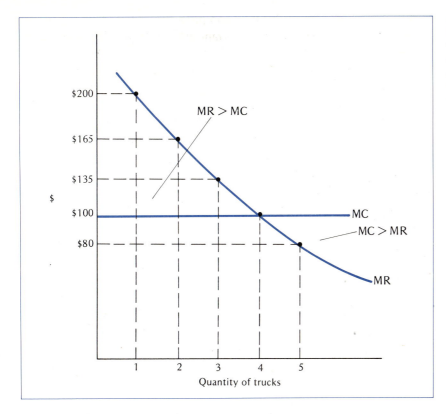

FIGURE 11-1: **THE INPUT–USE DECISION**
The firm must decide how many trucks to use. A maximum profit from this capital good can be achieved by adding trucks until the marginal revenue just equals marginal cost. This occurs when four trucks are used.

marginal revenue because it can be used for the most profitable deliveries. Both the truck and its driver can be kept busy earning revenues all day long. The second truck also adds to total revenue, but its marginal revenue is much less because of diminishing marginal returns. The second truck handles less profitable deliveries and may sit idle part of the time. It still adds revenues greater than the marginal cost but it is not as profitable to operate as the first truck.

The third and fourth trucks are also profitable (assuming that, as economists, we have added opportunity cost into the marginal cost of the trucks). The marginal cost of the fourth truck just equals the marginal revenues that it generates. If we use four trucks then profits are maximized. If we use less than four trucks, profits fall because we are giving up the use of profitable trucks.

Profits fall, as well, if more than four trucks are used. The fifth truck, for example, costs just as much as the first four to rent (has the same marginal cost) but suffers from diminishing marginal returns. The fifth truck may sit idle until another truck breaks down. Or it may be used on runs that generate low revenues. Because marginal cost exceeds marginal revenues for the fifth truck, deciding to use it will lower total profits. The profit-seeking firm, therefore, hires capital goods, natural resources, or any other input until the marginal revenue of the last unit just equals its marginal cost. These factors determine the firm's demand for productive inputs.

INVESTMENT: THE DEMAND FOR CAPITAL

Investment: in the economic sense, investment refers to the purchase of capital or human capital

Present-value calculation: a method of determining the current worth of future costs and revenues. The formula for present value is

$$PV = \frac{\text{future amount}}{(1 + i)^n}$$

for an interest rate i and time period n

Sometimes, as in the last example, a capital input can be treated as a variable input. The moving firm could choose to lease more or fewer trucks on a day-to-day basis. Hence the decision to rent one more truck was fairly simple. More often, however, firms must purchase the capital goods. They become fixed inputs in the production process, lasting years or even decades.

The potential long life of capital makes the firm's decision more complex. The firm must pay for the capital now, but the revenues that the **investment** makes possible are spread over many years in the future. How can the firm, in making the investment decision, compare these costs and benefits?

Suppose, for example, that your firm must decide whether or not to *purchase* a truck. The truck costs $40,000 now and will yield marginal revenues of $10,000 per year over a period of 5 years. Is the truck a profitable investment? On the face of it, the answer is yes. The current cost is $40,000 while the marginal revenues (spread over 5 years) add to $50,000. This looks like an investment with a 25 percent return! A good investment, indeed!

But wait a second. The revenues from this project are received over a relatively long period of time. Are the $10,000 revenues projected for the fifth year worth as much as the $10,000 received in the first year? Are costs and revenues spread over this time period comparable?

Economists suggest that money in the future is worth less than money now. There are many reasons for this. Inflation is one factor, but even without inflation most people would still prefer to have $100 now instead of $100 at some later time. Uncertainty is another factor. Future payments are less certain than payments now. But the basic difference between payments now and payments in the future has to do with opportunity cost. If you must wait 5 years for a payment, you are giving up the return that could have been earned on the next best alternative with funds received now. Waiting means going without revenues now and this opportunity cost must be considered in making business (and personal!) decisions.

If future payments are less valuable than present payments, how can the firm compare the two in deciding how many trucks to purchase? Economists suggest that this decision be made by **present-value calculation**. The present-value calculation is essentially a way to adjust future values for the opportunity costs of waiting—to separate the present value of that future payment from its opportunity cost.

To calculate present value, future payments are divided by the compounded interest return that is given up. The formula used is

$$\text{Present value} = \frac{\text{Future value}}{(1 + i)^n}$$

where i is the rate of interest and n the number of years until the future payment is made.

We can use this formula to make the investment decision by calculating the value of each of the 5 future $10,000 payments. For the sake of simplicity we shall use an interest rate of 10 percent. The first $10,000 is received in 1 year. Using the formula (with i = 10 percent or .10 and n = 1 year) we get

$$PV_1 = \frac{\$10,000}{(1 + .10)^1} = \$9091.$$

The present value of the second year's $10,000 marginal revenue is

$$PV_2 = \frac{\$10,000}{(1 + .10)^2} = \$8264.$$

The present value of the third year's $10,000 marginal revenue is

$$PV_3 = \frac{\$10,000}{(1 + .10)^3} = \$7513.$$

The present value of the fourth year's $10,000 marginal revenue is

$$PV_4 = \frac{\$10,000}{(1 + .10)^4} = \$6830.$$

Finally, a $10,000 increase in revenue not received for 5 years has a present value of

$$PV_5 = \frac{\$10,000}{(1 + .10)^5} = \$6209.$$

The total present value of the marginal revenues of $10,000 per year for 5 years at 10 percent interest is obtained by adding the individual present values, which amount to $37,907. (If you put $37,907 in a bank right now earning 10 percent interest, you can draw out $10,000 each year and not drain the account until the fifth yearly interest payment is made).

The truck, which looked like such a good investment a few pages ago, now looks like a loser. The present value of the marginal revenues ($37,907) is less than the marginal cost ($40,000) of the capital item. The truck, if purchased, will earn a loss, when the opportunity costs are considered.

The investment decision for this firm is shown in Figure 2. The profit-maximizing firm compares the marginal cost of a capital input with the present value of its marginal revenues. The investment decision rule calls for the purchase of capital until its marginal cost equals the present value of its marginal revenues.

Because present values must be considered in making capital investment decisions, the demand for capital depends on factors that make it different from the demand for other types of inputs. Because revenues are earned in the future as well as the present, anything affecting the present value of future payments also affects demand. In particular, the demand for capital depends on the interest rate and the length of time that the firm must wait for revenues.

Rising interest rates, for example, reduce the demand for capital, all else being equal. The higher interest rate means that firms must give up more interest income if they make an investment with future payoffs. This higher

FIGURE 11-2: THE INVESTMENT DECISION
The firm will invest when the present value of the marginal revenues that a piece of capital equipment will produce is greater than or equal to the marginal cost of that capital. The profit-seeking firm in this example will purchase 3 units of capital.

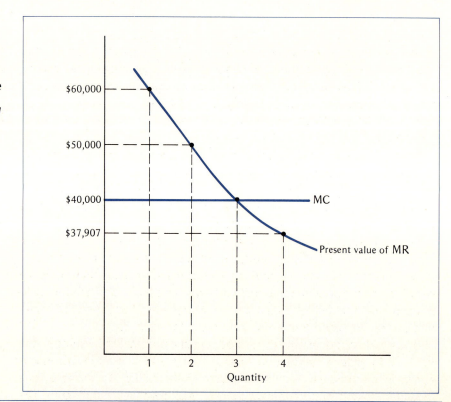

opportunity cost reduces the present value of investment revenues. Using the formula we can show that the present value of a $10,000 payment in one year is $9091 if the interest rate is 10 percent, but only $8770 if the interest rate is 14 percent (and $9800 if interest rates fall to 2 percent). The demand for capital is, therefore, inversely related to interest rates.

Opportunity costs of investment also vary inversely with the time period of the investment. Payments that are further in the future have higher opportunity costs and are therefore worth less. Revenues of $10,000 that are 10 years away have a much lower present value ($3860 at 10 percent interest) than those just 5 years away (present value of $6209).

If interest rates rise or firms must wait longer periods of time for revenues (all else—marginal costs and revenues—being equal) the demand for capital falls. Firms invest less for the future. Alternatively, lower interest rates and quicker returns (again, all else being equal) raise present values and encourage firms to purchase more capital. Since capital is generally the fixed input of production, these factors influence the extent to which firms adjust fixed input use over the long run and so affect virtually every aspect of the production process.

INPUT SUPPLIES: NATURAL RESOURCES

Inputs are generally produced by firms under the kinds of competitive situations described in previous chapters dealing with producer choice. Producers choose a production level such that marginal cost equals marginal revenue and so act to maximize profits. The production of inputs (like truck differentials, tin cans, or steel beams) takes place much as any other production.

This description of production does not, however, take into account problems encountered in some input markets—particularly markets involving **finite natural resources**. Because the total supply of these resources is limited, production today involves a trade-off: More today means fewer remaining finite resources to produce tomorrow.

Finite natural resource: a resource (like coal or oil) that cannot be reproduced

Let's take a moment to compare the production decision for a firm producing a finite versus a reproducible resource. When a bakery chooses to sell another loaf of bread, the only factors that enter into that production decision are the price that the loaf will bring and the cost of producing it. Making one more loaf of bread today does not affect the number of loaves that can be produced tomorrow, next week, or next year.

The situation is different for the producer of a finite natural resource. Any increase in today's production means a decrease in the amount that is available for production at some point in the future. To increase total revenues today, therefore, means to lower total revenues in the future. The finite resource firm must take into consideration the opportunity cost—the present value of the lost future sales—when more is produced today.

Let's look at a specific example. Suppose that you are the owner of a coal mine with 100 units of coal. To a certain extent, the mine is like a bank: It stores your coal and you withdraw coal from it as you wish, trying to maximize profits all the while. How much coal should you withdraw today? This depends on the price of coal today and the price of coal in future years.

Suppose that the price of the coal today is $10 per unit, and that you expect the coal will sell for $12 per unit after one year. Suppose, in addition, that the current interest rate is 10 percent for present-value calculations. If you produce all of the coal now, you receive $10 × 100 units = $1000 total revenue. If you wait a year to produce it, however, you will receive total revenues of $12 × $100 = $1200. This $1200 future revenue has a present value of $1091. It would be more profitable ($1091 versus $1000), in terms of present value, to hold off production for a year, assuming that your projection of the market price is correct.

If your coal firm chooses to produce today instead of waiting until tomorrow, you are paying a total of two costs. The first is the cost of marketing, production, and the like, which goes into our calculation of marginal cost. The second cost is the opportunity cost of the foregone future production—$91 in this case. The existence of this additional opportunity cost makes markets for finite natural resources different from those of reproducible goods. This can be seen in Figure 3.

If coal were reproducible, then the problem of rationing production over time would not take place. The firms in such an industry would end up producing where price equals marginal cost, at a level of total production shown by Q_r in Figure 3. This maximizes current profits but does not, for the

FIGURE 11-3: THE IMPACT OF RESOURCE LIMITS
Because this resource has a physical limit, the producer must take into account the value of lost revenues from future sales when current production takes place. The marginal resource cost (MRC), which includes this opportunity cost, is therefore greater than the MC. This causes the firm to produce fewer resources, saving some for future sale.

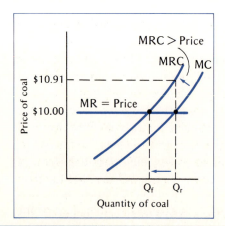

firm producing a finite resource, take into account lost future revenues. As the figure indicates, at quantity Q_r **marginal resource cost** (MRC)—which includes the opportunity cost of current production—is greater than price. The quantity Q_r then is not a profit maximum for this type of market. The revenues given up in the future are so great that the firm is actually losing money. Greater profits could be made by producing less now (and reducing current revenues) and more in the future (and increasing future revenues at higher prices). The profit-maximizing firm will therefore produce less than Q_r.

The firm selling a finite resource maximizes the present value of its total profits by producing at Q_f and selling at the equilibrium price. At this level of total output, the marginal resource cost of production exactly equals price. That is, the last unit produced sells for the production cost—including the cost of foregone future revenues. Any increase or decrease in current production from this level lowers the present value of total production for the finite natural resource.

Because of the existence of these lost future revenues, the individual firm in a finite resource industry produces a smaller quantity. This translates into a smaller market supply. With identical demand and identical production costs, prices will be higher and the equilibrium quantity lower if the good in question is a finite natural resource than if the item is reproducible. Market price will be bid up until price equals marginal resource cost—including the cost of foregone future revenues.

Marginal resource cost: the marginal cost of producing a limited resource including production, opportunity costs, and the present value of foregone future revenues

THE IMPACT OF PRICE EXPECTATIONS

The quantity of finite resources produced depends on demand, production costs, and the costs of the foregone future revenue that results from current production. Anything that changes future prices or revenues will alter the market equilibrium.

If prices are expected to rise in the future, this increases the present value of the future payments foregone when current production takes place. Production now carries a higher opportunity cost. Rising expected future prices cause firms to produce less in the current time period and more in future periods in order to take advantage of higher future profits.

If prices in the future are expected to fall, just the opposite reaction takes place. Falling future prices reduce the incentive for the coal mine owner to invest in the ground—to delay production in order to increase profits. When producers think that future prices will be lower, the opportunity cost of current production falls and they produce more now and have less to sell in the future.

The firm's production decision affects prices now and prices in the future. If, in expectation of higher prices, firms cut back production, this action tends to raise the current price (as market supply falls) and, as well, to reduce expected prices in the future. Since less is produced now, there will be more to sell later, thus increasing future supply and reducing the anticipated future price. Conversely, if firms expect future prices to fall, they will produce more now (bidding down the current price) and less in the future (helping to prop up prices then).

Expectations about prices have a large impact on the production decision for finite resources such as coal, natural gas, and oil. During periods of high energy scarcity, for example, oil and natural gas companies have been criticized for not producing their finite natural resources as fast as humanly possible. These companies are often blamed for creating a fake energy crisis by withholding fuel supplies. But based on the analysis just presented, their behavior is seen to result from rational business decisions. If prices for oil and natural gas are thought to be rising, then the fact of higher opportunity cost makes increased current production unprofitable. Indeed, if prices are thought to be rising, rational owners of finite resources will cut back on current production and withhold resources for future sale. The present value of the profits is maximized in this way.

Because the production decision for finite resources takes into consideration the present value of lost future revenues, the quantity produced is also sensitive to changes in interest rates. Falling interest rates, for example, increase the present value of future production. This increases opportunity cost. Falling interest rates, therefore, tend to cause firms to reduce current production and increase future production (they would rather have high revenues later than low interest income now). Rising interest rates have just the opposite impact. If interest rates are high, firms produce more now (often so that they can invest the revenues at the high interest rates themselves) and less in the future.

THE PROBLEM OF PROPERTY RIGHTS

Property rights: the legal and economic rights that accompany ownership or use of a good or service

The discussion of the production of finite natural resources has assumed a certain definition of **property rights**. Property rights are the legal and economic rights of ownership or use of a good, service, or resource.

All economic systems are built on a set of property right definitions. When you buy an apple, for example, you purchase with it a set of legal a and economic rights that determine what you can and cannot do with that apple and what others can and cannot do. You can eat it yourself, for example, or give it or sell it to another person. You may not, however, throw it through a store window, nor may others take the apple away from you without your permission. Property rights establish these sorts of rules for ownership or use. If property rights are altered (if, for example, you are allowed to eat your apple, but you are forbidden from selling it or from selling it for more than a given price), your economic behavior is altered as well.

Economists believe that people make economic decisions concerning the use of resources based on the types of property rights that prevail for those resources. For example, if an oil firm has full private ownership rights over a finite pool of petroleum, then the firm will ration production of that petroleum over time to maximize the present value of that fixed pool of oil. This definition of property rights does not hold in many cases, however, with disturbing results.

Some natural resources (finite and otherwise) are owned in common or have property rights that may be difficult to enforce. For example, who owns the fish in the ocean? Who owns the oil located beneath the ocean floor? When private ownership of a natural resource is impossible, that resource tends to become depleted too quickly. Fish in international waters, for example, are owned by everyone—which means that they are owned by no one. If an individual fisherman doubles his or her catch, the effect of this action on future catches is not immediately apparent to that fisherman. The fisherman may not be aware of how this action in any way reduces the amount of resources left. Because you do not own the fishery resource, doubling the catch reduces the amount that *others* catch, not the amount of your own future production.

In short, when a resource is owned in common, no individual producer takes into account the opportunity costs resulting from lost future production. Each individual firm produces a larger quantity (like Q_r in Figure 3) than would be the case if the opportunity costs were added to production costs.

This overproduction can rapidly deplete a natural resource. Many salmon runs on both the east and west coasts of the United States have been destroyed in this way. The disappearance of many species of whales from the oceans of the world is another example. Ignoring opportunity costs of a common resource can lead to the eventual extinction of that resource.

Oil and natural gas production is another area where this overproduction problem can show up. These resources are often found in large subterranean pools. If only one producer taps a given pool, then that firm must take into account the opportunity cost problem and be aware that more now means less later. Production is rationed carefully over time in this case.

But suppose that two competing firms tap into the same pool. If one produces more now, there is less left for both producers in the future. A race develops with each firm trying to produce more and more so as not to be left holding the empty bag when the oil or gas resource finally runs out. Overproduction takes place quickly here.

When the problem of common ownership prevails, the government often steps in to restore some sort of balance to the competing demands of present and future production. For example, much of America's forests are owned by the federal government. Logging is controlled to see that timber is rationed over time (although one can argue how well this rationing has taken place). Recent international agreements that expand national property rights to ocean fisheries, one might argue, are designed to reduce the potential overproduction that comes from common ownership of this resource.

UNSTABLE PRICES

The problem of limited supply is not nearly so restrictive in the case of producible items such as wheat or corn. Finite total resources mean that the amount of wheat that can be produced in any given time is limited—by the availability of land, seed, water, and so on—and any increase in wheat production means less production of some other good. In this sense, finite limits still apply. But, in another sense, the limit is less binding because an increase in wheat production today does not necessarily mean a decrease in wheat production in future years. When we produce wheat today we may have to give up corn today, but we don't necessarily have to give up either wheat or corn in the future.

But, there may still be a problem in these markets: the problem of unstable prices. The pricing problem arises from the uncertainty that producers face in making the production decision. Suppose that you are a wheat farmer. How much wheat should you produce? As has been noted in previous chapters, a competitive firm produces at the output level where price equals marginal cost of production. So this is the level of output that the farmer should produce. One problem remains, however. What will the price be?

Suppose you think that the price for the coming harvest will be $4.00 per bushel of wheat. If this is the price, then your farm should produce quantity Q_1 of wheat in Figure 4. If the price comes in as expected, you will maximize profits. If you are wrong in this price estimate, however, you could be in real trouble. If other farmers have cut back production or had their harvests reduced by natural disasters, then the price could be very much higher—like the $5.00 price shown in the figure. In this case, the farmer is giving up profits by not producing enough. If you knew that prices would be higher, you would have produced much more—quantity Q_2 in

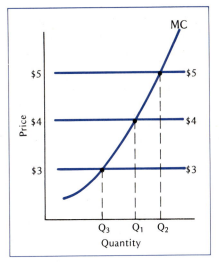

FIGURE 11-4:   PRICE UNCERTAINTY IN
THE WHEAT MARKET
*How much should the wheat farmer
produce? If it seems that the price this
year will be $4 per unit, then he or she
ought to produce amount Q_1. If the
price is different from $4, however, the
farmer will lose—a different amount
should have been produced.*

the figure. As it is, this small quantity supplied contributes to market pressures that drive up the price.

By guessing too low a price, the farmer gives up profits. If you guess too high, however, you also suffer. Suppose that other farmers had anticipated high prices and planted large crops or that mother nature was generous this year and harvests are unusually large. This causes the market price to fall to, say, $3.00 per unit of wheat. At this price, wheat farmers would have maximized profits by producing a small quantity Q_3 of wheat and devoting resources to other crops. As it is, having guessed too high, the farmer has produced more wheat than he or she should. Much of your wheat (the difference between Q_3 and Q_1) costs more to produce than it will bring on the market. If prices fall low enough, farm profits could be wiped out completely.

What should the farmer do? Profits are determined by changes in the market price. The market price, in turn, is affected by the production decisions of thousands of other farmers in several countries, the weather, and other natural forces that affect crop yields, and the demand for the product itself. Weather conditions in Russia can make and lose millions for farmers in Kansas.

This uncertainty as to future prices is a real headache for producers of producible resources. On what price should the farmer base production decisions? According to the **cobweb theory** (so-called for reasons that will become apparent in a minute) these producers may make decisions by projecting last season's price into the future. If the price of wheat last year was $3.00 per unit, then guessing that it will be $3.00 again this year may be as good an estimate as possible under the circumstances.

Cobweb theory: the theory that producers will base next year's production decision on this year's market price, causing unstable prices

This method of estimating prices can work pretty well. If demand and supply remain stable, then there is no reason to believe that prices should change very much from one season to another. But, if demand or supply is likely to change, this can set in motion some rather unstable price movements. The problem is illustrated in Figure 5.

Suppose that last year's wheat price was $3.00 per bushel. At that relatively low price, farmers did not make much money, so they decide not to be fooled again and produce only a smaller total Q_1, which maximizes producer profits at the $3.00 price. This production level would be fine if it turned out to be the equilibrium quantity for this market. But, as Figure 5 indicates, it is not. The equilibrium for this year occurs at a larger quantity and a higher price. In other types of markets, this problem would be easily solved: Prices would rise and producers, responding to the higher prices, would increase production to do away with the shortage. This is possible in many markets, but not here.

The size of the current wheat harvest was determined many months ago when the planting decision was made. Farmers are stuck with the small Q_1 quantity of their harvest. As a result, supply is temporarily limited to Q_1 and buyers will have to bid for the very scarce wheat. As Figure 5 shows, demanders are willing to pay a higher price of $5.00 per bushel for this small quantity of wheat. The price of wheat will therefore jump from $3.00 last year to $5.00 this year. Consumers will wonder why wheat costs so much and individual farmers will kick themselves for not producing more to take advantage of the unexpectedly higher prices.

FIGURE 11-5:   UNSTABLE PRICES
Because farmers thought the price would be low, they produced only a relatively small amount of wheat. This small quantity, however, sells for a high price. Price jumps suddenly from $3 to $5.

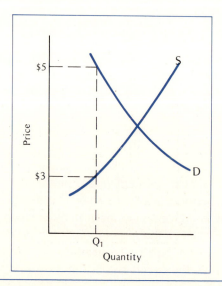

Price has now jumped once, and this instability is likely to continue as Figure 6 shows. Having seen prices go from $3.00 to $5.00, farmers will want to take advantage of high profits in the coming year (they hope). They will plant a very large quantity of wheat. At the expected price of $5.00 per unit for wheat, producers supply a very large amount of wheat. Sadly, consumers are not willing to buy that much wheat and so the price drops again.

The cycle can continue, as Figure 6 shows, with prices rising and falling from year to year. Finally, an equilibrium can take place, but don't count on it. The equilibrium shown here at the center of the cobweb is a point where the amount that farmers produce equals the amount that buyers want to purchase at the going price. The market moves toward this equilibrium, but will only reach it if nothing happens to change supply or demand in the meantime. A radical change in supply because of crop failures, bad weather, or new farming technology will put the cycle back into action, causing prices to rise and fall all over again.

The problem of unstable agricultural prices is one of the reasons for the U.S. government's farm price support programs (other reasons may be political in nature). In order to protect the producers from unstable prices and incomes, the government sometimes guarantees a price to farmers and accumulates stocks of goods to supply in case of poor crops. This helps reduce price fluctuations, but it can create other problems in the market. If the price if fixed too high, consumers will pay too much and too many resources will be used up in production. A growing surplus will be created.

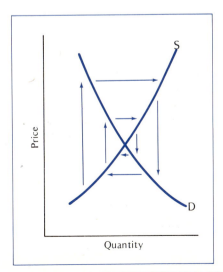

FIGURE 11-6: THE COBWEB CYCLE
In response to high prices, farmers produce a large quantity, which drives market price down. Because of the low price, they cut back on production and drive price up again. This cycle of unstable prices is often called the "cobweb."

Farm price programs have to balance the gains from stable prices against the losses that fixed prices inflict on the markets involved.

Cobweb cycles occur for a variety of agricultural goods and are apparent in many occupations as well. Engineers and teachers are in short supply now, but more people will enter these fields in response to rising prices. Boom and bust cycles for engineers and teachers have been very apparent in recent years.

REAL WORLD ECONOMICS: TRAINING AND EDUCATION PROGRAMS

PRESIDENT ANNOUNCES JOB TRAINING PROGRAM

WASHINGTON, D.C.—The President announced today plans for new federal job training programs designed to reduce hard-core unemployment in urban areas. The $5 billion program, which will be implemented with Congress' approval, over the next 3 years, will provide job training and experience for up to 300,000 unemployed urban workers.

"With this program, we hope to give workers the skills they need to compete in today's job market and to improve productivity in industry at the same time," the President said.

ECONOMIC ANALYSIS

Training and education programs represent an investment in **human capital.** By improving knowledge and skills, employers and individuals (today's college student included) hope to permanently increase productivity and therefore gain employment or improve employment prospects. Investment in human capital, like any other investment decision, is a risky one, however.

First of all, why would the President think that investing in human capital is a good way to reduce unemployment? Legal minimum wages prevail in many occupations. If the marginal cost of labor (because of the minimum wage legislation) is $4.00 per hour, then workers incapable of generating marginal revenues of at least $4.00 per hour stand little chance for jobs and are forced to compete for work in those occupations not covered by minimum wages or to go without wage income.

By training workers and increasing their productivity, the government hopes to increase their marginal revenues above that legally mandated minimum amount, making their employment profitable for private firms. The plan, therefore, is designed to move the unemployed off the public dole and onto private sector payrolls through job training.

Human capital: the stock of talent and skills that increase the productivity of labor

If this sounds like a good idea (and it does) then we must ask the question, Why does the government need to be involved here? Why don't the private firms (who would gain from the increased productivity) or the unemployed individuals themselves (who could train their way out of poverty) go out and purchase these training programs since it is in their own self-interest to do so?

In answering this question it is important to first note that individuals often do undertake investment in human capital as a way of increasing income. Enrollments in colleges, vocational training schools, and professional training programs attest to this. Firms often spend large sums training employees, counting on the increased productivity of those workers to make the investment pay off. Still, there are times when such investments are not made, despite clear economic justification. In these cases the government may want to step in.

Why don't poor people seek training to help themselves escape the grasp of poverty? The problem is often one of present value. The potential benefits (a probability of higher future income) must be weighed against a high present cost. At the interest rates that the poor must consider in making this decision (coupled with the uncertain nature of the future returns) this investment may not make sense. The fact that the money to pay for training is often unavailable makes investment an even more unlikely outcome.

For firms, investment in human capital is discouraged by a number of factors. Sometimes discrimination is the cause. Managers who make the economically unsound choice to discriminate against some workers on the basis of race, sex, or background may refuse to make investments that would otherwise be economically beneficial to both worker and firm.

A different problem occurs because of the nature of the property rights that firms own in their workers. If a firm undertakes an expensive training program, it hopes to earn a profit through the increased productivity of those workers over a period of time. But the worker is always free to change employers. If the worker receives training and splits, the investment in human capital is a bust for the specific firm that undertook it. The training may still act to increase worker productivity, but that investment may now benefit a competitor.

This inability to own workers makes firms less willing to invest in worker training or education projects. The projected future revenues from these projects are therefore reduced, and less human capital improvement is undertaken. The government may make a case for taxing firms in order to make human capital investments that may benefit the firms as a group; since the firms are unwilling to undertake the program individually. If this is the case, then the governmental job program might be a good gamble for the workers and for those who pay for it as well.

SUMMARY

1. Firms regulate their use of inputs depending upon the marginal costs of those productive resources and their marginal revenues. The profit-maximizing firm uses any given resource (all other inputs constant) until its marginal revenue equals marginal cost. Changes in either marginal costs or marginal revenues (due, for example, to changing output prices or productivity) alter the firm's demand for inputs.

2. The demand for capital is more complicated because capital must be purchased now, but revenues are earned in the future. Firms must use the tool of present value to compare these costs and revenues. The firm purchases capital to the point where its current marginal cost just equals the present value of its future marginal revenues.

3. Most inputs are supplied along the lines of the producer decision described earlier in the text. Natural resources supplies, however, may be affected by other economic events as well. In the case of a finite natural resource, opportunity costs (in terms of lost future revenues) must be considered. This makes the production decision different from that for a good without a finite production limit.

4. Some resource markets experience boom and bust cycles because of the lag between the time when production decisions are made and when the product itself can be brought to market. The cobweb model describes these cycles in markets for agricultural products, natural resources, and specific occupational groups labor markets.

DISCUSSION QUESTIONS

1. Suppose that a particular machine is guaranteed to produce marginal revenues of $1000 at the end of one year, $2000 at the end of the second year and $1000 a the end of the third year. Use the present value formula to determine the maximum amount that a firm will pay for this machine if the interest rate is 10 percent. How will this price change if the interest rate is 15 percent? Why?

2. Suppose that interest rates are currently rising. What effect do you expect this to have on the price of the finite natural resource oil? Explain your reasoning.

3. Do all cobwebs converge to an equilibrium price like the one illustrated in the text? Can you draw an exploding cobweb? What is the difference between these two results?

4. Because of the problem of enforcing property rights, individual firms may produce too much of a natural resource but undertake fewer worker training programs. Why does this hap-

pen? Is it possible for the government, using laws that define property rights, to change this result?

5. Economists have long observed price cycles involving beef, pork, and chicken prices. It takes several years to bring cattle to market, about a year to raise pigs, and only a few months to produce a marketable chicken. Given this information, what form do you think this cycle takes? Use the cobweb theory to derive your own version of the beef–pork–chicken cycle.

TEST YOURSELF

Indicate whether each of the following statesments is *true* or *false*. Be able to defend your response.

1. Capital goods are inputs that are not immediately used up in the production process.

2. A profit-maximizing firm purchases capital until the present value of future marginal revenues equals the marginal cost of the input.

3. The present value of a future payment increases as interest rates rise.

4. The present value of $1000 in one year is $847 if the interest rate is 20 percent.

5. Investment in human capital is designed to increase the productivity of workers.

6. Unlike investment in trucks, investment in human capital does not depend on interest rates.

7. If the price of a finite natural resource is expected to fall in the future, producers will supply more of the resource now.

8. Falling interest rates tend to reduce the quantity of a finite natural resource that is produced now.

9. In a cobweb cycle, high prices now lead to lower prices in the future because of shifts in demand curves.

10. Cob web markets always find a stable equilibrium.

12
Energy Markets

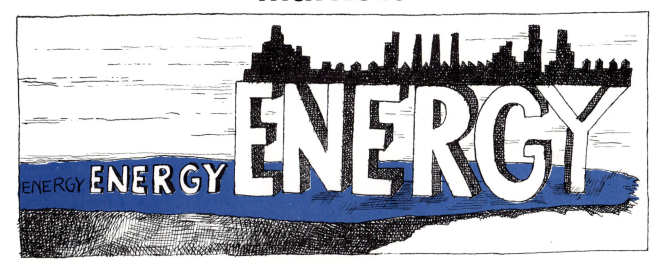

This chapter looks at markets that are in the news and will continue to be important to us individually and as an economy for a long time: the energy markets. This chapter answers some important questions about energy and economics, including the following:

What are the uses of energy? Why is it so important?
What are the sources of energy? What is the outlook for future energy supplies?
Why is the price of energy now and in the future important?
Will we run out of energy soon?
What impact do price controls have on energy markets?
Which is more important: energy or the environment?

Energy is the key to modern economic systems. As nations develop and become industrialized, they become more and more dependent on complicated energy systems. This heavy use of energy seems to be a consequence of economic growth. Natural though it may be, energy dependence represents a real problem in an age of increasing scarcity of energy resources.

ENERGY AND ECONOMIC DEVELOPMENT

Before going into the details of energy markets, let's take a look at some of the reasons for energy's importance in modern economies. The process of economic development is really one of specialization and exchange, much as these ideas were described in earlier chapters. In less-developed economies, exchange and specialization are of little use. Individual families provide most of the goods and services that they need. Food, clothing, heat, and entertainment are provided within the family unit without much dependence on outside sources.

As populations grow and the needs of the economy become greater, however, exchange and specialization become more and more important. In the agricultural sector of the economy, farmers find markets for their produce. They produce more food than they need and sell the excess, trading it for other desired goods. This process creates a double need for energy. First, to provide the extra food for sale often requires the use of more intensive or more sophisticated farming methods, which may use machines (and fuels to run them) or other energy-intensive items such as artificial fertilizers. At the same time, energy is needed to make exchange possible. Farm goods must be moved to market and the purchases of the farmers returned. Specialization and exchange here produce gains for all parties, but they also cause an increased demand for energy.

As the gains from specialization and exchange are further exploited, towns and cities are built. As individuals become more and more specialized in the goods that they produce, they need to be able to trade their own production for the large list of other items that they need. To make these exchanges easy and efficient, all the traders need to be relatively close together. This is the economic function of cities—to centralize markets and facilitate exchange.

As cities grow and exchange takes place, however, the demand for energy grows as well. This is the case for two reasons. First, as specialization becomes more advanced, more machines are used. At the same time, the increased numbers of exchanges also require more energy. With each trade, the goods must come to the people or the people must go to the goods. Transportation necessarily takes place. As cities grow geographically, more and more transportation will be mechanized. Food, the energy source for people, must be hauled long miles from farms, using more energy in the process.

Finally, as incomes rise because of the gains from exchanges, the demand for energy-related convenience goods such as refrigerators, stoves, electric lights, and cars increases. Energy use rises again.

Rising dependence on energy, then, seems to accompany modern economic development because sophisticated energy use makes possible greater specialization and exchange. This need not always be the case, of course, but these trends seem to have been closely associated in the past. We must learn about energy to understand the economics of the future.

PRICE, QUANTITY, AND SUBSTITUTION EFFECTS

Higher energy costs have three types of effects on the world economy that are important to us. The first is the price effect. Rising energy prices boost the prices of oil, natural gas, electricity, and the like directly, and increase a variety of other prices indirectly.

To give you an idea of the size of the price effects involved here, note the impact of the oil price increase of 1979. OPEC increased the world base price of oil by about 50 percent in the summer of 1979. This was a large price increase, to be sure, but oil was only one of the many energy sources that the United States used at that time and, in addition, the price increase directly affected only about half of the oil that the United States used. Even so, economists estimate that this rise in oil prices may have resulted in an increase in the national price level of about 2½ percent. This is a large increase to result from just one action. As other energy prices begin to rise to reflect the energy reality of the 1980s, we can expect to see even larger price effects.

Also important are the quantity effects of higher energy prices. Production processes that use energy as an input experience higher marginal costs. In the short run, these higher costs reduce supply and force up market price. (In the long run these effects may be moderated, depending on the ability of producers to adjust to higher energy prices.)

The resulting falling production of final goods translates into a falling demand for many of the resources discussed in this part of the text. Lowered quantities supplied and demanded create a number of economic problems like poverty and unemployment.

Finally, substitution and income effects have to be considered. As prices rise, consumers and businesses discover that their incomes stretch to cover fewer goods and services. The amount of goods in general that they can purchase falls and this aggravates the quantity impacts discussed above.

In addition, the substitution effects alter the way that consumers and businesses behave as they attempt to avoid some of the higher energy and energy-associated costs by substituting relatively lower-priced goods and services for those most directly affected by the higher costs. Insulation, a substitute in many cases for energy, should experience increased demand as energy prices climb. Higher demand here bids up the price of this item.

Energy-saving thermostats and fuel-efficient cars will also rise in price. Not everything will go up, however. Items that waste fuel, such as poorly insulated houses and gas-guzzling cars, experience less demand as energy costs more, and so these prices can be expected to fall somewhat.

In a world where everything depends on the price and quantity of energy, rising energy costs can be expected to send shock waves rippling in ever-larger rings throughout the economy.

ENERGY SUPPLIES

Why all this talk about higher energy costs? Energy is supplied by profit-maximizing firms. These firms supply scarce resources to earn maximum profits, given current demand, current prices, and expected prices in future years. Larger quantities of energy resources now must come at higher prices because of rising production costs and future opportunity costs.

Energy can come from a variety of sources. Which sources are used? The answer depends on price. Figure 1 helps explain why. Energy of a given type or form can be produced in different ways, but the cost of producing it varies widely. Oil, for example, can be pumped out of relatively cheap existing wells, or more expensive alternatives, such as offshore, Alaskan, OPEC, or synthetic oil, can be tapped. Each alternative has its own supply curve and its own price behavior. In each case, there is some minimum price needed to make production possible. Below that price, the alternative in question is uneconomic to supply.

At prices below P_1 in the figure, for example, no oil can be produced profitably. At prices between P_1 and P_2, firms profitably produce onshore oil, but other sources are not developed because price does not cover production costs. At prices between P_2 and P_3, firms are able to produce both onshore and offshore oil. Finally, at prices above P_3, oil from all three sources is made available to the market. The total supply of oil is the sum of the supplies from all available oil sources.

A look at the supply curve of Figure 1 illustrates several points. First, as with other supplies, quantity depends on price. Consumers who want more oil must expect to pay more for it, at least in the short run. Second, development of new energy resources depends on price, too. Low prices

FIGURE 12-1: ENERGY SUPPLIES

Energy (in this case, oil) is available from several sources with different supply curves. The supply of all forms of oil is the sum of these individual supplies. Price here determines both the quantity supplied and the way that it is produced.

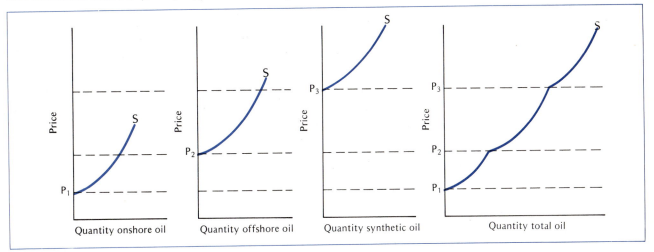

give no incentive for producers to voluntarily find new, more expensive ways to produce oil. Finally, this kind of supply curve suggests that the ultimate limits to oil production may be less a function of nature's abundance than society's willingness to pay. If oil's price were to increase a thousand times, significant new supplies might well be developed. But price here is the relevant limit.

ENERGY PRICE CONTROLS

Price is extremely important in energy markets because high price serves as a signal to generate energy from new sources using more expensive methods. When prices are not allowed to change in the face of market conditions, the problems created can be very severe. In spite of this, price controls are relatively abundant in energy markets. Because energy is an input in so many production processes, increases in energy prices raise costs throughout the economy and are a cause of inflation. One goal of price controls is to reduce this inflation. Let's take a look at what happens in energy markets when price controls prevail.

Suppose that we are dealing with energy supplied by oil and oil substitutes, as pictured in Figure 2. Here, we show four different sources of this type of energy. The first (cheapest) source of oil energy is oil produced by easily accessible onshore wells. The oil is relatively easy to extract and so

FIGURE 12-2: ENERGY PRICE CONTROLS

A price ceiling on oil creates a dual problem. It creates an initial shortage because a larger quantity than producers can supply is demanded at the ceiling price. In addition, by holding price down, it creates a long-run problem by delaying development of new energy sources.

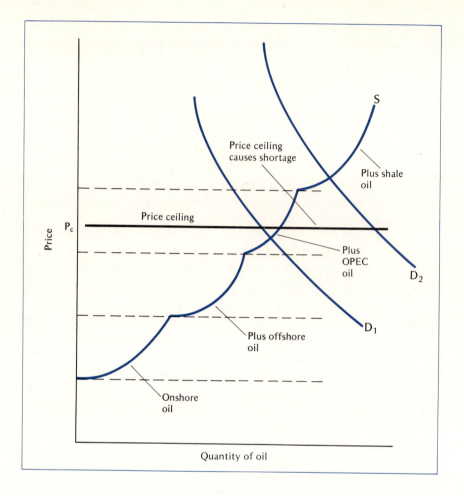

has a fairly low marginal cost. The second source is offshore oil wells. Because this oil has a higher marginal cost, it will only be produced when the marginal costs of onshore oil have risen high enough to make this method of production feasible. If demand and prices are low, no offshore oil will be produced.

The third source of oil here is imported oil. Because of high export taxes that OPEC countries levy on their oil, this energy is more expensive than even U.S. offshore production. The oil is actually cheaper to produce, but high transportation costs and high foreign government taxes (the OPEC way of controlling price is by setting these taxes) make this energy relatively expensive. The last source in this diagram (other sources exist) is oil derived from oil-shale deposits. This oil is very costly to extract and has the highest marginal cost shown here. This oil will be produced to increase total production, but only if the market price of oil rises above the marginal cost of oil-shale production. These different individual supplies of oil give us the supply curve shown in Figure 2. Oil production changes from one source to another as oil prices rise.

Now add price controls to this picture. Suppose that the government, in order to protect consumers from high energy prices and to reduce inflationary pressures in general, imposes a ceiling price P_c on oil from all sources. What impact will this have on the energy market? The impact depends on the demand for oil at the time that the price ceiling is imposed, and demand in the future. If demand is relatively low—D_1 demand curve in the future—then the price ceiling will have no impact. Here the ceiling price is above the market equilibrium and so limits only future price rises, but doesn't restrict current prices.

If demand increases to D_2, however, the ceiling will have a very real impact. At the higher demand, consumers wish to purchase more oil energy. At the ceiling price of P_c their demand is very high. Supply, however, does not respond to this higher demand. In order to produce the amount of oil that consumers wish, producers will have to change oil-production technology. Besides using more onshore, offshore, and imported oil, producers will also have to use oil-shale production methods to meet this new and higher demand. At the government-controlled ceiling price, however, this new source cannot be tapped. The new production source will only be used if market price rises to the higher oil-shale marginal cost. Lacking this, little change in quantity is apparent. The quantity supplied will remain constant, the quantity demanded will rise, and a shortage of oil will result. Those who can get the oil will, and others will have to do without; government rationing plans may have to be invoked.

In previous chapters we were concerned about price ceilings because they distorted economic decisions. Now we must look at a different aspect of price controls—their impact on energy sources.

By setting price ceilings, government agencies mean to lower consumer prices. They end up, however, restricting energy sources. In the preceding example, oil-shale production never takes place unless either prices are allowed to rise or some new technology drastically lowers oil-shale marginal costs. This is important because opening up a new energy source may not be a short-run proposition. It may take many years to bring a new energy source such as oil-shale into full production. The imposition of price controls, therefore, has a double impact. It creates shortages in the short run by allowing the quantity demanded at the control price to exceed the quantity that is supplied. It also creates long-run shortages by removing the important factor of increasing prices, which while inducing consumers to economize on energy use, allows for the development of the new energy sources that the economy needs.

OPEC AND THE SUPPLY OF OIL

Any discussion of energy supplies must mention the Organization of Petroleum Exporting Countries (OPEC). This oil cartel has been the dominant force in world oil markets since the early 1970s, and oil remains a key source of energy.

As noted in the preceding section, prices that OPEC charges for oil have relatively little to do with marginal production costs. Quantities of oil that cost tens of cents to produce are sold for tens of dollars. Oil profits are astronomical.

In looking at OPEC, two questions immediately come to mind. The first is how can OPEC charge such high prices for its cheap oil? Why would anyone pay $50 (or more) for oil that costs only a few dollars to produce? The answer to this question comes from two sides. The first is that high-priced oil may also be highly productive oil. As oil's price increases, its uses are limited to those which have a very high marginal product. Demand from these uses allows the high prices. The second part of the answer has to do with alternatives. If not oil, then what? At least in the short run, high-priced oil is the least expensive option for some producers and consumers. Hence the high demand even when price soars.

The second question about OPEC has to do with the stability of this cartel. A previous chapter pointed out the fact that cartels like OPEC are naturally unstable. The profits from cheating eventually doom the cartel's ability to raise price. Does this mean that OPEC is doomed and that we can expect oil prices to fall back to competitive levels when the organization self-destructs?

The answer to this double question is yes and no. Yes, the economic forces that plague cartels also exist for OPEC, and so OPEC's stability is like that of a spinning top—impermanent. But (the no part of the answer) that doesn't mean we can expect oil prices to return to their cheap pre-1973 levels. The forces that determine oil production are the forces of scarcity and choice. With oil scarce now and likely to be scarcer in the future, OPEC members with foresight can still profit by delaying production—by investing in oil left in the earth for future production. By rationing the scarce resource over time, OPEC members keep prices high—with or without the cartel organization.

MANAGING THE ENERGY PROBLEM

Rising energy demand coupled with supplies that expand only slowly, if at all (and sometimes actually contract) gives rise to a national and world energy problem. How do we cope with this problem? The answers depend directly on the question of price controls.

Managing a shortage of energy involves policies that act either to increase supplies, decrease demand (as through energy conservation), or both. Without price controls, the market performs these functions easily.

An energy shortage naturally increases the price of energy itself and of energy substitutes, and lowers the prices of goods that use up energy in large doses. These higher energy prices induce greater production and increased conservation. Quantity demanded falls as the quantity supplied increases. The shortage disappears.

While this way of reducing the shortage may be effective, different groups bear different burdens depending upon their ability to compensate for the higher energy prices. Very often the ability to adjust when energy prices rise depends on income or wealth.

When oil prices increased in 1979, for example, the *Wall Street Journal* reported that small-car prices suddenly shot up (as demand increased) and the prices of big, gas-hungry cars fell just as fast. One result of this was that poor people, who were least able to pay for the higher-priced gas, were also less able to avoid the higher prices by buying small cars. Toyotas, little Chevy's, and Volkswagens were suddenly unaffordable, and the big land-yachts were the only transportation to be had. Thus some poor people who use cars are hit with a double-whammy price hike. They both pay higher prices for gas and, through this peculiar chain of events, buy more of it too!

When price controls exist, energy prices don't rise (or at least don't rise as much). Thus price cannot be used to the same extent as an incentive to increase production and conserve scarce supplies. With prices fixed, other tools have to be employed: subsidies to suppliers (paid for, presumably, through higher taxes somewhere down the line), which stimulate greater supply, and regulations on demand (such as rules that require good gas mileage for cars or effective insulation for buildings), which act to reduce the quantity demanded.

If high prices impose a burden on the economy, managing a shortage with controls does so, too. Someone must pay to produce the increased supplies. Someone must pay for the cost of insulation and auto development. With prices rising, both of these ends would be accomplished voluntarily by producers and consumers.

Regulation has one further fault. If supply and demand are regulated by price, then producers and consumers have an incentive to lower cost by producing energy more efficiently and conserving more of it. Their attempts to lower cost focus on using less of the higher-priced commodity. When regulation is used, however, firms still pay a relatively low price for energy, and bear higher costs only when they obey the government's rules and laws. Saving cost, then, means getting around the regulations, not using less energy. This focus does little to accomplish the goal of conservation.

If burdens exist in either case—free market or controlled market with regulation—then the choice between them involves a weighing of the costs and benefits of each choice.

THE PARADOX OF NET ENERGY

Net energy: additional energy produced (MEP) minus additional energy used (MEC); the net addition to usable energy

When new sources of energy are being developed, as appears will be the case over the coming decades, many trade-offs must be considered. The usual economic choice of benefits versus opportunity costs applies. Is a new oil pipeline worth the cars, trucks, refrigerators, or twinkies that must be given up as resources are shifted? Another problem that must be considered, however, is energy production and the energy used in production.

The idea here is easy. When we produce energy (by, say, running a pump to gain oil from wells) energy must be used in the process. Sometimes the energy loss is relatively small so that the **net energy** produced is great. But this is not always the case. The building of pipelines, nuclear power plants, or solar-power stations is a process that is likely to consume absolutely huge amounts of energy. Still, these projects may be worthwhile, all else being equal, if the amount of additional energy they make available is large enough. As new energy sources are explored and old ones expanded, the problem of net energy will become more and more important. The problem is illustrated in Figure 3.

As more and more resources are devoted to the production of, say, solar power, the problem of diminishing returns eventually shows up. Additional resources devoted to any one kind of energy production yield lower **marginal energy production** (MEP in the figure), but come at a higher and higher **marginal energy cost** (MEC in the figure). So long as marginal energy production (MEP) exceeds marginal energy cost (MEC), the energy process makes available more energy than it uses, and so net energy is produced (although it is still important to bear in mind the opportunity costs involved in terms of alternative energy sources and the other goods given up). At some point, however, diminishing returns become so great that marginal energy cost exceeds marginal energy production. Here, negative net energy is produced—it takes two kilowatts to make one. Production of energy in this situation is clearly a mistake.

Marginal energy production (MEP): the amount of additional energy produced with additional resources

Marginal energy cost (MEC): the amount of additional energy used up in the production process

Why worry about this problem? Obviously, people will know when they have reached this negative net energy situation, right? No. That's the problem and the risk of energy development. Sure, if a scientist was running a simple generator and could measure both the total energy input and the total energy output directly, computing net energy and making net energy

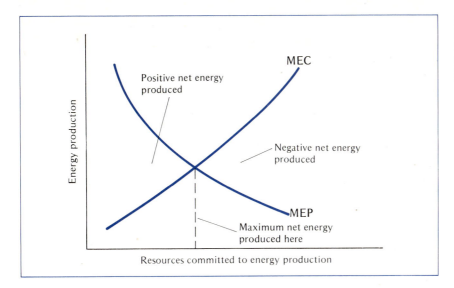

FIGURE 12-3:   NET ENERGY
*Producing energy uses energy.
Marginal energy costs (MEC) must be
weighed against the marginal energy
produced (MEP).*

decisions would be a simple affair. This ideal situation is not likely to prevail in the real world, however.

Energy output may be readily measureable since, in general, just one form of energy is produced and transmitted from a limited number of points. But how can the energy inputs be measured? They take so many forms. Electricity, coal, gasoline, oil, natural gas, and so on are all used. And they appear in so many different ways. What is the energy component of concrete used in construction? Of steel used in fabrication? Of the electrical devices necessary to operation? Of the planning and drafting and testing of the power plant?

All the various inputs into the energy production process use up energy and it is often difficult enough just keeping track of their money cost, much less their energy cost. When an energy production decision is made, therefore, it is very possible for marginal energy cost to exceed marginal energy production without those involved in the decision being aware of that fact! Appearances here are deceptive—what looks like energy production actually results in energy loss.

Production of negative net energy is clearly an undesirable situation. Yet (the paradox!) we might *rationally* and *economically* choose to *produce* energy using methods that yield *negative* net energy. How can this be? The key to the answer is to remember that society is motivated by opportunity costs. When we produce gasohol, we may be giving up more energy than we receive. But energy is not the only thing foregone. In producing energy, we may give up many other things. The negative net energy product may come at a lower opportunity cost than any other energy substitute and so may be a desirable product.

In the production of energy, it seems, all kinds of trade-offs must be considered: trade-offs between energy consumed and energy produced, and trade-offs between energy and all other goods as well. How society weighs these options determine the path for energy development.

ENERGY AND THE ENVIRONMENT

One of the crucial trade-offs that must be considered in examining energy markets is the trade-off between energy and the environment. Sometimes no trade-off is necessary. Programs that recycle cans and bottles, for example, conserve energy while often improving environmental quality at the same time. Such opportunities are limited, however. Once we are on the production possibilities curve for energy and environment (as shown in Figure 4), increases in energy production may result in a reduction of environmental quality. More energy can be extracted from coal supplies, for example, if that coal is burned dirty—in ways that can pollute the air. More coal can be produced, but it may require ripping up large quantities of the environment. This environmental damage can be repaired (or reduced through methods similar to those employed on the Alaska oil pipeline to limit environmental impacts), but these efforts also use up valuable energy resources, reducing the net amount of power that these activities produce.

This fact creates a hard and uncomfortable trade-off. When we acquire larger quantities of energy, we may have to give up both environmental quality as well as consumer goods (cars, boats, food) because of the additional resources devoted to energy production. The trade-off between energy and consumer goods can be made less severe, however, if the

FIGURE 12-4: ENERGY VERSUS THE ENVIRONMENT
At some point, a trade-off between energy and the environment must be faced. Since there will also be a trade-off between energy and goods, this creates a trade-off between goods and the environment. Will the environment suffer?

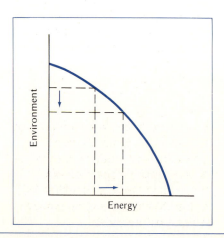

environment is allowed to suffer. That is, we may face the problem of deciding which is more important—more energy, more consumer goods, or a clean environment. Perhaps only one of these will be available at a time. Perhaps two out of three can be achieved. But, because of the trade-offs involved, at least one will have to be given up. Which one will it be?

ENERGY OFFICIAL PREDICTS WORLD PETROLEUM SUPPLIES TO RUN OUT BY 2025

WASHINGTON, D.C.—An official of the International Energy Commission today predicted that the world will run out of petroleum reserves by the year 2025 and perhaps sooner.

This shocking conclusion comes as a result of a study of current oil reserves. By comparing current world reserves (the total amount of oil currently discovered) with current and projected future energy use, the deadline of 2025 was uncovered.

"The world could run out of energy even sooner than our estimate if current oil use is not curtailed," a spokesman for the Commission noted. The Comission, in its report, called for rationing and conservation of petroleum supplies.

ECONOMIC ANALYSIS

This article is confusing because, on the one hand, the conclusions that it gives are correct. But, viewed through the economist's eye, the statements here are misleading and false.

The article is correct in a mathematical sense. If we take the amount of oil known to exist in the world today and divide that figure by the amount that is consumed yearly, then an energy crunch, where all oil supplies are drained off, does appear imminent. But is this mathematical certainty a realistic future? Probably not.

The key to understanding this problem is to understand the one variable that this report has left out: price. Both consumption and production of oil depend very much on price. When world oil reserves are calculated, we look not at some geological certainty—the total amount of oil that actually exists in the world. Rather, we see the amount of oil that has been discovered by profit-seeking firms. These firms are interested in oil that would be profitable to produce at current prices. Oil reserves, viewed in this light, are a function of the price of oil. Fifty years ago, the calculation of total oil reserves paid little attention to the vast quantities of oil located offshore under the ocean floor. These oil reserves were undiscovered and uncounted because it wouldn't pay anyone— at the prices then prevailing—to produce offshore oil. A comparison made then of oil reserves and oil consumption led to the conclusion that oil would run out before today.

REAL WORLD ECONOMICS: THE PRICE OF ENERGY

In looking at oil reserves then, we must bear in mind that, as oil reserves decline, increases in the price of this valuable resource will make production from new sources of oil profitable. This doesn't mean that oil won't eventually run out. But predictions that ignore the impact of rising prices on discoveries and production must be wrong.

Prices will also have an impact on consumption. It is easy to project more and more uses of oil for the future. After all, it is argued, oil prices have risen drastically over the past 10 years and the quantity demanded has increased, not decreased. Oil prices have gone up, it is true, but so have the prices of everything else. The real price— the relative price—of oil has

changed by a smaller amount over the years. The person who buys oil today gives up relatively little more of other goods than the trade-off that prevailed in the 1950s.

As the relative price of oil increases in the future, we can count on the fact that the more severe trade-offs will reduce the quantity of oil that is demanded. In looking at future price consumption, price cannot be ignored.

So, should we quit worrying about the energy crises and use all the oil we want? Obviously not. Future energy supplies will come at greater and greater opportunity costs. We can delay this problem and gain by conserving energy now. The energy crisis—rising opportunity cost—is real.

SUMMARY

1. Energy markets are important because energy is a basic ingredient in the process of specialization and trade that takes place in modern economies. Energy is used in production and transportation and for heat and other uses. Without energy, our economy would revert to a very simple, very primitive one.

2. There are many sources of energy, but each source depends on the price that is paid for energy. At low prices, wood and some coal energy will be produced. If the price of energy is very high, other sources, such as oil, will be used.

3. The price of energy is important for two reasons. First, it sets the trade-off between energy and other goods and makes us aware of energy's opportunity cost. Price, as well, serves as an incentive to develop new energy resources.

4. Will we run out of energy soon? No, if we are willing to pay the price in terms of other things that must be given up. If we are not willing to pay these prices, however, then there is an economic limit to the amount of energy that can be produced.

5. Price controls are particularly dangerous in energy markets because price ceilings not only hold down prices, but they delay production of energy from

new sources. Low prices, as well, reduce any incentive for conservation.

6. Which is more important: energy or the environment? This is a societal choice that must be made eventually. As the amount of energy used increases, this trade-off will become more important as the opportunity cost of energy increases.

DISCUSSION QUESTIONS

1. One source of oil noted in this chapter is imported oil. Suppose that, for national security reasons, Congress drastically limits the amount of oil that can be imported. How will this affect market supply and price? Will this encourage the development of new energy sources? Explain.

2. The government can keep energy prices low to consumers and still encourage the development of new energy sources by providing price subsidies so that, in effect, the government pays part of the cost of energy for consumers. Evaluate this policy.

3. Under what conditions will energy prices fall? Are these conditions likely? What effect will falling energy prices have on the economy? On firms? On consumers?

4. Is energy necessary to economic growth? Can the economy grow without expanding energy supplies? Defend your answer.

5. What is the energy crisis? Is crisis the right term for this?

TEST YOURSELF

Indicate whether each of the following statements is *true* or *false*. Be able to defend your response.

1. We will eventually use up the last barrel of oil in the world.

2. Rising energy prices reduce energy demand.

3. Use of energy substitutes can decrease the demand for energy.

4. No nuclear power will be generated until all oil–coal possibilities have been exhausted.

5. If better ways are found to produce energy from its sources, more energy can be produced using fewer resources.

6. Energy limits depend on the price of energy.

7. Price controls in energy markets increase the supply of energy.

8. Price controls in energy markets induce research to discover new energy sources.

9. Economic development uses energy to increase the gains from trade and specialization.

10. There is no energy crisis.

Part 4
Market Failures

13
Free Market choice

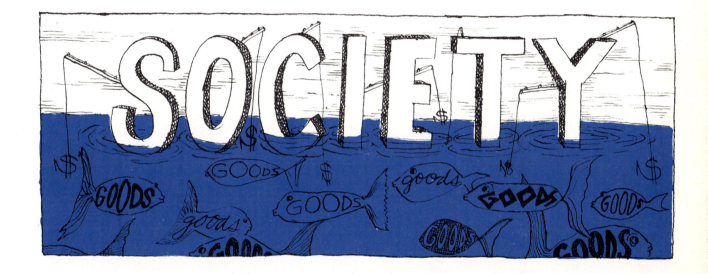

How do we choose? How does society decide which goods to produce and in what quantities? Several choice mechanisms exist. This chapter presents the case for the free market as a way for society to choose, and compares it to other ways of making economic choices. Questions answered include the following:

Why is the free market a desirable form of economic organization?
What advantages does the free market have over other ways of making choices?
What problems occur when choices are made with votes instead of dollars?

Scarcity and choice are economic facts of life. But how is the choice to be made? How are needs, preferences, and priorities expressed and communicated from consumer to producer and back again? Answering these questions is one of the fundamental concerns of economics.

What are the options? How can society make choices that affect income, welfare, and resource use? Three general methods of choice exist.

Free market choice is the practice of letting consumers and producers vote with dollars for the goods and services that they desire. Voting with dollars increases the value of goods that people want or need (providing an incentive to produce these goods) and reduces the value of undesirable items. Free market choice is a decentralized way of making societal choices. Individual buyers and sellers, each acting out of self-interest, make the choices that, in the aggregate, affect society.

A second way of making societal choices is **bureaucratic choice**. The government attempts to ascertain what is best for consumers and producers and then carries out the necessary production and distribution plans. **Command economies**, such as that of the Soviet Union, rely on bureaucratic choice to a greater extent than most Western nations.

Democratic choice involves individuals casting ballots, directly or indirectly, for their choices. The government, as a substitute for the free market, then implements the choices that are made at the polls.

Each of these choice mechanisms is useful and, in most nations, each is used to make at least some decisions. This chapter explores the subject of choice and focuses on the advantages of the free market as a way of making choices. The case for the free market is strong, but not perfect. The next three chapters look, in greater depth, at the conditions that lead to failure of free market choice and the need for other kinds of decision-making processes.

Free market choice: a decentralized method of making economic choices that relies on market mechanisms

Bureaucratic choice: a method of making economic choices that relies on central planning

Command economy: economic system where decisions affecting resource use are made by central planners

Democratic choice: a method of making economic choices that relies on the voting process

THE FREE MARKET ECONOMY

Free market economy: an economy where markets are allowed to work without government intervention

Many economists, including Nobel prize winners like Friedrich Von Hayek and Milton Friedman, think that a **free market economy** can be the solution to many of our most pressing social problems. If markets are allowed to function without government interference, they suggest, many of our important social and economic problems, such as unemployment, education, and energy, could be solved or the magnitude of these problems reduced. It is the lack of free markets, they submit, that makes these problems as big as they are. We have already seen some evidence of this in previous chapters. Minimum wages (and, indeed, most price controls) seem to have undesirable side effects, often creating more problems than they solve. Energy price controls can make the energy crisis worse, as we saw in the preceding chapter, by replacing rising prices with physical shortages.

There are several reasons why freely functioning markets are good things. First of all, free markets are just that—free. There is no coercion or force (such as the force that price controls use). The free market maximizes the number of voluntary exchanges. Whenever a control is imposed, it causes one side of an exchange or the other to lose. Because of controls, some previously beneficial exchanges are ruled out. With minimum wage laws, for example, no worker can offer to work for less than the legal minimum. The law rules out this voluntary exchange of labor for wages. In this case, possibly both sides of the market (employers and employees) lose.

THE INVISIBLE HAND

Adam Smith noted the exquisite paradox of the free market in 1776 in his *Wealth of Nations*. The market, he noted, is made up of individuals who are all motivated by self-gain. Buyers and sellers each gain by exchange, but each pushes for the lion's share of the gains. Somehow, however, the individual motives are transformed, through the forces of competition and conflict, into desirable social goals. As Smith put it:

Every individual . . . neither intends to promote the public interest nor knows how much he is promoting it . . . he intends only his own gain, and he is in this, as in many other cases, led by an invisible hand to promote an end which was no part of his attention.

Smith's "invisible hand" guides economic activity with a force that belies its invisibility. The power is the power of competition and conflict to mold private economic behavior and shape it in new ways. But what are the desirable social goals that the market makes possible?

The most important benefit of the market is **economic efficiency**. Production takes place, through free markets, in the most efficient way. Goods and services are produced at the least cost in terms of resources, goods, and services given up. The free market, in short, minimizes the opportunity costs of economic activity. To see that this is the case, we need only look at how the two sides of the market make economic decisions.

> Economic efficiency: production that takes place in the most efficient way—at lowest opportunity cost

Consumers make decisions on the basis of opportunity costs. If the price of pizza is too high (above the market equilibrium), the resulting surplus is a signal to producers and the economy that consumers consider the trade-off too great. The opportunity cost of buying a pizza is not worth the cost of producing a pizza. The market responds to this disequilibrium in two ways. First, a market surplus drives down price, reducing the opportunity cost of the good in question. Second, as price falls, sellers produce fewer pizzas and more of other, more desirable goods. In essence, the pizzas that came at an undesirably high opportunity cost are no longer produced.

Likewise, producers weigh opportunity costs when making production decisions. The quantities that they produce at any given price and the types of inputs and resources that are used, are all based on a clear calculation of opportunity cost. If hiring one more worker means giving up one machine, this opportunity cost will make itself felt in the producer decision and will, in the end, be reflected in market supplies, demands, prices, and quantities in all the markets involved.

Consumers maximize utility and producers maximize profits by minimizing the opportunity cost of their decisions. By making the best decisions, they give up the minimum of other goods and nothing can be gained by reorganizing consumption or production. The beauty of the market—and the reason for the ghostly nature of Adam Smith's invisible hand—is that this economic efficiency, this ability to minimize opportunity cost, comes automatically when perfect markets are allowed to operate freely.

BUREAUCRATIC CHOICE

Compare the wonder of Adam Smith's invisible hand with the very visible hand of bureaucratic choice. When centralized economic decision-making is used it can be very effective in accomplishing some ends. Economic growth in the Soviet Union, for example, has been very rapid. In part this is because planners were able to divert resources from the production of consumer goods to the production of industrial items like steel, heavy trucks, and so on.

But centralized decision-making is costly and inefficient. Consider for a moment the informational costs involved. In order to make any decision we need information about benefits and opportunity costs. In a market economy how do we get this information? Information about benefits comes from our reading (as consumers) of our individual preferences. No one can judge our preferences better than we can. Information about opportunity costs comes from prices. Prices tell us what we and (in a perfectly functioning economy) society must forego when a choice is made.

How do we collect such information in an economy that uses bureaucratic choice? Preferences, if not expressed in the marketplace, are hard to gauge. The preferences of planners and government and religious leaders may be substituted. Opportunity costs are difficult to estimate because, in the absence of a market economy, prices have little economic meaning. If planners set the prices then these prices represent the opportunity cost that the planners wish to advertise to consumers and producers—not necessarily the opportunity costs that society actually bears. The sophisticated use of mathematics and computer science by economists and planners can make bureaucratic choices more accurate, but at a tremendous dollar cost given the gains possible.

Bureaucratic choice is a costly and inefficient way to make economic decisions. Can it beat Adam Smith's invisible hand to the draw? From the standpoint of individual producers and consumers, the answer is no. Its principal advantage must be that it can divert resources, when authorities see the need, *away from* the choices that individuals would make. Central preferences can replace individual preferences in making resource allocation decisions.

SELF-INTEREST AND THE INVISIBLE HAND

In the end, the key to the wonder of the market choice, unlike bureaucratic choice, is that it relies on the motivation of self-interest. Each economic actor is attempting to make himself or herself as well off as possible. There is no abstract plan to follow nor planner-set goals to meet. When we each act in our own self-interest, we act, together, to produce the goods and services that we want efficiently and at the lowest possible opportunity cost.

Adam Smith's invisible hand, by relying on the motivation of self-interest, is a powerful mover indeed! We can explicitly analyze the benefits of the market's invisible hand—and see some of the ways that outside forces distort the hand's movements—by taking a look at the meaning of the market in a new light.

THE ECONOMIC PROPERTIES OF DEMAND

We have already discussed many properties of demand curves—how they shift, what they mean—but now let's ask a more basic question. In Figure 1, the demand curve shows that the quantity of guitars demanded in a particular market declines as price rises. At a price of $245 per guitar, a total of 101 guitars are purchased. At a little higher price, however, the demand is less. If the price is $248, only 100 guitars are purchased. And at a price of $250, the quantity demanded falls to just 99 guitars.

Why does this happen? If people are willing to buy 101 guitars at $245, why should they be willing to buy only 100 at $248? The difference in price isn't all that much. Why the change in buying behavior? It's possible to get very technical here. But in simple terms, why is the last customer willing to buy a guitar at $245, but not at $248? The answer to this question must be that the last customer thinks that, at a price of $245, the guitar is worth it (it

FIGURE 13-1: THE DEMAND CURVE FOR
GUITARS
*The demand curve shows the number
of guitars that will be bought at each
price. Why the different quantities?
Guitars supply different amounts of
benefits to different users. Each buyer
will weigh the marginal benefits
against the cost of the instrument. This
results in purchases for some and
nonpurchases for others at different
prices.*

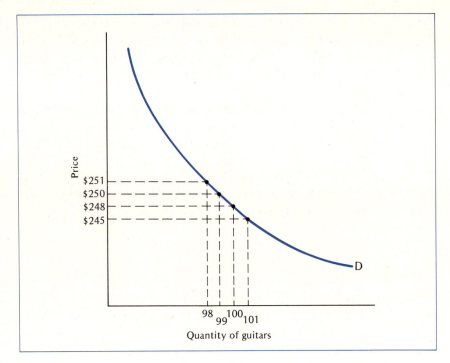

provides at least $245 worth of benefits). It is not, however, worth $248.
The same idea applies to the hundredth guitar (and all others, too).

The idea here is pretty simple. Consumers, through a marginal utility
process, compare the costs of each item, the benefits that the item provides
(utility), and the benefits that other items make available. A person will
spend $1 on an item only if it provides at least $1 worth of benefits.
Otherwise, the money is better spent on something that does provide $1
worth of benefits for each dollar spent.

Marginal benefit: the amount of additional
benefits derived from the purchase of an additional item

Using this idea we can think of the demand curve as a **marginal benefit**
curve. Here we measure benefits by dollars (with opportunity cost already
taken into account) instead of utility points. By showing how much an
individual is willing to pay for the last guitar, the demand curve gives a
measure of the worth or marginal benefit that that guitar provides. Since
each point on the demand curve shows the maximum amount that someone
in the market is willing to pay for the item demanded, each point on the
curve represents the marginal benefit that the last unit produces.

This marginal benefit idea helps explain why the demand curve is shaped
the way it is. To some people, a guitar provides extremely high benefit.

These folks, therefore, are willing to pay quite a lot of money for a guitar. These people inhabit the top part of the demand curve. They will buy for less if they can, but they will pay a very high price if they must—and that high price makes sense for them because they get very high benefits from the item that they purchase.

Other people receive very low benefits from a guitar. Because the guitar adds few benefits for them and opportunity costs are high, they are willing to purchase one only at a very low price. No one would pay $200 for a guitar that is likely to provide just $100 worth of benefits.

Think of your own demands in this light. Do you own a guitar? A diamond wristwatch? A houseplant? A dictionary? If you do, then it must be because, at the going price, the item provides at least as many benefits as costs (compared to other things).

TOTAL BENEFITS AND CONSUMERS' SURPLUS

The demand curve can be used to tell us something about the marginal benefits that an item produces—the demand curve can be viewed, in fact, as a marginal benefit curve for the reasons described above. We can also use the demand curve to tell us something about the total benefits that consumption of an item produces. This is illustrated in Figure 2.

Let us use the areas of different rectangles to estimate the benefits that items yield. In Figure 2, for example, we note that, if only one guitar is produced, someone will be willing to pay $500 for it. This first customer, therefore, must derive $500 of marginal benefits from this one guitar. Let's construct a rectangle 1 unit wide and $500 tall in the picture. The area of this rectangle is $1 \times \$500 = \$500$. This is how much the first guitar adds to total benefits.

Now let's do the same thing with the second guitar. We see that someone is willing to pay $495 for the second guitar produced. That means that this guitar must provide $495 worth of benefits. So, construct a rectangle 1 unit wide and $495 tall. The area of this rectangle represents the marginal benefits that the second guitar provides. Continue this rectangle-making with the third, fourth, and succeeding guitars. The third guitar will sell at $494, and so its marginal benefit can be represented by a rectangle of dimensions $1 \text{ unit} \times \$494 = \$494$ area.

Using this process we can represent the total benefits that a given quantity of guitars produces, by the area under the demand curve at that quantity. Figure 2 shows the total benefits produced by 99 guitars as the area under the demand curve up to 99 units. This is the sum of the benefits (area of rectangles) of the first guitar plus that of the second, third, fourth, and so on.

FIGURE 13-2: MARGINAL AND TOTAL BENEFITS FROM GUITARS
If the price that people are willing to pay for an item is the measure of the benefits that they receive from it, then the demand curve is also an indication of marginal benefits. The area under the demand curve shows the total benefits from each unit purchased.

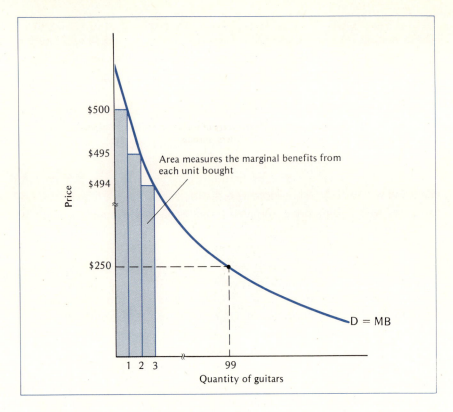

This measure of total benefits is useful, but it depends on the distribution of income and wealth that prevails in the economy. The poor may get high benefits from certain items but, because of their meager incomes, may be unable to participate in the market choice process. Their low income in effect robs them of their vote in the market. To the extent that their benefits don't show up in demand, then, this measure of total benefits underestimates the potential benefits of some goods.

By calculating consumer benefits in this way, we can see one more important property of demand in free markets. Suppose that the market price for guitars is $250. At this price, 99 guitars will be sold. Using marginal benefit theory, the purchaser of the ninety-ninth guitar buys it because the $250 guitar provides at least $250 worth of benefits. But notice who benefits the most from this sale. In order to sell 99 guitars, the price on all 98 previous guitars (assuming no price discrimination) must also fall to $250. The very first customer who is willing to pay up to $500 for one of these guitars is now able to buy one for just $250. That person, and the 97 other buyers who were willing to pay more than $250 for a guitar, get a

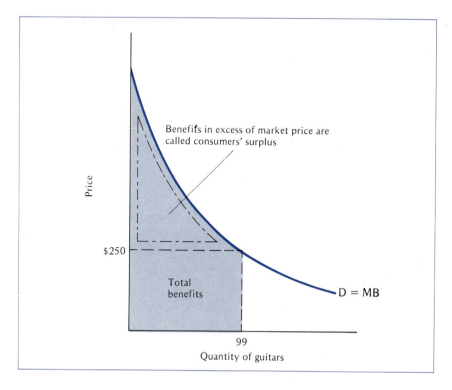

FIGURE 13-3: **TOTAL BENEFITS AND CONSUMERS' SURPLUS**
The area under the demand curve measures the total benefits received from some level of production. If the market price is $250, then 99 guitars will be purchased, giving total benefits equal to the shaded area above. Consumers' surplus is measured by the triangular area.

tremendous benefit from the market. They are able to buy an item that provides more than $250 worth of benefits for just $250. These extra benefits that they receive—benefits over and above the price that they pay for the item—are called **consumers' surplus**. As Figure 3 shows, many of the total benefits in any market take the form of such consumers' surplus— benefits that the consumers receive when they are able to pay less for an item than they are willing to pay.

Consumer surplus: the difference between the maximum price that a consumer is willing to pay for an item and the actual price that is paid

The other side of any market is supply—the sellers who make it their business to produce and sell goods at a profit. We have already spent a good deal of time exploring the methods that the suppliers use to maximize profits. For firms in competitive markets, profit maximization means producing at the output level where market price just equals the marginal cost of production (we assume here that the firm bears *all* costs of production). The last unit sold costs as much to make as is paid for it in the market.

In competitive markets, where this behavior prevails, we can tell how

THE ECONOMIC PROPERTIES OF SUPPLY

much an individual firm or an entire industry produces by looking at the marginal cost curve for that firm or industry. At any given price, the marginal cost curve shows the profit-maximizing amount of total output.

The supply curve for a competitive market is the same as the marginal cost curve for that market. This is shown in Figure 4. Why are the firms willing to sell 101 guitars at $257, but only 100 at $253? Production of the hundredth guitar adds $253 (marginal cost) to total cost. To sell it at $253 is good for the firm (since normal profit is included in costs)—to sell it for more than $253 is even better. But, under no circumstances will the firm sell it for *less* than $253. The ninety-ninth guitar will be sold only if the price that it receives is greater than or equal to marginal cost.

If the supply curve represents the marginal costs of production, then we can compute the total costs by looking at the area under the supply curve up to a particular quantity (actually, since MC measures variable cost only, the areas measure total variable costs and ignore fixed costs, but this doesn't matter for our purposes).

The first unit produced in this example has a relatively low marginal cost

FIGURE 13-4: THE SUPPLY CURVE AS A MARGINAL COST CURVE
Supply curves in competitive markets reflect the marginal costs of production.

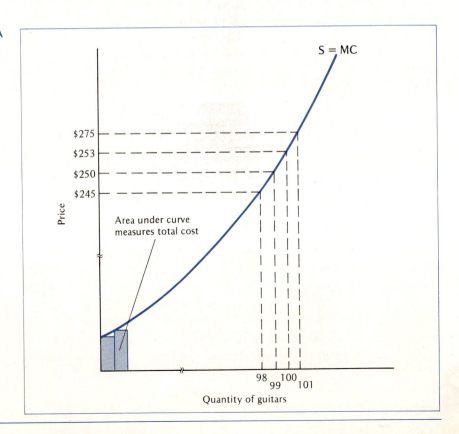

and so we show this marginal cost by the area under the supply curve for this quantity of production. When we continue to do this, we get a representation of total cost like that shown in Figure 5.

This picture, besides showing marginal and total costs, gives us a clue to why production is profitable even when price equals marginal costs. Suppose that 99 guitars are sold at a price of $250 each. Note that the last guitar sells for its marginal cost. But what about the first 98 guitars? As the figure indicates, each of these sells for $250 market price, but has a marginal cost of less than $250. On each of these items, the firm earns an operating profit—marginal revenue exceeds marginal cost.

This difference between total cost (the area under the supply or marginal cost curve) and total revenue (99 guitars × $250 each) is equal to what economists call **producers' surplus**. Producers' surplus is the amount that firms receive for their output over and above marginal cost. Since firms are willing to sell their goods for marginal cost, the producers' surplus represents the amount that they receive over and above the price at which they are willing to sell. This surplus is not all equal to profit—fixed costs

Producers' surplus: the difference between the price of an item and the minimum price at which the producer is willing to sell (marginal cost)

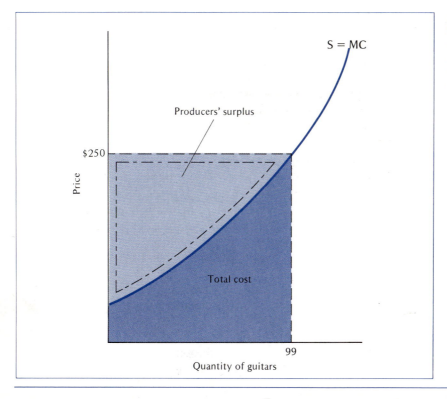

FIGURE 13-5: TOTAL COST AND PRODUCERS' SURPLUS
If the market price is $250, then 99 guitars will be produced and total cost will equal the shaded area. Producers' surplus will be equal to the triangular area.

must still be paid. Producers' surplus is, instead, the difference between minimum selling price (marginal cost) and the actual price received for an individual item.

MARKET EQUILIBRIUM: NET BENEFITS

Market equilibrium occurs when the quantity demanded at a given price equals the quantity supplied at that price. In Figure 6, for example, the market equilibrium for guitars occurs when the price is $250 and the quantities demanded and supplied are 99. We can discover this by inspection. Market equilibrium represents the limit to mutually beneficial exchange between buyers and sellers in this market. Given the costs and benefits apparent here, no more than 99 guitars can be voluntarily traded. This is one benefit of the free market equilibrium noted earlier, but there is another. From the point of view of society, the market equilibrium represents the best possible use of resources.

What is the goal of economic activity? One answer (the answer on which this discussion is built) is that economic activity is designed to produce societal **net benefits**. Net benefits are the benefits that society receives from the goods and services that are produced, over and above the resource costs of producing those goods. Net benefits are equal to the difference between the total benefits that production of an item makes possible and the total costs of producing those goods. When net benefits are positive, it means that we get more out of the resources than we put in.

Net benefits: the difference between marginal benefits and marginal cost or total benefits and total cost

FIGURE 13-6:   THE FREE MARKET MAXIMIZES NET BENEFITS
Net benefits are equal to the difference between total benefits and total costs. Graphically, then, net benefits are equal to the area between the supply and demand curve (the sum of consumers' and producers' surpluses).

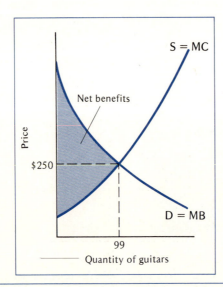

As can be seen in Figure 6, the market equilibrium has the property of maximizing societal net benefits. Net benefits can be found in this figure by subtracting the area under the supply curve (which represents total costs) from the area under the demand curve (which measures total benefits). The remaining area—the shaded triangular area in the figure—measures the net benefits that society receives from the free market exchange of guitars.

Note that, at the free market equilibrium shown here, every unit of production produces positive net benefits to society—for each guitar produced, marginal benefits exceed marginal costs. At the equilibrium, the total of these net benefits is as large as it can be (you may have already noted that net benefits are equal to the sum of consumers' and producers' surplus).

Government taxes, because they upset the market equilibrium, have the effect of destroying net benefits. This idea is illustrated in Figure 7.

Before the tax, this market was in equilibrium at a quantity supplied and demanded of Q_1. Since this is the free market equilibrium, net benefits are as great as they can be given the costs and benefits shown here. Now, suppose that the government imposes an excise tax on the output in this market. The tax, as we learned in previous chapters, shifts the supply curve back and to the left. Because suppliers must pay the tax, they increase their supply price and reduce the quantity that they produce. The new market

TAXES AND NET BENEFITS

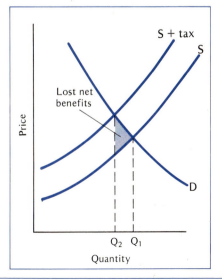

FIGURE 13-7: TAXES AND NET BENEFITS
Taxes raise prices and discourage production. In so doing, they reduce the net benefits available from production. Because the lower quantity Q_2 is produced, net benefits equal to the shaded area are lost.

equilibrium will be established at a higher market price and a lower quantity Q_2.

What has happened to net benefits here? Note that the imposition of the tax has *not* altered the marginal costs of producing this item. It takes exactly the same resources to make these goods with the tax as without it. Total and marginal costs of production have not changed (marginal benefits are the same, too). All that has happened is that the government is now collecting a fee whenever this item is sold.

Because costs and benefits are still the same, quantity Q_1 still acts to maximize societal net benefits. But, because the equilibrium quantity has been lowered to Q_2, this maximum is no longer attainable. Society loses the net benefits shown by the shaded triangle in Figure 7.

Taxes reduce societal welfare because they lower the amounts of goods and services that people purchase. Some items are left unsold not because they do not produce positive net benefits, but rather, because the tax price is too high. These goods are worth their cost, but not worth their tax-inflated price.

GOVERNMENT SUBSIDIES

Subsidies are something like negative taxes. When government subsidies are part of an expenditure, they pay part of the price. College students should be familiar with the idea of a subsidy because the price of college—tuition—is normally a subsidized item. When you pay $1000 in tuition, federal, state, and local governments add to your payment. You end up paying only part of the actual price of the education that you are buying.

Subsidies are relatively common in the economy. All government grants are subsidies of one sort or another. The food stamp program is a good example of a subsidy. When a consumer spends a certain amount on food, the government also pitches in to pay the price.

Subsidies distort the market and result in a greater amount of total production than would be the case without them. This is shown in Figure 8. When the government subsidizes the purchase of an item, the demand of that good rises, causing the demand curve to shift up and to the right. Since consumers are paying only a portion of the price, they demand a larger quantity at every price. The vertical distance between the new and old demand curves in this figure represents the size of the subsidy.

Even though the subsidy increases the amount of a good that we can purchase, it does not alter the marginal benefits that we receive from goods. As a result, subsidies can cause overproduction of the goods and services involved.

Without the subsidy, the market equilibrium would be established at a

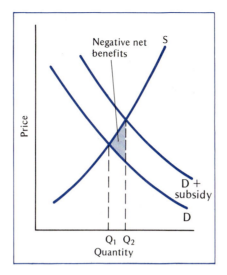

FIGURE 13-8: SUBSIDIES AND NET BENEFITS
A subsidy is a government payment. Because the government pays as well as the consumer, more of this item is purchased. Consumers are happy, but society suffers. The additional items have marginal costs that exceed marginal benefits and negative net benefits are created.

quantity Q_1 of output. This quantity maximizes net benefits, given marginal costs and marginal benefits as represented by the demand and supply curves. The subsidy makes it possible for consumers to purchase a larger quantity of output, but it does not alter a basic fact about these additional purchases: Each unit above the quantity Q_1 has a higher cost to society than the additional benefits that it provides. Consumers will buy these goods because they can afford to. But each one costs society more than society benefits. Negative net benefits result from the production of these goods. Society would be better off, from a cost–benefit point of view, if the goods had never been produced.

DEMOCRATIC CHOICE

So far we have looked at free market choice, where individual preferences move the invisible hand, and bureaucratic choice, where individual preferences may not be expressed at all. Democratic choice is a way of making societal decisions that fall somewhere in-between.

Democratic choice is less centralized than the bureaucratic alternative. Individuals get to vote to express their preferences. They vote at the ballot box, however, and not in the market. Under a system of bureaucratic choice, the central authorities essentially determine choices for all. Under a system of free market choice, each person chooses individually. When democratic choice mechanisms are used, all are allowed to vote, but majority rule prevails. Whereas, under a free market system, I can vote for symphony and you can vote for hard rock (and we *both* get only what we pay for), under a system of democratic choice, we both get what the majority has picked, and we both pay for it, too.

Politics these days has acquired a bad name and anything political is often viewed as corrupt or suspect. But politics is the process whereby individual preferences are assembled to form democratic choices that reflect those preferences. This process is sometimes easy to see (as in a New England town meeting where every citizen can directly express his or her preferences through speech and vote) and sometimes the link between individual choice and government action seems remote indeed (as when Congress acts).

To the extent that the political process is successful in formulating public policies that reflect individual preferences, this process is a necessary and desirable one. Many of the undesirable antics that are written off as playing politics are usually just attempts by individuals to express their preferences in the most effective way or by elected officials to respond to what they perceive as the public's utility function.

The analysis of democratic choice is complicated because voters infrequently consider directly the costs and benefits of government actions. More often, it is their elected representatives who make these decisions. Suppose, for example, that before the legislature is a special bill that will reduce property taxes for a small, specific group (say, for example, taxes on golf courses). This change will benefit a few people a great deal (those who run and use golf courses) but will make many more people a little worse off—all other taxpayers will find their property tax bills marginally higher as the tax is shifted from golf courses onto the remaining taxable property. If this law change is put before the public, it may be soundly defeated as the large number of losers will easily outvote the small number of gainers.

But suppose that, instead, the bill is considered by the legislature. Your local representative honestly desires to vote according to his or her constituents' preferences. But which constituents make their feelings known? Because their separate losses are so small, it doesn't pay any individual taxpayer to spend much time or money fighting the bill. For individual taxpayers, the costs of contacting their representative exceed any gains that might accrue. This is not the case for the golf course owners, however. Since they stand to gain or lose substantially, depending on how the vote goes, it does pay for them to spend time and money making their preferences known. The result is that the high gain that this bill will make possible for a few may outweigh the smaller individual loss (which could be large in the aggregate) of a larger number of nongolfing taxpayers.

The political process attempts to reflect the preferences of the population, but often ends up making decisions and judgments that do not accurately reflect those preferences. The problem is that each individual voter attempts to influence the legislative process based on the costs and benefits of so doing. If a few will gain substantially by new policies while many will lose only a little, chances are the desires of the majority will not show up in public policy consistently.

Even when the public votes directly for governmental policies, it may be difficult to figure out what it wants. There are many reasons for this: Not everyone votes, many issues are considered at once, imagery is often as important as substance. But the problems go deeper. One difficulty is that voters must choose between relatively simple options. The choice in the voting booth is not, What kind of educational system do you want? Instead, it is Do you want this system or not? or, at best, Do you want Plan I or Plan II? The mechanics of voting make reading the public's preferences difficult.

Suppose, for example, that a relatively simple choice must be made. There are three different kinds of educational packages before the voters (labeled Plan I, Plan II, and Plan III) to be voted on by just three voters (A, B, and C) as shown in Figure 9.

Voter A prefers Plan I to Plan II (and so will vote for I over II), prefers Plan II to Plan III (and will so vote), and prefers I to III. Voter B has different preferences, and so will vote for II over either I or III and III over I. Finally, voter C's preferences are different again, as this person prefers, in order, Plans III, I, and II.

Which of the plans does the public most desire? To find out, let's have the three voters consider the plans in pairs. Suppose that, in the primary

VOTING: WHAT DOES THE PUBLIC WANT?

	Plan I	Plan II	Plan III
Voter A	1	2	3
Voter B	3	1	2
Voter C	2	3	1

FIGURE 13-9: VOTER PREFERENCES
Voters here must choose among three governmental programs. Their preferences for each package are shown here ranging from 1 (most preferred) to 3 (least preferred). Which program does the public want?

election, we pit Plan I against Plan II. What is the result? Looking at the figure, Voter A votes for I, B chooses II, while C casts a ballot for I. Plan I wins. Now, in the finals, Plan I is pitted against Plan III. How are the votes cast this time? Voter A prefers Plan I to III and so votes for I. Voter B has the opposite preferences and casts a ballot for III. Voter C is the tie-breaker and votes for Plan III, making it the winner. The correct public policy, according to this voting scheme, is Plan III . . . or is it?

Suppose that we change the order of voting. Let's pit I and III in the primary election, with the winner facing II in the finals. Will the public choice be any different? Yes, indeed!

If Plan I and Plan III are considered at the same time, as we have just seen, Plan III is the winner. Plan III gains voter approval in the primary election. But what happens when it faces Plan II in the finals? Looking at Figure 9, we see that Voter A votes for II, Voter B chooses II as well, and Voter C casts a ballot for III. Plan II wins here on a two-to-one vote. So Plan II is the public's choice. Or not?

Finally, if we run Plans II and III in the primary with the winner facing I in the finals, the result will be (check this out) that Plan I is adopted.

This leaves us more than a little confused. Depending on the order in which they are considered, the voting process can result in Plan I, Plan II, or Plan III by majority vote (this may suggest why voting in primary elections is so important). Which is the public choice? It's not surprising that politicians are sometimes confused in reading public preferences.

THE ROLE OF GOVERNMENT: MARKET FAILURES

Comparing the three ways of making societal decisions, the case for the free market appears particularly strong. Why, then, is democratic choice used so frequently in even market-oriented economies? And why is the government, which has been seen here as a destroyer of net benefits, involved in so many areas of economic life?

The answer to these questions lies in the assumptions that were used in describing the free market. We have been describing perfectly competitive markets where demand accurately reflects the benefits that society really gets from goods, and supply is a true measure of society's marginal costs. But these perfectly competitive markets are rare. The economy is characterized, instead, by market imperfections. When competition is not perfect, a rationale exists for governmental intervention and the use of a mechanism other than free market choice to make decisions. The next three chapters take an in-depth look at these market failures.

SCALPERS GET BIG BUCKS FOR SUPER BOWL TICKETS

MIAMI—How much does a ticket to this Sunday's Super Bowl football game cost? It depends on whom you ask. The price on the ticket says $30, but the man in the trenchcoat is asking $200 for a pair. What goes on here?

The problem is one that plagues many sporting events, but is particularly noticeable at postseason football games like the Super Bowl (a game that matches the champions of pro football's American and National conferences), which is played here this week. The number of tickets available is set by the size of the stadium. And the price of the tickets is set by the NFL in an attempt to keep the game affordable to a wide range of fans. It's a good try, but to look at the prices that scalpers are getting, not one that is completely successful.

There were 75,000 tickets printed for this Sunday's game, and each sold initially for $30. These tickets were bought on a first-come, first-served basis. All 75,000 were quickly sold. Now, the only way to get a seat to the big game is to purchase one from a scalper—someone who buys tickets to events like this in order to resell them at a profit.

Scalping is illegal in this state, but that doesn't stop it from happening. Ads, carefully written to avoid identification, even appear in local papers.

The going price this year seems to be about $100 per ticket, sold in pairs. This amounts to a $70 per ticket profit.

"It's simply a matter of supply and demand," one scalper, who refused to be identified, commented. "People are willing to pay $100 each—some will pay more. So I'm really doing them a service. If it wasn't for us scalpers, some of these folks from out of town would have to watch the game on television."

The scalper denied that there was anything immoral in making such a large profit by reselling a ticket. "I'm a businessman like anyone else," he commented. "Sometimes you win, sometimes you don't. I lost a bundle on the 1979 Cotton Bowl game, for example. I bought a hundred tickets and then the weather turned bad. With freezing rain on the game day, I couldn't give the tickets away. I had to watch the game myself."

Scalping tickets may have its risks, but the Super Bowl looks like a sure thing this year and scalpers are surely making the most of it.

ECONOMIC ANALYSIS

Scalping is an example of a black market activity. Tickets are bought and resold at prices above the legal price. Figure 10 helps us understand why scalping takes place.

When there are only a fixed number of seats available to an event like this, and the price is arbitrarily set, as it has been by the NFL, then all kinds of economic problems are created. At a price of $30 per seat,

REAL WORLD ECONOMICS: TICKET SCALPING

FIGURE 13-10: THE SUPER BOWL TICKET PROBLEM
Super Bowl tickets are sold at a fixed price to the first 75,000 buyers. This creates a problem. Everyone who derives $30 or more in benefits from the tickets will wish to buy one—there may be 200,000 demanders! Only 75,000 tickets are available. The scalper serves a useful function by reselling.

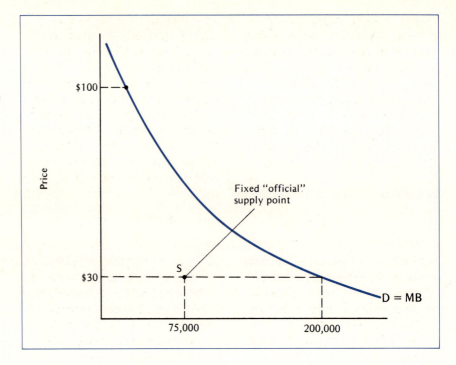

people will buy the tickets so long as they feel they will receive at least $30 in benefits from attending the game. As the figure shows, perhaps as many as 200,000 will be willing to buy the tickets at that price because the benefits of attending the Super Bowl are possibly very great.

A problem arises because the quantity of these seats is limited to 75,000 and the seats are not sold to the highest bidder but rather distributed in some more-or-less random fashion. This creates a problem because some people who get just $30 worth of benefits from the tickets will have them, while some people who would get $200 worth of benefits from the seat do not. This is the kind of

situation that leads to black market activities.

Suppose that you buy a Super Bowl ticket for $30 because you figure to get $45 worth of benefits. Your roommate, who likes football better, will get $200 worth of benefits from going and is therefore willing to pay you $200 for a ticket. Will you take the deal? Will you become a scalper? So long as there is a difference between the benefits you receive and the benefits that your roommate gets, there is a chance here for a mutually advantageous trade—but above the legal price of the tickets. This is the motivation of the black market.

The scalper in this story is correct when he says that he is doing a service to his buyers. The fact that they are willing to pay his high price for these seats indicates that they get more benefits from watching the game than he does. While he is earning producers' surplus, his customers are gaining customers' surplus, since they may be actually paying less for the tickets than their maximum buying price. Both sides of this exchange gain.

The scalper is also correct when he notes that this is a risky business. By buying tickets ahead of time, the scalper can take advantage of the fact that the true equilibrium price may be well above the market price of the tickets. In this case, scalpers win. But it is also possible for the tickets to be overpriced at $30. In this case, the scalper will get less than he paid for the tickets and learn a hard lesson in economics.

SUMMARY

1. Economic choices can be made in several different ways. Free market choice allows individuals to make their own choices. The invisible hand guides individual actions to pursue social goals.

2. The free market maximizes the sum of consumer and producer surplus. Consumer surplus is the benefit that buyers receive in excess of the price they pay. Producer surplus is the payment that sellers get in excess of marginal costs. In perfectly competitive markets, these net benefits are maximized.

3. Bureaucratic choice is another option. Bureaucratic choice is costly since the information that the market automatically produces about preferences and opportunity costs must instead be scientifically calculated. Bureaucratic choice is probably most useful when central authorities wish to impose preferences, not reflect them.

4. Democratic choice is another way to make collective decisions. Voting, however, is a complex process and there is no guarantee that the democratic process accurately reflects individual preferences.

5. Free market choice is desirable when perfect competition prevails. Where perfect competition does not exist, however, governmental actions may be desirable.

DISCUSSION QUESTIONS

1. Suppose that a market is perfectly competitive. What impact does a price ceiling have on the net benefits that it makes possible? A price floor?

2. Taxes destroy net benefits. Why, then, does the government impose taxes on many items? What possible reason can the government have?

284   FREE MARKET CHOICE

Where do the tax dollars go?

3. Under what conditions can markets change so that both consumer and producer surplus increase? Does this ever happen? Explain.

4. Is there any real difference between democratic choice and free market choice? After all, both allow consumers and producers to express their preferences. When would the same choice result under these two ways of making decisions? When would they be different?

5. The democratic choice mechanism has resulted in minimum wage legislation. Would the free market choice mechanism have brought about the same result? Why or why not?

TEST YOURSELF

Indicate whether each of the following statements is *true* or *false*. Be able to defend your choice.

1. Free market choice is a way of making decisions that allows individuals to vote with their dollars for the goods they want.

2. Individuals also vote with dollars when bureaucratic choice is used.

3. A command economy is an economic system where bureaucratic choice is the principal economic choice mechanism.

4. Western economies like the United States use all three choice mechanisms to some extent.

5. Consumer surplus is the difference between marginal benefit and price.

6. Producers' surplus is the difference between marginal benefit and marginal cost.

7. Net benefits are equal to the sum of producers' plus consumers' surplus.

8. Subsidies lower the price that people pay for a product and so encourage them to purchase more of it.

9. A price floor results in too much production and negative net benefits.

10. Majority-rule voting is an accurate way to determine public preference.

14
Market Failures: Externalities

Free market choice is not always the best way to allocate resources. Sometimes the market breaks down and the government must step in to improve the results of market actions. This chapter examines the market failure caused by externalities. Questions answered include the following:

What is an externality? What is the difference between an external benefit and an external cost?

Why does the market fail when externalities are present?

What is the appropriate government action when faced with externalities?

What is a public good and why does the government often act to produce public goods itself?

Externality: an externality is produced when all the costs or benefits of an economic decision do not accrue to the party making the decision

An **externality** is created when there is a breakdown in the structure of private property rights. The prevailing scheme of private property holds that, when I purchase (or rent) a good or service, I pay all the costs associated with the provision of that item and, in return, I have the legal right to receipt of all the benefits produced. Property rights are designed to create a closed system wherein the purchase decision (which is a weighing of costs and benefits) takes into account *all* the costs and benefits involved.

When a person or firm makes an economic decision, we have been assuming that all the costs and benefits of that decision are borne by the decision-maker. When you purchase a hamburger, for example, this action does not normally inflict any costs on your neighbors, nor provide any benefits to them. You pay for the hamburger, bear the cost of producing it, and receive the benefits of its production. For most goods, this system of property rights works well and many economic decisions have little effect on third parties.

However, it may be more often the case that decisions by one party *do* impose costs or benefits on others. Suppose, for example, that you decide to cook your hamburgers on a smoky outdoor grill. Your neighbor receives benefits from the delicious smell of your cooking or bears a cost in terms of charcoal air pollution. Your decision to cook burgers here affects you but it also affects those around you. In this case, say that an externality has been produced. Your decision has had a **neighborhood effect** and the costs and benefits of your actions extend well beyond your backyard. Externalities are a frequent fact of economic life.

Neighborhood effect: an externality

Economists divide externalities into two basic types. **External benefits** (sometimes also called **positive externalities**) occur when one person's actions cause others to benefit. If you paint your house or landscape your yard, for example, you benefit from these actions in obvious ways, but your neighbors also benefit. Both esthetically (they look on a more beautiful scene) and economically (by improving the looks of the neighborhood, you increase the values of both your house and those of your neighbors).

External benefits: benefits of an economic decision that accrue to third parties in a transaction

Positive externality: an external benefit

External benefits can be generated in both obvious and subtle ways. Education is often cited as an example of a good that produces external benefits. When you pay tuition to go to college, society gains in a number of ways. Your income will be higher (benefiting you, of course) but it also means that there will be more goods and services available to others, benefiting them. As a result of your education, you will pay more taxes (lessening the burden for others), vote more intelligently (perhaps!), and be less likely to harm others through crime (or at least be party to a better class of crime). You benefit from your college education, but so do many others who neither receive the education nor directly pay for it. These parties are the beneficiaries of external benefits.

External costs (sometimes called **negative externalities**) are produced when one person's actions impose costs (either monetary or otherwise) on others. Anyone who has a roommate who snores or a friend who smokes cheap cigars is familiar with the concept of external costs. Pollution is a classic example of an external cost. Suppose that you live near a plant that produces smoke and soot. When the plant goes into production, it bears most of the costs of producing the things that it makes. It pays for materials, labor, utilities, and the like. But you also pay a cost. You bear part of the cost of production in poorer health and a less desirable environment.

External costs can be generated in many ways. Some, like the snoring roommate or the barking dog next door, may be rather trivial costs and of little consequence. Others can be severe. In the 1970s, for example, scientists discovered that the propellant in the aerosol sprays then in use had the potential of damaging the ozone layer of the atmosphere. This phenomenon had a number of consequences, one of which was that skin cancer could increase dramatically as the ozone barrier deteriorated. People who were spritzing themselves with deodorant were causing other people to suffer cancer and other serious ills. The costs here were high and, in spite of conflicting scientific evidence, the government saw fit to ban widespread use of the chemicals that were suspected of causing this problem.

To get an idea of the frequency with which externalities are generated, it is a good idea to make a list of daily activities in which you are affected by others' actions or which produce external costs or benefits borne by others. What externalities are presented in school? When driving a car or riding a bus? In shopping? At meals? Many of these externalities are small, admittedly, but some are very important. In 1979 the world waited to see where an externality—the space station, Skylab—would come down (it hit Australia). Although seldom so dramatic, externalities affect our economic decisions and therefore daily distort the verdict of the market.

External costs: costs of an economic decision that accrue to third parties in a transaction

Negative externality: an external cost

PRIVATE VERSUS SOCIAL COSTS AND BENEFITS

Externalities upset the market because when they are present, demand and supply curves no longer reflect all the costs of producing goods nor all the benefits received from their purchase and use. The forces of supply and demand are essentially private forces based on the existence of private property rights. Producers and consumers normally take into account *only* the costs and benefits that they pay and receive when they make a market decision. Supply, therefore, reflects only **private costs** and the supply curve reflects only **marginal private costs**. Profit-maximizing producers take into consideration only the (private) costs they must bear, not the costs that others may suffer on account of their actions.

Private costs: those costs accruing to the producer of an item

Marginal private costs (MPC): the additional private costs of an additional unit of output

Social costs: the total costs of an economic decision; private costs plus external costs

Marginal social costs (MSC): the additional social costs that result from additional production

Private benefits: those benefits that accrue to the purchaser of an item

Marginal private benefits (MPB): the additional private benefits produced when an additional unit of output is made available

Social benefits: the total benefits of a decision; private benefits plus external benefits

Marginal social benefits (MSB): the additional social benefits produced when an additional unit of output is made available

External costs cause private costs to be different from **social costs**. Social costs are the total costs of an action to all members of society. Social cost includes both the private costs and the external costs that an action creates. When no external cost is present, private and social costs are equal. When external costs are present, however, social costs are greater than private costs. The supply curve, which reflects marginal private costs, fails to truly reflect **marginal social costs**.

When external benefits are produced, much the same difference exists. Demand curves reflect **private benefits**. When you purchase a Coke, you weigh the cost versus the benefits (private benefits) that you receive. The demand curve, therefore, reflects the **marginal private benefits** that a decision produces. When external benefits are present, however, private benefits differ from **social benefits**. Social benefits include both private and external benefits. When you paint your house, as previously noted, this action creates both private benefits (your house increases in value) and external benefits (your neighbors' houses are also worth more). Social benefits exceed the private benefits that you receive from your action. Demand curves may reflect marginal private benefits, but they do not take into consideration the **marginal social benefits** that are produced.

The discussion of free market in the preceding chapter assumed that demanders and suppliers receive all the costs and benefits of their actions—that no externalities are produced so that private and social costs and benefits are equal. This is the case in many markets, and when this condition holds the market is the best form of economic organization because it does maximize the net benefits of economic activity. When social and private costs and benefits differ, however, problems result and market intervention can be desirable.

EXTERNAL BENEFITS

When external benefits are present, the difference between social benefits and private benefits creates a reason for government intervention in the market. The case of external benefits is illustrated in Figure 1. In this diagram, we assume that no external costs are present. Since this is the case, the supply curve reflects private costs and social costs at the same time (with no external costs, private and social costs are equal). This is not the case on the demand side, however.

The demand curve reflects the marginal *private* benefits that the purchase of this good—education—provides. But, since education provides benefits for those who do not actually purchase the training, social and private benefits are different. Suppose that we add the external benefits to the demand (or marginal private benefit—MPB) curve. The new curve that we

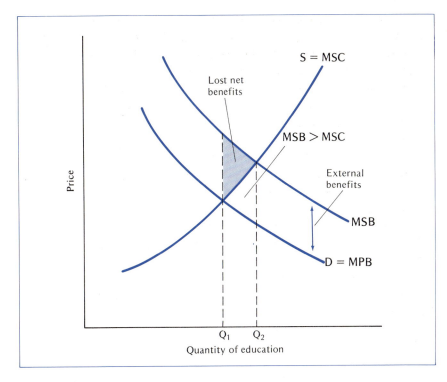

FIGURE 14-1: EXTERNAL BENEFITS FROM EDUCATION
Because education produces external benefits, marginal social benefits (MSB) exceed marginal private benefits (MPB). The market equilibrium Q_1 is therefore too low. Additional net societal benefits can be gained by increasing production to Q_2.

get can be called the marginal social benefit (MSB) curve. This curve reflects *all* the benefits that society derives from the purchase of educational services—both those benefits that students receive and those accruing to third parties.

Because of the difference between social and private benefits, the free market is inefficient in determining how much education should be produced. As the figure shows, if the free market is left on its own, an equilibrium quantity of Q_1 units of education will be produced and sold. This level of total production maximizes *private* net benefits. As can be seen by examining Figure 1, the purchase of any additional units of education will involve private costs that exceed private benefits. There is, therefore, no reason why the market, responding to private motivations, would produce a quantity of education greater than Q_1.

But is this the best level of education for society? A close examination of Figure 1 indicates that it is not. Suppose that one unit more than Q_1 of education is produced. As already noted, the private costs of this production would exceed the private benefits produced. But private and social benefits differ here. The next unit of education has high cost, but even higher social benefits! Indeed, additional net social benefits are available as production is expanded to a level of Q_2 units of education.

The best level of educational production for society occurs at Q_2. Here, the marginal social cost of education equals the marginal social benefit from education. Social welfare is improved because society is earning as many net benefits as it possibly can. If any quantity of education less than Q_2 is produced, society is giving up net benefits that could have been possible. If the market is allowed to work freely, the social net benefits shown by the shaded triangle in Figure 1 will be lost.

When external benefits are present, the free market fails in that it produces too little of the externality-laden item. Individual buyers respond to private benefits, they purchase the right amount of goods for themselves, but deny society benefits that could come from additional purchases. The government has a role here. By increasing the amount of externality-bearing goods that are produced, the government can increase society's net benefits and make the population better off. But how can this be done?

A governmental action that can increase production was discussed in the preceding chapter: the subsidy. A subsidy can be a harmful policy because, in an externality-free market, it results in the overproduction of goods. In the case of a good that yields external benefits, however, subsidies can have very desirable results. The use of a subsidy is shown in Figure 2.

When education's external benefits are taken into account, the market equilibrium quantity of education, Q_1, is seen to be *too little*. But suppose that the government pays high subsidies, either directly or indirectly, to the consumers of education. The existence of the subsidy lowers the effective cost of education. Students now consume additional education with higher cost, but pay a lower market price (tuition and fees) because the government subsidy makes up the difference. The subsidy lowers effective tuition rates and increases the amount of education consumed. If the subsidy is chosen correctly, it can result, as Figure 2 shows, in the social net benefit maximizing quantity of education being produced.

This is a nice theory, but does it apply to the real world? You have only to look around you to see that it does. Federal, state, and local governments provide literally billions of dollars annually in subsidies to all levels of education. Primary and secondary education is free or low cost (the subsidy accounts for most of the costs here, resulting in an extremely low market price). Tuition at institutions of higher education is very low in heavily subsidized institutions (state universities and community colleges) and even relatively expensive private colleges and universities charge lower tuition rates than they might on account of the federal and state subsidies that they receive.

Education is not the only external benefit-producing item that receives

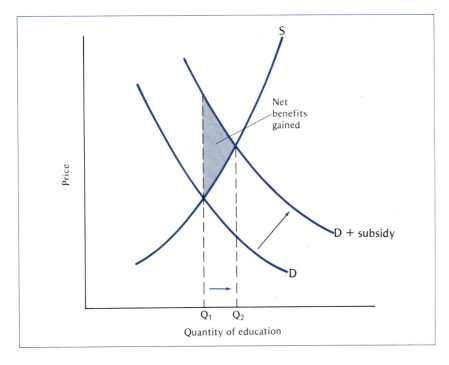

FIGURE 14-2: A SUBSIDY FOR
EDUCATION
*A subsidy can solve the problem of the
external benefits that education
produces. The subsidy lowers the price
that consumers pay for education and
so increases the amount consumed
from Q₁ to the socially desirable Q₂.*

such subsidies. Parks, for example, produce significant private benefits, but external benefits are provided as well. Admission to parks is therefore set below the marginal cost of their operation through subsidies designed to increase consumption of park services to the socially desired level. Other activities such as the construction of roads, the building of bridges, and various charitable organizations benefit from public subsidies because of the external benefits that they produce.

When external benefits exist, the market produces too little of the goods involved. Government intervention in the market is desirable because it can lead to the increase in socially desirable production. Subsidies are a good way for the government to increase this production.

EXTERNAL COSTS

External costs also cause market problems that call for government intervention. External costs are generally ignored by the firm unless those who bear the costs make their presence known through lawsuits or other actions. But this is not often the case. Sometimes the people or firms who bear the external costs can be far away or economically isolated. Those who stood to suffer from higher skin cancer rates due to the deterioration of

292   MARKET FAILURES: EXTERNALITIES

the ozone layer, for example, might not have been aware of the change or that aerosol sprays were the cause. There would be little chance of their getting compensation from the producers of the external costs.

The problem is the one shown in Figure 3, using the market for spray deodorants as an example. Here we assume that there are no external benefits produced by deodorant (a questionable assumption) so that the demand curve and the MSB curve are the same.

If demand here reflects social benefits, the supply curve does not reflect social costs. Supply here is based on the marginal private cost (MPC) of production. But, as discussed earlier, additional costs accrue to people who don't buy spray deodorant and are not involved in its purchase. When these social costs are added, we get the marginal social cost (MSC) curve shown in Figure 3. This curve reflects the total costs of producing this product— both the private costs that the manufacturers bear and the social costs that third parties to these transactions are forced to suffer.

If the market is left on its own, the forces of supply and demand bring about a market equilibrium at quantity Q_1 and price P_1 for this product. At this price, marginal private costs and marginal private benefits are equal— private net benefits are as large as they can be. But what about the social benefits?

This is an undesirable level of production from society's point of view.

FIGURE 14-3: EXTERNAL COSTS AND THE OZONE LAYER
Because of external costs, the marginal social cost (MSC) of deodorant production is greater than the marginal private cost (MPC). The market produces too much aerosol spray deodorant and charges too low a price compared with the socially desirable level Q_2.

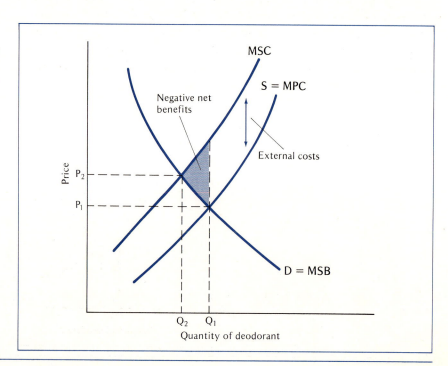

Look at the last unit of production here. The marginal social cost of the Q_1 unit produced is clearly higher than the marginal social benefit. This last unit is a social loss—it costs society more to produce than society receives in benefits. This good should not be produced from a social standpoint!

The best level of production here is Q_2, which sells at price P_2. At this level of production, social net benefits are maximized. The MSC of the last unit produced just equals its MSB. Society gains by restricting production— the gain is shown in Figure 3 as the shaded triangle of negative net benefits that the market produces.

When external costs are present in a market, the free market system produces *too much* of the good involved and charges too low a price. By producing too much of the good, the market produces too many external costs.

How can this problem be solved? One way is to deal with it as the government actually did in the aerosol spray case. The government determined that the risks were very great and simply banned the specific kind of spray that caused the damage. This is an example of the use of government regulations to impose changes on firms in society.

A different way to handle this was suggested in the preceding chapter. The government can reduce the consumption of an externality-producing good by imposing an excise tax on it. This is illustrated in Figure 4.

An excise tax has the impact of increasing the price of an item and lowering the amount produced. The tax raises the supply price and consumers respond by purchasing less. As Figure 4 shows, if the tax rate is chosen correctly, the tax can raise price and lower quantity to the levels desired by society. The power to tax, it is often said, is the power to destroy.

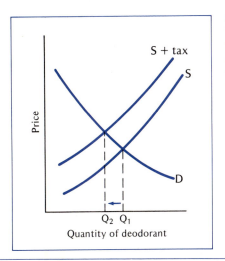

FIGURE 14-4: TAXES AS A SOLUTION TO EXTERNAL COSTS
By imposing a tax on deodorant, the quantity of this item produced is reduced to the Q_2 level, which is socially desirable.

Here taxes can be used to destroy the unwanted external costs of production.

Taxes are often used in this way. The use of gasoline, for example, produces the external cost of air pollution. Hence, federal and state governments impose taxes on gasoline that raise its cost and lower the amount of it burned and the amount of pollutants produced. Can you think of other items that are taxed? Do they generate negative externalities?

OPTIMAL POLLUTION

One of the interesting things that the study of external cost points out is that all pollution is not necessarily bad. Indeed, from an economic point of view, it would be a mistake to stop all pollution! Some pollution is bad, but there is an optimal amount of pollution that economists feel should be produced! This interesting conclusion is illustrated in Figure 5.

This is the market for steel. One of the problems with steel production is that it generates pollutants that inflict external costs on those who live around the steel factories. This is the classic externalities problem as discussed in the previous section. The market overproduces steel at quantity Q_1. Because of the external costs that steel production imposes, the most desirable level of steel manufacture is the lower quantity Q_2 in Figure 5. The government has reason to step in and restrict steel production to that level.

Note, however, that Q_2, the amount of external costs produced, is not

FIGURE 14-5: SOME EXTERNAL COSTS ARE NECESSARY
Even though steel production produces external costs, it is not desirable to completely destroy these costs because that would mean ending steel production. At Q_2, some external costs still remain, but they are offset by the social benefits that steel itself makes possible.

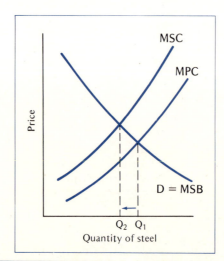

zero! There is still some pollution generated (although not as much as before government regulation was imposed). Why is this so? Why isn't all pollution done away with? It is a matter of costs and benefits, as the figure indicates. Suppose that we further reduce pollution by producing even less steel. The external costs will be reduced, but so will the social benefits. In fact, we will be giving up goods (steel) with a very high benefit in order to gain a relatively small reduction in external cost. The opportunity cost of further reducing pollution is too high.

At some point, the costs of reducing pollutants is greater than the benefits. This is perhaps best illustrated in Figure 6. This figure looks at the amount of pollutants that can be removed from the air around the steel factory. Removing the pollutants involves costs and benefits. Those who benefit from pollution control are those who suffer the external costs of steel production—those who must breathe the air and work in the environment around the steel factory. They benefit from pollution abatement, as the figure indicates. Their benefits increase as more of the air is cleaned, but the problem of diminishing marginal returns is apparent. The marginal benefit curve shows that clearing the worst pollutants out of the air yields more additional benefits than does any activity that removes the very last ones. Diminishing marginal benefits from pollution control exist.

The costs of pollution control must also be considered. As the figure

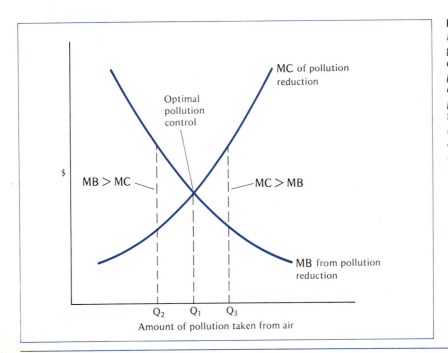

FIGURE 14-6: OPTIMAL POLLUTION
Removing pollutants from the air generates benefits, but also imposes costs. At Q_1 the marginal benefit from pollution reduction equals its marginal costs. This is the optimal level of pollution reduction. Point Q_3 provides too much pollution reduction—the benefits are not worth the costs—the air is "too clean." For the opposite reason, the air is too dirty at Q_2.

shows, marginal costs rise as more and more pollutants are removed from the air. The first pollutants may be removed with a simple filter, but the last ones require sophisticated equipment, which drives up marginal cost.

At some point, where the marginal benefit from pollution control equals its marginal cost, it is no longer economical to clean up the steel factory's emissions. Q_1 is the optimal level of pollution control in this case. At a pollution level of Q_2 it makes sense to further clean up the air because the marginal benefit from doing so is greater than the marginal cost. But it is possible to go too far in removing pollutants. To remove a quantity Q_3 of pollutants from the air around the steel factory involves marginal costs that greatly exceed the marginal benefits that such actions produce. This is a waste of resources from a societal point of view.

Just as there is an optimal level of external costs, there is also an optimal level of external benefits. Just because education generates benefits does not mean that an infinite amount of education should be produced.

Not everyone should go to college and a government subsidy plan that would make this possible would be a grave error. External benefits should be subsidized until the marginal benefit derived is just equal to the marginal cost. Just as we stop fighting pollution at some point, we also quit trying to educate everyone at another.

EXTERNALITY POLICY OPTIONS

Government actions can increase net benefits whenever external costs or benefits exist by altering the verdict of free market choice to induce more production (if external benefits can be produced) or less (when external costs are present). There are essentially four ways for the government to accomplish these changes in market behavior. Taxes and subsidies, as we have just noted, are two ways of altering market forces. Taxes reduce consumption, and subsidies can be used to increase the quantity of goods that are produced and consumed.

Taxes and subsidies are attractive from an economic point of view because they essentially preserve the role of the market as an allocator of resources. By imposing taxes or subsidies, the government alters costs and benefits, but the forces of supply and demand still prevail so that the market can respond to changing conditions effectively.

Another way for the government to promote the proper production of externalities is for it to step in and produce the proper quantity of goods itself. The government provides schooling, as well as bridges, roads, and parks rather than providing subsidies for the private production of these items. Each of these goods provides significant external benefits. Note that any of these items *could* be produced by the private sector, and roughly the same amount could be supplied if the proper government subsidy were available. This is how the railroads were built. Substantial government subsidies were given to encourage the expansion of the transportation system and many subsidies of private enterprise continue.

Finally, the government can alter private production through regulation. As noted before, the government simply banned certain kinds of spray propellants when the environmental damage that they cause was discovered. Regulation here was substituted for either a tax on the ozone-destroying matter or a subsidy of alternative kinds of propellants.

Regulation is frequently used to deal with externalities. Sometimes the regulation is cheaper or more efficient in dealing with externalities than taxes, subsidies, or some other kind of program. A good example of this is the system of **zoning** that prevails in the United States. Zoning is the practice of restricting the property rights of land ownership. Under a zoning scheme, only certain land uses (residential property, industrial, commercial, and so on) are permitted in a given area. The idea behind zoning is that every type of land use produces certain externalities. Single family houses produce one set of external costs and benefits and steel factories produce other, decidedly different, external benefits and costs. When adjacent land has a similar use, these external costs and benefits may wash out with little effect. So, for example, the leaves that fall from the tree in your yard into your neighbor's are not a significant external cost problem if his tree's leaves also pollute your property. Barking dogs on each side of the fence are compatible, if not completely soothing. Likewise, a steel mill and a chemical plant located side by side may produce externalities that are not inconsistent. In fact, their adjacent location may facilitate transportation networks and so save money. Shopping malls are built on the idea that each store in the area creates positive externalities to every other one.

Now, suppose that we mix up these three land uses. When the family home is placed next to both the department store and the steel mill, the externalities no longer mix and everyone is likely to lose. The idea behind zoning is to keep like land uses together (because their externalities mix well) and keep different kinds of land uses apart (because mixing these externalities makes everyone worse off).

The goal of zoning could be produced in other ways than regulation. The government could allow people to build whatever they want wherever they want (the result might well be the same as if zoning prevailed) and then tax those that produced the external costs (barking dogs would carry a particularly burdensome tax) and provide subsidies to external goods. Alternatively, the government could build everything (so that the proper

Zoning: government regulations on legal land use

items were produced) and sell it to private owners. Either of these solutions would be costly and inefficient, however. The use of zoning regulation represents a reasonably good way to affect the proper production of externality-laden goods.

LIMITS TO GOVERNMENT ACTIONS

Should the government step in whenever externalities are produced? Before answering this question, ask yourself if the government has a policy (tax, subsidy, public production, regulation) in every case you can think of where an externality is produced. Certainly, the government steps in in many cases (air pollution resulting from auto emissions, for example). But not in all cases. Why not?

When the number of people affected by an externality is small, private negotiations are a simple way to solve the market problem. All the families in a neighborhood can get together and induce the dog owner to silence his animal. When costs and benefits are easily quantified, other private solutions are possible. If you cut down a tree in your yard, and it falls into mine, putting a hole in my roof, I can sue you in court to recoup the damages. The existence of the court allows me to impose on you the external costs you create and, in addition, forces you to take this possibility into account when you make the fateful decision.

When these conditions are violated, however, private actions to deal with externalities are less successful. If the groups involved are large or widely dispersed (so that collective bargaining is difficult) or if external costs and benefits are difficult to measure or their existence hard to prove, public policy may be needed to replace private actions. But government actions that produce benefits (increase net societal benefits) are costly, too. The government has a role only if the gains are worth the cost.

Determining whether this condition is met is a real problem for policy-makers. Take the problem of cigarette smoking, for example. It is hard to deny that the smoker produces an external cost to nonsmokers in the vicinity. In fact, scientific research shows that the cigarette smoke is not only smelly and irritating, but that it also carries a real health hazard to nearby nonsmokers (and to the smokers also). What is the appropriate government policy with respect to this widespread form of external cost? Some local governments have taken the step of banning smoking from public places like elevators (although enforcement of this law is difficult) or to guarantee nonsmokers "separate but equal" facilities at restaurants and the like. These actions, where they have been taken, certainly reduce the external costs produced, but at a cost to government and the public in general. What is the optimal amount of cigarette pollution and how much would it cost for the government to take actions to reduce it to this level? This is not an easy question and so illustrates the problem of public policy in the area of externalities.

PUBLIC GOODS

The existence of external costs and benefits is not the only reason for government involvement in market activities. There are situations, in fact, where governments may need to actually take over markets—supplying goods and services, setting prices, and making production and distribution decisions. This is often the case with **public goods**.

A good or service is a public good if it has the property that one person's consumption or use of the item does not diminish the amount of the good that others can consume. Note that this *does not* mean that a public good is anything produced by the government for the public. Some items that the government supplies do qualify as public goods, but many others definitely do not.

A classic example of a public good is a lighthouse. Once one person erects a lighthouse (in order to keep ships from running aground on a rocky shore) everyone else is able to use the lighthouse's services whether they have contributed to the construction of the lighthouse or not. It would be impossible (or, at least, extremely costly) to keep **free riders** from using the lighthouse's services without also restricting those who have paid for the service. But the use of the lighthouse by nonpayers in no way diminishes the services provided by the owners of the lighthouse.

Another example of a public good is national defense. Suppose that there were no national army, navy, or air force to protect us from foreign invasion. Now suppose that a group down the street organized an army to protect their property from invading groups. It would be impossible for them to protect their property and lives without also supplying you with that protection (if the enemy got as close as the next block, their game would be lost). Therefore, in order to protect themselves from invasion, they must also protect you and your neighbors. Once the good "national defense" is supplied, all can benefit from it whether they pay for it or not.

As you can see, the idea of a public good is closely related to the idea of externalities. There is a difference, however. When you purchase an item that generates external benefits (such as education, for example), third parties receive benefits, but the benefits they receive are somewhat *different* from the benefits that you receive. As well, you are likely to receive *more* private benefits than others receive external benefits. The difference between private and social benefits exists, but it may not be very great. This is not the case with a public good.

Public good: an item that has the property that one person's consumption of the item does not diminish the ability of others to consume it as well

Free rider: an individual who benefits from a good or service without making payment for that good or service

When someone purchases an item that is a public good, then everyone else receives roughly the *same* benefits as the purchaser. Suppose, for example, that there is a swamp located near your house. If you pay to have the swamp drained in order to protect your own health, everyone else in the neighborhood will get exactly the same kind of benefit, and they each will likely benefit by about the *same* amount as you do, even if they don't help finance the project. The difference between private benefits and social benefits here can be very great. The external benefits that a public good produces are likely to be many times larger than any private benefits received. This creates market problems as illustrated in Figure 7.

The demand curve in this diagram represents the private benefits of those individuals who want to have this good the most and are willing to pay for it. Private demand derives from their private benefits. All others are free riders—they wait for someone else to pay for the good. As a result of this free rider problem, there is a very great difference between demand and the marginal social benefits that the public good makes possible. If left to its own, the market results in relatively low production of the public good. At this small quantity of production, the private market is in equilibrium, but

FIGURE 14-7: PUBLIC GOODS
Because free riders will not participate in the market, the difference between demand and marginal social benefits (MSB) is very large when public goods are present. If no government action is taken, only Q_1 units of the public good will be produced and a large amount of net benefits (the shaded area) will be lost.

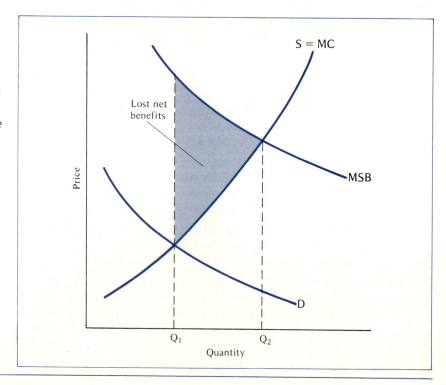

marginal social benefits far exceed marginal social costs. Many societal net benefits are lost because of the small level of private production.

The existence of public goods causes a double problem. The first is equity—the free riders simply don't pay for the benefits they receive. The second, and probably more important, problem is one of efficiency. Because of this free-rider problem, market choice results in *too little* production of public goods. The market choice mechanism breaks down.

Government actions are desirable where public goods exist and many government activities can reasonably be classified as the production of public goods. National defense is a public good, as are highways. The National Weather Service is also a public good. Television and radio are public goods, although not provided by the government directly. The government provides a subsidy here to encourage production of these services by allowing television and radio stations to have limited monopolies. Higher profits plus government regulation of the communications industry encourage production of these public goods.

One reason for the heavy government involvement in the provision of public goods is that often a public good will not be produced at all unless the government steps in. This is illustrated in Figure 8. Shown here is the market for a public good relating to national defense—a nuclear submarine fleet. These vessels, by increasing the level of national security, provide benefits that are shared by all citizens. There is a problem, however. Because the marginal cost of providing this sub fleet is so high, not a single one would be produced if the decision were left to the market. Most folks would be free riders and those who were willing to even consider buying would not gain enough private benefits from this action to make the purchase of the sub system possible. In the absence of governmental action, therefore, the equilibrium market quantity of these subs is zero.

Yet, there is good reason to build the sub fleet. As Figure 8 shows, the marginal social benefits from this public good are very high. By letting the market work and not building the fleet, very great social net benefits are lost (shown by the shaded area in the picture). Without government interference no subs will be built, and so the government has a role here—to step in and create a market, making construction of these items possible. All benefit and, through taxes, all may help pay the cost.

One of the problems with providing public goods is to decide just what is the socially optimal quantity to produce. Since demand curves tell us little about the benefits that society receives, the decision of how much to produce is often full of uncertainty. This uncertainty, of course, is one of the reasons that governmental budget policies are so controversial. Should the national defense budget be cut, expanded, or held at the same level as last year? The answer depends on whether marginal social costs are greater

FIGURE 14-8: PUBLIC PRODUCTION OF PUBLIC GOODS

If the market were left alone, no submarines (a possible national defense public good) would be produced. The marginal cost easily exceeds the benefit that any individual buyer would receive. Yet, for society, the benefits are worth the cost. Government production and operation of the subs is the answer. The net benefits this produces are shown by the shaded area.

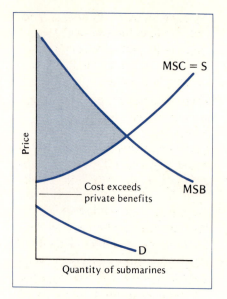

than, less than, or equal to marginal social benefits. Both of these factors are hard to measure objectively, leading to wide disagreement about policy prescriptions.

REAL WORLD ECONOMICS: FREE MARKET OR DEMOCRATIC CHOICE

FREEWAY ISSUE KEY IN TUESDAY ELECTION

PIGTOWN (SPECIAL)—Voter attitudes toward the proposed new freeway extension in Pigtown will be the key to next Tuesday's municipal election, according to incumbent mayor Wink Porker.

"There is broad support for improving the freeway within the business community and in the parts of town that aren't directly affected," Porker noted in a pre-election press conference, "But voters in the neighborhood where the freeway would pass have organized community groups to oppose the action. I can see both sides of this debate and haven't made up my mind yet. I support the proposal to put the issue on next year's ballot as a special referendum."

Porker's opponent in the mayor's race, Virginia Hamm, has come out against the freeway extension. The election, therefore, gives voters something of a choice on this issue, but the mandate may not be clear-cut.

ECONOMIC ANALYSIS

Free market choice, as this chapter has shown, is an imperfect way to make economic decisions when externalities or public goods are present. But democratic choice may not be a perfect solution either.

In one sense, the proposed freeway extension would be a public good. Porker's use of it wouldn't directly reduce Hamm's benefits from the freeway's existence. In addition, the highway would create a number of external benefits. Businesses located along the highway could count on increased volume and folks who have to travel the route might save time because the highway would be faster and safer. Based on these factors, the freeway plan looks like a good idea. But there is more.

The freeway also generates some negative externalities. Congestion will appear where it did not previously exist. Pollution and parking problems may crop up as well. Noise, smell, and other factors reduce the value of residential land near the new freeway while increasing the value of commercial property—a reason for business support of the plan.

These external benefits and costs are difficult to measure, and so bureaucratic choice, where the government simply decides whether the highway will be built, is not a perfect plan. Democratic choice, as in this voting situation, is also inaccurate. The market, as we have seen, cannot guarantee the perfect societal choice, either.

Does the choice mechanism make a difference then? It sure does (just ask the voters). But the science of economics here can only help us ask the right questions: What are the costs? What are the benefits? Which is greater? It does not provide the perfect answer.

SUMMARY

1. Externalities exist whenever all the costs or benefits of an economic decision (production, consumption) do not fall to the individual making that decision. When some of the benefits of a decision accrue to third parties we say that external benefits have been created. When costs are imposed on third parties, it is called an external cost.

2. The free market breaks down when externalities are present. If an external benefit is produced, then social benefits exceed the private benefits on which market decisions are made. The market will produce too little of the benefit-yielding item. When external costs are present a different problem appears. Social costs exceed the private costs on which production decisions are made. The market produces too many of the external cost-producing items.

3. Government policies can be chosen to correct market failures and increase social welfare. External benefits can be encouraged with the use of subsidies to increase consumption. External costs, on the other hand, can be reduced through taxation, which discourages

production. Government regulations are sometimes more effective in accomplishing this reduction in external costs.

4. A public good is an item that is shared by all. If one person purchases a public good, all others can be free riders and derive the benefits of the good without paying for it. Public goods, like goods that produce external

benefits, are not produced adequately in the market—in some cases public goods with high social benefits are not produced at all in free markets because no one individual can afford to make the purchase. Government subsidies and government production of public goods can be used to increase social welfare.

DISCUSSION QUESTIONS

1. Is it possible to produce too much of a good that produces positive externalities? Why? Give an example of a good with external benefits that may be produced in oversupply. How does this happen?

2. Are taxes used to regulate all goods that produce external costs? Are regulations applied to the rest? Are there any goods that produce external costs that are left free, their quantity more or less determined by the free market? Why hasn't the government intervened?

3. Suppose that, in order to increase the production of a good that gives external benefits, the government must impose a tax on another good that *also* has external benefits. What is the impact here? Are there any conditions under which such a policy would make sense? What are they?

4. Why is there such a large difference, in the case of a public good, between the market demand curve and marginal social benefits? What makes up the demand curve for a public good, given that it is possible to be a free rider?

5. You are a fan of your local pro football team. If the stadium is sold out by Friday, the big game will be shown on local television. If not, no local television coverage is possible and only those in the stadium will see the game. Use the theories of this chapter to determine whether or not the price of a ticket to this game reflects the marginal benefits that the game produces.

TEST YOURSELF

Indicate whether each of the following statements is *true* or *false*. Be able to defend your choice.

1. Public goods produce external benefits.

2. No public goods would be

produced if the free market were allowed to function on its own.

3. An apple is an example of a public good.

4. All goods produce either external benefits or external costs.

5. Price controls can be used as a way to control the amount of external costs produced in a market.

6. Taxes are the best way to encourage external benefits.

7. Regulations can sometimes correct an externality with less disruption to a market than other solutions.

8. Subsidies are one way to encourage the production of public goods.

9. An outdoor concert by a symphony orchestra fits the definition of a public good.

10. A symphony orchestra is a good that produces many obvious external benefits.

15
Market Failures: Monopolies

Markets can fail because of monopolies and so-called natural monopolies. When this happens, there is an economic case for government intervention. Monopolies can generate benefits, too, and so not all monopolies are controlled. This chapter answers many questions about governmental actions in this area, including the following:

Why does the government need to control monopolies?

How does government monopoly policy work?

If monopolies are bad, why does the government create monopolies through patent and copyright laws?

What is a natural monopoly?

What is the appropriate governmental policy in dealing with a natural monopoly?

Monopoly power, when it exists, gives producers the upper hand in the market. Consumers may still be price-takers—individually unable to influence market price—but producers can be price-setters and so gain potentially higher profits. This advantage exists in monopoly markets and, to a lesser extent, in markets characterized by monopolistic competition and oligopoly.

Does free market choice lead to the efficient production and distribution of goods and services in monopoly markets? This chapter aims to find out.

MONOPOLY PROBLEMS

We already have a suspicion that monopolies are a source of economic problems. Monopolies don't produce the same amounts of goods that competitive producers would in the same situation.

When a market is characterized by competition, the industry marginal cost curve is also the market supply curve. A competitive market, as in Figure 1, therefore finds equilibrium at a market price P_c with a production quantity Q_c. When monopoly prevails, the free market does not choose this level of production. The monopolist acts to maximize economic profits by picking a level of production Q_m where marginal cost equals marginal revenue. The monopolist then sells that level of output for the highest price consistent with demand. This results in a market price P_m in Figure 1.

The monopolist, therefore, charges a higher price than would prevail in competitive markets, and produces less to boot. Consumers pay more and get less. This may make them suspicious of the role of the monopolist, and with good reason, as Figure 2 shows.

Let's assume that neither external costs nor external benefits are present in the market shown here. That is, the demand curve reflects all the benefits that the consumption of this item produces and the marginal cost curve shows costs for both the firm and society. Even without externalities, the presence of the monopolist creates problems.

The monopolist equates marginal costs with marginal revenues. But revenues and benefits here are not equal. Marginal revenue represents the additional cash that the firm gets from additional production. Marginal benefits show the extra benefits that extra production makes possible. This difference between marginal revenue and marginal benefit causes the monopolist to display antisocial behavior.

The sin of the monopolist is one of omission. By restricting production, the monopolist robs society of unproduced net benefits. The difference between the production level that the monopolist picks and that which

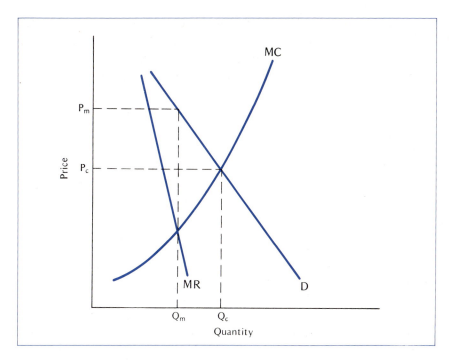

FIGURE 15-1: MONOPOLY PRICING AND PRODUCTION
The monopolist charges a higher price P_m and produces a lower quantity Q_m than competitive firms would in the same market.

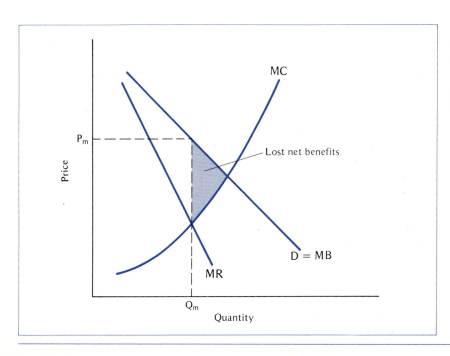

FIGURE 15-2: MONOPOLY PROBLEMS
Because the monopoly produces less and charges a higher price than competitive firms would, given the same costs and demand, the monopoly lowers social welfare. The lost net benefits from monopoly actions are shown by the shaded area.

would prevail in a competitive situation is made up of items that yield positive net benefits. Not enough resources are allocated by monopolists to the production of these desirable goods.

Monopoly is also undesirable because of the pricing policy that prevails in these markets. In a competitive market, goods are priced at their marginal cost. In a monopoly market, price is set well above the marginal cost of production. People give up more resources (in the market price) for goods than are used to produce these goods (as measured by marginal cost). The exchange here is rigged in favor of the monopoly supplier.

GOVERNMENT MONOPOLY POLICY

If free market choice results in too little production by monopolists, can government policies correct the problem? Several solutions are possible.

1. SUBSIDIES. Whenever private market decisions result in too low a level of output, subsidies are an answer. By granting subsidies to consumers (which increase demand and therefore marginal revenue to the monopolist) or by giving the payments to the producer instead (which effectively lower the marginal costs of production) the government can induce the monopolist to increase production and generate higher net benefits.

The problem with subsidies, from the government's perspective, is that they represent yet another public expenditure. Tax dollars must be raised and this can create problems in other markets. Also, the need for these subsidies must compete with needs for public expenditures in other areas where public goods exist or externalities prevail. Since public dollars to subsidize monopoly production go into the pockets of the monopolist—who may earn economic profits already—this plan is not likely to be popular among voters.

2. PRICE DISCRIMINATION. Another plan that causes the monopolist to increase production to the socially desired level is price discrimination. Price discrimination is the practice of selling the same thing to different buyers at different prices. If the monopolist is allowed to be a perfect price discriminator, then the market's problems will be solved.

Perfect price discrimination is the practice of selling each individual item produced at the highest possible price (as shown by the demand curve). Since the demand curve shows that the first item produced generates

Perfect price discrimination: the ability to charge each individual demander the highest possible price

very high marginal benefits, then someone is willing to pay a very high price for that one first piece of production. The second unit should go for a high price, too, but less than the first, and so on. Perfect price discrimination is accomplished by auctioning production off, one piece at a time, to the highest bidder. It may be impossible in practice, but a clever firm (with government help) may be able to accomplish something very much akin to it.

Why consider a price discrimination scheme? The answer is suggested by Figure 3. When the firm can sell each piece of output to the highest bidder, then each demander pays an amount equal to the marginal benefit that he or she receives. Different prices can be charged to different buyers, and so the firm does not have to cut price on all its production to sell one additional unit.

The result is that marginal revenue is equal to the demand curve for the perfect price discriminator. Each additional unit is sold for the demand price while the price of previous output is unaffected. The perfect price discriminator produces where marginal cost equals marginal revenue. Because the demand curve is now also the MR curve, however, this monopoly production point is the same as would prevail in a perfectly

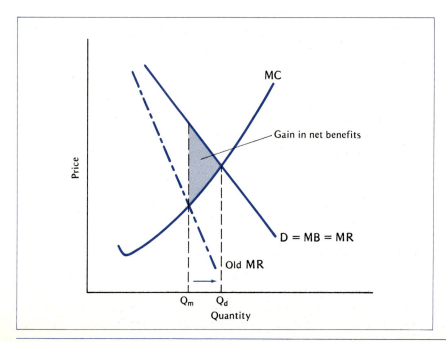

FIGURE 15-3: PERFECT PRICE DISCRIMINATION
If the monopolist is able to use perfect price discrimination, the marginal revenue and demand curves are one and the same. The monopolist will increase production to Q_d, which maximizes both monopoly profits and social net benefits.

competitive market. The monopolist produces amount Q_d in Figure 3, well above amount Q_m, which would occur if price discrimination were not allowed.

Perfect price discrimination is obviously difficult to achieve, but any form of price discrimination, however crude, tends to increase monopoly production and so increase societal net benefits. Many regulated monopolies, such as the telephone company, railroads, and public utilities, are allowed to charge different customers different prices partially for this reason.

The problem with price discrimination, however, is that it changes the distribution of net benefits in the market. Under normal circumstances societal net benefits are pretty well divided between the seller (who benefits in the form of producers' surplus) and the buyer (who gains consumers' surplus). By allowing perfect price discrimination, however, the government alters this balance. This is illustrated in Figure 4. Since each good is sold at its highest demand price, all of the difference between demand (marginal benefit) and marginal cost is gained by the producer. No consumer surplus is generated. The monopolist, who earns economic profits in any case, gains even higher profits when this solution is used. Social well-being improves, at least in theory, because more benefit-yielding goods are produced. But the new distribution of benefit is not likely to prove very popular. Most buyers will prefer the old monopoly system since, for most of them, the monopoly price is less than the new price discriminator's price. The only ones likely to vote for this solution are the

FIGURE 15-4: WINNERS AND LOSERS WITH PRICE DISCRIMINATION
Without price discrimination, the net benefits from production are shared by the producer and the consumer. Giving the monopolist the right to discriminate may increase the total of these net benefits, but it also changes the distribution—all the benefits go to the monopolist.

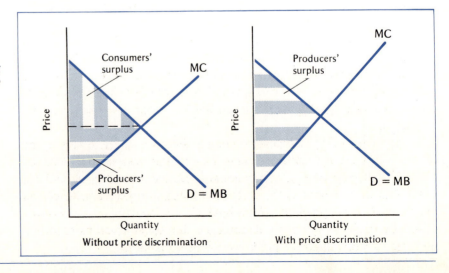

monopolists (who stand to gain profits) and those who would otherwise be denied production because of the monopolist's restricted output, but who could buy if the price discrimination alternative were enacted. Since the first group is likely to outnumber the second group (and clearly does in the real world), price discrimination is seldom used to solve monopoly problems.

ANTITRUST REGULATION

A problem with subsidies and price discrimination is that, in order to bring about the proper monopoly behavior, it may be necessary to take money from taxpayers or consumers and give it to the monopolist. A method that works in the opposite direction is **antitrust legislation**. **Trust** is just another word for a monopoly. Through antitrust legislation, the government tries to restore competition to monopoly markets.

The **Sherman Antitrust Act** makes it a federal crime to engage in monopoly activities and provides penalties for anyone caught doing so. The **Clayton Antitrust Act** adds penalties for acts such as price discrimination that unregulated monopolies engage in. These two laws, and others that Congress has added from time to time, put the federal government firmly in the antimonopoly field.

Antimonopoly laws also work by discouraging monopolists from actually acting like monopolies. If the monopolist knows that by bearing monopoly profits he is likely to be attacked by trustbusters, then the firm is more likely to behave like a competitor, lowering prices and increasing production. By doing this, the firm may be able to retain some of its monopoly position and still earn some economic profits, while giving the appearance of acting like a competitive firm.

It should be noted here that it is not monopoly *per se* that is bad. If only one supplier exists, but that supplier sells at a low price, then it may not make any difference that a single firm monopolizes the market. It may make a difference, however, if the single firm means a smaller choice of goods or poorer quality of goods — then even the low price won't substitute for competition.

Even while working to increase competition in markets, however, the government also takes actions to create monopolies. Barriers to international trade, artificial barriers to occupational entry, and rules or regulations that affect production costs and the costs of substitutes or complements can all increase the market power that firms hold. Government policy is a two-way street: Monopolies are openly discouraged, but some government regulations reduce competition in otherwise efficient markets.

Antitrust legislation: government laws that seek to outlaw or regulate monopolies

Trust: a monopoly

Sherman Antitrust Act: a federal law, passed in 1890, which makes most normal monopoly practices illegal

Clayton Antitrust Act: a federal law, passed in 1914, that outlaws monopoly pricing practices such as price discrimination

TRADE-OFF: PATENT MONOPOLIES

If monopolies lower social welfare, and government policies that break up, tame, or take over monopolies are appropriate, then why does the government act to foster and create monopolies? By issuing patents, for example, the government gives individuals limited monopoly power. The holder of the first patents in xerography was able to take advantage of monopoly power in the photocopying industry. Why does the government allow this? The answer is that monopolies can be a mixed blessing. While they reduce welfare by lowering production, they can sometimes add to welfare in other ways.

Patent monopolies, by rewarding innovation, encourage technological progress. We are all better off because of the constant search for improvements that the patent monopoly must go through in order to keep its competitive edge.

Is the patent monopoly bad? It depends on whether the gained benefits of innovation, which generate the public good of knowledge, exceed the monopoly loss due to lower total production. The government, it seems, has decided that the patent monopoly is acceptable, as current laws encourage this type of business. The government must have decided that the gain exceeds the monopoly loss there. Are all monopolies that the government creates by, say, restricting market entry, desirable because they foster the creation of external benefits? No. When barbers gain market power through government regulation, forces other than a desire for economic efficiency are at work.

COSTS AND BENEFITS OF MONOPOLY REGULATION

Many monopoly (or just uncompetitive) market situations are tolerated by the government because the costs to society of restoring competition to the market exceed the benefits that doing so makes possible. Suppose, for example, that one grocery store in an isolated community is able to exercise some monopoly power in pricing. True, the store may be earning monopoly profits and robbing the community of net benefits by selling a smaller quantity at a higher price than competitive markets, but what will it cost to change the situation? How easy will it be to determine if the higher price results from monopoly power or just higher costs? How should the community go about regulating the grocery business? Should it force the store to divide in two? Should price be set by the town council? Should the community bribe a second store to open its doors?

Even in a simple case like this, the problem of dealing with monopoly welfare loss may cost more than it is worth. Only in really important cases, where the net benefit loss is very large, does regulation of monopolies make sense from a cost–benefit point of view. We live with a trade-off here. Monopoly power may be less damaging in many cases than the socially desirable alternative of regulation.

NATURAL MONOPOLIES

Natural monopoly: a natural monopoly exists in a market when no more than one firm can operate with nonnegative economic profits

In most circumstances, monopolies exist because of an undesirable lack of competition in a market. In other cases, however, monopolies are desirable because they are the most efficient form of market organization—more efficient than perfect competition. These are cases of **natural monopolies**.

A natural monopoly occurs in a market if, because of the relationship between production costs and market demand, only one firm can profitably exist. The presence of even one competitor results in negative economic profits, for all.

Under what conditions do natural monopolies exist? One case is shown in Figure 5. Marginal costs are very low in this market—meaning that competitive firms will be forced by competition to sell at very low prices. There is nothing wrong with this—lots of markets are characterized by low prices and are not ripe for monopoly. The principal difference here has to do with the fixed costs of production. Notice that fixed costs in this figure are very high relative to marginal costs. At a certain quantity, marginal costs

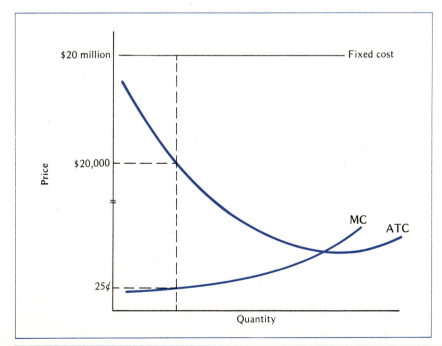

FIGURE 15-5:   THE NATURAL MONOPOLY
If a competitive firm operates in this market, it may be forced, by competition, to price at marginal cost (25¢) when average total costs are $20,000. These competitive firms will go out of business. A monopoly is the only form of business that can successfully produce under these conditions.

may be just 25¢, but the fixed costs amount to $20 million! Any competitive firm that prices at marginal costs—25¢ in the picture—will quickly go out of business (or never go into business in the first place)—because it will be unable to pay the fixed costs. If this market is characterized by a large number of competitive firms, each producing a relatively small amount and pricing at marginal costs, then they will all go out of business because none of them will earn a profit! Monopolies in general may not be desirable, but natural monopolies are clearly preferable to the alternative—no firms at all in these markets and, as a result, no goods or services produced!

In what kinds of markets are natural monopolies found? A number of natural monopolies come to mind: water, power, and sewer systems; telephone companies; natural gas companies; and subways among them. Indeed, most of the public utilities that we deal with are natural monopolies in this sense. Try to imagine a large number of competing telephone, sewer, or electric light companies, each making the large initial investment and trying to sell its services for today's relatively low rates.

Public utilities are not the only examples of natural monopolies, however. Pharmaceutical companies are private firms that are natural monopolies. A new miracle drug may have a marginal cost of production of just a few cents, but may require literally billions of dollars of fixed costs (research to invent the drug, test it, and perfect it) in order to make production possible. If competition were allowed, no single firm could afford to invent these wonder drugs, since they would bear the fixed costs (and the losses) but would be forced to compete in production. Through a combination of patents and secrecy these natural monopolies keep monopoly power, charge something akin to monopoly prices, and give us the new drugs that we need.

PRICING OF NATURAL MONOPOLIES

Given the fact that monopolies are necessary in the kinds of markets described above, what is the appropriate pricing and production policy for these firms? What is the best policy for the public? For the firms themselves? As we have seen in the past, this is an area of some conflict. What's good for General Motors (if GM were a natural monopoly) is not necessarily good for the United States. Figure 6 shows the problems of monopoly pricing.

The natural monopolist may normally pursue a monopoly pricing policy. This involves selecting a production level Q_m where marginal revenue equals marginal cost and selling that level of output for the highest price that the market will bear—price P_m in this figure. This policy maximizes monopoly profits and, as Figure 6 shows, allows the natural monopolist to earn a profit. The monopoly price P_m is greater than the average total cost of

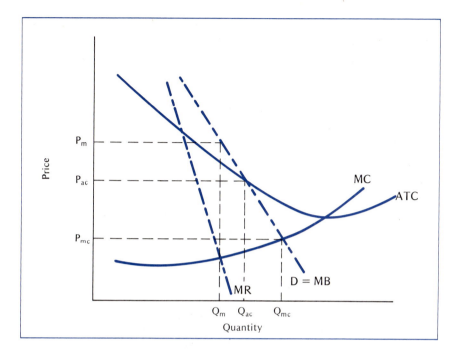

Price
P_m
P_{ac}
P_{mc}
MC
ATC
MR
D = MB
Q_m Q_{ac} Q_{mc}
Quantity

FIGURE 15-6: PRICING FOR A NATURAL MONOPOLIST
The natural monopolist maximizes profits by pricing at P_m and producing quantity Q_m. Societal net benefits are lost here, however. The firm breaks even if average cost pricing is used (P_{ac}), but some net benefits are still foregone. Net benefits are maximized if marginal cost pricing (P_{mc}) is used and output is expanded until marginal cost and marginal benefits are equal (Q_{mc}). The firm runs at a loss at this price, however, and must make up the deficit somehow.

that level of production, and so positive profits are earned. The natural monopolist stays in business.

There is a problem, however. Like any other monopoly, a natural monopoly lowers social welfare by its monopoly production practices. At the monopoly output level Q_m, the marginal benefits of additional output far exceed the marginal costs. The net benefits from production can be increased if the monopolist expands production. Here is an interesting paradox. The monopoly is better than competition because no market can exist at all with competition, and net benefits will amount to zero. But with the monopoly, the potential gains in terms of net benefits can be much greater if production expands.

When this situation exists, the government often steps in to regulate or, in some cases, take over the natural monopolies. One step that is often taken is called **average cost pricing**. The idea behind average cost pricing is that the natural monopoly should produce as much as possible, so long as it pays its own way or breaks even from a financial point of view. What does this mean in terms of the market? Figure 6 shows the situation.

Average cost pricing dictates that price be set equal to the average total cost of production. This takes place at quantity Q_{ac} and price P_{ac}. At this quantity and price, a larger amount of production is made available, and so more net benefits are produced and social welfare is enhanced. Prices are

Average cost pricing: the setting of price charged by a natural monopoly at the level that covers total cost; price is set equal to average total cost

lower than those which prevail under monopoly pricing, too. More of the surplus here falls to consumers and less is gained by the producers. Since the firm breaks even, it is neither exercising its monopoly power nor draining the governmental treasury. Still, there are problems with this policy.

So long as price exceeds marginal costs, society gives up net benefits and welfare. At the average cost price, as the figure shows, marginal benefits from additional production still exceed their marginal costs. Even greater production will make social welfare rise. But to expand production will mean selling at a price below average total costs. If this occurs, the firm loses money and must either go out of business or be subsidized by a public agency.

From society's point of view, efficient production takes place if the natural monopolist adopts **marginal cost pricing**; if the natural monopolist behaves as a competitive firm and produces where price equals the marginal cost of production. This is desirable from a social welfare point of view because such a policy will maximize the net benefits from production. Marginal benefits and costs will be equal and as many net benefits as possible will be produced.

But this will create a problem, as well. Marginal cost pricing, as the figure shows, means a price that is less than average total cost. The firm loses money and must gain a subsidy in order to stay in business.

This may help explain why many natural monopolies are owned and operated by arms of the government. In order for them to produce as much social welfare as possible, they are forced to run at a loss. Subsidies are needed to finance the production of benefits, and these subsidies are perhaps most easily paid if the natural monopoly is already owned by the government.

Those natural monopolies that do not run at a loss deprive the economy of net benefits. But even these are seldom allowed to use their monopoly power. Average cost pricing is more the rule here. The firm breaks even at the price set by government regulators. The telephone company and many other natural monopolies, their rates set by federal and state agencies, pursue this kind of pricing policy.

Average cost pricing may be an acceptable compromise between the loss in social welfare and the problem of financing deficits that marginal cost pricing produces. Still, it is sometimes possible to pursue marginal cost pricing *without* running deficits. A price-discriminating natural monopolist, for example, can make enough additional revenue by charging three prices to three different groups to make marginal cost pricing of the unprofitable last units produced possible. This is often done by electrical companies that offer different rates for commercial, industrial, and household customers.

The firm can break even (or even earn a small profit) and still use the marginal cost pricing concept to maximize social welfare.

Other methods can be used to make up the deficit, too. Sometimes firms impose fixed use fees in addition to their regular price in order to make up the fixed costs. Telephone subscribers, for example, normally buy a fixed number of calls whether they use them or not and are only charged for certain other services such as long-distance dialing. The fixed monthly fee covers the fixed costs of production and allows something like marginal cost pricing of the other services. Similar schemes are employed in water and sewer markets, too.

REAL WORLD ECONOMICS: U.S. POSTAL SERVICE

POSTAL SERVICE MUST PAY WAY SAYS SENATE MONEY LEADER

WASHINGTON, D.C.—The U.S. Postal Service will give up its deficit-ridden ways and show a profit if Senator Myron Gotrocks has his way.

Gotrocks is minority leader of the Senate subcommittee, which is considering this year's request for a larger federal appropriation to cover the Postal Service's deficit. "The Post Office ought to be run like any other business—it should show a profit or go out of business. If they can't at least break even, then I'm in favor of selling out to a private firm that can," Gotrocks said at a press conference following today's testimony by the head of the Postal Service. Senator Gotrocks did not say if his interest in ending the Post Office deficit extended to raising postage rates.

ECONOMIC ANALYSIS

Is Senator Gotrocks right? Should the postal service turn a profit? Why doesn't it at least break even? With a little information and the ideas developed in the preceding few chapters we should be able to figure out quickly whether Gotrocks is right or wrong.

First, a little information is necessary. The U.S. Postal Service is a quasi-public concern, which means that it is run by the government and regulated by the government, but is in competition with private-sector firms. The Post Office has a government-decreed monopoly in the first-class mail service—no one else can deliver this item. The Post Office competes for delivery of other types of mail, however. The United Parcel Service (UPS) currently provides most of the competition for packages (UPS actually delivers more packages than the Post Office), and various others compete in specialized areas such as special delivery mail and the like.

For the sake of argument, let's suppose that the Post Office is able to use monopoly power. If it is a monopolist, should it earn a profit? The answer to this question may be no. The Post Office may be a natural monopoly. As we have already seen, social welfare is maximized in the case of a natural monopoly when the price that is charged is set equal to marginal costs. In this case, however, the natural monopoly sets a price less than average total cost and actually loses money (this explains the postal service's deficit—they are charging prices below ATC in an attempt to maximize social welfare, not profits).

If the Post Office is a natural monopoly as discussed in this chapter, then there is good reason for the operating deficit. Profits should be avoided because they are a sign that price is too high and, as a result, the amount of net benefits generated is too low. But there is evidence that this is not the case. The success of the profitable United Parcel Service suggests that this may be a situation where the principle of natural monopoly does not apply. The Post Office monopoly may be an undesirable government creation. Perhaps competition could work in the postal delivery market. If this is the case, should the Post Office run a profit? Again, the answer is probably no.

The Post Office is in the business of information transmission. By linking people through ideas, the Post Office is increasing the amount of information available within the economy. This service is one that is highly likely to produce external benefits to the economy. The person who receives mail is not the only one who benefits by the process. Others gain benefits and society gains as well because of the spread of information that the Post Office makes possible.

If mail delivery does generate external benefits, then a firm that maximizes profits, as we learned in the preceding chapter, will charge too high a price and not produce enough mail delivery services. A subsidy that induces higher output and lower prices is needed to increase the amounts of external benefits generated and to increase social welfare as well.

Even if the Post Office is not a natural monopoly, a subsidy can be justified on the basis of externalities. If the postal service *is* a natural monopoly, then a deficit is doubly justified and society is best off with the situation as it now prevails, and will be worse off if the Post Office pays its own way.

There is one final explanation for the Post Office's problems. They may be acting as a monopolist (in first class mail) and *trying* to earn a profit but failing to do so. Not every monopoly is profitable, after all. We might call this situation an unnatural monopoly. Were it not for government help, this business would be out of business.

There is reason to believe that this situation may be the case for the Post Office and for other public service firms, as well. Metropolitan transit systems (buses, trains, subways) seem to lose money no matter how hard they try.

If the market were allowed to operate, these firms would quickly go under. Here government plays a useful role in keeping firms in business either through public provision of these services or by governmental subsidies. The government has a role here because of the importance of the services that these firms provide and because of the external benefits that they make possible.

Is Senator Gotrocks correct then? In general, he probably is not. There are good reasons for the continuing Postal Service deficit and, on the basis of a natural monopoly or externality argument, we can say that the Post Office should not even break even—a deficit may be highly desirable from a social point of view.

But we must temper our comments with caution. The money to finance the deficit must come from somewhere. Taxes can create social losses in other markets while they increase social welfare here. If the loss that society must endure in order to provide the subsidy to the Post Office is great, then the Senator may have something.

SUMMARY

1. Government regulation of monopolies is necessary because monopoly pricing and production practices reduce social welfare. The monopolist produces too little total output, causing a loss in the net benefits from production.

2. The government uses a variety of tools to influence monopoly production. Subsidies can be used to increase monopoly output, as can the use of price discrimination. More used, however, is the government's power to regulate production directly or to break up monopolies into competitive firms. Often just the threat of government action is enough to make monopoly firms act like competitors and increase output. The current loss from monopoly power is likely to be very small because of the success of governmental actions in this area.

3. Monopolies may be undesirable, but there are trade-offs here too. The monopoly may generate external benefits in terms of innovation, new knowledge, and new inventions. These external benefits may balance the costs that monopolies impose. Government patents and copyright laws encourage the limited formation of monopolies in order to encourage the production of these external benefits.

4. A natural monopoly exists when average costs are greater than marginal costs at levels of output consistent with competition. Many competitive firms would go out of business under these conditions. Monopoly is the only form of market organization, therefore, that can survive in these markets.

5. Natural monopolies produce benefits by their very existence, but still lower social welfare when they pursue monopoly

pricing practices. Society is best off when marginal cost pricing is used by natural monopolies, but some way has to be found to finance the deficit that results.

DISCUSSION QUESTIONS

1. This chapter makes a case for regulating monopolists in order to increase social welfare. Does this case also apply to a cartel? What impact does a cartel have on social welfare? Explain.

2. Suppose that you need to raise taxes in one market in order to finance subsidies in another. Which type of market does it make the most sense to impose the tax on: the monopolist or a market where perfect competition prevails?

3. Is product differentiation a good thing? What impact does it have on social welfare? Explain.

4. If you were a monopolist, which type of government control would you prefer: regulation, subsidies, or a license to price discriminate? Which would you prefer if you were the monopolist's customer? Why?

5. Suppose that a monopolist produces external costs. What is the proper governmental policy in this case?

TEST YOURSELF

Indicate whether each of the following statements is *true* or *false*. Be able to defend your choice.

1. Monopolists tend to sell at a price above marginal cost and produce a quantity below that which would prevail at perfect competition.

2. The reason that monopolies are bad is that they sell at a price in excess of marginal benefit.

3. If a profit-maximizing monopolist is not a perfect price discriminator, then it produces too little total output.

4. A price discriminator is one that sells to all at the highest price that anyone will pay.

5. When perfect price discrimination takes place, marginal benefit and demand are the same.

6. Fear of regulation can be enough to make a monopolist behave like a competitive firm.

7. Patent monopolies may be tolerated by the government because the monopoly loss is not very large.

8. Natural monopolies always lose money.

9. The telephone company is not an example of a natural monopoly because it earns a healthy profit and is not run by the government.

10. If the telephone company is a natural monopoly, it should lose money in the public interest.

16
Scarcity and Choice: The Poverty Problem

Poverty is a serious problem, a problem that even rich nations have thus far been unable to lick. This chapter looks at the poverty problem and the trade-offs that are necessary when economic policies are considered. Questions answered include:

How serious is the poverty problem in the United States? Who are the poor? Which groups are most affected by poverty? Why are they poor?

What kinds of government policies can be used to reduce the poverty problem?

What kinds of trade-offs exist in antipoverty programs?

Poverty: inadequate earnings when compared to a benchmark standard of living

"The principal difference between the rich and the poor is that the rich have more money." Mark Twain said it, and he was probably right in many ways. Still, in looking at the economic problem of **poverty**, the differences between families with different incomes and the causes of those differences are most important.

Economists define poverty much as Mark Twain might have. Poverty is simply the fact of inadequate earnings—income that is incapable of sustaining some minimum standard of living. That minimum living standard (and therefore the poverty line) varies depending on who is setting the standard and how, but we can all agree on the existence of poverty, regardless of the technical definition used.

The poverty problem is an important one for many reasons. From a moral or ethical point of view, one questions the justice of an economic system that makes some so rich and leaves others perennially hungry. Poverty is an important problem from an economic standpoint because its existence alters the results of free market choice.

Under a market system, people vote with their dollars for the goods and services that they desire. People who want more apples can secure them by voting in the marketplace—buying apples with dollars. In this kind of system, however, a person's ability to influence market actions is limited by his or her market power—limited by income. Poor people, viewed in this light, have less of a vote in market decisions. To a certain extent, the poor are disenfranchised in the free market choice mechanism.

FIGHTING POVERTY: THE RECORD

Absolute poverty: poverty as measured by real income—the ability to purchase goods and services

How serious is the poverty problem in the United States? How successful have antipoverty programs been?

Poverty can be measured in several ways, and two of these are presented in Figure 1. One way to gauge the severity of the poverty problem is to look at a measure of **absolute poverty**. Absolute poverty is defined in terms of the amounts of goods and services that households can purchase. A family is said to be living in absolute poverty when their real income is below some standard of acceptance—when they haven't enough money to purchase some minimum standard of goods and services.

As Figure 1 shows, the United States has made real progress in solving the poverty problem according to this measure. According to the figure, over 20 percent of the population lived in absolute poverty in the 1960s. The proportion of people below this poverty line was cut in half by 1975. This indicates a rising standard of living, which extended even to the very poor. Reducing absolute poverty by so much so fast is an admirable achievement,

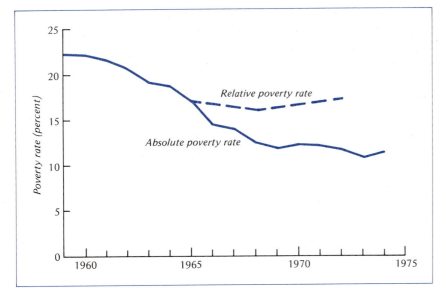

FIGURE 16-1: ABSOLUTE AND RELATIVE POVERTY RATES, 1959–1974
Figure from "Income Security Policy" by John L. Palmer and Joseph J. Minarik, in Setting National Priorities: The Next Ten Years *edited by Henry Owen and Charles L. Schultze, Brookings Institution, 1976.*

especially considering the fact that, because of high inflation, the population in general experienced falling real income during part of this period.

Pride in the fall in absolute poverty must be restrained, however. Those with substandard incomes still amount to a relatively large proportion of the population, and those who remain in poverty are quite likely those who it is hardest to help. Indeed, the quickest way to reduce the poverty numbers is to help only those closest to the poverty line. The very poor—those with the most severe economic problems—may be relatively unaffected. The gains in better living standards that we have seen here are important, but they are not enough.

Poverty is not just an absolute problem, it is also a problem of relative income distribution—the gap between the rich and the poor. **Relative poverty**, as shown in Figure 1, compares the poor not with a fixed standard of living but with their neighbors. How did the poor do, compared to other groups in the economy? The gains made in fighting absolute poverty were not achieved here. Relative poverty continues at about the same rate as in the past. The poor may be richer, but the rich are richer, too. The poverty gap remains about the same. The 1 percent of families with the highest incomes have about as much money after taxes as do all the families in the poorest 20 percent of the population. The top one-fifth of the families have about as much after-tax income as the poorest three-fifths. These unequal distributions have prevailed for years and even President Lyndon Johnson's great War on Poverty does not seem to have changed it much.

Relative poverty: poverty in relation to the incomes of others

FIGURE 16-2: RICH VERSUS POOR
Evidence suggests that the poor have not been helped so much by a redistribution of income from the rich to the poor (a movement from A to B) but rather by general economic growth that has allowed both groups to gain (A to C).

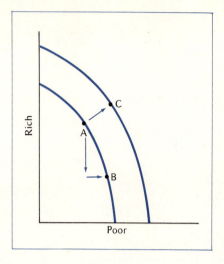

How is this paradox possible? How have the poor been able to gain absolutely (higher real incomes) but not relative to the rich? The answer may be suggested by Figure 2. People often assume that the poor are helped by governmental "Robin Hood" programs, which take from the rich and give to the poor (shown by a movement from A to B in Figure 2). Such programs make the poor absolutely better off and increase their incomes relative to the now "poorer" rich. But it appears that the real change in the poor's income has come instead as a result of economic growth. Economic growth (shown as an outward shift in the PPC in the figure and a movement from A to C) increases the poor's real income, and that of the rich, too. Both gain in absolute terms, but the relative differences (the rich–poor gap) remains about the same.

WHO ARE THE POOR?

Poverty strikes virtually every age, sex, and ethnic group in the United States. Yet, as an economic illness, poverty infects some groups relatively more than others. Poverty is much more frequent among blacks than whites in the United States. Blacks make up about one-third of all poor families. Poverty is a more frequent phenomenon among women as well. This is particularly the case among women who head households (who are the principal source of family income). The old and the young are also more

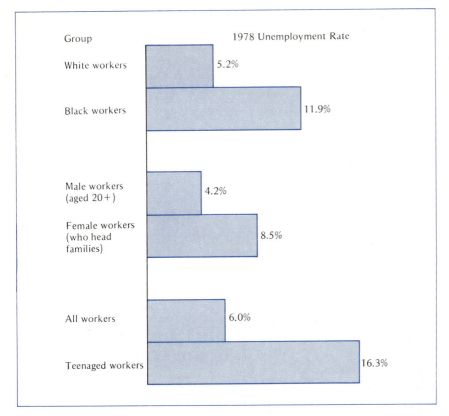

Group   1978 Unemployment Rate

White workers — 5.2%

Black workers — 11.9%

Male workers (aged 20+) — 4.2%

Female workers (who head families) — 8.5%

All workers — 6.0%

Teenaged workers — 16.3%

FIGURE 16-3: POVERTY AND UNEMPLOYMENT
Blacks, females, and the young bear substantially higher unemployment rates than other groups. These figures for 1978 are typical of those which have prevailed in recent years.

likely to be numbered among the poor. The old face the declining income that comes at the end of their active working years. The young are bound by the inadequate earnings of their parents and families, and by poor employment prospects.

Evidence of this distribution of poverty in the United States is seen in unemployment statistics like those presented in Figure 3. Blacks, women who head families, and teenagers have unemployment rates that are often more than twice those of other groups. The old are not separately measured in these unemployment statistics because they often do not participate in the labor market. Poverty and their age keep them from even looking for work in some cases.

These four groups—blacks, women, the old, and the young—face the highest poverty levels. They share the problem of low income, but do they share other problems? Why are they poor? The causes of poverty are as diverse as the groups that share it.

CAUSES OF POVERTY

Studies of the poverty problem, like those reported in Richard Perlman's *The Economics of Poverty*, have uncovered the economic problems that lead to the existence of poverty. Solving the poverty problem in the United States is essentially a problem of dealing with these causes.

A first cause of poverty is unemployment. People who cannot find work (or who must settle for part-time work) are less able to earn the income necessary to lift them from their poverty. The solution to this problem involves finding ways to make the poor more competitive in the labor market.

A related cause of poverty is inadequate education. Very often the poor cannot find good jobs (or cannot keep them) because they have poor educations or inadequate general working skills. Clearly a person who cannot read well is at a severe disadvantage when looking for a job. Poor education can make poverty hereditary. The children of poor parents may be forced to leave school at an early age to find work and contribute to family income. The poor education that caused poverty for the parent is passed down, by force of circumstances, to the children.

Discrimination adds to the poverty problem. Groups that suffer prejudice bear higher poverty rates. Laws in the United States ban discrimination in most labor markets and so should reduce this problem, but discrimination is a difficult nut to crack.

Discrimination can take many forms. When the word discrimination is mentioned, most people think of the overt forms that racism or sexism take ("I won't hire her because she is black or female!"). This sort of discrimination is the kind that most laws are designed to reduce. Overt discrimination is unprofitable from both the employer's and employee's point of view. In order to exercise prejudice, the employer must pay a cost. Discriminating employers refuse to hire qualified black or female workers because of their race, sex, or age, suggesting that, implicitly, white, male, or middle-aged workers of lesser qualifications get hired instead. If markets were truly competitive, nondiscriminating employers would take advantage of the skills of the best workers regardless of sex, age, or race, and so produce products at lower costs than discriminators. In perfect markets, therefore, discriminators pay for their prejudice with profits. But the existence of less-than-perfect competition in many markets reduces the penalty for prejudice and makes government policy necessary.

While overt discrimination is a problem, discrimination can also take more subtle forms. A firm that hires only college graduates, for example, may be perfectly willing to employ qualified blacks, but actually hires very few. The existence of other problems that reduce the number of blacks who graduate from college also reduce their ability to gain employment here.

Doing away with these forms of indirect discrimination is a much more complicated problem than simply ordering a prejudiced personnel manager to hire people based on ability to produce, not sex, age, or skin color.

Discrimination, unemployment, poor education—these causes of poverty are interrelated and are all tied up in the labor market. These problems prevent the poor from joining the productive, income-producing working world. Goverment policies try to get to these causes, but the facts of scarcity and choice still come into play. Let's look at several governmental policies that try to get to the roots of the poverty problem and examine the winners and losers that they create.

TRANSFER PAYMENTS

Transfer payments are government payments to groups and individuals where no good or service is returned in exchange for the payments. A transfer payment is, in effect, a one-way transfer of cash. Welfare payments, unemployment benefits, and social security payments are examples of transfer payments. Transfer payments represent one of the major weapons in the fight against poverty in the United States.

Transfer payments are designed to deal with the poverty problem that Mark Twain observed. By giving the poor money directly, transfer payments try to solve their problem.

Transfer payments have a number of interesting effects, as Figure 4 notes. We can, first of all, examine the impact of transfer payments on the budget lines of two groups: the recipients of the transfer payments (the poor) and

Transfer payments: a transfer of money from one group to another without a corresponding payment of goods or services, e.g., welfare and unemployment benefits

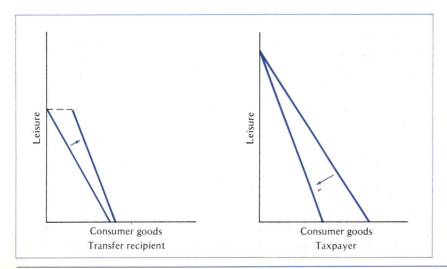

Consumer goods
Transfer recipient

Consumer goods
Taxpayer

FIGURE 16-4: WINNERS AND LOSERS WITH TRANSFER PAYMENTS
The transfer payment recipient finds an expanded purchase possibilities curve with transfer payments. Taxpayers find that their real income has fallen as taxes (used to finance transfer payments) shift the PPC in.

those who must finance the payments (the taxpayers). For the transfer payment recipient, the goverment payment alters the trade-off between work and leisure. As the figure shows, the additional payments make a larger quantity of consumer goods available to the poor. Their standard of living should improve and move them out of the absolute poverty level. The principal goal of transfer payments is to have this desirable income effect.

There is an income effect at work with taxpayers, too, however. The taxes that must be paid in order to make transfer payments possible reduce the real incomes of those not in poverty. They find that each hour of work brings home fewer consumer goods than before because more taxes are taken from each paycheck. They suffer a loss in real income. The trade-off is clear—some must lose in order for others to gain under this Robin Hood kind of program.

Another trade-off is affected, too. By lowering the after-tax wage rate, the transfer payments tax alters the trade-off between work and leisure for taxpayers. Consumer goods now have a higher opportunity cost in terms of the leisure that must be given up in order to acquire them. Less work may be offered and a larger quantity of leisure consumed. Workers, on the margin, may choose to consume nontaxed leisure over taxable consumer goods.

This labor–leisure trade-off affects the poor, too. Transfer payment programs are often set up to help only the needy. If a poor person gets a job and earns money, the amount of the transfer payment is reduced. This means that if the poor workers makes $1 of income, he may stand to lose up to $1 of government payments. If he spends all his time working, he may be less well-off than if he was idle and collected the full payments. The transfer tax alters the labor–leisure choice for the poor person as well as the taxpayer. *Both* groups may find it less profitable to work and more satisfying to spend their time at leisure activities.

WHAT KIND OF TRANSFERS?

Even though transfer payments reduce work incentive, they seem to be a necessary piece of any antipoverty plan. But what form should the transfer payments take? There are two schools of thought here. Some policy-makers favor cash transfers and support the movement toward a **negative income tax** while others suggest a policy of **in-kind transfers.**

In-kind transfers are gifts of goods and services, not money, to poor people. Medical care, counseling, food, and housing are supplied to the poor directly through government-owned low-income housing, for example, or indirectly through programs like food stamps. Cash transfer programs give the poor money and allow them to use it in any way they wish.

The difference in philosophy between these two programs is not difficult to see. Those who favor cash transfers suggest that the poor are best able to determine what goods and services they need. If they take transfer dollars and spend them on lottery tickets, it must be because this gamble leaves them better off than any alternative. People who favor in-kind transfers have decided that the government knows what the poor need better than the poor do themselves.

The ultimate form of cash transfer program is a negative income tax plan that automatically gives cash (the negative taxes) to people who fall below a poverty line. The poorest families get the biggest negative tax payments. As family income rises, transfers decline and eventually positive taxes are collected as family income exceeds the poverty level.

MINIMUM WAGES

Minimum wages represent an attempt to cure the poverty problem by regulating wages in the labor market. Like other government antipoverty policies, minimum wage laws create winners and losers. In this case, however, the losers are not always those who pay taxes, but the poor themselves. The problem of minimum wages is illustrated in Figure 5.

The whole idea of minimum wages is to set the wage rate artificially above that which would otherwise prevail in the labor market to help low income workers. In many markets like the labor market for skilled

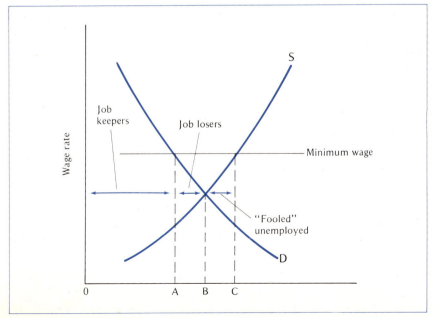

FIGURE 16-5: MINIMUM WAGE EFFECTS
Minimum wages make workers OA better off because they get higher wages than would prevail in the free market. Workers AB are unemployed, but could have worked if the minimum wage were not enacted. Workers BC would not have been employed anyway, but are drawn into the labor market by the existence of high wages, even if no jobs are available.

electronics workers, supply and demand factors have already pushed the wage rate above this minimum level and minimum wage laws have no impact. In those markets where wages are very low, minimum wages have their largest impact.

The minimum wage laws affect three groups in different ways. One group wins, as Figure 5 shows. Those workers who are able to retain their jobs (job keepers) in the face of governmental wage restrictions (shown by segment OA in the figure) gain. Without minimum wages, they will be paid at the lower market wage rate. With these laws, they get more income for the same work. These people are clearly better off.

But minimum wage laws reduce employment and so create losers, too. The group of job losers shown by segment AB in Figure 5 lose. Because wages are above the equilibrium level, they cannot find work, which would have been available if the labor market were allowed to function freely. The labor supply curve suggests that these folks would rather work at the lower market wage rate than be unemployed at the higher minimum wage. The government makes these groups losers. Unless they can do something to increase their productivity they will become unemployed.

The third group affected by minimum wages is the workers represented by segment BC in Figure 5. This group is what economist Bruce Mann calls the "fooled unemployed." They are only part of the labor market because the government announces that the minimum wage rate is high (at the low market wage rate they would not search for work). Minimum wages for them create a false hope of a job that, as the figure shows, just does not exist.

Minimum wage laws, it seems, make some poor better off while making others worse off. And, to the extent that the artificially high labor price causes inflation (higher prices of final goods), unemployment (with the higher taxes that remaining workers must pay) or substitution of other inputs for low-productivity minimum wage workers, many other groups can be affected as well.

JOB TRAINING AND EDUCATION

Transfer payments attempt to solve the poverty problem by bypassing markets altogether and giving the poor money. Minimum wage laws intervene in labor markets to give the poor higher incomes by short-circuiting the economic forces that result in their low wages. Education and job training programs attempt to produce the same results—higher incomes for the poor—in a very different way.

Training programs try to look beyond the simple statement that the poor are poor because they don't have enough money. The market, we have seen, rewards the ability to produce. By increasing the poor's ability to produce, the logic goes, it will be possible to place them successfully into the labor market and free them from the shackles of poverty. This idea is illustrated in Figure 6.

By providing education and training to the poor, it should be possible to increase their ability to produce. This training will be seen, in the market, as an increase in the marginal revenues that these workers can generate for employers. Assuming a sufficient demand for the final output, an increase in worker productivity translates into an increase in the demand for labor. Wage rates and employment should rise for the poor, at least partially solving the poverty problem. But there are problems with training programs.

First, the existence of transfer payments may make the poor unwilling to take a chance on these training programs. Training means foregoing leisure or a certain small income in order to take a chance on another occupation and the possible loss of government benefits currently received. A bird in the hand may be preferred to an uncertain turkey in the bush.

The second problem is that these programs must be paid for with tax dollars. This creates winners and losers, as noted in the discussion of transfer payments. If higher taxes reduce the demand for consumer goods, they may also reduce the demand for the labor for which the poor are training. If the poor are educated to become, say, plumbers' assistants, this does them little good if high taxes force people to do their own plumbing.

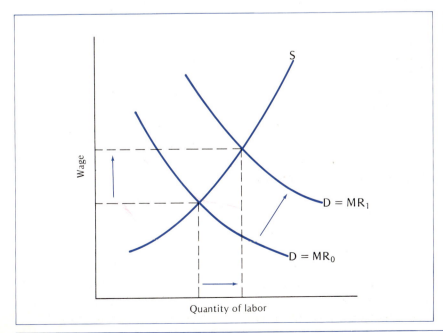

FIGURE 16-6: EDUCATION AND THE LABOR MARKET
Training can increase the productivity of workers. This can produce an increase in the demand for labor, which eventually results in higher wages and high employment.

Finally, this is a risky proposition. Training is an investment in the future that pays off if the present value of future benefits exceeds the current cost. Training provides many possible benefits to the poor person who is part of the program (higher income, self-esteem, standard of living) and the public as well (greater tax collections, higher total production, fewer future transfer payments). For the successful trainee, the costs—even if quite high—may be justified by the present value of the high future benefits. But not all such programs will be successful and not all taxpayers, government decision-makers, or potential program participants are likely to have much foresight. Day-to-day pressures may force such long-run solutions aside. Taxpayers, faced with high tax levies today, may not be willing to wait for benefits far down the road. They may ask for cheaper programs with tangible benefits now. The trade-offs must be weighed, and those with uncertain future benefits are certain to suffer.

PUBLIC EMPLOYMENT PROGRAMS

The final solution that we will look at here is the variety of government programs that attempt to affect the labor market by providing job opportunities in the public sector of the economy. These programs, as Figure 7 shows, increase employment by having the government artificially increase the demand for labor. Wage rates may not rise (if minimum wage laws apply that already create surplus labor supply), but the number of people working certainly does rise. Incomes go up for those hired, and this represents a

FIGURE 16-7: PUBLIC EMPLOYMENT PROGRAMS
Public employment attempts to increase employment by artificially increasing the demand for labor from D to D + G (G stands for the additional government demand for workers).

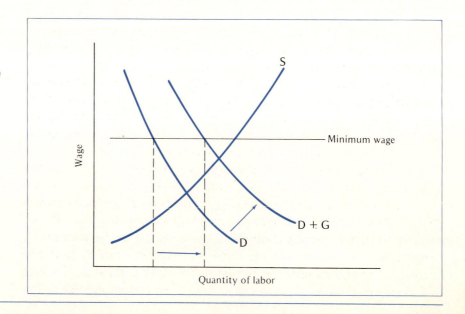

Quantity of labor

solution to the poverty problem so long as hiring is directed toward the poor groups (not always the case).

As with any other program, public employment projects force trade-offs. The first is that, like any other government plans, this one must be financed through taxes either now or later (if borrowing is used to pay the bills currently produced). Winners and losers are created as taxes are levied.

Public employment imposes other burdens, too. One of the most dangerous is the inflation that can result as employment rises. Higher incomes breed higher demands. If demand rises and supply does not, then higher prices will prevail in markets around the economy.

Instead of risking this inflation by increasing government employment, the public sector can try to accomplish the same end by taking actions that stimulate the expansion of business firms. As firms expand, their demand for labor rises and employment may rise as well. This creates the kind of economic growth pictured in Figure 2, which seems to have benefits for all groups in the economy. Alas, it may not be popular to try to help the poor by providing benefits to rich corporations, especially if the gains that the poor make may be only indirect and perhaps a long time in coming.

COSTS OF GOVERNMENT ACTION

Because the government must exist in a world of scarcity along with the rest of us, any choice that it makes is likely to produce costs. The government must consider opportunity costs when making its decisions because the resources that it commands within governmental budgets and within the economy are strictly limited. There are two opportunity costs for the government. The first opportunity cost—the one that public decision-makers are most likely to be aware of—is created by the government's budget constraint. If more money is spent on transfer payments, less will be left for training programs for the poor, expenditures on national defense, subsidies for public utilities, and construction of parks and highways. Which use provides the greatest net benefits? What is the impact all around if one less dollar is spent on project A and one more dollar devoted to project B? Who will gain and who will lose? Is the loss worth the gain?

The second opportunity cost that the government must face is the opportunity cost of the funds spent in the private sector. Every time tax dollars are collected, taxpayers must give up the goods and services that those dollars could have purchased instead. There is a direct loss in real income and utility among consumers. Is the benefit of the government program worth the loss that the taxpayers make in order to fund that program? This second opportunity cost is every bit as real as the first one but, because it shows up in society's budget constraint and not in the government's, it is often ignored. These opportunity costs reduce the extent to which net benefits can be produced and make the case for government policies less persuasive.

Antipoverty programs are affected by governmental direct costs—this is what Arthur M. Okun has called the "leaky bucket" problem. Suppose that we are taxing Peter, who is rich, to pay Paul, who is living in poverty. Let's assume, to make life easy, that everyone agrees that it is a good idea to take $10 from Peter and give it to Paul. Even Peter agrees that this is a desirable action because of the externalities that he expects this plan will produce.

Now, let's introduce the government's leaky bucket. Suppose that, in order to take from Peter and give to Paul, we must pay government employees to collect the tax, process the funds, and screen Paul to make sure that he needs the money. Suppose, therefore, that Peter gives up $10 but that, because of direct governmental costs, Paul is able to receive just $5. Is the plan worth it? Peter still loses, and Paul still gains, but direct costs have driven a wedge between the two.

Many government (and, indeed, private sector) antipoverty programs suffer from the leaky bucket dilemma. Some leakages are necessary. But how much loss is too much? At what point, because of the leakages, does the cost become too great?

Clearly, governmental actions are a trade-off. Benefits may be generated by government programs, but there are many costs to be considered, as well. In many cases, public policies that produce benefits for some groups must be denied because of the costs that are borne by others. Paradoxically, however, the voting process may lead to just such programs being implemented if the distribution of benefits and costs is uneven. And voting cannot guarantee an accurate reading of public preferences, either.

The basic problem of society remains the same as it was in the first chapter of this book. Scarcity exists for us all. Opportunity costs must be faced. And choices must be made. This is the economic world.

REAL WORLD ECONOMICS: THE SOCIAL SECURITY TAX

CRITICS OF SOCIAL SECURITY MEET WITH CONGRESSIONAL GROUP

WASHINGTON, D.C.—Leaders of groups representing the working poor met with congressional representatives today to discuss changes in the social security law. The critics wish to lobby for a change in the tax and benefit structure of social security.

"The current social security system is biased against the poor. The social security tax takes a large bite of the working-poor's income and provides only a meager retirement income," a spokesman for the poor-people's lobby noted, calling for a change in the funding and increased benefits from the governmental program.

ECONOMIC ANALYSIS

The social security system is interesting to economists and others for a variety of reasons. Social security demonstrates the problems of scarcity and choice that the government must deal with and the winners and losers that are created when the public choice is made.

For the individual (poor or not) the social security system represents a trade-off. With limited amounts of resources, it is not always possible to live high on the hog now and in the future, too. The social security system faces that trade-off and forces it upon workers. The system taxes current workers and pays these revenues to those who are now retired. The tax comes out of your paycheck, goes to Washington, and is immediately sent on its way to some retired individual around the country. The worker is worse off, but the income of the retired family rises, making them better off.

Because one must generally pay social security taxes in order to receive benefits, another kind of trade-off is made. Workers pay now (while they are working) in order to receive benefits later

(when work has stopped). Because the social security tax falls on wages and salaries only (as opposed to income from investments and stocks and bonds) the tax tends to hit the poor harder than other groups within the economy.

Is the social security system a good thing? It apparently depends on who you are and your point of view. Studies have shown that, from a present value perspective, social security may be good for the poor and not so good for other groups. The poor can probably expect to receive benefits from social security that have a present value greater than the taxes that they will pay. Other groups are not so fortunate. Today's college students (who, by and large, are not in poverty groups) will pay social security taxes with greater present value than the benefits that they will receive.

If this is the case, then why are these people complaining about social security. After all, the poor win, don't they? Apparently, they don't think so. Because the poor have so little, each dollar they give up now in taxes has very high utility. The taxes hurt them now and the fact that they will receive a dividend in higher benefits in the future may not seem to cover the loss.

1. The poverty problem is a serious one in the United States. It affects between 10 and 20 percent of the population (depending on the poverty measure used). Absolute poverty has been reduced in the United States in recent years, but relative poverty remains about the same.

SUMMARY

2. Poverty strikes most groups to some extent. Blacks, women, the old, and the young bear a disproportionate poverty burden. Unemployment, poor education, and discrimination are causes of poverty in these groups.

3. Governments use many types of policies to reduce poverty. Transfer payments give money to the poor. Minimum wage laws attempt to increase in-comes artificially by propping up wage rates. Training programs try to make the poor's labor more valuable. Public employment programs offer an employer a last resort.

4. Antipoverty programs force trade-offs. The poor, the government, employees, and employers all face the problem of scarcity and deal with the opportunity costs that result.

DISCUSSION QUESTIONS

1. What other options are available in dealing with the poverty problem? Do these plans also create winners and losers? List two other ways of increasing poor people's incomes and state the winners and losers from each.

2. Economic growth makes all income groups better off. Does it force any trade-offs or do these gains come without opportunity cost? Explain your answer.

3. If education is one solution to the poverty problem, why must the government get involved? Why don't the poor invest in education and training themselves?

4. Why should the elimination of poverty be a public policy as opposed to a purely private concern? Is poverty the result of market failures?

5. Suppose that your local government wishes to hire more police. List all the costs of this action. Who will benefit from this? Who will lose? How should we decide whether or not to increase spending on the police?

TEST YOURSELF

Indicate whether each of the following statements is *true* or *false*. Be able to defend your choice.

1. The government does not face the same problems as other parts of the economy because of its greater access to resources.

2. Economic growth has lowered absolute poverty while having little affect on relative poverty.

3. Relative poverty is a measure of the goods and services that poor families can afford to purchase.

4. Absolute poverty refers to the absolute difference in incomes between the rich and the poor.

5. Transfer payments cause poor and rich alike to work harder by providing incentives to consume more goods.

6. Minimum wage laws increase the number of people looking for work—these are the "fooled" unemployed.

7. Government programs have an opportunity cost in terms of alternative government programs that could have been funded instead.

8. Government programs have an opportunity cost in terms of private goods that could have been purchased instead.

9. The government must step in whenever external benefits are produced in order to increase the net benefits to society.

10. Discrimination increases poverty for blacks and women, but probably does not cause poverty among the young and old.

Suggestions for Further Reading

This section gives a chapter-by-chapter listing of readings that may be used to supplement or expand the treatment of economic problems, theories, and policies given in the text. These readings include articles from magazines, books, and economic journals that should be available at most college libraries. Many of the articles also appear in books of readings for introductory economics courses.

In addition to the specific articles referenced here, certain periodicals can be counted upon for understandable presentation of current economic events. These include *Time, Newsweek,* and *U.S. News* magazines, *The New York Times* and *The Washington Post* and, most particularly, *The Wall Street Journal.*

Those articles which are particularly difficult are marked with an asterisk(*).

CHAPTER 1: SCARCITY AND CHOICE

1. Scarcity and choice in the United States is discussed in the interesting article by J. Irwin Miller, "Changing Priorities: Hard Choices, New Price Tags," which originally appeared in the *Saturday Review* (January 23, 1971).

2. A different set of opportunity costs is analyzed in an important little book by Arthur M. Okun, *Equality and Efficiency: The Big Tradeoff* (The Brookings Institution, 1975).

*3. For a good discussion of the trade-offs and problems that economic growth brings with it, see "Growth and Antigrowth: What Are the Issues?" by E.J. Mishan, which originally appeared in *Challenge* (May–June 1973).

CHAPTER 2: SPECIALIZATION AND EXCHANGE

1. No student of economics should miss reading Adam Smith's vivid description of the pin factory as an example of specialization and exchange. It is described in his *The Wealth of Nations*, Book I, Chapter 1.

2. Some rather sophisticated economic policies can be derived from the theory of comparative advantage. For an example of this, see an interesting book by Jude Wanniski, *The Way the World Works*, (Simon and Schuster, 1978). Of particular interest is Chapter 5.

*3. Students with exceptional mathematical skills might enjoy the quantitative treatment of comparative advantage contained in *International Trade* by Akira Takayama (Holt, Rinehart and Winston, 1972), Chapter 4.

CHAPTER 3: DEMAND AND SUPPLY: THE MICRO SIDE

1. An interesting look at how markets work in the worst of times can be found in an article by R.A. Radford, "The Economic Organization of a P.O.W. Camp," which was first printed in *Economica* (November 1945) and can be found in many economics reading books.

2. For insights into the nature of the conflict and competition that takes place in the market, see "Grocery War" by John A. Prestbo in *The Best of the Wall Street Journal* (Dow Jones, 1973).

3. When markets break down, due to government regulations or other events, the results can be severely damaging to those involved. The anatomy of a market failure is outlined in "The Gas Price Fixers" by Tom Bethell, *Harper's* (June 1979).

CHAPTER 4: MARKETS AT WORK

1. An interesting use of the concepts of elasticity of demand can be found in "The Demand for Higher Education" by Michael S. McPherson in *Public Policy and Private Higher Education*, edited by David W. Breneman and Chester E. Finn, Jr. (The Brookings Institution, 1978).

2. Many different factors can affect markets. An unusual analysis of markets at work is "Attendance and Price Setting" by Roger G. Noll in *Government and the Sports Business*, edited by Roger G. Noll (The Brookings Institution, 1974).

3. For more examples of markets in action, the student is advised to simply read any day's *Wall Street Journal*.

4. For a more in-depth analysis of elasticity, see intermediate microeconomic theory texts such as *Price Theory and Applications* by Jack Hirshleifer (Prentice-Hall, 1976) Chapter 5.

5. Students may be interested in the results of the article by Charles T. Nisbet and Firouz Vakil, "Some Estimates of Price and Expenditure Elasticities of Demand for Marijuana Among UCLA Students," *Review of Economics and Statistics* (November 1972).

CHAPTER 5: CONSUMER CHOICE

1. A very complete discussion of the economic meaning and uses of utility is found in "The Meaning of Utility Measurement" by Armen Alchain, *American Economic Review* (March 1953).

2. Many kinds of choices are affected by economic variables. The decision to consume crime—to undertake criminal acts—is one such choice. An interesting treatment of this problem is found in "Criminal Behavior and the Control of Crime: An Economic Perspective" by Timothy H. Hannan, *Federal Reserve Bank of Philadelphia Business Review* (November 1974).

3. Many government agencies attempt to measure and quantify costs and benefits when making decisions. A good discussion of this formal cost–benefits analysis is found in Chapter 7 and 8 of *Public Finance In Theory and Practice* (2nd edition) by Richard A. and Peggy B. Musgrave (McGraw-Hill, 1976).

CHAPTER 6: PRODUCTION AND COST

1. Students who have trouble with the cost and revenue curves presented here should spend some time with any of the many economics workbooks and study guides that are available in most college bookstores and libraries.

2. A good general presentation for the relationship among marginal, average, and total costs and revenues is found in Chapter 3 (Marginal Analysis) of *Economic Theory and Operations Analysis* (4th edition) by William J. Baumol (Prentice-Hall, 1977).

CHAPTER 7: PRODUCER CHOICE: MONOPOLY

1. The ideas of monopoly and the related concept of monopsony are discussed in most intermediate theory texts. A very readable example is *Intermediate Microeconomics: Theory, Issues and Applications* by Roger LeRoy Miller (McGraw-Hill, 1978).

2. A good general discussion of monopoly is contained in "The Concept of Monopoly and the Measurement of Monopoly Power" by Abba P. Lerner, *Review of Economic Studies* (June 1943).

CHAPTER 8: PRODUCERS IN COMPETITIVE MARKETS

1. More detailed treatments of the topics covered in this chapter can be found in any intermediate theory text. See, for example, Chapters 9 and 10 in *Intermediate Microeconomics and Its Applications* (2nd edition) by Walter Nicholson (Holt, Rinehart and Winston, 1979).

2. An interesting discussion of the role of fixed and marginal costs together with elasticity of demand in a specific market is found in "A Note on Textbook Pricing," by Paul M. Horvitz, *American Economic Review* (September 1965).

*3. An interesting, but sometimes difficult discussion of these topics is found in an article by Joan Robinson, "What Is Perfect Competition," *The Quarterly Journal of Economics* (November 1934).

CHAPTER 9: IMPERFECT COMPETITION

1. A lengthy but interesting article by Reuben A. Kessell looks at some topics covered in this chapter. It is "Price Discrimination in Medicine," *Journal of Law and Economics* (October 1958).

2. A good general description of different market structures is found in "Monopoly and Competition: A Classification of Market Positions" by Fritz Machlup, *American Economic Review* (September 1937).

*3. A very difficult article especially selected for the mathematically inclined is written by Don Patinkin,

"Multiple-Plant Firms, Cartels, and Imperfect Competition," *The Quarterly Journal of Economics* (February 1947).

4. An interesting discussion of why firms seek regulation is found in "The Theory of Economic Regulation" by George J. Stigler, *Bell Journal of Economics* (Spring, 1971).

CHAPTER 10: LABOR MARKETS

1. A good discussion of the causes of current labor market problems is an article by Steven P. Zell, "Recent Developments in the Theory of Unemployment," *Federal Reserve Bank of Kansas City Monthly Review*, (September–October 1975).

2. A look at wage differentials is interesting as done in the article by Mary Hamblin and Michael J. Prell, "The Incomes of Men and Women: Why Do They Differ?" the *Federal Reserve Bank of Kansas City Monthly Review* (April 1973).

3. A more detailed introduction to the economics of the job market is a book by Richard B. Freeman, *Labor Economics*, (Prentice-Hall, 1972).

CHAPTER 11: CAPITAL AND NATURAL RESOURCE MARKETS

1. These topics are covered in more detail in most intermediate theory texts including *Intermediate Microeconomics: Theory, Issues and Applications* by Roger LeRoy Miller (McGraw-Hill, 1978).

2. Capital markets are discussed in detail in William Baumol's *Economic Theory and Operations Analysis* (4th edition).

*3. Robert M. Solow has written an excellent article describing the economics of natural resource markets. It is "The Economics of Resources

and the Resources of Economics," *American Economic Review* (May 1974).

CHAPTER 12: ENERGY MARKETS

1. A good, readable article that describes the problems faced in energy markets is "The Gas Price Fixers" by Tom Bethell, *Harper's* (June 1979).

2. A short book by S. David Freeman presents a good overall description of recent energy problems: *Energy: The New Era* (Vintage Books, 1974).

3. A perspective on the economics of energy and energy resources is found in an article by Nathan Rosenberg, "Innovative Responses to Material Shortages," *American Economic Review* (May, 1973).

4. David C. White has written an interesting article, "Overview of the Energy Shortage Situation: How Real Is It and What Are the Options for the 1970s and the Necessary Policy Decisions to Make Them Viable?" *Business Economics* (September, 1974).

CHAPTER 13: FREE MARKET CHOICE

1. Milton Friedman takes a look at the market economy and the role of government in *Capitalism and Freedom* (University of Chicago Press, 1962).

2. For a look at how economies work when markets aren't allowed to function freely, see the descriptions of Soviet economic life in *The Russians* by Hendrick Smith (New York Times Book Co., 1976).

3. Nothing beats Adam Smith for Adam Smith. See his *Wealth of Nations* (Everyman's Library, 1964).

CHAPTER 14: MARKET FAILURES: EXTERNALITIES

1. A good discussion of pollution externalities is found in an article by Larry E. Ruff, "The Economic Common Sense of Pollution," *The Public Interest* (Spring, 1970).

2. Externalities disrupt markets and call for public policies. This is illustrated for the case of farm and open lands in "Alternative Policies for Preserving Farm and Open Lands" by Michael Veseth, *American Journal of Economics and Sociology* (January 1979).

*3. A difficult but very important article is "The Problem of Social Cost" by Ronald Coase, *Journal of Law and Economics* (October 1960).

4. The problem of externalities and the prisoner's dilemma that they can create are discussed in "The Economics of Urban Renewal" by Otto A. Davis and Andrew B. Whinston, *Law and Contemporary Problems* (Winter, 1961).

CHAPTER 15: MARKET FAILURES: MONOPOLIES

1. A good general discussion of the monopoly problem is found in an article by Sheldon W. Stahl and C. Edward Harshberger, "Free Enterprise Revisited—A Look at Economic Concentration," published in the *Federal Reserve Bank of Kansas City Monthly Review* (March 1973).

2. A good discussion of the welfare losses due to monopoly is contained in *Intermediate Microeconomics* by James P. Quirk (SRA, 1976) Chapter 14.

3. Discussions of several different regulated monopolies are found in *Regulation: A Case Approach* by Leonard W. Weiss and Allyn D. Strickland (McGraw-Hill, 1976).

CHAPTER 16: SCARCITY AND CHOICE: THE POVERTY PROBLEM

1. An interesting discussion of the poverty problem appears in "Standards of Income Redistribution" by Martin Rein and S.M. Miller, *Challenge* (July–August 1974).

2. Lester C. Thurow has written an important book about the poverty problem and government policies that deal with it. The book is *Generating Inequality* (Basic Books, 1975).

3. An outstanding overall discussion of this governmental problem appears in an article by John L. Palmer and Joseph J. Minarik, "Income Security Policy," which appears in *Setting National Priorities: The Next Ten Years*, edited by Henry Owen and Charles L. Schultze (Brookings Institution, 1976).

4. The excellent little book cited in the text is *The Economics of Poverty* by Richard Perlman (McGraw-Hill, 1976).

Glossary

Absolute advantage: the ability to produce more total output with a given amount of resources

Absolute poverty: poverty as measured by real income—the ability to purchase goods and services

Absolute value: the value of a number regardless of its sign. The absolute value of both +4 and −4 is 4, for example

Accounting profits: profits calculated ignoring opportunity cost as a cost to the firm

Antitrust regulation: government laws that seek to outlaw or regulate monopolies

Atomistic competition: competitive markets where individual buyers and sellers are as small, relative to the market, as atoms are relative to the items they form; another name for perfect competition

Average cost: total cost divided by the quantity of production; the mean cost of production

Average cost pricing: the setting of price charged by a natural monopoly at the level that covers total cost; price is set equal to average total costs

Average revenue: total revenue divided by the quantity of output

Barriers to entry: factors such as high entry costs or government protection, which prevent competitors from entering a market

Barter economy: an economy where exchange takes place without money; goods are exchanged for each other directly

Budget line: same as purchase possibilities curve

Bureaucratic choice: a method of making economic choices that relies on central planning

Capital: long-lasting productive resources such as plants, equipment, and factories

Cartel: an organization of firms in a market designed to exercise monopoly control by restricting supply

Choice: the problem of deciding among several alternatives, not all of which can be obtained at the same time

Clayton Antitrust Act: a federal law, passed in 1914, that outlaws monopoly pricing practices such as price discrimination

Cobweb theory: the theory that producers will base next year's production decision on this year's market price, causing unstable prices

Coincidence of wants: the condition prevailing when the items that one person wishes to receive are the same as those the other person wishes to exchange; the condition necessary for exchange

Command economy: economic system where decisions affecting resource use are made by central planners

Comparative advantage: the ability to produce a good or service at a lower opportunity cost

Complement: goods that are used together are called complements; toast and jam, coffee and sugar, and hamburgers and french fries are all examples of complements

Complete specialization: when an economic unit produces only one good or service; specialization in one aspect of production to the exclusion of all others

Constant returns: the condition prevailing when each resource adds as much to production as the one before it; equal productivity of resources

Constant returns to scale: constant long-run average costs

Consumer burden: the part of a tax that consumers pay in the form of higher prices for the taxed goods

Consumer equilibrium: the situation that prevails when the consumer allocates resources to maximize utility

Consumers' surplus: the difference between the maximum price that a consumer is willing to pay for an item and the actual price that is paid

Copyright: the right to exclusive use of a publication, recording, and so on

Corporation: a form of business organization where a firm has many owners each of whom has only limited liability for the debts of the firm

Decrease in demand: a change in income, tastes, and preferences, or some other determinant of demand, which causes the quantity demanded to be lower at every price (shown by a shift to the left in the demand curve)

Decrease in supply: a change in costs of production, technology, or some other determinant of supply, which causes the quantity supplied to be less at every price (shown by a shift to the left in the supply curve)

Decreasing returns to scale: rising long-run average costs

Demand: a description of the buyer side of the market; demand looks at how the amounts and kinds of goods and services people wish to buy are determined

Demand curve: a curve that shows the quantity of a good or service that buyers wish to purchase at every possible price

Democratic choice: a method of making economic choices that relies on the voting process

Diminishing marginal product: a situation where the addition to total product of a unit of input declines as the number of inputs used increases

Direct relationship: a direct relationship exists between A and B if they increase or decrease together, i.e., an increase in A implies an increase in B

Economic efficiency: production that takes place in the most efficient way—at lowest opportunity cost

Economic profits: profits in excess of the opportunity costs of the firm

Economics: the social science that studies the production and distribution of goods and services in a world of scarce resources

Efficient: an efficient use of resources is said to occur when it is impossible to use resources differently to produce more of every good or service

Elastic demand: a good has an elastic demand if quantity demanded is responsive to changes in price; the elasticity coefficient is greater than one

Elasticity coefficient: the elasticity coefficient is defined to be

$$E = \frac{\% \text{ change in quantity demanded}}{\% \text{ change in price}}$$

Elasticity of demand: a measure of the responsiveness of quantity demanded to changes in price

Equilibrium for the firm: the profit-maximizing (P = MC) level of production for the firm

Equilibrium price: the one price where the quantity supplied equals the quantity demanded; neither a surplus nor a shortage exists at the equilibrium price; all exchanges desired at this price can be completed

Excess demand: a situation where the quantity demanded at a particular price exceeds the quantity supplied at that price

Excess supply: a situation where the quantity supplied at a particular price exceeds the quantity demanded at that price

Exchange: the voluntary trading of goods or services

Exchange rate: the ratio of goods in exchange; the rate at which two goods trade

Explicit costs: costs that the firm must pay to other firms or businesses

External benefits: benefits of an economic decision that accrue to third parties in a transaction

External costs: costs of an economic decision that accrue to third parties in a transaction

Externality: an externality is produced when all the costs or benefits of an economic decision do not accrue to the party making the decision

Finite natural resource: a resource (like coal or oil) that cannot be reproduced

Firm: a group of people organized to produce and sell goods and services

Fixed costs: costs that do not vary with the level of production in the short run

Fixed inputs: resources whose use does not change with the level of production in the short run

Free market choice: a decentralized method of making economic choices that relies on market mechanisms

Free market economy: an economy where markets are allowed to work without government intervention

Free rider: an individual who benefits from a good or service without making payment for that good or service

Game theory: a method of analysis that analyzes economic decisions by examining strategies and payoffs as if a game were being played

Human capital: the stock of talent and skills that increase the productivity of labor

Imperfect competition: markets where the assumptions of perfect competition do not hold, but monopolies do not exist either

Impossible zone: the area that lies outside the production possibilities curve; combinations of goods and services that cannot be produced with existing production methods and available resources

Income: the amount of money received in a given period of time

Income effect: when the price of an individual good increases or decreases, this affects the consumer's ability to purchase that good and all other goods. This change in purchasing power has an impact on the quantity of goods demanded and is called the income effect

Incomplete specialization: specialization that is not complete; production becomes specialized, but some other goods are also produced

Increase in demand: a change in income, tastes, or some other determinant of demand that causes the quantity demanded of some good to rise at every price (shown by a shift to the right in the demand curve)

Increase in supply: a change in the costs of production, technology, or some other determinant of supply that causes the quantity supplied to increase at every price (shown by a shift to the right in the supply curve)

Increasing returns to scale: a firm that experiences falling long-run average costs

Indifference curve: a graph that shows all the different combinations of two goods that produce the same total utility

Industry: the collection of all firms that produce a particular product

Inefficient: a method of production that does not produce the maximum possible totals of goods and services from available resources

Inelastic demand: a good has an inelastic demand if quantity demanded changes relatively little when price changes; elasticity coefficient is less than one

Inferior good: a good with a negative income effect; a good that experiences falling demand when income rises

In-kind transfers: transfer payments that take the form of goods or services rather than money

Innovation: technological improvements that reduce costs, increase quality, or both

Inputs: factors of production; goods and services that are used in the production of other goods and services (labor, raw materials, and so on)

Inverse relationships: an inverse relationship is said to exist between A and B if an increase in A results in a decrease in B (A and B move in opposite directions)

Investment: in the economic sense, investment refers to the purchase of capital or human capital

Isocost: a graphical device showing all the combinations of two inputs that can be purchased for the same total cost

Isoquant: a graphic device showing all the different combinations of two inputs that can be used to produce the same level of total output

Labor union: an organization of workers designed to increase their market power

Law of diminishing returns: the economic law that holds that, in general, additional resources used in production are less productive than the resources already in use; declining marginal product; like other laws, diminishing returns does not hold in every case

Law of variable proportions: the marginal product of any one input changes as the quantity used varies relative to other inputs

Long run: a period of time long enough so that firms may alter plant, size, technology, and so on

Macroeconomics: the study of the operation of the national economy

Marginal benefit: the amount of additional benefits derived from the purchase of an additional item

Marginal cost: the change in total cost resulting from a one-unit change in production

Marginal cost pricing: the setting of a price charged by a natural monopoly at the level equal to marginal cost (the same as would prevail under competition)

Marginal energy cost (MEC): the amount of additional energy used up in the production process

Marginal energy production (MEP): the amount of additional energy produced with additional resources

Marginal opportunity cost: the opportunity cost of consuming an additional unit of a good or service

Marginal private benefits (MPB): the additional private benefits produced when an additional unit of output is made available

Marginal private costs (MPC): the additional private costs of an additional unit of output

Marginal product: the amount of additional production that results when an additional unit of a resource is used in production, all else held constant

Marginal resource cost: the marginal cost of producing a limited resource including production, opportunity costs, and the present value of foregone future revenues

Marginal revenue: the added revenues that result from the sale of an additional unit

Marginal social benefits (MSB): the additional social benefits produced when an additional unit of output is made available

Marginal social costs (MSC): the additional social costs that result from additional production

Marginal utility: the amount of additional utility derived from an additional unit of a good or service

Markets: formal or informal economic institutions where goods and services are exchanged

Microeconomics: the study of how individual economic decisions are made

Models: simplified descriptions of real world processes designed to increase the understanding of the real world behavior

Money: anything generally accepted in exchange for goods and services and in payment of debt

Money wage: the wage rate expressed in the number of currency units paid per hour of work

Monopolistic competition: competition. among firms that because of product differentiation, can act as limited monopolists

Monopoly: a market where there is only one seller

Mutually advantageous exchange: exchange that benefits all trading partners

Natural monopoly: a natural monopoly exists in a market when no more than one firm can operate with non-negative economic profits

Negative externality: an external cost

Negative income tax: a proposal that would pay transfer payments to the poor directly through the income tax system

Neighborhood effect: an externality

Net benefits: the difference between marginal benefits and marginal cost or total benefits and total cost

Net energy: additional energy produced (MEP) minus additional energy used (MEC); the net addition to usable energy

Oligopoly: competition among just a few firms that together dominate a market

Opportunity cost: the cost of an economic action as determined by the value of the opportunities foregone

Output: the result of the production process

Partnership: a firm with two or more owners

Patent: a government grant of exclusive use of a new idea or invention

Patent monopoly: a monopoly created by the exclusive access to a patented invention or process

Perfect competition: a market situation characterized by large numbers of buyers and sellers, identical products, and no barriers to entry or exit

Perfect price discrimination: the ability to charge each individual demander the highest possible price

Perfectly inelastic demand: the situation that prevails when the same quantity is demanded at every price

Positive externality: an external benefit

Present-value calculation: a method of determining the current worth of future costs and revenues. The formula for present value is

$$PV = \frac{future\ amount}{(1\ +\ i)^n}$$

for an interest rate i and time period n

Price: the amount of money required in exchange for a unit of a good or service

Price ceiling: a maximum legal price

Price discrimination: the practice of charging different prices to different buyers for the same good or service

Price floor: a minimum legal price

Price-setters: firms, like monopolists, that can set any price for their goods because of their control of the market

Price-takers: competitive firms that must react to changes in market price but have no control over that price themselves

Private benefits: those benefits that accrue to the purchaser of an item

Producer burden: the burden of a tax borne by producers in the form of lower after-tax price for the taxed item

Producers' surplus: the difference between the price of an item and the minimum price at which the producer is willing to sell (marginal cost)

Product differentiation: the practice of creating a real or perceived difference among similar products in a competitive market

Production functions: show the relationship between the resources used and the production that results

Production possibilities curve (PPC): a graphic device illustrating the maximum possible combination of goods that can be produced with given technology and available resources

Profit: the difference between revenues and costs to a firm

Property rights: the legal and economic rights that accompany ownership or use of a good or service

Poverty: inadequate earnings when compared to a benchmark standard of living

Private costs: those costs accruing to the producer of an item

Public good: an item that has the property that one person's consumption of the item does not diminish the ability of others to consume it as well

Purchase possibilities curve: a graphic device showing the maximum possible combinations of two goods that can be purchased with given income and prices

Real wage: the wage rate expressed in terms of the amount of goods that can be purchased with an hour's work

Relative poverty: poverty in relation to the incomes of others

Returns to scale: the relationship between inputs and outputs over the long run

Revenue: the amount of money spent on an item; price times the quantity bought and sold

Scarcity: the situation that prevails when desires exceed resources

Sherman Antitrust Act: a federal law, passed in 1890, which makes most normal monopoly practices illegal

Shortage: a situation where quantity demanded exceeds quantity supplied

Short run: a period of time such that some inputs and costs are fixed

Social benefits: the total benefits of a decision; private benefits plus external benefits

Social costs: the total costs of an economic decision; private costs plus external costs

Sole-proprietorship: a firm with a single owner

Specialization: use of resources that results in the more efficient production of one good

Stockholder: part-owner of a corporation

Subsidy: a government payment to an individual or group, generally designed to encourage certain economic actions

Substitutes: goods that perform the same function are termed substitutes; coffee and tea, hamburgers and hot dogs, and pens and pencils are examples of pairs of substitutes

Substitution effect: when the price of an individual good changes, consumers tend to purchase more of relatively cheaper goods and less of relatively more expensive substitutes

Supply: a description of the seller side of the market; supply looks at the factors that determine the amounts and kinds of goods and services offered for sale

Supply curve: a curve that shows the quantity of a good or service that producers wish to sell at every possible price

Surplus: a situation where the quantity supplied exceeds the quantity demanded

Tangent: a pair of lines or curves that have only one point in common, but do not intersect or cross, are said to be tangent to one another

Technical efficiency: a production process that does not result in wasting of resources

Technology: the process by which inputs are combined to produce goods and services; changes in technology involve changes in the processes that are used to make goods and services

Total product: the total amount of output produced with given inputs

Total revenue: the sum of all revenues from the sale of a product

Trade-off: the situation that prevails when one or more options must be given up when a choice is made

Transfer payments: a transfer of money from one group to another without a corresponding payment of goods or services, e.g., welfare and unemployment benefits

Trust: a monopoly

Utility: a measure of well-being, used to compare choices

Variable costs: costs that depend on the level of production in the short run

Variable inputs: resources whose use depends on the level of production

Wage-lag effect: the increase in employment that takes place because higher output prices increase labor demand for individual firms, causing employment to rise until wage rates also increase

Zoning: government regulations on legal land use

Answers to "Test Yourself"

CHAPTER 1: SCARCITY AND CHOICE

1. True
2. True
3. False
4. False
5. False
6. True
7. False
8. False
9. False
10. True

CHAPTER 2: SPECIALIZATION AND EXCHANGE

1. False
2. False
3. False
4. True
5. False
6. False
7. False
8. True
9. True
10. True

CHAPTER 3: DEMAND AND SUPPLY: THE MICRO SIDE

1. False
2. True
3. False
4. False
5. False
6. False
7. True
8. True
9. False
10. True

CHAPTER 4: MARKETS AT WORK

1. False
2. False
3. False
4. True
5. True
6. True
7. False
8. False
9. True
10. False

CHAPTER 5: CONSUMER CHOICE

1. False
2. False
3. True
4. True
5. True
6. False
7. True
8. True
9. True
10. False

CHAPTER 6: PRODUCTION AND COST

1. True
2. False
3. True
4. False
5. True
6. False
7. True
8. True
9. False
10. False

CHAPTER 7: PRODUCER CHOICE: MONOPOLY

1. False
2. True
3. False
4. True
5. False
6. True
7. True
8. False
9. True
10. True

CHAPTER 8: PRODUCERS IN COMPETITIVE MARKETS

1. False
2. True
3. False
4. False
5. True
6. True
7. False
8. True
9. True
10. False

CHAPTER 9: IMPERFECT COMPETITION

1. True
2. True
3. True
4. True
5. True
6. False
7. False
8. False
9. False
10. True

CHAPTER 10: LABOR MARKETS

1. False
2. True
3. True
4. False
5. False
6. True
7. True
8. True
9. False
10. False

CHAPTER 11: CAPITAL AND NATURAL RESOURCE MARKETS

1. True
2. True
3. False
4. True
5. True
6. False
7. True
8. True
9. False
10. False

CHAPTER 12: ENERGY MARKETS

1. False
2. True
3. True
4. False
5. True
6. True
7. False
8. False
9. True
10. False

CHAPTER 13: FREE MARKET CHOICE

1. True
2. False
3. True
4. True
5. True
6. False
7. True

8. True
9. True
10. False

CHAPTER 14: MARKET FAILURES: EXTERNALITIES

1. True
2. False
3. False
4. False
5. True
6. False
7. True
8. True
9. True
10. False

CHAPTER 15: MARKET FAILURES: MONOPOLIES

1. True
2. False
3. False
4. False
5. True
6. True
7. True
8. False
9. False
10. False

CHAPTER 16: SCARCITY AND CHOICE: THE POVERTY PROBLEM

1. False
2. True
3. False
4. False
5. False
6. True
7. True
8. True
9. False
10. False

Index

A 0
B 1
C 2
D 3
E 4
F 5
G 6
H 7
I 8